FAR EASTERN AND RUSSIAN INSTITUTE
PUBLICATIONS ON ASIA
NUMBER 17

The
Gate
of
Darkness

Studies on the
Leftist Literary Movement
in China

by TSI-AN HSIA

University of Washington Press / Seattle and London

10007790 02
T 0C 00 435365

PREFACE

WHEN our friend and colleague Hsia Tsi-an was one of us and shared his studies and ideas in the discussions of the Modern Chinese History Project, there was always the problem of holding to the topic at hand this brilliant and sparkling mind which was forever looking beyond the issue of the discussion. Hsia Tsi-an's search for knowledge and understanding and his realization of the interrelationship of all the topics he was dealing with led him across a wide field of personalities and their problems. In this search, the burning issue which occupied our friend among all others was the survival of the spark of intellectual and emotional freedom under the pressure of totalitarian attempts to remake man in the image of a preconceived doctrine. The scope of Hsia Tsi-an's thinking was such that he attempted to fathom the thought and emotions of the people he studied, as well as the realities of the politics of that crucial period during which much of Chinese intellectual tradition— cut off from the sources of its past—was diverted to the political purposes of the Communist organization. For communism used the critical faculties of the writers to attack the past and thus clear the field for its own system, which these writers saw only as an idealized promise for the future rather than in its reality.

Hsia Tsi-an attacked this vast issue of the totalitarian scheme and its victims through studies of individuals, their role and their fate—studies which, combined, were to illustrate the complex human reactions to this Communist method of penetrating and using the human mind for its preconceived order. Approached in this way, Hsia Tsi-an's task was limitless. His fertile imagination, his quick grasp of problems, led him to include more and more people, more and more situations and political issues of the time in the scope of his investigations. And it was not easy for his friends to help him in rounding out his series of studies into one book of interrelated essays without curbing his drive, imagination, and willingness to explore other aspects of that over-all problem. We felt there was time for the work to grow and never imagined that Tsi-an's early and unexpected death would leave us only those parts of the whole story that he had been able to touch on. He could not give us the connecting link of his introduction which he planned to expand, he could not restate or rewrite his separate pieces, let alone undertake that second volume of further studies that we talked about.

The essays that Hsia Tsi-an wrote and that form the content of this volume approach the main theme through people of very different character and importance and through the treatment of many aspects of the problem of doctrine and freedom. The cast assembled by Hsia Tsi-an for his dramatic story does not consist of great writers, with the one exception of Lu Hsün. In fact, several of Hsia Tsi-an's characters were not really writers at all but rather political agents. And even Lu Hsün in the last period of his life (Lu Hsün and the League) is no longer truly a writer but rather a tortured person, agonizingly searching for his and the writer's role in the revolution in which he believed. His creativity had ended much earlier— in 1926—according to the study by William Schultz to which Hsia Tsi-an refers and with which he agrees. The twilight zone is dealt with by Hsia Tsi-an in his piece "Aspects of the Power of Darkness in Lu Hsün," and the title which his brother selected for the book, "The Gate of Darkness," echoes this theme. But what then becomes really the subject of Hsia Tsi-an's concern is the personal problem of attitude and conscience of representative figures in the group of writers of the time and of their relationship to the party and its purposes, rather than the problem of the writing itself.

It is an odd and uneven fellowship of people that Hsia Tsi-an brings together to cover the whole scope of the problem as he sees it. There is Ch'ü Ch'iu-po, the "tenderhearted Communist," a schizophrenic person who tries to retain a little islet of individualism when surrendering himself to the party. Ch'ü's writings on his trip to Russia demonstrate his melancholy emotions, linked to nature. The feelings he expresses in describing the scenery through which he passed show that "his creative genius was never fully engaged in the reports on one of the greatest human dramas enacted right before his eyes." Indeed, it is surprising to see the hesitations of this man during what was still an early stage of communism, when the illusions of many were still intact and the chaos that Ch'ü Ch'iu-po witnessed might still have been regarded as constructive. The romanticism of Ch'ü's emotions, to which he returned in his testament before his execution, expresses a mold of thought that prevented him from becoming a hardened fighter for the cause—a true Communist. To Hsia Tsi-an this was shown in the "feebleness, perfunctoriness, or rather halfheartedness with which he wrote." And it is of historical interest that Ch'ü Ch'iu-po's "Superfluous Words" were published in the same journal, *I-ching,* that had contained the "confessions" of earlier condemned Chinese revolutionaries. It was this halfheartedness that not only prevented him from surrendering his mind to the revolutionary purpose with which he played but also kept him from applying the harshness of the Comintern's verdict of deviationism against a Communist colleague, Li Li-san, when the latter strayed from the path. Ch'ü Ch'iu-po's inability to forget his instincts kept him from success in Communist leadership and led eventually to his destruction.

The last of the essays written by Hsia Tsi-an and the one which he had no time to polish before his death was a study of a very different figure. Chiang Kuang-tz'u was a hack writer, shallow and pompous, who was popular at the time because his display of emotions appealed to the "barely literate youth." In Hsia Tsi-an's view, Chiang was not much worse than other such popular authors of the time, whose romantic personalities rather than their faulty technique helped them to sell their stories. Chiang Kuang-tz'u's unwillingness to submit to the party and its discipline led to his being condemned as bourgeois; but his name was later, after his death, restored to the list of literary worthies who helped the revolution. To describe his usefulness from the party point of view, the Communists in an ideologically fitting explanation, spoke of the "petit-bourgeois" contribution that he had made to the revolution. Chiang Kuang-tz'u's attempt to combine his desire for personal license with a romantic participation in revolution led to conflict. This conflict in itself might have been a subject for literary treatment, but Chiang Kuang-tz'u was obviously too bad a writer to bring this out. His is the story of a popular author who did not fit into the pattern but was useful to the Communists at that time for his romantic appeal.

The "Enigma of the Five Martyrs" deals with five Communist agitators, executed by the Nationalists, of whom only one could possibly be described as a writer at all. To claim them as martyred writers was a Communist device to use these men's fate for propaganda among intellectuals, always willing to fight for that freedom of the writer which communism, once in power, would never grant. The political aspect of this story, the indication that these "martyrs" had been betrayed and led to their death by the Communists themselves wanting to get rid of members of a dissenting faction, adds a particularly sinister note of double intrigue applied for the glory of the party.

The central piece among these essays and Hsia Tsi-an's main topic is the story of "Lu Hsün and the League of Leftist Writers," told in two sections. It reveals the Communist use of a man who was without doubt the outstanding writer of the time in China and who was used to bring as many of the secondary figures as possible into line through the organization of a writers' group that served the Communist purpose. Lu Hsün was then discarded when his limited, direct, and naïve approach to the doctrine he had learned kept him from understanding or following the new twist of the line. Through some of its leading literary representatives, the party had earlier flattered Lu Hsün and humored him along. But when the leadership moved to Yenan, this contact was disrupted, and the local party hacks in Shanghai did not have the touch that could sway the man and overcome his self-assertion. The frustration and bitterness in the last period of Lu Hsün's life are clearly shown in the account by Hsia Tsi-an, who seems to believe that it was this break that may have helped to hasten Lu Hsün's death. Lu Hsün died in time to remain the intellectual hero of the Communist revolution, the role for which he had been singled out by being given the accolade of Mao Tse-tung's own words. If he had lived, he would probably sooner or later have had to be condemned and purged. As it was, he became the prime example of a writer with little insight into the strategy and politics of the time but with a naïve faith in the doctrine and a willingness to use it for the principles of intellectual freedom in which he believed and to whose destruction he unknowingly contributed. The League had served its purpose. The united front demanded new symbols and the temporary use and exploitation of broader concepts of nationalism which Lu Hsün could not reconcile with his own revolutionary faith.

To those of us who believe in the indestructibility of the human spirit, Tsi-an's story has not ended here. To his friends he himself represented that spark that will live on. He had that extraordinary combination of an understanding of the great Chinese heritage and of the modern emancipation movement that made him a proof of the writer's role in our time. Even though he was not able to give the final touch to his essays or to his own introduction, Tsi-an left us a piece of work that clearly shows the theme with which he was concerned and his own spirit and approach. In our plans to publish it as a memorial to our friend, we have turned to friends who have shared the loss and with whom we wanted to join in our effort. It was with his brother that Tsi-an corresponded about his work and plans, and we have asked his brother to give the book, in his introduction, that meaningful connection and personal intimacy with Tsi-an's thought that only a brother could provide. He has added his own profound knowledge of the time and its problems to the story of Tsi-an's description of his own work.

The fate of the writers and intellectuals in modern China is an issue that concerns not only those of us interested in the story of Communist China and its problems. What Hsia Tsi-an deals with is a major problem of our time in a world in which totalitarian control has been extended over many countries, threatening the survival of a most basic human freedom—the freedom of creative thought. In this book Hsia Tsi-an has probed the effect this system had on a number of its victims, and in so doing he has given us a work that combines the results of his scholarly research with his own perceptive contribution as a writer in the modern Chinese literary tradition which communism attempts to destroy on the mainland today.

FRANZ MICHAEL

May 27, 1968

ACKNOWLEDGMENTS

SOME of the essays gathered in this volume have appeared in slightly different form in scholarly journals. "Ch'ü Ch'iu-po" and "Twenty Years after the Yenan Forum" were published in *The China Quarterly* (1966 and 1963 respectively), and "Aspects of the Power of Darkness in Lu Hsün" in *The Journal of Asian Studies* (1964). The "Enigma of the Five Martyrs" appeared as No. 2 in the Research Series of the Center for Chinese Studies, Institute of International Studies, Berkeley, 1962. "The Phenomenon of Chiang Kuang-tz'u" (1964) and "Lu Hsün and the Dissolution of the League of Leftist Writers" (1959) are published here for the first time.

CONTENTS

Introduction, by C. T. Hsia   xv

Ch'ü Ch'iu-po: The Making and Destruction
of a Tenderhearted Communist   3

The Phenomenon of Chiang Kuang-tz'u   55

Lu Hsün and the Dissolution of the League
of Leftist Writers   101

Aspects of the Power of Darkness in Lu Hsün   146

Enigma of the Five Martyrs   163

Twenty Years after the Yenan Forum   234

Index   263

INTRODUCTION

M^Y elder brother Tsi-an Hsia died of a cerebral hemorrhage on February 23, 1965, at the age of forty-nine. When the shocking news reached Taipei, many of his friends there wrote articles for the local newspapers and magazines to commemorate his achievement as a teacher and man of letters. Not having read his recent works in English, they were only vaguely aware of his enhanced reputation as a creative scholar in modern Chinese studies during his last six years in America, but they were unanimous in affirming his importance as a salutary influence upon the literature now being produced in Taiwan. In the commemorative issue of *Modern Literature Quarterly* (July, 1965), one of his disciples wrote, "Ever since the mainland was lost to the Communists, no one had played as important a role in keeping Chinese literature alive and in fostering new talent among younger writers." [1] This claim was made in all seriousness despite Tsi-an's slim body of creative writing. As a lecturer and, later, professor in the Foreign Languages Department of National Taiwan University, my brother had more than any other teacher encouraged promising students to write, and as founder and editor of the *Literary Review* (*Wen-hsüeh tsa-chih,* 1956–60), he had tirelessly subjected their manuscripts to criticism and revision before publishing them and thus prepared these young writers for their eventual maturity and independence. He himself had written a number of seminal critical essays to correct taste and foster excellence, but in the recollections of his student-writers, he had done far more by giving them his unstinted friendship whenever they dropped in on him to seek his advice or just to chat.

I have stressed Tsi-an's singular importance as a decisive influence among Taiwan's younger writers because, beyond his personal friends, perhaps few Western readers of the present book, even though they had

[1] Liu Shao-ming, "Huai Tsi-an hsien-sheng," *Hsien-tai wen-hsüeh chi-k'an,* No. 25, July, 1965, p. 5.

greatly admired his short story "The Jesuit's Tale" (*Partisan Review,* Fall, 1955)[2] and other English writings, could be aware of the creative role he had played in Taiwan, and earlier on the mainland, as a teacher at Kuanghua University, Southwest Associated University, and National Peking University. True, it was only upon his arrival on these shores in March, 1959, that Tsi-an began his most productive phase as a scholar, but the same keenness of intellect and warmth of heart apparent in his English writings had characterized his earlier roles as teacher, editor, critic, and occasional story-writer and poet. To those who have taken the pains to compare his translations from English with the original, he would also appear to be one of the most sensitive and accomplished translators of his generation in China. In translating a volume of classical American prose (Irving, Thoreau, Hawthorne, and others),[3] he has not only recreated its rich cadence without at all sacrificing accuracy but, in so doing, introduced a new suppleness to the *pai-hua* idiom.

This awareness of Tsi-an's important role in his own cultural tradition is especially pertinent to a just appreciation of the present volume. Its preparation entailed years of extensive research, but it is not a book that could have been written by someone less vitally concerned with the future of Chinese culture. Born in 1916, Tsi-an was himself inescapably nurtured upon the ideals and aspirations of the May Fourth period; in turning to a study of his immediate literary heritage after having played an active part in the current literary scene, he was driven by the desire to recapture the historical reality of an earlier period in all its tragic complexity. He could have written a straightforward, factual account of the leftist literary movement of the twenties and thirties, or prepared a series of biographies of its representative authors or critiques of their works. Such studies, each embodying one particular discipline, would have been still very useful, but to my brother they would have simplified and therefore distorted the total cultural picture. In his preface to its second edition, Jacques Barzun says of *Darwin, Marx, Wagner* that "an essay of this sort is clearly not pure

---

[2] This story was written during Tsi-an's first trip to America as an exchange graduate student in the Department of English at Indiana University for the spring semester of 1955. After spending the summer in New Haven, he went back to Taiwan. A story of the same period, "The Birth of a Son," has been posthumously published in *Literature East and West* (Vol. IX, No. 4, Dec., 1965).

[3] *Mei-kuo san-wen hsüan,* Vol. I (Hong Kong: World Today Press, 1958). All the selections were translated by my brother, except for one essay by Emerson, which was translated by Eileen Chang. Tsi-an also translated Arthur Koestler *et al., The God That Failed*; Godfrey Blunden's novel, *A Room on the Route*; Manes Sperber's novels *The Burned Bramble* and *The Abyss.*

biography, history, or criticism; it is a selection and fusion of all three, which is sometimes called cultural criticism." [4] Among books on modern China, I can recall very few titles that have applied as fruitfully the multiple approaches of cultural criticism and fused them with as much literary distinction as my brother's study.

The method is ideal for Tsi-an's purpose. Of the writers he has chosen to exemplify the leftist literary movement—Lu Hsün, Ch'ü Ch'iu-po, Chiang Kuang-tz'u, and a quintet of inconsequential authors posthumously honored as the Five Martyrs—only Lu Hsün can be called a classic, since his finer works can be read with enjoyment independently of their biographical and historical contexts. But even for Lu Hsün, his creative sterility during the last decade of his life cannot yield its full cultural significance unless seen as a consequence of his embroilment in polemics and politics. Tsi-an says of Chiang Kuang-tz'u that his worth lies in his literary worthlessness, and of the Five Martyrs that it is only the circumstances of their death that could justify a study of their lives. Such remarks are not just flights of paradox: they underscore the point that for many writers of the leftist period it is only in the full recreation of their biography and politics that they yield their representative value at a particular juncture of Chinese culture and emerge as meaningful, sympathetic, and indeed tragic literary figures. With their differing literary talents and education, these writers are in retrospect all unquestioning supporters of the May Fourth tradition, in their demand for personal emancipation, social justice, and national rejuvenation. Their aspirations are none the less real even if they seldom capture that reality in their writings. They used the pen to combat tradition, and many would gladly have laid it down to take up more violent forms of struggle against the enemy. But even among those who had early embraced communism, few could have suspected that they would sooner or later have to contend with an enemy who compromised their personal and patriotic integrity at every turn while cynically exploiting their aspirations and in the process all but dooming their literary careers. It is the tragic irony of modern Chinese history that the Communist revolution should now appear as the rightful and logical successor to the May Fourth Movement. But with the leftist writers at least, their early faith in communism has only rendered more poignant their subsequent disenchantment with the Communist Party and their belated attempts at defying its decree that they prostitute their talent in strict furtherance of its political objec-

[4] *Darwin, Marx, Wagner: Critique of a Heritage* (2d ed. rev.; New York: Doubleday [Anchor Books], 1958), p. ix.

tives. Happy were the Five Martyrs who had died as victims of the Communist maneuver for power without ever having reached the further stage of disillusionment!

But I must let my brother speak for himself about the nature of his work. In June, 1964, he had written a "Draft of the Preface to a Book on the Leftist Literary Movement in China." He was about to embark upon his annual summer trip to Seattle to engage in further research on his book, and he wanted to take along the preface, which he had drafted in Berkeley, to show his colleagues at the Far Eastern and Russian Institute of the University of Washington, in preparation for its publication. As he had repeatedly told me in his letters, he was not happy about that draft and had intended to write a much longer introduction to the leftist literary movement. But when he returned in the fall to his work as research associate linguist at the Center for Chinese Studies, University of California in Berkeley, he had to divide his attention between the book and the writing of a monograph on Chinese education for the Center's Current Chinese Language Project. The preface had remained unrevised when on February 21, 1965, which was a Sunday, Tsi-an went to his office to work as was his wont and suffered a fatal stroke. But even as it stands, the piece bears the distinctive stamp of my brother's style and states succinctly the intention of his book. It is given below in its entirety:

DRAFT OF THE PREFACE TO A BOOK ON
THE LEFTIST LITERARY MOVEMENT IN CHINA

The name of the leftist literary movement in China may call to the reader's mind either of two things. One is the Chinese Communist theory about the progress from bourgeois democratic revolution to proletarian revolution in modern China. The Chinese writers after the May Fourth Movement are said to have shared the universal fate of the intellectuals of the petty-bourgeois class: they had to make their choice between the progressive and the retrogressive forces. Those who joined the leftist movement actually helped Mao's revolution, but they were supposedly promoting the progress of history. They were more than prophets who foresaw the "liberation"; they were fighters who used their weapons, which included their pens, to bring about the future. Though the number of leftist writers was never large and the quality of their writing was, to say the least, uneven, they are understood to represent the most important school of writing in modern China, and their importance was due to their contribution to the revolution rather than to the aesthetic value of their work.

Such a theory, neat within the ideological framework, agrees largely with the Marxist interpretation of history. It also provides a drama of struggle and triumph: how a group of intellectuals began by spurning the old China and then defied everything in their pursuit of the revolutionary ideal. Their appearance on the literary scene is said to have been a historical necessity: an act in the inevitable process which culminated in the victory of Mao Tse-tung. Now Mao is in power, and whatever is done under his dictation is interpreted as a realization of the ideals that the leftist writers fought for thirty years ago.

But a different drama is possibly also known to those who happen to have lived through the period concerned or to have read and thought about it in a way free from the one-sided Marxist influence. It was a drama fraught with deeper emotional problems and sometimes even baffling for its complex motivation. First of all, the alliance between the Communists and writers with no party affiliation was not an easy one. The conflict in the movement itself was not always caused by dispute over policy; but principles were involved. People who cherished some degree of conscience, whether humanistic or artistic, perhaps could never work together with professional revolutionaries bent upon one single purpose. And the Chinese experience was not unique. In the parallel period, a number of talented writers were attracted to similar movements in the United States and Europe. They left behind a record of the awakening and betrayal of social conscience and a library of inferior literature, which its authors might today feel ashamed to acknowledge. The final failure of the movement, in countries other than China, afforded an education in disillusionment which was helpful to the maturing of the writer's mind. Disillusion was the Chinese experience too, but when a Chinese leftist writer has outgrown his naïveté, probably he has also lost his freedom of expression.

The severest critic of the leftist writers in China happens to be my brother in his book *A History of Modern Chinese Fiction.* To them he applies a standard of criticism which requires insight, perception, independent interpretation of life, analysis of motives, and a kind of wisdom which balances ardent hopes with a knowledge of practical impossibilities and human weaknesses. Most leftist writers, of course, could not pass the test, and Chih-tsing pronounced them failures. His criticism offended the Czech scholar, Mr. Průšek, who would have given a higher estimate of the writers whom Chih-tsing downgraded. The exchange between Chih-tsing and Mr. Průšek, which appeared in the pages of the *T'oung Pao,* has perhaps aroused interest in a subject hitherto little studied by sinologues, namely, modern Chinese literature. What seems to me significant about their exchange is that Chih-tsing has not only vindicated his critical stand but has also demanded a fresh look at a subject in which scholarship is so often mixed with propaganda.

But because of the critical nature of Chih-tsing's book, he has to leave out certain aspects of the leftist literary movement. He draws sufficient attention to the vehemence in the utterances of the leftist writers, but he does not dwell upon the equal vehemence in their extraliterary activities. What concerns me is the conflict between politics and art, a dilemma experienced by many a leftist writer all the world over, and it was this that spelled the failure of the movement. In the 1930's the Communist Party's irksome interference with the writer's private life, private beliefs, and private ways of writing worked rather toward alienation from those whose service it wanted to exploit. The literary policy of the Chinese Communist Party has not changed much, but has grown very powerful.

But before the party became so powerful, the dilemma was more keenly felt, because individuals had still then the dignity to match the party's power. A spiritual drama is noticeable in the lives of the leftist writers of whom I have written. These writers found themselves confronted with immense freedom and also immense responsibility after the May Fourth Movement. Immense freedom, because of the falling apart of the old Chinese social system; and immense responsibility because of the wonderful opportunity to shape the future to their liking. With the contemporary scene, they were certainly dissatisfied. Ever since 1911, revolution had been an obsessive thought with many intellectuals, and the Russian model of 1917 seemed to afford the best example of what a revolution should be. Many embraced communism of their free will; in it they found a cause worthy of them, to which they would dedicate their talents and, if necessary, their lives. But what began as an individual commitment was finally caught in the mechanism of the Communist Party apparatus. One had to obey orders and observe discipline. The individual wish for change, the individual assertion of freedom, and the individual gesture of defiance and rebellion had to be merged in the collective will and concerted action. There may have been little difficulty in believing in the utopia promised by "scientific" socialism, but to accept at the same time the infallibility of the cadres who directed the collective will and conducted the concerted action demanded too much of a sacrifice, since in some instances it may have been a sacrifice of principle.

The fate of individuals in a collective movement can be tragic; and the purpose of my work is to recreate that tragedy. Courtesy will be extended even to the Communists, who, if treated as individuals, seem to be also capable of thoughts other than political. In the historical juncture I am concerned with, the Chinese Communist Party was weak. The internal power struggle during the first decades of its history left not a few comrades bewildered, disgusted, or simply disheartened. Those involved in factious fights demonstrated a meanness which rather belied their inspired talk. This state of confusion in China, in one way or another created by Moscow, was confounded by directives from the same source, directives peremptory but often self-contradictory, being reflections of the internal strife within the Soviet Party. All this was painful to many a Chinese comrade whose inducement to join the party was perhaps the ideal of a better world. Caught between the "rightist" and the "leftist" deviation, cadres entrusted with underground activities in the cultural and literary circles did not always know which line to follow. Their difficulty was greatly increased by the necessity either to defy or to evade the severe measures adopted after 1927 by the Kuomintang to smash the rebellion.

As I propose to write the history of the leftist literary movement in China, I have no personal experience to relate. I have never had an affair with any kind of Marxist movement. Since no smoldering cinders are burning in my heart, I do not find in me the necessity to repudiate an old love. The kind of study I make is biographical and historical, but not autobiographical. I got my materials only from research, that is, from reading in the library; nothing in my book is personal, except my observations and remarks. I have not had a chance to interview the *dramatis personae,* some of whom are still alive. Unfortunately there has not been in China a Stephen Spender, an Arthur Koestler, a George Orwell who could return to tell the story about a journey to the left. Hu Feng, Ting Ling, or Feng Hsüeh-feng might have been the ideal person to write a spiritual autobiography of the leftist writer in China, but they have been made silent. My book may supply this want. Where I fail in intimacy, I hope the reader will find compensation in my detachment and, perhaps, my scholarship.

As originally planned, then, Tsi-an's book would have consisted of a series of essays on leftist writers and their relations with the Communist Party. The chapters on "Lu Hsün and the Dissolution of the League of Leftist Writers," on Ch'ü Ch'iu-po, Chiang Kuang-tz'u, and the Five Martyrs belong to that series. My brother had also planned to include two articles published respectively in the *Journal of Asian Studies* and *The China Quarterly:* "Aspects of the Power of Darkness in Lu Hsün" and "Twenty Years after the Yenan Forum." Though differing somewhat in form from the other chapters, they are crucial to an understanding of the leftist literary movement. "The Power of Darkness" not only complements the portrait of Lu Hsün given in the biographical chapter; it illustrates at length the critical principle implicit in my brother's discussion of all the other authors, namely, that a writer is condemned to superficiality unless he draws fully upon the resources of his inner self. "Twenty Years after the Yenan Forum" fittingly summarizes the trends of leftist writing to be discerned in the authors studied and recreates the historic occasion when a literary dictator repudiates these trends and ushers in a new era of Communist literature.

The reader is surely entitled to know whether my brother would have revised some of these chapters had he lived long enough to see his book through the press. By June, 1964, Tsi-an had established himself as a scholar of rare originality and versatility in the field of modern Chinese studies. He had published two brilliant monographs on Communist Chinese society and language entitled *Metaphor, Myth, Ritual and the People's Commune* and *A Terminological Study of the Hsia-fang Movement*, and a third, *The Commune in Retreat as Evidenced in Terminology and Semantics*, was scheduled for publication later that summer. He had read several papers at scholarly meetings and published important articles in learned journals.[5] Above all, he had completed all the chapters of the present volume except the one on Chiang Kuang-tz'u. In their dittographed forms ("Enigma of the Five Martyrs" was published in Berkeley

---

[5] Besides "Twenty Years after the Yenan Forum" (*China Quarterly*, No. 13, Jan.– Mar., 1963) and "Aspects of the Power of Darkness in Lu Hsün" (*Journal of Asian Studies*, Vol. XXIII, No. 2, Feb., 1964), Tsi-an published "Heroes and Hero-Worship in Chinese Communist Fiction" (*China Quarterly*, No. 13), "Demons in Paradise: The Chinese Images of Russia" (*Annals of the American Academy of Political and Social Science*, Vol. 349, Sept., 1963), and a review of Victor Purcell, *The Boxer Uprising* (*Journal of the American Oriental Society*, Vol. 83, No. 3, Aug.–Sept., 1963). He also wrote "Taiwan," an appendix to my *History of Modern Chinese Fiction, 1917–1957* (New Haven: Yale University Press, 1961).

as a separate study),[6] they had elicited unanimous high praise from qualified readers. Gratified by the reaction, his colleagues at the University of
Washington therefore urged my brother to complete his study as soon as
he could, especially since it had already grown to considerable size. Upon
arriving in Seattle that June, Tsi-an agreed to write one more chapter and
an introduction before submitting his work for publication. But at heart he
felt he should still undertake more; he confided to me in a letter dated
June 24:

> My urgent task now is to complete my book on the Left League. Two
> chapters are yet to be written. The chapter on Chiang Kuang-tz'u I plan to
> complete here in two months' time. . . . The other chapter is a general dis-
> cussion of the Left League, and since this topic entails endless research (e.g.,
> about the early career of Chou Yang), I have till now postponed tackling it.
> But nevertheless I hope to have it done by Christmas, or perhaps even by
> Thanksgiving. Another chapter, "Lu Hsün and the Dissolution of the League,"
> I plan to rewrite . . . and lengthen considerably. I would like to describe
> in minute detail Lu Hsün's relations with the Communist Party and the advo-
> cates of proletarian literature, and the careers of Hu Feng and Feng Hsüeh-
> feng (to aim at an original presentation is difficult, but unless I do so, I feel
> I'll be doing less than full justice to these two "men of rectitude"). Further-
> more, I would like to discuss at some length the satiric *tsa-wen* of Hsü Mou-
> yung published in 1956–57, which seem to me to have made the author the
> inheritor of Lu Hsün's mantle (neither Hu Feng nor Feng Hsüeh-feng is his
> equal in literary talent). This task may take up some time.

Four weeks later, in a letter dated July 18, Tsi-an envisaged a further
expansion of his book:

> [My friends at] the University of Washington expect me to complete the
> book by writing one more chapter on Chiang Kuang-tz'u and then go right
> ahead with its publication. On their part it is sheer good will, but I can't
> help feeling embarrassed:
> For, first of all, I want to examine thoroughly the anti-Lu Hsün and anti-
> Mao Tun campaigns of 1928. That year the Creation Society and the Sun
> Society were also engaged in controversy, though I am not too clear about
> the issues involved. It seems that the Creation Society advocated proletarian
> literature, and the Sun Society revolutionary literature. To what extent these
> two societies really differed in their views on literature (of course, there is
> plenty of evidence they were at the same time merely exploiting their rivalry)
> and whether they represented two camps of opinion among Soviet writers

---

[6] *Enigma of the Five Martyrs: A Study of the Leftist Literary Movement in
Modern China* (Berkeley: Center for Chinese Studies, Institute of International
Studies, University of California, 1962). The chapter on Ch'ü Ch'iu-po has been
posthumously published in *The China Quarterly*, No. 25 (Jan.–Mar., 1966), under
the title "Ch'ü Ch'iu-pai's Autobiographical Writings: The Making and Destruction
of a 'Tender-hearted' Communist."

at that time—these problems all merit careful study. I could organize these problems around a chapter called "The Formation of the Left League."

Secondly, a most intriguing phenomenon was the greatly diminished influence of the former members of the Creation and Sun societies once the Left League was established. The latter group appeared especially enfeebled after the expulsion of Chiang Kuang-tz'u from the party. Lu Hsün had a very strong *ego* [English in the original]; when he thought of this, he must have fingered his mustache and smiled—years later, when Feng Hsüeh-feng wrote about this period, he, too, was filled with evident personal satisfaction. Lu Hsün lost his power [within the League] probably at the time when Chou Yang gained power. But soon after that, Hu Feng arrived on the scene. As things developed, Lu Hsün headed the Left League faction out of power, while the *upstart* [English in the original] Chou Yang headed the faction in power. As to how this came about, I am not too clear. But the elation of Lu Hsün during the early phase of the League (he continued to satirize the Creation and Sun societies, forgetting that they were now his comrades on the same front— the Trotskyite Wang Tu-ch'ing was filled with anger when writing about the humiliations endured without a protest by the Creation Society) and his sulking resentment during the later phase are also matters worthy of further investigation. This chapter would relate how power changed hands within the Left League. (Probably, when Feng Hsüeh-feng was in power, he would defer to Lu Hsün and consult him on everything, but later Chou Yang showed him scant respect.)

Thirdly, in connection with the dissolution of the Left League, I would like to make a good study of Hsü Mou-yung. In 1956 he said he had kept his silence for twenty years, but suddenly during the Hundred Flowers period he felt inspired to write a good number of satiric essays. These essays were superb. We really ought to collect them into a book, to prove that the Lu Hsün style is not yet dead.

Fourthly, due credit should be given to Lu Hsün's praiseworthy works as an introducer of Soviet literature. In the twenties the Soviet Union really went through a "Hundred Flowers" period; flourishing then were many schools of writers eventually liquidated by Stalin. Lu Hsün was interested in (1) the diversity of Soviet literature . . . ; (2) the fellow-traveling writers—in their sympathy for the suffering people and their concern with style and technique, these writers had probably continued the glorious tradition of Tsarist Russian literature. Lu Hsün could be called an indefatigable learner, even though he didn't understand the futurism of Mayakovsky, the symbolism of Pasternak and others, and the Formalist critics. As he saw it, there existed strong ties between Soviet and Tsarist literature. This understanding differs greatly from ours, living as we do in a post-Stalin period. "Lu Hsün and Russian Literature" would be a good topic. . . .

If I want to make a thorough study, I am afraid I would have to devote a few more years to it.

It is a great pity that Tsi-an was felled in his prime and could not continue with his definitive investigation of all aspects of the League of Left-Wing Writers. But since he had had no serious intention of incorporating all these chapters in the present book (he would have had to write a second volume), if he were to oversee its publication, it would remain pretty much as it now stands except that he would have provided an introductory chapter in place of or in addition to the preface and considerably expanded the chapter on the dissolution of the League. He would probably also have introduced some minor changes in the chapter on Chiang Kuang-tz'u. He had read all the works of Chiang he could get hold of, but there were still a few titles he had not seen. However, since Chiang's works are all stereotyped, the reading of additional material would have been mainly to satisfy my brother's conscientiousness as a scholar and could not have affected the portrait of the author given in the chapter.

But the chapter on the dissolution of the League remains a different story. Like the rest of the biographical chapters, it is, of course, an engrossing story told with consummate skill. Even though Tsi-an was relatively new to his subject when he began research on this chapter in 1959, by the time he was through, he had read so deeply in Lu Hsün's letters and diaries and other original sources that the resultant portrait of the author in the year of his death—1936—is grimly memorable and startlingly different from anything we find in the standard biographies. Nevertheless, in the course of his subsequent research in the Left-Wing League, my brother had devoted so much of his attention to the personalities and careers of Chou Yang, Hu Feng, Feng Hsüeh-feng, and Hsü Mou-yung—all major protagonists in the literary debates of 1936—that it remains a genuine loss to scholarship that he could not have incorporated some of his findings in the chapter as he had wanted to.

Tsi-an did not give his book a main title. I hope the title I have chosen, *The Gate of Darkness,* would have met his approval. The phrase *hei-an-ti cha-men* 黑暗的閘門 appears in a passage by Lu Hsün quoted in the chapter "The Power of Darkness":

> Let the awakened man burden himself with the weight of tradition and shoulder up the gate of darkness. Let him give unimpeded passage to the children so that they may rush to the bright, wide-open spaces and lead happy lives henceforward as rational human beings.[7]

Lu Hsün wrote the passage in 1919, only five months after the fourth of May, at a time when to most enlightened Chinese intellectuals the tradition itself appeared as the main obstacle to progress. In the preface to his first collection of stories, *Na-han* (1923), Lu Hsün has further elaborated on this metaphor so that the gate of darkness now appears as a windowless

---

[7] See below, p. 146–47.

iron house in which the Chinese are contentedly asleep, with little hope for awakening.

But if in 1919 Lu Hsün is mainly concerned with the task of shouldering up the gate of darkness to give "unimpeded passage" to his countrymen seeking liberation from the tradition, by 1936 he is tottering under the weight of another gate of darkness whose final descent has denied the Chinese their access to "the bright, wide-open spaces." Lu Hsün, of course, could not then relate his personal struggle with the Communist literary commissars in Shanghai to the eventual entrapment of hundreds of millions of his countrymen behind that gate: he could only confide to his more intimate correspondents his own sense of pain and humiliation: "I always feel that I am bound in an iron chain while a foreman is whipping me on the back." [8] But the oppressive imagery remains unchanged: the erstwhile intellectual giant that took upon himself the task of shouldering up the gate of tradition is now a Samson shorn of his strength, bound to an iron chain and tending the mill of Communist propaganda with always the foreman's whip behind his back. It was not until 1942 that writers gathered at the Yenan Forum on Literature and Art witnessed the official lowering of the gate of darkness against all their hopes for freedom. But if with their puny strength they could no longer hope to lift that gate, they have at least continued to bore holes through it to admit some gleams of light. Hu Feng, the most dauntless of Lu Hsün's followers, saw the gate of darkness as a solid wall of iron. In 1951 he confided to one of his friends defiantly, "When the time is ripe, I am willing to cut off my head and hurl it against that stinking wall of iron so as to shatter it." [9]

My brother's book, therefore, records the tragic dilemma of writers caught between two ponderous gates of darkness. While they appeared successful in their collaborative effort to shoulder up the gate of tradition, each was sooner or later trapped behind another gate of darkness or else crushed to death under its weight. In that respect they are characteristic of the May Fourth period as a whole rather than merely of the leftist literary movement. For leftists and non-leftists alike, the May Fourth tradition postulated a new way of life, a quest for national and personal fulfillment. In the chapter on "Twenty Years after the Yenan Forum," Tsi-an has singled out three main trends of that tradition—realism ("the realism of nineteenth-century Europe in as diversified styles as there could be from

---

[8] See below, p. 113.
[9] C. T. Hsia, *A History of Modern Chinese Fiction, 1917–1957*, pp. 327–28.

Tolstoy to Balzac"), sentimentalism (humanitarian and romantic love), and the satiric style as exemplified by the essays of Lu Hsün—only to find that these are precisely the targets of ridicule and attack in Mao Tsetung's talks at the Forum:

> As a matter of fact, "petty-bourgeois" realism, sentimentalism, and satire were all denounced as wrong. Henceforth, literature and art were to serve solely the party under Mao, in the name of the workers, peasants, and soldiers. Realism would be used for the praise of "progress"; love would bear the stamp of "class nature"; and satire would be directed only against the prescribed enemy. The change was great.[10]

Since 1942 the countless writers subjected to persecution and punishment on the mainland have been precisely those who defied Mao's directives to speak out for the necessity of realism, the sanctity of human love and sympathy, and the importance of maintaining an independent satire.

If the leftist writers are distinguishable as a group from the non-leftist, it is by their greater naïveté or courage to act upon their beliefs, their predisposition to romanticism, in their writing as in their behavior. It is a unique contribution of Tsi-an's book that, in exploring the careers of Ch'ü Ch'iu-po, Chiang Kuang-tz'u, and the Five Martyrs, he has been able to capture the essence of their individual romanticism, in all its noble and ludicrous manifestations. Lu Hsün, temperamentally a non-leftist, was capable neither of the heroism of Ch'ü Ch'iu-po, who journeyed to the Land of Hunger (Russia) in quest of truth, nor of the megalomania of Chiang Kuang-tz'u, who styled himself the Byron of China. But it is good to remember that, in his formative years, even the creator of Ah Q was under the spell of the English romantic poet.

On the mainland and Taiwan alike, the Fourth of May is still annually greeted with pious cant. While agreeing that the date marks a period of spiritual renewal for China, my brother appears far more realistic in his appraisal of its actual achievement. Its tragic thesis notwithstanding, his book abounds with comic vignettes of authors driven to foolishness or desperation by their abstract passion for love or revolution. But even the excesses of a revolutionary romanticism are always looked upon by Tsi-an with ironic respect not untinged with genuine admiration; for him they express the exuberance of idealism and they are the reverse of the sinister. Given time, one outgrows one's immaturity, even though writers like Chiang Kuang-tz'u, who would not have taken up the writing profession in any other than the May Fourth period, seemed doomed to lifelong

[10] See below, p. 240.

adolescence. Tsi-an repeatedly observes that from the early twenties to the middle thirties, the *pai-hua* language has steadily gained in precision and expressiveness and the literature itself has markedly matured. And it would have continued to reach higher levels of achievement as the standards of criticism improved and the writers themselves, chastened of their delusion and conceit, developed a greater sense of artistic responsibility. But, of course, this period of further potential growth coincided with a new era of increasingly effective Communist control over all media of expression.

With the fate of the Chinese writer since 1942 the present book is only incidentally concerned. Nor is it primarily concerned with the literary history of the preceding period. Rather, with an astounding wealth of telling detail and astute commentary, my brother has chosen to retrace for us the spiritual odysseys of several of its writers confronted with "immense freedom" and "immense responsibility." They often abused their freedom, and they never fully lived up to the challenge of their responsibility. But, on the other hand, they never abdicated their freedom or their responsibility, even though they were already in various ways victimized by the Communist Party. Against the darkened literary scene on the mainland today, their lives enshrine for us the blaze of hope that once enkindled the May Fourth Movement.

* * *

Since the above was written in December, 1965, a new Cultural Revolution has swept over mainland China, and among its better-known victims have been veteran Communist writers who had enjoyed positions of trust within the party since the early thirties. Far from being antiquated by the revolution, therefore, the present book has actually gained new importance as an objective background study of Mao Tse-tung's current attempt to reorganize his propaganda machine and rewrite literary and political history. In compliance with his decree to discredit the cultural past, Mao's new corps of propagandists have even denigrated the leftist literature of the thirties, hitherto officially acclaimed as a heroic record of creative Communist endeavor under Kuomintang oppression, as on the whole the sinister product of petty-bourgeois minds either pathetically ignorant or defiantly unheedful of his literary policy (that policy, of course, was not fully formulated until 1942). Consequently, the three acknowledged leaders of the Left-Wing League—Lu Hsün, Ch'ü Ch'iu-po, and Chou Yang— have been much in the news, not merely in the historic context of cultural reappraisal, but in the over-all revolutionary context of Mao's fanatic determination to transform his subjects into totally obedient instruments of his will. Though at the time of my brother's death these three had equally enjoyed a spotless reputation for party loyalty (Ch'ü Ch'iu-po, however, was castigated by Premier Chou En-lai at an unpublicized meeting of party leaders held in 1964), Lu Hsün alone has remained unscathed by the revolution. He appears, in fact, more revered than ever, since the people are still urged to read him, while the works of nearly all other major Chinese writers, traditional and modern, have disappeared from bookstores. But his enjoyment of continued party adulation has been made possible only by minimizing his intellectual and creative independence. Whereas in 1940 Mao Tse-tung had saluted Lu Hsün as "the chief commander of China's cultural revolution" prior to his own rise to power, the speakers at a monster rally staged in Peking on October 31, 1966, to commemorate the great writer all saw fit to praise him as Mao's most beloved and obedient disciple. Thus his widow, Hsü Kuang-p'ing, declared, "For Lu Hsun, our great leader Chairman Mao was the reddest sun in his heart. . . . In those days the invincible thought of Mao Tse-tung was the supreme guiding principle for Lu Hsun. . . . Acting under the guidance of Mao Tse-tung's thought, Lu Hsun was a most courageous fighter who breached and stormed the enemy citadel on the cultural front." [11] (Lu Hsün, of course, could have had scant acquaintance with Mao's thought, since at the time of his death nearly all of Mao's most influential tracts and books were yet to be written.)

Specifically, Lu Hsün has been cited as Mao's most obedient soldier holding aloft "the banner of the proletarian revolutionary line" [12] in literature in connection with the nationwide campaign to brand Chou Yang as the principal saboteur of that line during the decades when he was entrusted with the task of its implementation. Despite the detectable signs of his disaffection in the early sixties, when his regard for literary values had finally gained the upper hand over his allegiance to Mao (in that respect he, too, could be seen as a "tenderhearted" Communist), Chou Yang's earlier record of zealous party service was of course beyond reproach. But that record could be easily altered, and among other instances of his supposed dissidence and deceit, his dispute with Lu Hsün over the slogans has been rewritten entirely in the latter's favor (the fact that Lu Hsün's prin-

[11] *Chinese Literature,* No. 1 (Peking, 1967), p. 37. Six speeches given at the rally are featured in that issue.
[12] *Ibid.,* p. 37.

cipal ally in the quarrel was the infamous Hu Feng has been conveniently forgotten). Mindful of Chou Yang's recent downfall, the reader should follow my brother's account of the whole episode with a keener awareness of the irony of history.

Ch'ü Ch'iu-po, for years the only party helmsman of the pre-Mao period to have been spared official Communist condemnation, has also become the object of repeated vilification since the Cultural Revolution: even his grave has been defaced by the Red Guards. His traducers have triumphantly cited his *Superfluous Words,* so sympathetically analyzed by my brother as the last testament of a tenderhearted Communist soul-sick over a life misspent in politics, as the key document in support of his being a Communist renegade cringing before his captors.

Modern Chinese history will continue to be rewritten to suit the changing needs of the Communist Party, and for years to come, even after the present revolution has spent its fury, cultural leaders of an earlier period will play in the news their instructive but falsified roles as simple heroes and villains. In the following studies of Lu Hsün, Ch'ü Ch'iu-po, and several representative writers of lesser note, however, such distorting labels will be totally out of place, as the author recaptures their dilemmas and ordeals for us in all their historical and psychological complexity.

C. T. HSIA

February, 1968

THE GATE OF DARKNESS

Studies on the Leftist Literary Movement in China

CH'Ü CH'IU-PO:
THE MAKING AND DESTRUCTION
OF A TENDERHEARTED COMMUNIST

I

I⊤ is in one capacity that a Communist is generally known—as a tough, dedicated fighter. His individuality is often lost in the mass movement. Whatever private concerns he has, his tastes, sentiments, and worries are beyond our ken. Living dangerously and always on guard against enemies both inside and outside the party, he cannot afford to be other than secretive. He may even be reticent about the useful work he has done for the party, since all glory must go to the incomparable strength of the masses, the correctness of Marxism-Leninism, and the right direction from the man at the top.

A mere member of the party or a cadre is as a rule an example of self-denial. His ideas of truth will not of course prevent him from concealing or distorting facts. As a product of that hardening and depersonalizing process known as endless "strife," one Communist is scarcely distinguishable from another, so far as his personal qualities are concerned. The limits to his mental outlook and intellectual range are as well known as his limitless resources of dissimulation. His passions are known to run in but one channel, and his ideas are cast in one mold. He may be ruthless, ambitious, vindictive, mendacious, and disputatious, but these qualities can hardly be called individual; they do not indicate so much a personal character as the character of a rigid type, which is jealously kept uniform.

So whenever we write about a Communist, we think of him as a type, with all its familiar traits. We can trace his career, but we can hardly identify him as an individual human being. Our research so often stops at the façade he has carefully built up. Whatever is hidden behind—a well-oiled machine or a burning evangelical spirit, as the appearances suggest, or some mixtures incompatible with the faith—we generally do not find out.

But even from the records of the party, we know that its members are not so simple in character. Before the emergence of what Djilas terms the "new class" in a Communist state, almost all Communists are recruits and converts who come from different social origins. Their mental compositions, from a Communist point of view, are "impure" and not all "political education" can surely wash them clean. Though the party demands complete surrender, it can hardly claim total victory over a man's inner life. The "tail" that has been scissored may take on a new growth, and the fire of hatred, if not replenished, can wane.

The Communists themselves are not unaware of this. The successive rectification campaigns are designed to meet just this problem: to reinforce strict conformity. It would be unfair for us to underestimate the scope, thoroughness, and deadly effectiveness of the thought control of the party, or the severity with which the individual members discipline themselves, for therein lies the strength of the party. The Communist movement could not have grown to such magnitude without a vigilant awareness of the inherent elements of dissolution and the ruthless measures taken against them.

The emphasis the campaigns receive only indicates that dissension, whether hidden or open, does exist. And the dissenters are not always Communists of another brand who interpret a common faith in a different way; there are those who strike at the very roots of the faith. They are the doubters, the disillusioned, the idealists who find the new order scarcely better than the old. There are also those who have come to grudge the heavy price they have paid for the right to join the revolution. And the price is the loss of their personal freedom.

We do not know much about the inner life of "hardhearted" Communists, save that they get along well within the limits of the dogma and discipline set by the party. Some are even in a position to impose them. They have successfully remolded their personalities; they are perfect adjusters. But the life of a "tenderhearted" Communist, we can imagine, is miserable. He is too weak to become a good revolutionary fighter, though he has to put up a show of toughness. Trying to quit involves too many practical difficulties; moreover, the party may have still some lingering meaning for him. But to stay on is to suffer all the frustrations, indignities, and hypocrisies. His conscience, which he has somehow kept alive, cannot deliver him from the dilemma. He is constantly aware of his personal tragic errors as well as the errors of the party, but he is also beset by solitude. In the air of mutual suspicion that envelops his life, he cannot communicate his true feelings to his comrades; but he has lost contact with the old non-Communist world. As an individual, he is no match for the party in strength, and he may not be able to offer a system that can take the place of communism. But with all his weaknesses, he has maintained a little islet of individualism which refuses to be swallowed up by the dark, turbulent seas all around. As the doubter, the worrier, the silent, introspective rebel, he is a much more interesting character than his tough colleague. The very existence of this isolated, troubled soul is a silent protest against the totalitarian movement. His terrible experience is one of the most memorable human dramas in which not only his personal fate but the fate of humanity is on trial.

Though the "tenderhearted" Communist has appeared as the tormented, meditative hero of many a political novel, he is no mere imaginary character. His existence is illustrated by the examples of the Koestlers, the Spenders, the Djilases, and the Ssu-ma Lus, whose vivid descriptions of their first-hand experiences reveal as nothing else can the feelings and thoughts of a Communist in bewilderment. But there may be many more within the Communist Party who have not so luckily resolved their doubts, or who are only awaiting an opportunity to speak out in their own voice. Until such an opportunity arises, the silent disloyal must be classified with the silent loyal.

Nothing can induce us to describe Ch'ü Ch'iu-po (1899–1935) as a disloyal Communist, but what makes him such a fascinating study is that he was a writer and that he wrote at great length about himself. In the bulk of his works written between 1923 and 1934 we hear only the voice of one who spoke for the party, though the voice sometimes also has personal conviction in what he was writing about. But the two books he wrote during his first trip to Soviet Russia (1920–22), *A Journey to the Land of Hunger* and *History of the Heart in the Red Capital,* are remarkable for an astonishing candor. The books are not mere travelogues or propaganda but are concerned with the author's mental state in the critical years in poverty-stricken Russia when he was changing from a non-Communist into a Communist. Then after more than a decade of bitter struggle, he reviewed his life in a prison in Changting, Fukien, and wrote, in addition to a few lyrics, his testament, *Superfluous Words.* The last document, in the form that is available, is one of the most intimate records of the soul of a Communist.

Today Ch'ü Ch'iu-po is honored as a martyr,[1] and his good name as a

---

[1] "The remains of Comrade Ch'ü Ch'iu-po, who was executed by the KMT reactionaries twenty years ago in Changting, Fukien, were interred in the Martyrs'

worthy leader and comrade, once fallen into disgrace, has been rescued by a resolution of the Central Committee under the direction of Mao Tse-tung.[2] Mao is a man of long memory. The coolness or unkindness shown him by his former "bosses" in the party, Ch'en Tu-hsiu, Li Li-san, Ch'en Shao-yü, or Ch'in Pang-hsien, he will never forgive, but his relations with Ch'ü are known to have been more cordial. There may have existed between the two men a certain degree of friendship or mutual respect.[3] If so, it would seem natural for Mao to have some concern for the posthumous reputation of Ch'ü. But Ch'ü's distinguished career should also speak for itself. He will be long remembered for the part he played in the struggles against the "patriarch" of the party, Ch'en Tu-hsiu, in 1927. His policy of riots in 1927 and his conciliatory attitude toward Li Li-san, the author of the famous "tough line of action," in 1930 have been called into question by his comrades, but they reflect no discredit on his eager desire for revolution. His arrest and execution only crowned a long record of struggle marked by the spirit of self-sacrifice. If he was not an unusually clever schemer or able organizer, he was at least a quite formidable fighter.

Ch'ü is also known to have been a man of letters, and there is no doubt that he used his pen bravely and diligently in the service of the party. His

---

Cemetery at Pa-pao-shan, Peking, on June 18." Hsinhua News Agency, June 18, 1955. *Jen-min jih-pao,* June 19, 1955.

[2] "Comrade Ch'ü Ch'iu-pai, who was supposed to have committed mistakes along the line of conciliation, was a party leader of prestige and did much useful work (mainly cultural) even after blows were dealt to him, and died a hero's death in June, 1935, at the hands of the KMT executioners." Mao Tse-tung, "Resolutions on Some Questions in the History of Our Party," *Selected Works* (New York: International Publishers, 1956), IV, 183. See also *ibid.,* the note on p. 340, ". . . he was attacked by the 'Left' doctrinaire-sectarians and excluded from the party's central leading body."

[3] "Comrade Ch'iu-po was very respectful toward Comrade Mao Tse-tung. . . . [After only a part of Mao's lengthy] 'Report on an Inspection of the Agrarian Movement in Hunan' . . . was published in *Hsiang-tao (Guide Weekly),* its editor, Peng Shu-chih, was not willing to publish the remainder. . . . Ch'ü, then in Wu-han, not only published the full text as a book but also wrote a preface to it." Hsiao San, *Jen-wu yü chi-nien (Personalities and Reminiscences)* (Peking: San Lien Bookstore, 1952), p. 221. Ch'ü also taught at the Training Center for the Agrarian Movement, which was under the direction of Mao in Canton. See Wen Chi-tse, "Comrade Ch'ü Ch'iu-po's Battling Life," *Hung-ch'i p'iao-p'iao (Red Flags Are Flying)* (Peking: Chinese Youth Publications Association, 1957), V, 93. In Kiangsi, he was said to be on cordial terms with Mao, though he did not get along well with other Communist leaders. See Hsüeh-hua, "Introduction to *Superfluous Words,*" *I-ching,* Vol. II, No. 25 (Mar. 5, 1937), p. 19.

name has become inseparable from the Leftist Literary Movement in Shanghai. He knew how to express himself in lucid Chinese, and his mastery of the Russian language was a rare ability among the Communist leaders of his time. Besides his elucidation of the Communist theory, especially on literary subjects, he endeavored to put language to its best use as a weapon for agitation and propaganda. He aimed at a larger audience and advocated a "language for the masses," to be distinguished from the *pai-hua,* which he disdained as scarcely more lively than the "dead" *wen-yen* it was supposed to supersede.[4] He went so far as to deplore the poor readability of Lu Hsün's translations,[5] a criticism which, though it confirmed the opinions of "bourgeois" critics like Liang Shih-ch'iu,[6] Lu Hsün could only take gracefully, since it came from a friend who had the linguistic demands of the masses in view. The useful work Ch'ü did in this direction is recognized by the party. Though not all his critical views are accepted today,[7] Ch'ü's name as a writer has been perpetuated by the publication of his literary works (not his political writings), in a set of four imposing volumes.[8] As Lu Ting-i, Minister of Propaganda of the Chinese Communist Party, put it, "His noble qualities and the meritorious deeds he did in his lifetime will live forever in the hearts of the people; they are immortal." [9]

But before Ch'ü assumed the halo of immortality, he revealed himself, in his two early works, in a character quite different from the heroic image brandishing his pen against a background of surging masses. His is an alto-

[4] See the five essays on Literary Revolution and Language Problems in *Ch'ü Ch'iu-po wen-chi (Collected Works)* (Peking: People's Literary Publications Association, 1953), II, 593–704.

[5] See his two letters on translation to Lu Hsün, *Collected Works,* II, 917–42.

[6] Liang's essay on "Mr. Lu Hsün's 'Hard Translation' " appeared in the *Hsin-yüeh (Crescent Moon),* Vol. II, Nos. 6 and 7 (a combined issue). Lu Hsün's rebuttal "Hard Translation and the Class-Nature of Literature" is found in *Lu Hsün ch'üan-chi (Complete Works)* (Peking: People's Literary Publications Association, 1957), IV, 155 ff.

[7] Ch'ü wrote in 1932 an essay on the "Revolutionary Romantic," which looks disapprovingly at the "romantic elements" contained in a leftist novel, *Ti-ch'üan (Spring from the Earth),* written by Hua Han. This essay is found in an earlier collection, *Luan-t'an (Vulgar Music)* (Shanghai, 1949), but is excluded from the authorized *Collected Works.* One reason is perhaps that "revolutionary romanticism" is an essential part of the literary policy of the Chinese Communist Party under Mao Tse-tung. Kuo Mo-jo believes that one of Mao's poems, "Tieh lüan hua" is a "typical combination of revolutionary realism with revolutionary romanticism." *Wen-i pao,* No. 7, Apr. 11, 1958.

[8] For publication data see note 4.

[9] *Jen-min jih-pao,* June 19, 1955.

gether much more complex and lonely character. Enthusiasm for revolution is probably there, but that is only one of his many facets. We are able to see him more or less in depth, and he is found to be affectionate, sentimental, meditative, idealistic, capable of absorption in scenes of natural beauty, introspective to the point of self-pity, and haunted by a sense of loneliness. These are the qualities customarily associated with a poet in the traditional Chinese sense rather than with a revolutionary. But then his revolutionary career had barely begun. There was plenty of time ahead for him to overcome his weaknesses, and to hammer this fragile material, which was not only adulterated with all forms of sentimentality but marred by a serious case of tuberculosis, into a first-rate fighter.

A tenderhearted Communist is but a halfhearted, and therefore a poor, Communist. The inevitable question is, "How successfully did he transform his character?" It is hard to conceive how the young writer whose love for his parents, cousins, friends, and the wild flowers and moonlit night made such poignant reading could have developed into a revolutionary whose name was equated with terrorism, blind fury, and relentlessness, especially after the series of notorious riots staged under his leadership. To make that possible, he must have discarded his tender half, since the two sides of his character were irreconcilable. But here an interesting psychological question arises: Can a person be entirely cut off from his past? Can his early training be wiped out, his memory suffocated, and his mental habits all reformed? He may accomplish this to a certain degree by the power of his will. But can he control his subconscious mind? Hard work may help. To drive oneself at a feverish rate so as to exhaust oneself mentally and physically is a proven measure against dangerous thoughts. That was how Ch'ü treated himself most of the time. But now and then leisure was forced upon him, as relapses of his tuberculosis would require a rest cure. Those days spent in a sickbed perhaps brought him no peace of mind. Then he was arrested and put in prison. A period of enforced idleness, together with other circumstances, such as the interrogation by the Kuomintang officials, softened up his defenses against his own past. With the loss of his freedom, his mind, paradoxically, was set free. As his thoughts roamed, the urge for self-expression returned. The few poems he wrote then are all nostalgic in nature, and in *Superfluous Words* he came to understand himself better when he admitted to his "dual personality." Which one is the real Ch'ü Ch'iu-po, the fighter or the ruminating sentimentalist? Perhaps both, if we believe that a split personality is not impossible even with a Communist.

II

On January 29, 1899, Ch'ü Ch'iu-po was born into a family in Chang-chow, Kiangsu, that had for generations "smelt of the scent of books." His grandfather, a high official under the Manchus, left behind a considerable fortune which, however, was quickly dissipated. After a few comfortable years in early childhood, Ch'iu-po was soon to experience a poverty which was degenerating from the genteel sort into the abject. His father, who was responsible for the decline of the family fortunes, must have been one of those decadent young men so often found in the mandarin houses in China in the late nineteenth and early twentieth centuries. Accustomed to elegant living and luxuries, they did not know how to earn their own bread. To seek employment was thought to be beneath them; and anyway they were not good at anything except dabbling in art and indulging in refined idleness. They were intelligent but weak-willed, full of good intentions but short in spirit for any kind of exertion. The changing times, hurried on by the advent of the republic, caught them unprepared. Ch'iu-po's father, who, among all the possible hobbies, chose occult Taoism, managed to live for years on the family treasures—paintings, calligraphy, art objects, and fine furniture. Among Ch'iu-po's experiences in his teens were his constant visits to the pawnshop. The landed property must have been liquidated at the same time, for the family had to find shelter in the "clan temple."

After the shiftless, opium-smoking[10] father had gone to the province of Shantung to accept a position as a schoolteacher, which promised only subsistence pay, the burden of raising a family of six children[11] fell upon the shoulders of the mother. The good woman seems to have been the prototype of the daughter of a mandarin house who, while practicing the virtues of patience, meekness, and modesty, had much more character than the man she was destined to marry. She was sensitive, intelligent, narrow-minded, and fiercely proud. In her might even be found domineering quali-ties, for she was trained since girlhood to rule as a daughter-in-law and

[10] No other source mentions that Ch'ü's father was an opium smoker, but Ch'iu-po himself admitted to this in an interview held in prison in 1935. Li K'e-ch'ang, "An Interview with Ch'ü Ch'iu-po," *Kuo-wen Weekly*, Vol. XII, No. 26 (July 8, 1935).

[11] I do not know exactly how many children she had. But Ch'ü noted, at the time he was leaving for Russia, that he and two younger brothers were in Peking, and two other younger brothers and one younger sister were in Hangchow. They had to depend on relatives only after their mother's death. *A Journey to the Land of Hunger, Collected Works,* I, 8.

eventually as a matriarch over a large household. The man could afford to forget about the world in his hobbies, but the woman had no way of escaping from the day-to-day problems of housekeeping. The task confronting Ch'iu-po's mother turned out to be more than she could cope with. For with all her accomplishments, she shared the fatal weakness of the gentry class; she did not know where to look for a source of income. The best she could do was to live frugally and to haggle energetically so as to get the most out of what little was left of the family collection. The family inevitably ran into debt. So in addition to all the humiliations, she had now to answer the dunners.

Regular education for the children was something that a family of high standing like the Ch'üs of Changchow could not afford to neglect even in its reduced circumstances. Ch'iu-po was a bright student in both the primary and secondary schools he attended. But one year before his graduation from the Changchow High School, when he was sixteen *sui,* he was compelled, for financial reasons, to quit. Considering the four younger brothers and one younger sister who needed to be fed and educated, he got a job in the neighboring district of Wusih as a schoolteacher. Thus he not only saved the family from the expenses of his own education but began to support himself. But instead of bringing satisfaction to the heart of the mother, this became another source of sorrow. She hated herself for not being able to keep in school a son in whom she saw great promise for learning.

Soon afterward Ch'ü's grandmother died. The old lady had seen much better days while the grandfather was living but now for years had been suffering from paralysis and had become a grumbling, pathetic figure. The daughter-in-law must have had a hard time in catering to her needs. The expenses incurred by her long illness were also beyond the means of this particular branch of the Ch'ü clan. To get rid of the burden, Ch'iu-po's mother suggested moving the old lady to Hangchow so that she could be better taken care of by one of Ch'iu-po's uncles who was in better circumstances.[12] But the travel proved fatal, as the grandmother died after she arrived in Hangchow.

The whispers that had been exchanged among the relatives now became audible. They all amounted to so many accusing fingers pointed at the

---

[12] The uncle could be the "fourth paternal uncle," on whom Ch'iu-po's brothers were to depend for support. He was probably also the uncle who had served as magistrate of certain districts in Chekiang (mentioned in Li's "Interview," cited in note 10).

harassed woman, Ch'iu-po's mother. It seemed that she was unwifely, so that her husband had to leave home; she was unmotherly, so that she would not let her son finish high school; she was undaughterly, so that she would hasten the invalid mother to death by moving her about. These criticisms, in addition to the difficulties with the dunners who became particularly importunate at the end of the lunar year, drove her to despair. She ended her life by taking an amount of the phosphorous heads of red matches watered down with a quaff of tiger-bone wine. On the night of the second day of the first moon, in the year of *i-mao* (February 19, 1915),[13] Ch'iu-po rushed home from Wusih when he heard the news. He was not too late to witness the terrible scene, with his mother lying in bed, the box of matches and the bottle of wine.[14]

His mother's suicide was one of the most terrible blows in Ch'iu-po's life, a trauma which was perhaps never healed. As he reflected on the incident in 1920, on the eve of his departure for Russia, he said:

My mother has been driven out of this universe by Poverty; my father is nothing but jetsam cast off by the same force, . . . The large family system . . . was first quivering and shaking, and then it will topple and gradually become lost to sight. I shall take up one phase of this social phenomenon— the dying system of the large family in China, a phase that I have personally witnessed and participated in. I can only see that day after day this system is drawing closer to its end. The best one can say of the system is that under it everybody lives a dry, static life. On the side of its evils, one can see that because of the conflict of economic interests and the looseness of family ties, especially between husband and wife, the members of such a family—fathers, sons, brothers, sisters-in-law, uncles—while staring blankly at each other under the mask of Confucianism, will stop at nothing to give vent in secret to their jealousy and hatred, to grumble, to murmur, to curse, and to kill with their venomous tongues. The relations between man and man have troubled me as a great puzzle. The meaning of life is absolutely obscure to me. Though I believe I have within me a harmonious chord, no harmonious music can I play.

In my childhood, I received tender and loving care from my mother. My

[13] The date, the second day of the first moon, is agreed upon by Wen Chi-tse, "Comrade . . . ," *Red Flags Are Flying*, V, 81; Ts'ao Tzu-hsi, *Ch'ü Ch'iu-po ti wen-hsüeh huo-tung* (*Ch'ü Ch'iu-po's Literary Activities*) (Shanghai: New Literature Publications Association, 1958), p. 5; and Shang-kuan Ai-ming, *Ch'ü Ch'iu-po yü wen-hsüeh* (*Ch'ü Ch'iu-po and Literature*) (Nanking: Kiangsu Literary Publications Association, 1959). Shang-kuan Ai-ming said that the day was February 19, 1915, in the solar calendar, but I checked on the calendar and found it to be February 15. Yang Chih-hua (Ch'ü's widow) does not give a definite date. She only refers to February, 1915. "In Memoriam, Ch'iu-po," *Red Flags Are Flying*, VIII (1958), p. 26. The other biographers stress poverty as the cause of the suicide. Yang Chih-hua brings in the interesting factor of relatives' accusations.

[14] Wen Chi-tse, "Comrade . . . ," *Red Flags Are Flying*, V, 81.

soul was nourished by the landscape known in the south of the Yangtze, the delicate hills and lovely waters, and my body, by the *lu* [a tasty fish like perch] from Sungkiang and the cabbage from Hsi-hsiang. My heart was delighted by the natural tunes of the insects chirping under the sheds laden with beans or melons; refreshed by the poetical ideas flowing in with early morning breezes against a fading moon; and warmed by subtle, innocent love affairs, the gentle brushing of a curl of hair, the hushed sweet small talk. Alas! Good friends, intimate friends, loving relatives, tender care, generous help—they have all vanished like a dream. Even so, the merciless society, like a stern mathematics teacher, has posed before me a most difficult, almost astronomical problem which, to my sadness, I have not yet been able to solve. But some "inner urge" is driving me onward—me who only by a narrow chance have escaped turning into a callous, misanthropic recluse under miserable circumstances. I have steeled my heart to part with my aged father, my brothers, cousins, and all relatives and friends and set out on my journey westward.[15]

So the family was broken up. After several months spent in mourning, Ch'iu-po, with the aid of various uncles and cousins, left home and ventured into the world. What he took with him was the bitter-sweet memories described above. The small world he left behind was not altogether hateful. It had at least contained something he treasured dearly, his mother's love. Compared with the cities he was going to visit, Wuchang and Peking, both cultural and revolutionary centers with enough intellectual activities to challenge the growing powers of the young man, his native town had been narrow in its intellectual horizon but not without quiet beauty and artistic tradition. Even when he was too young to be sent to school, he had learned to recite the famous T'ang poets at his mother's knee. His father taught him to paint and he studied the carving of seal stones with an uncle.[16]

Life might have been happy but for poverty, to which indeed he attributed his mother's death, the dissolution of his family, and the jealousy and hatred inside the clan. And poverty was to pursue him even in the big cities. Whatever grudges he bore against his relatives, he was to continue to rely on their help. For the clan system, or the large family system as he called it, was an odd mixture of conventional virtue, genuine humanity, and hypocrisy. Among its many functions, it provided a sort of social security—a bereaved, penniless member of the clan could always get the money to buy a coffin for the deceased, and an orphan would not be left in the world uncared for. The system also provided some schooling which he could not have obtained elsewhere. A child was expected to learn proper manners from the elders, but he was exposed to the ugly side of

[15] *Journey, Collected Works,* I, 13–14.
[16] Ts'ao Tzu-hsi, *op. cit.,* p. 3.

life demonstrated in the behavior of those he was taught to revere. At a tender age he had to accept vice and injustice as facts of life. A sensitive youth, particularly if he was snubbed by the better-off branches of the clan, could only rouse himself by rebellious thinking to avoid being depressed by what he saw around him.

As to Ch'iu-po's school education, it bore the marks of that period of Chinese history. Lessons in patriotism, public duty, and modernization permeated the curriculum, and even militarism was taught as a way of national salvation. Ch'iu-po received some sort of military training after the news of the Wuchang uprising in 1911 reached his high school, though he was then only a boy of twelve.[17]

When Ch'iu-po was taking a boat up the Yangtze, he had emerged from this complicated background a little dazed, without quite understanding the forces that had been working on him. The major political events, the founding of the republic and the fall of Yüan Shih-k'ai, had passed by, leaving him unimpressed. He described himself in retrospect as an escapist,[18] in the sense that he had been wholly absorbed by the world of poetry, classics, and inspiration (*hsing-ling*). Now his mother's death had deprived him of the last protection against the necessities of everyday life; he had to fend for himself, if not for his younger brothers and sister.

The aims he set for himself were not high: to go back to school, and if possible, to get a college diploma so as to qualify himself for a better position than the one he had occupied as headmaster of the obscure school at Wusih. The future was open for him, but the path he had been treading was much the same as the one followed by many other young men of his generation. To seek independence in big cities while keeping up the genteel tradition was in the minds of those who, in spite of their tastes and inclinations, suddenly found that they could no longer live with their families. Ch'iu-po was then more melancholy than rebellious, intent upon seeking his own fortune rather than denouncing the society that made such adventure necessary. He was to continue to enjoy the help and warmth provided by the clan system. He did not go to nearby Nanking or Shanghai, where he would have been alone in a strange world, but to Wuchang in the mid-Yangtze Valley, where his cousin Shun-po was ready with brotherly help, which included, if not a great deal in the way of cash, at least a home and mature advice. Ch'iu-po would have to depend on him for years to come.

[17] Wen Chi-tse, "Comrade . . . ," *Red Flags Are Flying*, V, 80.
[18] *Journey, Collected Works*, I, 21.

Ch'iu-po might have turned his attention to the political and social problems in his new environment, but under the influence of another cousin, a Mr. Chou, he devoted more time to the subtle and challenging art of composing classical Chinese poetry. Under the same influence, he discovered a "revived interest" in Buddhism. Such studies necessarily furthered his introverted tendencies, while his juvenile ideas about a "political solution of social problems," he later admitted, had to wither before they had a chance to bud forth.[19] He was even induced into a mystic state of peace.

For a short time Ch'iu-po attended the Foreign Languages College in Hankow. It was perhaps his cousin's transfer to Peking that led Ch'iu-po to make a trip there sometime in 1916. He was denied enrollment at the National Peking University because he could not pay the tuition, but the lecture halls of the august institution were open to him, as well as to many other young men who then swarmed to the capital to quench their thirst for learning. What impressions Ch'en Tu-hsiu or Li Ta-chao made on him then were not on record, though he later joined the Socialist Studies Group formed under Li's direction.[20] In the summer of 1917 he was admitted to the Russian Language College, a tuition-free training school for foreign service, affiliated with the Ministry of Foreign Affairs. It was clear that Shun-po, himself a government employee,[21] would like to have his young cousin follow in his footsteps in the government service.

Ch'iu-po was gradually taking in Western ideas, but he persevered in his own plans of study. He worked very hard, with the aid of his Buddhistic studies, toward a personal solution of life's problems which kept baffling him. He might have become a poet and philosopher in his own way, while leading the philistine life of a career diplomat. What changed him was the May Fourth Movement. Indeed, no one has more right to the title of a man born of that movement. From then on he had to revise his views to

[19] *Ibid.*, p. 22.

[20] In 1920 Li Ta-chao started the organization of Socialist Studies Small Groups at several schools in Peking as well as the Communist Small Group. The latter was more closely related to the Third International. Wang K'e-feng, *Wu-szu yün-tung yü chung-kuo kung-ch'an-tang chih tan-sheng* (*The May Fourth Movement and the Birth of the Communist Party*) (Nanking: Kiangsu People's Publications Association, 1958), pp. 34–35. According to Wen Chi-tse, Ch'ü joined the Socialist Group. "Comrade . . . ," *Red Flags Are Flying,* V, 85.

[21] According to Cheng Chen-to, Shun-po was a *k'e-yüan* of the Ministry of Foreign Affairs. "A Few Anecdotes in Comrade Ch'ü Ch'iu-po's Early Life," *Hsin kuan ch'a* (*New Observer*), No. 12, June 16, 1955. But Ch'ü himself told the interviewer in prison that Shun-po was an employee of the Ministry of War. Li K'e-ch'ang interview cited in note 10.

fit into the Marxist doctrine he came to accept, and revolutionary activity began to take precedence over poetical and religious meditation. He was the best authority on the progress from an aspirant yogi to a would-be commissar through those critical years. In *A Journey to the Land of Hunger* he said:

The three years from my arrival in Peking to the eve of the May Fourth Movement were the most solitary in my life. I had then no friends. The new bureaucrats in the capital, with their "republican" way of living, disturbed me as a source of painful irritation. I became more and more convinced of my misanthropic views of life with the three years' study of philosophy. But a change had come over my mind, since I felt then a positive disgust which took the place of my earlier escapist attitude. My interest in classical studies led me to the ambition to reform such studies through a revival of the "Modern Text School." My attempts at solving life's problems through Buddhism resulted in another ambition: to humanize Buddhism and practice altruism as contained in the idea of Bodhisattvahood [*p'u-sa-hsing*]. These were the vain and boastful wishes of a young man, but they epitomized the dualistic view of life evolved in my solitude. I allotted a part of my time to preparing for the discharge of my "worldly" duties—training for a career in which I was supposed to make a livelihood. Another part of my time was used on the "transcendental" level, for I had also to prepare myself diligently for the "service" [*kung-te,* a Buddhistic term] of saving China by cultural means. I never relaxed in my philosophical studies, which added heavily to the load of work at the Russian Language College. That I had to live like an ascetic and to study more than eleven hours a day was only a manifestation of my pursuit of the dual aims. Social intercourse could not have a place in my life. I studied Russian because thereby I could some day eat my own rice; for the rice I then ate was not mine but my cousin's. My parasitic existence could not fail to stimulate me, now and again, into thinking about social problems, the problem of the relationship between man and man.
A bright path gradually revealed itself out of my studies in Buddhism: I believed that the world was to be saved through the practice of Bodhisattvahood and that everything was impermanent, including the social system. But such a philosophy could not hold long when the May Fourth Movement sucked me in like a whirlpool. My solitude was finally broken. My comrades in the Peking Social Service Club:[22] Ch'ü Shih-ying (an uncle), Cheng Chen-to, Keng Chi-chih, and Chang Chao-te (the last two being my schoolmates at the Russian College) all, like myself, joined the movement with an unbelievable fury.[23]

[22] *She-hui fu-wu-hui* in the original. But the name should be more correctly Society Promotion Society, a social service branch of the YMCA, Peking. *Wu-ssu shih-ch'i ch'i-k'an chieh-shao* (*An Introduction to the Periodicals in the May Fourth Era*) (Peking: People's Publications Association, 1958), I, 320, compiled by the Research Room, Editing and Publication Bureau of Marx-Engels-Lenin-Stalin's Works, Chinese Communist Party.

[23] As to his activities during the May Fourth Movement, he was arrested together with eight hundred others and imprisoned for three days. Wen Chi-tse, "Comrade . . . ," *Red Flags Are Flying,* V, 84. On the very day of the demonstration, he came home spitting blood. Hsiao San, *op. cit.,* p. 218.

We were all aware of the deep-seated maladies of the society to which we belonged but were yet ignorant of their cure. Feelings alone, however, ran so strong that restlessness could no more be contained. That was, so far as I can see, the real significance of the student movement. There was a demand for change, and that demand came out in an outburst. It had then at least its shocking and rousing effects, for as Prince Kropotkin said, "One riot does more than thousands of books and pamphlets."

The unhappy situation of those eight and nine years after the founding of the Republic had to produce a reaction. Then the ideological revolution as reflected in *La Jeunesse* and *New Tides* joined forces with the public sentiments in the student movement; and they together raised cataclysmic waves that shook through all China. The patriotic movement had actually a deeper meaning than mere patriotism. The taste of colonialism, in its full bitterness, had never come home to the Chinese until then, even though we had already had the experience of several decades of foreign exploitation behind us. The sharp pain of imperialistic oppression then reached the marrow of our bones, and it awakened us from the nightmares of impractical democratic reforms. The issue of German possessions in Shantung, which started the national uproar, could not be separated from the larger problem. The industrial powers of the modern world are beset with the problems of capitalism, which takes the form of imperialism in the colonies. It was because of this that the student movement in China inevitably leaned toward socialism. Our social problems became further complicated with the bankruptcy of the clannish rural economy, which took away the basis from the old social structure. The problems of Confucianism, women, labor, and social reform, the literary problems centered on the vernacular, and the philosophical problems related to the view of life all rose up at the same time; they have ever since revolved around the social thinking of new China.[24]

Like many other sensitive youths of that time, Ch'iu-po did some thinking of his own. His active interest in social problems could be seen from the articles he contributed to *The New Society,* a magazine published, curiously enough, under the sponsorship of the YMCA and edited by Ch'iu-po and some of the friends mentioned above.[25] Here are some titles: "The Family of the Chinese Intelligentsia"; "The Time for Reform Has Arrived"; "The Labor Problem of China and of the World"; "The Spoils of Knowledge"; "Victims of the Social Movement"; "On the New Christian Corporate Life in the USA" (to which he objected); "Society and Evils"; "The Society of the Future and the Countercurrents of Today"; "The Pan-Labor Theory of A. Bebel" (of which he approved); and "Whose Weapon Is This—La grève, le sabotage?" The French words in the last title were perhaps meant to show off the author's linguistic ability, but more probably to cover up the dangerous thoughts contained in "strike"

[24] *Journey, Collected Works,* I, 22–24.

[25] About the details of the *New Society,* see *Introduction to Periodicals,* pp. 320 ff. The titles of Ch'ü's essays are found on p. 326.

and "sabotage," which, in Chinese, could easily be recognized by the police.

The magazine had a life of only six months; it was banned on charges of containing socialist propaganda. The charges may have been true, but not all its contributors were sympathetic with Bolshevism. Ch'iu-po was on the left, while the others such as Cheng Chen-to, the literary-historian-to-be but then a student in the School of Railway Management, and Ch'ü Shih-ying, Ch'iu-po's uncle (a student of philosophy at Hui-wen College who later got his Ph.D. at Columbia, taught philosophy at Yenching University, and actively supported the Rural Reform Movement under Dr. James Yen), were for a more mild, idealistic line in their editorial policy as well as in their sophomoric political program. But as Ch'iu-po did not insist on something which he did not think he really understood,[26] no serious quarrel split the small group. This handful of young men, while drifting apart, could still see that they agreed more than they disagreed. The differences that alienated Hu Shih from Ch'en Tu-hsiu, or that tore asunder the Young China Association, leaving only two mutually antagonistic groups of Communists and extreme Nationalists,[27] simply did not happen to them.

Although Ch'iu-po objected to its idealistic connotation, he accepted the name *Humanité* to be used on the cover of their new magazine that succeeded the defunct *New Society*.[28] Only one issue was out, to which Ch'iu-po contributed "The Voice of the Heart," a poem that did not attempt to conceal his idealism. Ch'iu-po was leaving for Russia when the YMCA came up with an apology that it was no longer in a position to continue its financial support. So *Humanité* was forced to cease publication, but the small group of writers launched a more venturesome enterprise, the Literary Research Society, which made history.[29]

[26] "No one at that time understood the meaning of the materialistic view of history." *Journey, Collected Works,* I, 24. This statement of Ch'ü's is definitely applicable to his small group. Whether he held the same view as people like Li Ta-chao and Ch'en Tu-hsiu is doubtful.

[27] The Young China Association was the predecessor of the rightist Young China Party, but its early members included such eminent Communists as Mao Tse-tung and Li Ta-chao. The struggle inside the Association was one of the most interesting phases of Chinese ideological and political history in the early twenties. For a brief account see *Introduction to Periodicals,* pp. 235 ff.

[28] The first issue of *Humanité* was published on August 15, 1920. See *Introduction to Periodicals,* pp. 328 ff.

[29] Four of the founders of the Literary Research Society were originally associated with the *Humanité*: Cheng Chen-to, Ch'ü Shih-ying, Keng Chi-chih, and Hsü Ti-shan.

III

Ch'ü Ch'iu-po went to Russia as a correspondent of the *Ch'en pao* (*Morning News*) of Peking.[30] The offer, which came a few days after the publication of *Humanité*, was tempting. It meant an opportunity to travel, to see the socialist revolution at first hand, and to earn his independence. The annual pay of $2,000 (Chinese currency) was a considerable jump from the $6 a month he got as a schoolteacher in Wusih.[31] But he was also warned of the hardships and perils in a land torn by civil war and afflicted with utter destitution. Relatives and friends tried indeed to dissuade him from making the hazardous trip, but in vain. He agreed that Russia was a Land of Hunger, but could they not see that the appellation had an allegorical meaning? To seek death by starvation was in the noble tradition of Confucian idealism. He was only doing what was expected of a Confucian superior man; and no consideration of material comfort or personal safety should be allowed to interfere with the pursuit of lofty ideals. Soviet Russia was his promised land, the fulfillment of his devout wishes. He reminded them of the little essay *On the Land of Hunger* by the eighteenth-century scholar Kuan T'ung, which reads:

The Land of Hunger is located at the extremity of the Cosmos, separated from China by immeasurable distances. Bare is the land where no rice, sor-

---

The Society was founded in January, 1921, when Ch'ü Ch'iu-po was in Russia. Both *A Journey to the Land of Hunger* and *History of the Heart in the Red Capital* were listed as publications of the Literary Research Society.

[30] Li Ta-chao might have been an influence behind the appointment. "The Peking *Ch'en pao* was formerly known as the *Ch'en chung pao* (*The Morning Bell*), an organ of the Progressive Party, headed by the bourgeois reformers Liang Ch'i-ch'ao and T'ang Hua-lung. The same political group became later the Constitution Research Society, or, in its better known name, the Research Clique. At the inception of the *Ch'en chung pao* (Aug. 15, 1916), its editor-in-chief was Li Ta-chao, only recently returned from Japan. . . . He was discharged from service, however, after only two months because of differences in opinion. . . . In September, 1918, eight newspapers in Peking were banned on account of their publication of the news about Japan's huge loan to Marshal Tuan Ch'i-jui. Among them were the two papers of the Research Clique: *Ch'en chung pao* and the *Kuo-min kung-pao*. In December of the same year, the *Ch'en chung pao* resumed publication under the name of *Ch'en pao*. In February, 1919, its page 7 (or supplementary page) went through a reorganization. Li Ta-chao, who had acquired some rudimentary knowledge about communism, was brought back to work on it. From then on the paper made it clear that it was favoring the new cultural movement." *Introduction to Periodicals*, p. 95.

[31] The amount paid by the *Ch'en pao* was revealed in his interview. Li K'e-ch'ang, *op. cit.* The amount paid by the school in Wusih is given in Shang-kuan Ai-ming, *op. cit.*, p. 3.

ghum, wheat, bean, cow, sheep, chicken, pig, fish, turtle, melon, or fruit ever grows—nothing that nourishes the human being. Those who are desirous of attaining unto it must first rid themselves of appetite, in the same manner as the Taoists who practice breathing exercises and claim that they can thereby live without food. The first stages of the journey are unendurably hard; but if fortitude should urge the traveler on, the destination may be reached within less than ten days. The entrance will take him into an open, bright country which looks as if it were a new universe. Then management falls into disuse and thought comes to a stop. There is no occasion for hustle and bustle, no need for paying calls. One becomes completely at ease where one is beyond the reach of the cries of one's children, the vituperation of one's wife and concubines, and all manner of sarcasm, insult, frivolity, and derision that human society inflicts. But in spite of all these benefits, the common people, minding the hardship encountered in the initial stages of the journey, strive with every possible means to avoid the road that will take them thither. If, as ill luck would have it, they come within sight of it, they will become regretful and allow themselves to be dissuaded from proceeding further. Therefore the land is barred to all but those who go against or deviate from the ways of the world, or those who choose the paths of integrity, honor, propriety, and righteousness. Nevertheless, unless they are unshakable in their determination to accept death for the sake of truth, they will turn back even when they have almost arrived.

At the beginning of the Chou Dynasty, King Wu was raising an army against the House of Yin. The brothers Po-yi and Shu-ch'i thought it dishonorable to eat the rice of Chou, so they made a trip successfully from Mount Shouyang to the Land of Hunger. They became the first known settlers in this Land. . . . [Then follows a short history of the Land. The settlers were all who died of Starvation. But there were also those who failed to reach it because of their lack of purpose.] . . . Alas what country is the Land of Hunger indeed? Why is it so inaccessible? As one who has long despaired of this world, I am making preparations for the journey. Hence I write this note from the studies I have made.[32]

Ch'iu-po replied to his goodhearted friends, who in a morality play would assume the names of Prudence, Timidity, or Complacency, in this fashion:

Our thought should not be allowed to remain in confusion. Though we may think we do not owe society anything, we owe ourselves the supreme duty of satisfying our inner demands. It would be futile for me to argue with you, since realistic theories have laid the foundation of human life for thousands of years. However, we should, within the limits of our capacity, do the utmost to meet the demands of our hearts and, at whatever cost, endeavor to realize our private wishes. Kuan T'ung of the Ch'ing Dynasty identified the Mount Shouyang of Po-yi and Shu-ch'i as their Land of Hunger where they were starved to death. Their real demands were psychological, far more powerful than their economic desire for subsistence, i.e., to eat the dishonorable rice

---

[32] Kuan T'ung, *O-hsiang-chi,* can be found in many anthologies. My source is *Han-fen-lou ku-chin wen-ch'ao,* Vol. 86.

of the Chou. I shall find in the Soviet Union my Land of Hunger. Let us ignore the facts of hunger and cold, that there one will have nothing to eat, nothing to wear, and so forth; the significant fact is that this is the first country that has realized socialist revolution; it is the center of world revolution where the Western and Eastern cultures meet. I shall not be troubled by the means I take to make the trip possible. . . . I know I am not qualified for the task assigned me but I'll go as a newspaper correspondent; I should not accept the offer but I have accepted it; nor shall I ask excuse for my ambition in my attempt to lead our thoughts, with my power of persuasion, to the right path out of the ideological confusions as reflected in *Ch'en pao*. I believe there is no private possession of thought, and that's why I have made up my mind to go.[33]

The paradox of Ch'iu-po's life is shown in this little farewell speech. When he took an early train the next morning and left for Manchuria, he was led, as it were, by a gleam of red light. He was fired with enthusiasm, not unmixed with some pride in the sacrifices he was ready to make, but melancholy, too, at the thought that he would miss all that was hateful and dear to him in China. He could feel the emotions that assailed him, but he could not see the essential conflict in his attitude. To plunge into the revolution if only to report on it (and his reports were to clear the ideological confusions produced by the May Fourth Movement in China) and at the same time to satisfy the reporter's "inner urge"—there was nothing incompatible, so far as he could see then, between the two purposes of his mission. He was not yet fully aware of the scope or variety of his "inner demands."

We see from his own statements that he longed for many things that a revolutionary should never tolerate. Even when he was babbling about the bright future, about a universe filled with "red light" and a land covered with "red flowers stained in blood," [34] he found it hard to sever his ties with the Land of Black Sweetness,[35] the old China with its intricate family relationships and aesthetic ideals. He had to resist the tender love he felt for all the persons, places, and things he had held dear since childhood. Such human weaknesses must be a part of his "inner demands," but what an impediment they turned out to be to his "urge" for spreading the socialist revolution! When the living conditions in the Land of Hunger became hard to bear, his yearning for the Land of Black Sweetness grew strong. For the two terms represent two different attitudes of life, two sets

[33] *Journey, Collected Works,* I, 27.

[34] Introduction, *ibid.,* p. 5.

[35] *Hei-t'ien-hsiang* connotes "sleep." In the Introduction, *ibid.,* pp. 3–5, he characterizes the lethargic, comfort-loving Chinese as "sleepers."

of values, and he was caught in between. The conflict would continue to torment him throughout his life. He never resolved it.

Meanwhile, before he left China, he had a ritual to perform, bidding farewell to his relatives and friends. He visited his father in Tsinan, Shantung, and then stopped at Tientsin before returning to Peking. The relatives he saw all spoke of their uneasy circumstances and unhappy family life. He had to write to obtain an extension for the family debts in his native town. (It is surprising that this responsibility should have been left to the son, who had barely attained manhood, rather than to the father.) His exercises in classical poetry and prose were collected and edited at his father's behest.[36] He wrote to the friends of his childhood as if he would see them no more. "The meaning of my departure from China was tantamount to 're-nunciation of the world.' " [37] "I did not know when I should come back once I had left, and I did not care about the loss of my life. My letters were written with the intent, therefore, that they should carry a farewell forever." [38] The premonition proved correct, for when he returned more than two years later, he had already entered a "new life." The affectionate youth who felt so keenly the saddening effects of the autumn wind, the rustling willows and reeds, the withered grass, and the darkening clouds which accentuated the several scenes of parting, was to come home a Communist whose revolutionary duties would forbid him to resume his normal relationships in life.

One of the friends he visited in Tientsin was Chang T'ai-lai, a schoolmate in the Changchow High School. Chang would play an important part in Ch'ü's life. It was he who introduced Ch'ü into the Communist Party. And it was he who was to die in the Canton Insurrection in 1927 as the victim of Ch'ü's policy of riots. In 1920, Chang was already a member of the Socialist Youth Corps.[39] Ch'ü must have found something exciting

[36] I don't know whether the collection has ever been published.

[37] Introduction, *Journey, Collected Works,* I, 15.

[38] *Ibid.,* p. 16.

[39] "His original name was Chang T'ai-lai, also Chun-mu. He changed it to Chang T'ai-lei after he joined the revolution." Wang I-chih (Chang's widow), "In Memoriam, T'ai-lei," *Red Flags Are Flying,* V, 13. Ch'ü gave his name as Chang T'ai-lai, *Journey, Collected Works,* I, 28. Chang's activities in 1920 are summarized in *Men and Politics in Modern China, Fifty Preliminary Biographies,* ed. Howard L. Boorman (New York: Columbia University Press, 1960), p. 20. "By 1920 he had become active in radical politics in Shanghai. In August of that year when Ch'en Tu-hsiu with the help of Voitinsky, organized the Chinese Socialist Youth Corps, Chang became one of its first members. . . . He was in Tientsin in October, 1920, when Ch'ü Ch'iu-po, then not yet committed to communism, passed through there on his way to Russia. Chang

in the radical views of his chum. The two young men, in the company of two other friends, discussed "Chinese social life" for a whole night.

The two co-founders of *Humanité,* Cheng Chen-to and Keng Chi-chih, who was to win fame as a translator of Russian literature, presented Ch'ü with a farewell poem typical of the doggerel that passed under the name of "new poetry" at that time:

> The whistle is blowing, once and again, to hurry;
> The wheels are rolling, rolling, slowly.
> You are going . . .
> Going into the Red Light . . .
> The whistle has broken our hearts,
> Our hearts are rolling away with the wheels.[40]

The epistle from his philosophical uncle Ch'ü Shih-ying was also in character. Besides quotations from Tagore and Bergson, two of the most popular thinkers in 1920, it offered some comforting thoughts:

> We are going to part for just a little while,
> But I believe:
> We are still living in the great harmony of the universe.
>
> Harmony—Oneness. . . . [41]

In the poem that Ch'iu-po sent back to them are found the significant lines:

> To urge me ahead, the Universal Will;
> To greet me, the Natural Harmony.
>
>   If it is said,
>   Honey is extracted from flowers,
>   And flowers wither after honey is made,
>   But turn your head and look . . .
>   What flourishing and what splendor! [42]

If Ch'iu-po had formulated any theory of his own out of his philosophical studies, it was an eclecticism, a cross of Ch'ü Shih-ying's idealism and

---

was then probably assisting Li Ta-chao in organizing in north China a Socialist Youth Corps modeled after the one which had been set up earlier in Shanghai." About Chang's role in introducing Ch'ü into the Communist Party: "February, 1922. Ch'iu-po joined the Communist Party through the recommendation of Comrade Chang T'ai-lei." Yang Chih-hua, "In Memoriam . . . ," *Red Flags Are Flying,* VIII, 27. Ch'ü himself added Chang Kuo-t'ao in his interview with Li. "The next year [1921], Chang Kuo-t'ao, Chang T'ai-lei, and others, came to Russia. They introduced me into the Communist Party." Li K'e-ch'ang, *op. cit.*

[40] *Journey, Collected Works,* I, 28–30.
[41] *Ibid.,* p. 31.
[42] *Ibid.,* p. 33.

Chang T'ai-lai's materialism. His earlier "misanthropic views" had given way to optimism. He accepted the inevitability of socialist revolution, but that, to him, was more a stage in spiritual evolution than a necessity conditioned by economic factors. In interpreting historical materialism in a metaphysical framework of Buddhism plus Bergsonism, he was advancing a heresy in the pure Marxist's eyes. He philosophized on several occasions in the two books, but with the dominant concepts of Universal Will and Current of Life; he always seems to favor a dualism, if not downright idealism. This, of course, he had to drop after he joined the Communist Party. But then perhaps metaphysical speculation ceased to be of any interest to him.

The Living Force in the universe, or the Third One [besides subjectivity and objectivity] is present everywhere and complete in itself. It is the Prime Mover, which is neither itself moving nor rests stable. The harmony felt in a person's heart and the echoes he finds in his environment are the proofs of the universal truth. As the living force, it does not attach itself to appearances, but it is found in appearances. Thus its reflections can be perceived. It exists in personality and in society; but it also exists in non-personality and non-society. It seems to be the Third One, but it is not the Third One.[43]

Paradise and the sacred status of labor are not the products of the pen of the intelligentsia. They are to be found in the progress of the actual life of the proletariat. Spiritual comfort, the harmony between matter and mind—when the "universal motions" reflect upon and stimulate each other—is made possible by nothing but the Inner Strength of the human being. The motive behind the evolution of an individual, a race, or mankind as a whole is the necessity for, or the demands made upon, the Inner Strength to cope with economic life.[44]

These observations he made while he was still in China. In the postscript to *A Journey to the Land of Hunger* (dated October, 1921, when he had been nine months in Moscow), he still manifested a predilection for Buddhistic concepts and symbols:

Human history throughout the centuries is but a series of visions, one nightmare quickly succeeded by another, which appear in one's consciousness as in the moment when the blood is rushing to the heart. Therefore we cannot have more than faint impressions of them. Social phenomena, with all their endless involvements and myriad reflections, cannot also but leave faint traces, because they are only so many undulations of the heart-wave. Everything in human life rests on Reality, just as so many rivers find their home in the heart-sea. . . . The heart-sea is ever in motion and the heart-wave heaves and rolls in every possible manner. They compose this phantasmagoric world of ours. The closer we are to awakening, the more real, and probably also the

[43] *Ibid.*, p. 11.
[44] *Ibid.*, p. 44.

more terrible, the dreams appear. Since the heart-sea is all pervasive, so the world is in one dream; but since the heart-waves rise and fall in all grotesque shapes, the starlight they catch glitters with a brilliance that is different from here to there. . . . [Then the author stretches the metaphors and alludes to himself.] So long as the compass points in the right direction I shall some day make a circuit of the universal heart-sea and return to my real Homeland.[45]

In an entry in *History of the Heart,* dated December 24, 1921, only two months before he became a Communist, he wrote:

Unite Ego with Non-Ego and there is likeness. Oppose Ego to Non-Ego and there is the awareness of the uniqueness of personality.
There must be a way to unite the two; and that is Love.
It is nothing censurable for a child to like to play. But if he does not know that there is Mother's bosom for him to return to, then he will become lost in his play. He will experience fear. Our prideful nature, if not improved by Love, will become likewise our curse.[46]

Rhapsodic and obscure musings like these and, more prominently, the "mood pieces" outbalance factual reports in the two books, especially the second one, *History of the Heart in the Red Capital,* which covers an eventful year (February, 1921, to March, 1922) spent mainly in Moscow. This is what he asked the reader to expect from a book titled *History of the Heart.* More information, he said, was provided in a third book, *On the Russian Revolution,*[47] which I have not had a chance to read. But since Ch'ü describes it as a "social science treatise," containing "observations on history and interpretations of institutions," [48] it would not be of much help to our understanding of his personal life. The interesting question is whether Ch'ü's *heart* responded to the social upheavals and human sacrifices with the same force that it responded, say, to the landscape. He never lost his feeling for natural scenery. Lake Baikal, the Urals, and the Russian steppes, with their weird bleakness and their hidden gigantic power braving the rigors of winter, caught his imagination, and he left some vivid passages

[45] *Ibid.,* pp. 90–91.

[46] *History of the Heart, Collected Works,* I, 173.

[47] "Comrade Ch'iu-po wrote another book of studies on Soviet socialism. It was sold to a certain publisher. But under the pressure of the Northern warlords and then the KMT Government, it never had a chance of getting published. The manuscript was destroyed in a fire during the war in Shanghai in 1932." *Ch'ü Ch'iu-po chu-i hsi-nien mu-lu* (*A Chronological Catalogue of Ch'ü Ch'iu-po's Writings and Translations*), compiled by Ting Ching-t'ang and Wen Tsao (Shanghai: Shanghai People's Publications Association, 1959), p. 99. The title Ch'ü used was "O-lo-szu ko-ming lun." Hsiao San said it was "A Revolutionary History of New Russia." The publisher identified was the Commercial Press, *ibid.,* p. 98. See also note 3.

[48] *History of the Heart, Collected Works,* I, 97.

of writing into which he unmistakably put his heart. It is this kind of vividness that we would expect of his descriptions of the human scenes of the revolution. But we are disappointed. Judging from the style, his imagination was not much stirred by what he had come so far to see. In his reports on one of the greatest human dramas, we are struck by the feebleness, perfunctoriness, or rather, *halfheartedness* of his descriptions. His books are not enlivened by the portrait of a single memorable character or a single memorable scene of mass movement which could have justified his illusions about the Communist revolution. The flatness of style only indicates that he was not thrilled or enraptured by what he was seeing, for he could be more effective when he chose. A demonstration in the Red Square is dismissed in two or three lines:

A vast field, where thousands of Red Army, infantry, cavalry, artillery, the militia units of labor, the military training units of the Communist Party, workers both men and women, children and youths, paraded in formations. Eulogies from the delegates of various nations. Shouts of cheer.[49]

Lenin was faintly etched in his memory, so far as his reports indicate, as one whose large head made an impressive silhouette and whose tone of voice sounded "determined."[50] The Kremlin, the setting of many interviews and conferences, was noted for its "magnificent tall walls and splendid old architecture," and also, as he went on in his absent-minded exploration, for its "smooth, shining floor, resplendent columns, and sculptures by famous Italian artists."[51] He did not reserve his literary skill for the revolutionary fervor of the ordinary people either—those nameless Ivans on whom so much of the success of the revolution would depend. The general impression is that none of them seemed either happy or enthusiastic about what the revolutionists were doing in their name.

But then neither was our author happy. The vast Eurasian country was truly a Land of Hunger. Famine left its terrible scars everywhere, and the N.E.P., recently put into effect, could at best elicit some faint shadow of a grim smile out of the ubiquitous gloom. The miserable material conditions turned his attention further inward, and there dark moods rose like dark waves in his "heart-sea." It was only by accident that he did not lose his enthusiasm altogether. His health deteriorated so badly that he was almost a human wreck at the time he was accepted into the ranks of the Communists.

[49] *Ibid.,* p. 127.
[50] *Ibid.,* pp. 128–29.
[51] *Ibid.,* pp. 103, 128.

A Journey to the Land of Hunger and *History of the Heart in the Red Capital* are records of his personal "heart-waves," registered in a language that borrows heavily from the vocabulary of the Chinese lyrics and Buddhistic scriptures that made up his early studies. He did not write them for the proletariat or for the semi-educated but for the class to which he himself belonged: literate readers who had been brought up on classical Chinese and were now readjusting themselves under the impact of Western cultural forces. It was their tastes that largely determined the manner and matter of the new literature born of the May Fourth Movement.

Self-expression, a main trend in Chinese literature, was further encouraged by Western models and precepts. It has never been sufficiently emphasized what fertile soil Chinese lyricism provided for the transplantation of European romanticism, interpreted as the awakening of the individual soul. But the vernacular movement, with its accompanying literary theories, rather facilitated the gush of sentiments for the literati and resulted in a large number of literary productions notable for eager self-expression. Clamor for fighting, for battles specified or unspecified, and for victory in the battles; the magnified projection of the writer as a hero, a lover, a martyr, or as one who feels and suffers more deeply than the rest of humanity; a stupefied and dislocated psyche which insisted on opening its wounds to the view of the world—such were the literary fashions of the twenties in China, and Ch'ü was not far above the fashions.

Today, Ch'ü's two books are dated. They have the special flavor of that period when literature belonged to a small minority, when prose could be indistinguishable from poetry, or vice versa, when the *pai-hua,* though accepted as a vehicle for literary creation, had still to rely on the *wen-yen* for its richness, precision, and evocative power. The best parts of Ch'ü's two books are elaborately written, too elaborately, perhaps, for the purposes of journalistic reporting. But Ch'ü's literary talent is unmistakable; he is at his lyrical best when he describes his moods, and they are plenty, in all the shades of melancholy. The tone, the texture, and the choice of words are evidently those of a man who has made an effort to study classical Chinese poetry and who does not want to conceal his effort. As a whole, his two books are characteristic of the immediate literary products of the May Fourth Movement; for the elaborate style and oversentimentalization seem passé today. But it is an ironic comment on the cultural scene of China in the early twenties that Ch'ü's eulogy of Soviet Russia, which must be among the earliest of the kind, should be overladen with sighs of personal grief. Since it comes from Ch'ü Ch'iu-po, this incongruity is especially re-vealing. We cannot say for sure how much fire he possessed as a person, but his early writings show a sickly pallor.

IV

Ch'ü and two friends, Li Tsung-wu and Yü Sung-hua, who also went as correspondents for *Ch'en pao,* traveled in the company of a Mr. Ch'en, the newly appointed Chinese consul-general to Moscow, and two of his staff. They took the land route by railway through Manchuria. But everything was not well along the Manchurian border. They did not know for certain, when they started, how seriously land communications were disrupted by the battles fought between General Semenov's "Whites" and the Far Eastern Republic. The only reassurance they got from Mr. Urin, represen-tative of the Far Eastern Republic in Peking,[52] who signed their visas, was that they would have a share in whatever privileges or facilities in the way of transportation might be granted to the Chinese consular officers.

After the Shanhaikwan Pass, they were entering Manchuria, with its strong marks of Japanese and Russian colonialism. Mukden looked very much like a Japanese city. The Chinese coolies, noisy and eager to offer their services, who used to be the first to meet the travelers leaving the train, were not to be seen at the Mukden station. They were under the strict con-trol of the Japanese, and only a Japanese railroad clerk knew where to find them. But it was at Changchun that Ch'ü experienced his first taste of a severe northern winter fraught with a misery that was more Russian than Chinese. As he stepped out of the station, on the early morning of October 20, what greeted him was a vast, empty field, closed in by rows of bare, shivering trees. Frost was everywhere, hard as ice, and the fallen leaves were being blown about by the wind.

Several Russian-style horse-carriages were waiting. Some of the cabmen were Russian, wearing dirty, oily fur hats. The hair of the fur was trembling so violently in the wind that it went as far as to brush against and cover up the eyebrows. That gave the Russian face a look even sadder than usual.[53]

The Russians seemed to be very much in charge of the Chinese Eastern Railway, though a promise had been made by the Soviet government that

---

[52] Urin is Ch'ü's spelling; otherwise spelled Yourin. He was the Soviet plenipo-tentiary to negotiate commercial treaties with the Peking government. A. K. Wu, *China and the Soviet Union* (New York: John Day, 1950), pp. 140 ff.

[53] *Journey, Collected Works,* I, 35.

it would be returned to China.[54] One Russian who offered to buy tickets for the young travelers charged them more than the actual fare. A third-class carriage which Ch'ü peered into was occupied by Russians lying about in a disorderly fashion. The floor was covered with cigarette butts and spit, and the stench threw him back. The second-class compartments, in which the Chinese group was accommodated, looked much better, but a closer inspection revealed dust about half an inch thick on the seats. The windows, the window curtains, and all the fixtures seemed to be falling apart in various stages of dilapidation. When the engine started to move, the train began to shake with a disconcerting instability, unlike anything he had experienced on the Peking-Mukden line (under Chinese management) or the Southern Manchuria line (under Japanese management). Fatigue finally lulled him to sleep.

When they arrived in Harbin, they learned they could go no farther until transportation across the border was resumed. They put up in a hotel and spent several weeks in anxious waiting. Harbin, cold, dirty, and expensive, was not a cheerful place, and distance was now mingled with despondency. Ch'ü and his two friends began to talk about abandoning their original plan and returning to the Land of Black Sweetness.

Ch'ü's shrinking at the first frustration on the journey after his earlier bravado may seem ridiculous. But Ch'ü was after all no Hsüan-tsang, no paragon of a faith triumphant over difficulties material or spiritual, and his trip to Russia had nothing heroic in it. If he presented himself correctly in his own record, he was not a man of will but a man of sensibility. It is rather his frailty and his frankness in confessing to it that wins our sympathy. His moods changed too readily with the changing circumstances, and his visions and hopes were not an incitement to action but something to be fondled in private. Hardships he could endure to a certain extent, but they were not a challenge to a soaring spirit that seeks to transcend them. This first sign of wavering was a minor matter compared with the despondency that assailed him in Moscow.

Life was at least not so hard in Harbin, and he could beguile himself by taking in impressions of a town that was half Chinese and half Russian. If he was not yet in the Land itself, he was blessed with ample opportunity to study the manners and behavior of the people who originally belonged there. Even among the local Chinese population, the influence of Russian

[54] According to the Second Soviet Declaration (September, 1920), "the Chinese Eastern Railway was only to be put under joint control—not to be returned to China without compensation as under the earlier offer (July, 1919)." Wu, *op. cit.*, p. 139.

philistinism and Russian squalor was remarkable. The Chinese *nouveaux riches,* who had risen from the position of office boys in Russian business concerns, now had Russian wives and surrounded themselves with luxuries in their *dachas.* The Chinese merchants transacted business with the aid of "pidgin" Russian. The local intellectuals were graduates of the Russian Language College who served as officials and clerks. Their parochial views and bureaucratic habits estranged them from the young alumnus who aimed at much higher things in life. Indeed, he shuddered to think that some day he might become one of them, fill a menial post, and inherit all their ignorance and vulgarity.

The lower classes toiled in their mute and stolid way as they had for centuries. If they had altered in any way under foreign influence, it was that their uncleanliness seemed to have been made worse by the bad examples set by the *russkii muzhik.* Specimens of the latter—cabmen or beggars—came across his way almost daily. What particularly offended Ch'ü's sensitive southern nose was the smell of the unwashed bodies of the "Northern Chinese" and the Russians.

The conscientious pilgrim kept reminding himself that these people, disgusting as they were as individuals, constituted the masses to whom he had to endear himself. Reason would embrace what was repulsive to the senses. The ugly things that he saw in life, here, as later in Moscow, had to be explained away, so that he could uphold the truth of the theory he found in books. So the superficial affinity of the malodorous shabbiness of the Chinese poor and the Russian poor was interpreted as real "cultural fusion," a "mutual understanding" of two peoples, unimaginable to the promoters of Sino-French or Sino-American intellectual cooperation in the southern cities.[55]

Harbin was Russia in miniature, with a perhaps complete cross-section of Russian society: peasants, workers, merchants, capitalists, generals, and bejewelled and perfumed women. But it was also a Russia of the happier old days, one that was not yet visited by Hunger and the intense bitterness of revolution. The Russians in Harbin partook of the bounty produced by the rich soil of Manchuria. High piles of foodstuff could be seen all along the railway from Harbin northward—exports earmarked for Russia that could not be shipped because of civil war. At the local celebration of the October Revolution, which Ch'ü attended as a private guest, the jubilant atmosphere was broken by a Communist from Moscow, who reminded his

[55] *Journey, Collected Works,* p. 41.

fellow countrymen indulging in a drinking bout that back home nothing better than black bread could be had and even that not in sufficient amount.

Battles were fought between the Whites and the Reds only a few hundred miles away, and General Semenov was suffering one defeat after another (which meant, for the stranded travelers, that the way to Siberia would soon be clear), but in Harbin the revolution was not a bloody affair except for a few political assassinations, which had occurred before Ch'ü's arrival. Here it was a fight between newspapers, which, hawked in the streets by Russian-speaking Chinese newspaper boys, were avidly read by the followers of the two camps. The Union of Railway Workers (probably for the Russians only) was composed of Bolsheviks, Mensheviks, social revolutionaries, and socialists of other kinds. No rivalries and jealousies in that organization were remarked by Ch'ü. In the face of a still powerful White opposition, backed by the Japanese, the revolutionaries were probably well united.

After more than fifty days the word finally came that Semenov's forces had been routed and that he was retreating toward Vladivostok under Japanese escort. The road beyond the border station of Manchouli was clear. A special train, sporting the five-colored flag of the Chinese Republic, was ready for the consular officers, to whom diplomatic privileges were evidently accorded. The group went aboard on December 8, but the train did not move until the tenth. During the interval, they made necessary preparations against Hunger. Stores of food and kitchen equipment were procured and carried to the train. They would cook their own food all the way—a wise precaution, as it would soon prove. The three young men continued to feed on the same wheat flour they had bought in Harbin even months after they had arrived in Moscow. Perhaps they also sold some in the market, for Ch'ü noted that it would become a source of income for them.[56]

The group stopped at Manchouli for four days, and at Chita, the capital of the Far Eastern Republic, for more than two weeks. Chita, at forty degrees below zero, Réaumur, was suffocatingly cold. A few minutes' walk in the open covered Ch'ü's overcoat with a layer of frost, and he began to complain of his lungs. Another source of worry was his incompetence. The deeper he penetrated into Russia, the more he realized that it was too great a task for an "immature" (his own word) youth with only inadequate training to report on this vast land and the first socialist revolution of the

[56] *Ibid.*, p. 53.

world. He could converse in Russian only with difficulty, and as for Communist theory, he admitted that he received valuable information, though still rudimentary, from the pamphlets, magazines, and books he had access to in Chita.

The delay of the special train at Chita was caused by red tape which involved confirmation and reconfirmation from both Peking and Moscow. For Ch'ü the time was well spent, though anxiety would again creep into his mind in a depressed moment. He took up a cramming session in Marxism, while picking up more Russian phrases to acquire a proficiency in that language. Living was more expensive here than in Harbin, and the people were grumbling about the lack of sugar and tea. Ch'ü found nothing distasteful in the black bread he tried in a Russian home, but it was not a genuine specimen he had eaten, as he was later to find out. Rumors were rife about the real misery deeper inland and in European Russia. Irkutsk was "one hundred times worse" according to a man from there. The man was an intellectual, but Ch'ü felt no sympathy with the first blasphemy he heard on the journey.

"Ha! Communism indeed! The Bolsheviks know nothing but killing, and then. . . ." His "dogmatic" head of the intelligentsia type was outlined in the moonlight, which, though faint under the subtle shadows of the clouds, was intensified by the reflections from the snow. The head was nodding, bristling all over with hair and beard, while the upturned black fur collar revealed a tattered tie dangling on an unscrubbed neck, and the voice continued, muttering: "They themselves have good food and fine clothes—to call them Communists!" [57]

The Chinese vice-consul at Chita, another alumnus of the Russian Language College, tried to dissuade Ch'ü from proceeding on the journey. A Russian girl, in a sable stole, burst into emotion upon hearing of his destination: "Horrible! Horrible! Going to Moscow . . ."

At Irkutsk, the Chinese vice-consul gave a party which for Ch'ü was the initiation into the Land of Hunger. He swallowed a piece of the "Soviet black bread." "Its bitterness and sourness, with an odor of rotten grass mixed with mud, was something no Chinese has ever tasted." [58] The meal happily also included chicken and fish, delicacies obtained from the farmers who traded in the black market. Since Irkutsk was the first Soviet Russian city he visited, Ch'ü was curious to know what the people thought who had accepted Hunger as a fact of life. So at the gathering after the dinner, he

[57] *Ibid.,* pp. 62–63.
[58] *Ibid.,* p. 76.

asked the Russian engineer, a thin old man, who lived under the same roof as the vice-consul, whether he was a Communist.

The engineer put down his pipe, and a voice expressive of mockery, but with undertones of sadness, came out of his hoarse throat: "Me? A Communist? Ha! . . ." Somebody interrupted and, pointing to a girl, said, "But she is." I turned to ask her about the platform of the Communist Party. The girl registered puzzlement on her ridiculously powdered and rouged face. Giggling, she uttered a few words, and then stopped, as if she were overcome with shyness. But the engineer snatched the words from her. "The platform is perfect! Excellent! But only dreams, illusions . . . rifles, jails, jails, . . ." The man was an employee in the railway. He had gone to jail three or four times for his "lazy-strike" and his insults to the Bolsheviks. But prison terms did not mend his ways. The Soviet government, having no engineer of its own, had to retain him in service.[59]

At Omsk the lock on their pantry car was wrenched open, and someone spirited away ten *pud* (about 300 *chin*) of wheat flour. Mr. Ch'en was furious, but nothing could be done. Episodes like these, and the spectacle of tattered and shivering human figures at various stations where the train stopped, were a terrible experience. But if it taught Ch'ü any new lesson, it was that old vices bred of the old society had to be combatted and that socialist revolution could not be accomplished, as if it were a miracle, "in a test tube." [60] However distressed he might be by personal worries—and they were overwhelming—Ch'ü was careful not to express doubts about the validity of socialist revolution. That seems to have been a faith which stood unshaken by cold facts, which was never completely extinguished in his blackest moods, and which was only strengthened by his non-Marxist ideals.

Meanwhile, the train roared on, "rushing against whipping wind, and emitting a harsh, groaning sound as it was crushing over ice and snow." [61] At the approaches to Moscow, it "rubbed against thousands of crisscross shadows of the boughs of snowy trees that stood in rows, now dense and now sparse, along the two sides of the track. Where there was an opening, the icy beams of the crystal-like moon shot in a flash into the windows of our compartment. So through flashes and dancing lights, our train pushed on, and Moscow was near. Parts of the city, glowing with electric light, could now be seen. Also distinguishable in the darkness were the wisps of smoke from the factory stacks, which looked as if they were panting." [62]

[59] *Ibid.*, p. 77.
[60] *Ibid.*, p. 79.
[61] *Ibid.*, p. 80.
[62] *Ibid.*, p. 84.

At about eleven o'clock in the night, January 25, 1921, Ch'ü Ch'iu-po arrived in the Yaroslavsky Station in Moscow. "Under the chilly moon, and amidst the hubbub of the crowds in the railway station, I knew I was in the Land of Hunger. . . . Moscow, situated at the peak of the waves of the heart-sea of the European proletariat, was surging with the warm blood of the Russian laborers. . . . The child from the Orient was now feeling within him the rise of his inner strength." [63]

If his "inner strength" rose at the end of the long journey which took about two months to complete, it did not sustain him for long. There were no doubt periods, during his stay in Moscow, of concentrated, dispassionate study which produced the third book mentioned above and the series of informative articles published in *Ch'en pao*.[64] There were exciting moments too—his meeting with Lenin, for instance, and more important, his reunion with Chang T'ai-lai, but they are summarily dealt with, if at all, in the *History of the Heart*.

As a visitor with a regular source of income, Ch'iu-po did not have to share the fate of the famished Soviet masses in the terrible year of 1921. He could avail himself of whatever was sold on the market under the N.E.P. of March that year, before he had exhausted the private hoard he had brought with him from China. Then, at the newly established University of the Toilers of the Far East, he obtained a position as an interpreter and lecturer, which may have paid him handsomely. One of the old-time students recalls that Ch'ü used to invite them to a rice dinner. They relished the delicious change from the black bread which was their sole sustenance, but they wondered where he got the rice.[65]

Ch'iu-po's unhappiness was induced by illness, loneliness, and the cheerless aspects of human life, as well as nature, in Russia. But even more serious was the dilemma in which he found himself caught. His was not simply the case of a sensitive, homesick youth, with a complaint in the lungs, traveling in an unpleasant alien country. For its very unpleasantness embodied the man's ideals. He could quit the unlovely place, but could not so easily leave his ideals behind. The Bolshevik revolution, still at an experimental stage, had few solid achievements to provide cheer and comfort, while the disconcerting evidence of public discontent or apathy was

---

[63] *Ibid.*

[64] The *Introduction to Periodicals* has fourteen titles of Ch'ü's correspondence on serious subjects published in the *Ch'en pao* from June, 1921, to November, 1922. For the dates of these and other articles, see Ting and Wen, *op. cit.*

[65] Wang Hung-hsün, "The Baptism of the Great October," *Red Flags Are Flying,* Vol. **IV**.

abundant. The necessity of defending it in writing, to convince himself no less than the readers in China of the truth and goodness of all that was going on, must have caused great inner strain. The hard facts of revolution, which had been forced upon his attention ever since he entered Siberia, had sobered the hotheaded youth of the May Fourth Movement. Natural harmony, once a basic tenet of his juvenile metaphysics, was nowhere to be found.

Each of the two personalities within him was demanding undivided allegiance, but to pay them equal attention was impossible. One urge was to follow his natural inclination, to satisfy the longing for mildness, tenderness, pretty objects, and a cozy atmosphere; the other was to pursue what reason taught to be right, to accept unquestioningly the revolution in its wholeness, together with the harshness, ugliness, and abnormality that accompanied it. If no compromise could be effected, he had to make a choice. It is remarkable that he joined the Communist Party at a time when his physical strength was at its lowest ebb, when what he needed was apparently more rest, not more struggle. But for him there would be no rest until he attained peace of mind. By becoming a Communist, he entered a new life. He had been weak and solitary, but now he was to be supported by the organized strength of the party. He had been divided within himself, but now the revolutionist in him could dominate. All the sleepless agony during those critical months before he joined the party was a symptom of this inner struggle.

The only Russian in the book that spoke intimately of his experiences of the revolutionary years was a soldier, about thirty years of age, but with telltale wrinkles on his brow, who worked in a military academy. Unlike the other Russians the author met, the man had no complaints to make. He was not one of the dumb masses but was remarkably articulate. He had acquired serenity through resignation to long years of suffering. The greatest moment in his life was an altruistic deed which was perhaps more basic to humanity than any socialist theory. It was in this man, intrinsically kind and generous who lived to help people, a true ascetic who humbly accepted his lot in life but who nevertheless remained an idealist, a cadre who seemed to have a soul of his own, that Ch'ü found the deepest sympathy. He felt that there was a "communion between two souls" as his host began to talk, over a cup of hot tea, in the dingy, littered room, partitioned from a formerly elegant parlor but now filled with dark shadows which the light from a dim lamp helped to create rather than to dispel.

Alas! How can a young man from China understand the profundity of the Russian soul? One has to live through all this in order to appreciate it. . . . The trenches in Germany . . . explosions of the grenades, the airplanes circling overhead, one's feet in mud and water. Every cannon shot was a shock which left the heart trepidating for more than ten minutes. It was not fear. As one became accustomed to it, one was numb. The eardrums would tingle even in sleep. Day and night, one felt not oneself, but an unreality where one was suspended. Your home, your country, your parents, your brothers, love, all gone. . . . We were released from military service after the October Revolution, and I had a reunion with my wife in Petrograd. . . . Then in the country, I was made a secretary of the village soviet. . . . The insurrection of the Whites . . . and the Soviet Government required 3,000 conscripts from our village. That morning, when I was counting the heads of the recruits gathered in the railway station and making them sign their names, the scene was filled with lamentation: "Dear Ivan, don't forget me after you have gone. . . ." "Vassily, will you come home alive? . . ." Then rifle shots. . . . The peasants rushed in . . . I felt my whole frame was trembling as if cold water was running on my spine. My lungs were expanding, my breath became short, and I lost touch with the world except for the shouts and curses that rang in my ears: "No conscription!" "The Soviet go to hell!"

I found myself in a barn when I reopened my eyes. . . . I came to Moscow and found a job in the military academy. . . . One day I went to the province [to visit his wife]. . . . It was two o'clock after midnight that the train reached the station. There was another two verst for me to walk. It was raining and the ground was slippery. I had a hard time walking with the loaves of bread in my hand [the black bread he had saved in Moscow to feed his wife.]. I felt fatigued, as I had not slept well on the train. On my way I met an old woman, tottering under a large sack of potatoes. She asked for help when she saw me. I agreed, took up the burden from her, and carried it to her home. I did not leave her place until I saw everything was in good order. Then, as I resumed my journey home, I felt relieved. The sorrows that had troubled me when I got off the train were gone. I felt exceedingly happy. In rendering service to others, one forgets about oneself and one is at ease. To keep thinking about oneself is only a form of self-torture. When I arrived home, it was already past four o'clock. I lay down with an easy conscience. Can you see the difference between my mental state at that moment and my feelings when I was in the battlefield or when I was working as the secretary of the village soviet? [66]

The story of this petty officer of the Red Army was an object lesson for Ch'ü to ponder over. Never in his life, particularly not at this time in Russia, had he experienced such joyful relief which made life meaningful. He could appreciate the sadness and weariness of the traveler, hurrying home at midnight in the rain and on a dark, slippery country road. He could easily draw a parallel with his own predicament. He might eventually reach

---

[66] *History of the Heart, Collected Works,* I, 134–36.

his *own* home, but with a fatigue and depression which not even the sight of his dearest ones could relieve. To make himself happy, he had first to give a helping hand to some old woman and place her burden on his shoulders. The shortest route to his own home, where happiness would be waiting, seemed to be by way of the home of someone else that he had helped. That was essentially the meaning of Bodhisattvahood, which had constituted his earlier beliefs.

By enlisting in the Communist Party, he was apparently neglecting his private needs, but he believed that only thus could he realize happiness in life. He never made an explicit statement like this, but a study of his inner struggle before he joined the party would lead us to believe that if there was any selfish motive behind this irrevocable and even rash move, it was that he was desperately in need of peace, purpose, and strength. This little episode, which occurred in September, came in good time to point out to him a way. As to the implied criticism of the Bolshevik regime in the story, he rather neglected it.

The first crisis came around August. In a short rhapsody, dated August 5, he wrote:

The sky was clear and cloudy by capricious turns, and there was now a drizzle. My heart was darkened in sympathy. On the muddy, slippery Moscow streets, paved with jagged cobblestones, the busy pedestrians seemed all to walk with a limp. The children at the street corners, hawking cigarettes, and the salty smell of meat and fish from the grocery had somehow a disturbing effect. . . .

I felt all the more ill after I was back in my apartment. A few days ago, the doctor found a lesion in my left lung and advised me to go home. Wasn't it that I again spat blood yesterday? I was laid up for one month in July,[67] and I felt that I had become lifeless, and that my soul was wearing away. . . . Oh, return to me my character, return to me the energy I would need for social service! Alas! the wind, the cold, and the thick snow of the North, the black bread and the rotten meat that makes up one's nourishment.

By ten thousand *li* I am separated from home—how can I enjoy once more the tenderness and the affections? The manners, the climate, the sky are all so different from those at home. A whiteness that fills up the universe for five long months—the weird, phantomlike drifts of snow—the pressure in the air that almost deprives one of the power of breathing. Ice—snow—storm— how can those compare, as spiritual nourishment, with the scenes of the South of the Yangtze—the bright, colorful springtime and the autumnal flowers, in rich array, each trying to surpass the other?

[67] The Third Congress of the Comintern was held June 22 to July 12, 1921. Georg von Rauch, *A History of Soviet Russia* (New York: Praeger, 1959). Ch'ü wrote a brief report on it on July 6. *History of the Heart, Collected Works,* I, 128–29. He might have fallen ill afterward.

But the culture and the fertility of the South is doomed. It will turn into, nay, it has already become, a colony. The British overlords are there. . . .

Rising with the obscure thoughts in a delirium, with anxiety and fever, there appear the indistinct shadowy dreams of the South: the golden flowers of the rape, the translucent pond, the peach blossoms. . . .

Alas, the mind is unfixed, the nostalgic dreams are haunting to no purpose. I am gone far in illness, or am I? [68]

The poem "Moon of the East" was written on the cloudy night of September 16 (the Mid-Autumn Festival in the Chinese calendar). It contains not one cheering note, but suggests unmistakably a disappointment in his "inner demands" symbolized by the hidden moon.

Wandering over ten thousand *li,* here in this land of hunger and cold.
It is said, "Snowfall begins in the eighth moon under the Barbary sky";
Though nothing is here but the dreary autumnal touches, the subtle chilliness.
But my "Moon of the East" is hidden, behind the clouds of the Red Capital.

.   .   .

Roundness, the perfect shape, will appear only in dreams,
Memory is hard to bear under the lamp.
My regret is for the thickening cloud,
Which allows not a single beam of hope to penetrate.[69]

Feverish, coughing, and spitting blood, Ch'iu-po felt that he was too ill to work. And his growing awareness of his incompetence in newspaper work had compelled him to consider terminating his service with *Ch'en pao.* Nine days after he composed the poem, he wrote to Yü Sung-hua, who had left in May, that he was determined to go home. Now of the three correspondents, only Li Tsung-wu would remain. Yü had left because he did not know Russian, but now in Berlin he probably could better discharge his duties as a foreign correspondent. It seemed that Ch'ü alone would end up in ignominious failure.

But he was not so soon to admit defeat. He lingered on. He procrastinated for the ostensible reason of the difficulties of transportation. The Trans-Siberian Railway was still not running on time, and his luggage was greatly increased by the books he had acquired. And then, he canceled the plan altogether. He did not leave until some fifteen months later (December, 1922).

[68] *Ibid.,* pp. 129–30.
[69] *Ibid.,* pp. 136–38.

His hesitation to pack saved for the Chinese Communist Party one of its early leaders. It is hard to conceive how he could have regained his self-confidence if he had departed at that time out of disgust, if not entirely with Russia, at least with himself. Ch'ü Ch'iu-po might have come to be known as a professor of Russian literature or simply a writer whose favorite subject was the tribulations of the heart. The Communist International could still send back a man as able, or even abler, to promote revolution in China. But Ch'ü would have forfeited his share in the mass movements that were soon to erupt in China. It was unlikely that he would have ever become a "martyr," though he might still have died young, a tubercular and a sad man who had come within sight of the highest ideal of life but, owing to his weakness, had missed it. What made all the difference was that he stayed on.

Though it is hard to verify the dates, the offer from the University of the Toilers might have come at a time[70] when he had sunk to the lowest depths of dejection. The Chinese students who were to attend that university had arrived, about forty-two in all, the elite of a rising generation, the flower of the revolutionary spirit, but whatever credentials they carried with them, they were handicapped by their slight acquaintance with the Russian language.[71] They could not follow lectures in Russian; their reading ability was doubtful. No good Russian-Chinese dictionary was then available, the one published in Harbin being unreliable. Of the Russian faculty, only one member, V. S. Kolokolov, spoke Chinese. But in the opinion of Ch'ü, not even Kolokolov, who was brought up in China and had a Chinese name, could do an adequate job in interpretation.[72] The language problem might have seriously retarded the training program and upset the timetable for world revolution prepared by the Kremlin. To avoid delay someone suggested the names of the two Chinese correspondents, and so both Ch'ü and Li were hired.

Ch'ü was to teach Russian as well as to prepare a Chinese version for the courses in indoctrination. The additional work would of course do his

[70] Wang Hung-hsün mentions that the university was established in summer and the class started in the autumn. By autumn he might mean September. *Red Flags Are Flying,* Vol. IV.

[71] Ts'ao Tsing-hua, known for his translations from Russian, has an interesting article about his difficulties with the Russian language while attending the University of the Toilers. "Tidbits of My Reminiscences of Ch'iu-po," *Wen-i pao,* No. 11, June 15, 1955.

[72] Kuo Chih-sheng is the man's Chinese name. When Ch'ü first arrived in Moscow, he received help from Kolokolov, official interpreter assigned by the Commissariat for Foreign Affairs. Ch'ü said that Kolokolov did not translate well, but they became fast friends anyhow. *Journey, Collected Works,* I, 88.

health no good. But its rewards were more than monetary. He could now live independently of the *Ch'en pao*. He was brought into closer contact with Communists, both the veteran Russian and the fledgling Chinese, and their company might somehow have relieved his loneliness. The homework he did for the indoctrination courses also imparted a meaning to his life as nothing else could. In struggling with ideological matters where a mistake in translation might be viewed with suspicion as the allegation of a heresy, he was gradually led into the arcana of orthodox Marxism-Leninism. He was no longer an amateur who would compound Marx with Buddha and Bergson. He was receiving strict theoretical training, a necessary preparation for the revolutionary career to come.

But he still had chinks in his armor to mend, monsters to slay, and enemies to subdue before the quest for supreme Marxist-Leninist truth could be accomplished. Homesickness, quite unworthy of a revolutionist, was still doing its worst to harass him. For more than six months he had been anxiously expecting a letter from his home. He became ashamed of his weakness. He observed:

A part of my ego was becoming strange. The "social self" within me was mocking at me and laughing at me from the shadows of darkness.[73]

When in November he finally received a letter from his brother, which bore the postmark of March, he burst into tears. A phrase meant to be comforting particularly struck him. What did it mean that "everybody at home is well"? Was not his brother sensible enough to see that they no longer had a home of their own, that their mother had been killed by poverty, "leaving her tender love as her only legacy," that the brothers were scattered, living as parasites, that his own "home" was now this Land of Hunger, that the old gentry class of China was doomed? The questions that had previously troubled him rushed back in the excitement of drinking in the long anticipated letter from "home." But the answer to them, if once vague, now became clearer:

There will be a day, all the gentry class will be proletarianized. Then we shall do whatever we can do. There will be such a day. . . .[74]

On December 12 he was moved to a sanatorium. There, his mind became more restless. He had been comparing himself to Raskolnikov, who always "asked more of life." [75] Now he was haunted by another hero of

[73] *History of the Heart, Collected Works,* I, 161.
[74] *Ibid.,* p. 164.
[75] *Ibid.,* p. 166.

Russian fiction, Rudin, the ineffectual intellectual. He found that the conflict between heart and head, between romanticism and realism, had turned him into what Turgenev called a "superfluous man."

> Alas! Regret, lamentation, sorrow. . . . I used to regard myself as unusual, but looking back, can I find anything unusual about me? How ridiculous! "What indeed can you do? Why not identify yourself with the masses?" Reason has reached a conclusion, but the force of inertia is too great. . . .[76]

In the antiseptic quietness of the hospital bed, he had also his moments of peace—peace not emerging as a solution to his problems, but rather a faint recapitulation of the days of innocence when the conflict had not yet been so sharply formed. He would imagine himself strolling under the willows along the Nan-wan-tzu in Peking. In another instant, he was revisiting the country home of his aunt, in a village outside the Northern Gate of Changchow, snugly ensconced in the bend of the Bracelet Creek.[77] In January, 1922, he translated two poems by Tiutchev, one entitled *A Moment* and the other, the much celebrated *Silentium*.[78] The mystic joy and the sense of "oneness with nature" contained in them may have brought relief to a mind more diseased, perhaps, than the body. But as a stretch of agonized introspection would follow a transient mood of lyrical serenity, he had to disown them both. The source of his restlessness, as he repeatedly discovered, was his overindividualized self. What he learned from Turgenev (to identify himself with the masses) and from the petty officer of the Red Army (to render service to others in order to forget about himself) would become for him the supreme lesson in life, something more valuable than the treatment of his tuberculosis. Sometime in January he was allowed to leave the sanatorium to attend the Congress of the Toilers of the Far East.[79]

---

[76] *Ibid.*, p. 171.

[77] *Ibid.* About Bracelet Creek, see Shang-kuan Ai-ming, *op. cit.*

[78] *History of the Heart, Collected Works*, I, 175–78.

[79] "After the first session of the Conference in Irkutsk [held in November, 1921] its delegates traveled to Moscow and then to Petrograd, where they were joined by new delegates. Their deliberation continued from January 21 to January 27, as the First Congress of Toilers of the Far East, sometimes spoken of as the First Congress of the Peoples of the Far East." X. J. Eudin and R. C. North, *Soviet Russia and the East, 1920–1927* (Stanford, 1957), pp. 145–46. Ch'ü apparently did not go to Irkutsk, though he attended the meetings held in Moscow and Petrograd. Here I have to argue with Wen Chi-tse about Ch'ü's status at that time. Said Wen: "In early February, 1922, Comrade Chang T'ai-lei, a founding member of the Chinese Communist Party, came to Moscow. Through his introduction, Comrade Ch'ü joined the CCP. After that, he, together with Chang T'ai-lei and other comrades, was appointed by the party to attend the Congress of the Peoples of the Far East, in the spring of 1922." Wen Chi-tse, "Comrade . . . ," *Red Flags Are Flying,* V, 90.

He felt a momentary exultation at the release from the regimen of the sanatorium. The Congress itself revived his enthusiasm. Upon this he wrote an
essay, "Morning Glory," which perhaps is more symptomatic of a hectic
brain than of a real sense of joy:

> Look at the Far East, how bright the purple and red flames shine forth as
> they spin! The blazing clouds, just sprouting, but how roaringly they shoot
> towards the firmament! How fierce, how dazzling, the wheel of light is spinning!
> Ah, morning glory, morning glory! [80]

Ch'ü followed the delegates to Petrograd, as the meeting place was shifted,
and there again with a typical absent-mindedness he noted the impressions
of the meeting:

> The sombre, dim lights filled the hall, but the red light shone forth in every
> direction. The voice of the Orientals, cheers, shouts, applause, the Inter-
> nationale. . . .[81]

After the meeting, he tried to walk two *verst*. Under the arctic night, he
found the freezing air unbearably oppressive. He met a woman (probably
another delegate), who supported him all the way back to the hotel. Blood

---

This statement is questionable on several points: (a) Chang T'ai-lei was very active
in Russia throughout 1921. It was he who drafted the invitation to the Congress.
He conferred with the Far Eastern Secretariat in Irkutsk, and debated with M. N. Roy
in the Third Congress of the Comintern; Eudin and North, *op. cit.,* pp. 139–47.
Ch'ü must have seen him on the occasion of the Comintern Congress, though he
was silent on the subject in the *History of the Heart.* What did they talk about then?
Did Chang try then to introduce Ch'ü into the party? (b) If Ch'ü joined the party
as late as February, 1922, then it was after, and not before, he attended the Congress
of the Peoples of the Far East, which, according to the Russian sources quoted by
Eudin and North, was held in January. (c) Again, if Ch'ü did not join the party
until February, then he attended the Congress as a "non-party" delegate (even possibly as an interpreter). He could not share the official duties with Chang T'ai-lei
who was already a member of the CCP. There were fourteen "non-party" members
in the Chinese delegation. Allen S. Whiting, *Soviet Policies in China, 1917–1924*
(New York: Columbia University Press, 1953), p. 299.

Hsiao San is likewise confused on these points: "In the spring [which month?]
of 1922, the Congress of the Peoples of the Far East was convened in Moscow.
Comrade Ch'iu-po and others, representing revolutionary organizations in China,
actively participated. At that time, Lenin showed love and respect toward Comrade
Ch'iu-po." Hsiao, *op. cit.,* p. 98. Does the following remark made by Ch'ü on
December 3, 1921, suggest that he was then no more a fellow traveler but a member
of the Communist Party? "Of course I am only a common foot-soldier, but I am
enrolled with the pioneers of the world cultural movement which will not only
open a new road for the world but also restore glory to ancient China." *History
of the Heart, Collected Works,* I, 166.

[80] *Ibid.,* p. 178.
[81] *Ibid.,* p. 181.

again came out with the cough. He was laid up for four or five days, regretting the opportunity he missed to report on the city of Peter. On February 7, senseless, he was carried back to Moscow. And the routine of the sanatorium started again.

The Communist sources, with questionable authority, assert that Ch'ü Ch'iu-po joined the Communist Party in February, 1922.[82] From Ch'ü's own accounts, February of that year may possibly have been the climacteric month. For two or three days before he collapsed in a Petrograd hotel, he was actively enjoying the leave of absence granted by the sanatorium. It was probably on one of those days that he took the decisive step. But we have to point out that he spent the remainder of the month in sickbed and that his moods were not altogether improved by his newly won status. One week after he was moved back to Moscow, that is, on the thirteenth, he wrote "Snow in Russia," a poem which, especially if read side by side with the more famous and more vigorous work on snow by Mao Tse-tung, reveals a soul that was miserably shrinking, groaning, and perplexed by the spectacle of a "vast, white dream" that seemed to be the only thing left of the living universe.[83] He was still recuperating in the sanatorium on March 20, the day he wrote the concluding piece of *History of the Heart*. It was remarkable for a more optimistic tone:

> The world is real; man is living.
> The real world must be made to appear from the dreamlike life. Everything in reality is living; everything that is living is also real. Since activities for the new culture are in the real world, those who work in the real world are also in the midst of life. They are all living.[84]

V

How much our knowledge about the Communist movement in the twenties and the thirties would be enriched if Ch'ü Ch'iu-po had continued to keep a record of his inmost thoughts after he had joined the party. But he

[82] See Yang Chih-hua, note 39, and Wen Chi-tse, note 79. Lu Ting-i, Director of Propaganda, Chinese Communist Party, reported at Ch'ü's funeral in 1955 that Ch'ü joined the party in 1922, but no month was given. *Jen-min jih-pao*, June 19, 1955. Ch'ü's own account (note 39) is vague. It only says that he joined the party after his meeting with Chang Kuo-t'ao, Chang T'ai-lei, and others. It might have been either 1921 or 1922. Hsüeh-hua, who published the *Superfluous Words*, offers another date, which is plausible. "In May, 1921, Chang T'ai-lei came to Moscow and recommended him to the Communist Party. In September, as Ch'ü was employed by the University of Toilers, he became a regular member of the party." *I-ching*, Vol. II, No. 25 (Mar. 5, 1937), p. 19.

[83] *History of the Heart, Collected Works*, I, 182–83.

[84] *Ibid.*, pp. 194–95.

had to break off the habit. To prattle away the secrets of his revolutionary activities would have been tantamount to treacherous betrayal. Even in *History of the Heart* he was careful not to say a thing about Chang Kuo-t'ao, Chang T'ai-lei, and other Chinese visitors who were in Moscow to confer with the Third International. If he did not successfully get rid of the doubts, worries, and longing for the amenities of life, he had to conceal them so as not to jeopardize his position in the party. That he should sanction the publication of *History of the Heart* without expunging the sections that smack more of individualism than of Marxism is indication enough that he did not wish to have his past buried.

If the book succeeded in arousing admiration for Soviet Russia, it was nevertheless to have a counteracting effect in promoting the self-centered, maudlin tendencies of the new literature in China. In the introduction to the book, dated August 4, 1923, he advanced an heretical opinion which would permit literature to serve the individual. "The personality of the author should be somehow brought forth in a literary work." [85] Even though he was already a member of the Central Committee of the Chinese Communist Party when he wrote this, it is obvious that his thoughts still needed to be corrected. And they were corrected to a considerable degree. There is hardly any evidence of the intrusion of the author's personality in the large body of theoretical studies and propaganda he later produced. It should gratify him to think that of all his bodily and spiritual weaknesses, he conquered at least one—exhibitionism.

But in 1933, when he was no longer a commanding figure in the party as a result of intraparty strife, he wrote an essay, curiously indicative of a relapse into the dark moods with which we are familiar. Here again he was writing a chapter, though a brief one, of the history of the heart. It is one of a group of thirteen essays which he wrote while living in close company with Lu Hsün. To hide their authorship, for Ch'ü was on the "wanted list," Lu Hsün allowed them to be published under one or the other of his own numerous pseudonyms. Lu Hsün went so far in assuming the responsibility for them that he included them in the collection of his own works. All except one of the thirteen essays by Ch'ü are found today in Lu Hsün's books, and the one exception is entitled "Childhood." There must have been something in its weak sentimentality that even a fellow-traveling "fighter" like Lu Hsün found objectionable. That it should have come from the pen of a true Communist is almost inconceivable.

Those who have not found meaning in their life hold especially dear their

[85] *Ibid.,* p. 97.

youth and childhood. Romantic reminiscences do not arise from a new discovery that childhood is really wonderful but from a feeling of decline that
comes after one has reached middle age. . . . He who sees his life "floating
away like a dream" is also the one who has taken much from the world but
given back little. Such a man will inevitably feel a deathlike fatigue, so much
so that he does not have even the strength to take anything more from the
world. The sad awareness of age and impotence will weigh on him like lead.

When one cannot move ahead, he wants to retrace his footsteps, to recover
the ground that has already been traveled. I wish for the return of innocence
so that I might regain the joy of learning. How sorrowful the stoppage of
growth is!

Bygones will remain bygones, and the future is yet to come. What do I
mourn for? I ask myself.[86]

A far more revealing account is of course *Superfluous Words,* which he
wrote in prison while awaiting death. This was perhaps the best time in
his life to say what he liked about the Communist Party and himself. All
scruples about his personal safety were then gone. The worst punishment
he could expect for a bold statement of an unfailing, undying, and ever-
growing faith in communism was death, and he was prepared for it. On the
other hand, he could not have cared less about what his comrades might
think of him. The walls of prison had separated them from him, and if he
chose he could use his own criteria in reviewing his past, rather than the
criteria of the party. As it turned out, in *Superfluous Words,* an intimate
autobiography, it is not Ch'ü the apologist for Marxism, but Ch'ü the self-
analyst, who is speaking. But we must guard against the rash conclusion
that he was finally disenchanted. He perhaps remained a Marxist to his
death, one who might not find Marxism entirely satisfactory, yet a Marxist
nonetheless.

He confessed in unequivocal terms to his "dual personality," and we may
accept him as such: a revolutionary hypochondriac, a socialist-minded
aesthete, a sentimental hater of the old society, a practitioner of Bodhisattvahood trained in Moscow, a pilgrim in quest of the Land of Hunger who
could not stand the black bread, or, in a word, a tenderhearted Communist. *Superfluous Words* does not register a new development in his character; it only confirms the impression of him given by his two early books.
The valuable addition to our knowledge that the autobiography supplies,
in regard to Ch'ü Ch'iu-po or possibly any other Communist who faces a
similar dilemma, is that not all the fires of revolution can steel a revolutionary made of base metal, and that human nature, however one chooses
to define it, is not subject to complete transformation under the most thor-

---

[86] *Collected Works,* I, 441–42. Concerning the thirteen essays, see *ibid.,* p. 456, note.

oughgoing thought control. Ch'ü Ch'iu-po the secretary of the party, the theoretician, the leading leftist writer, and Ch'ü Ch'iu-po the prisoner remained essentially Ch'ü Ch'iu-po the young man who sighed over the clouded moon in Moscow and uttered a despairing cry at the mysterious, appalling Russian snow.

Superfluous Words, in the form that we know it, begins with a short preface and is divided into six chapters: (1) "Historical Misunderstanding"; (2) "Fragile Dual Personality"; (3) "Marxism and I"; (4) "Blind-riot-ism and Li Li-san Line"; (5) "Man of Letters"; (6) "Farewell." The preface reads:

WHY MUST I SPEAK?

Since words are superfluous, then why must I speak? Having come to the end of my life—what remains of it can no more be counted by years—I may as well leave them unsaid even if I really have something to say.

But, as ill luck will have it, I am involved in "historical entanglements." Even today, people may take me to be this or that. About their blame or censure, I do not care a bit; it is their admiration that staggers me. My only wish is that the young men would never model their lives after me; that they would not take my former writings as truly representing a certain doctrine. Hence I have to write down these final words, to make a clean breast of myself, before what is left of my life is completely extinguished.

Owing to a "historical misunderstanding," I began, fifteen years ago, to engage myself, no matter how reluctantly, in political work. It is because of this reluctance that I have never succeeded in performing any task satisfactorily; when my hands were busy with one thing, my mind was occupied by something else. I was forbidden by the circumstances, neither had I ever the time, to speak out my mind. There was an assigned role which I had to play. Now that I am completely disarmed and dragged out of the ranks and have only myself left, the impulses to speak out my innermost thoughts have become irresistible—I feel more strongly the need for a thorough exposure of the facts about my heart. The urge for self-analysis, natural to the petit bourgeois, but detested by the Bolshevik, cannot but have a free play at last.

I will keep on writing even with the knowledge that this work will probably never reach my intended readers or that it is not worthy of publication. Man will always like to use his gift of speech. Sometimes he feels relieved if he can talk only in a few sentences and he will not care what kind of readers he may get. It is especially so with me on the eve of my "annihilation," for this is my last chance to speak.

CH'Ü CH'IU-PO, in a prison at
Tingchow
May 17, 1935 [87]

In the text he repeatedly emphasizes his ineptitude and distaste for political work. He says he must classify himself with the "Man of Letters,"

---

[87] *I-ching,* Vol. II, No. 25 (Mar. 5, 1937), pp. 19–20.

not the writer or the literary critic in the modern sense, but a shiftless, fainthearted, and self-deceiving nonentity whose only strength, as the Chinese of the old times would say, lies in "singing of the wind and toying with the moon." [88] With the painful seriousness of an egotist who resents being misunderstood, he hammers on this point:

> I think that it is really a "historical misunderstanding" for a man of my disposition, capacity, and cultural training to become a leader of the Chinese Communist Party. I am no better than a "half-baked" man of letters; to this last minute I have never cured myself of my "chronic literary habits." From 1927 on I gradually lost interest in politics until I became completely unconcerned in the past year, the year I spent in Juichin. I did my work only perfunctorily; I did not even care to learn of politics on the national scale. The reason was of course on one hand my poor health and lack of energy which resulted in a state of utter exhaustion, and on the other hand, my distaste for the kind of work which was contrary to my temperament and inclination but which took up more than ten years of my life, when I served first as a "political interpreter" and then as a political worker. It has been indeed a misunderstanding, a nightmare.
>
> I have no intention of clearing myself of any responsibility when I make this confession. I will never try to shirk, or for emotional reasons, to excuse or minimize my responsibility in my relations to the Communist Party or the "party-state" of the Kuomintang. I mean only to tell the truth before I die. In a word, I am a common literary man who has ironically borne the title of a leader of a certain political party for so many years. If it is not a "historical misunderstanding," then what is it? [89]

These confessions, if they can be accepted as truly from Ch'ü, would demand a reappraisal of his character and position in history. He would lose the honor due a revolutionary and martyr. It is not surprising, therefore, that his official biographers in Communist China never use *Superfluous Words* as a source of material. They seldom mention it. They would rather reject it as spurious.

Hsiao San said in the *Lives of the Martyrs,* a collection of authorized biographies published in 1936:[90]

> The patriotic poems composed by Comrade Ch'iu-po, during his imprisonment and at the time of his execution, together with his will contained in his letters, were all witnessed by newspaper reporters. Comrade Ch'iu-po obviously wanted to deliver, through the service of the gentlemen of the press, a message to the whole nation, to make a last appeal, as he was himself bidding farewell, for resistance against Japan and national salvation. But under the pres-

---

[88] *Ibid.,* Vol. II, No. 27 (Apr. 5, 1937), p. 6.

[89] *Ibid.,* Vol. II, No. 25, p. 22.

[90] Publisher unknown, p. 185. The book, "published in celebration of the Tenth Anniversary of the Chinese Communist Party," is available in the Far Eastern Library, University of Washington, Seattle.

sure of reactionary forces, what appeared in the newspapers to pass for Comrade Ch'iu-po's works, after his heroic death, were not in their original form. Some letters and documents are obvious forgeries, published by the enemy for the purpose of damaging Comrade Ch'iu-po's good name.

An objection may be raised about the term "original form." It can be presumed that Hsiao never saw any of the manuscripts. Yang Chih-hua, Ch'ü's widow, noted in 1958 in Peking:

At the time, Ch'iu-po wrote a number of poems and a book, *Superfluous Words,* but they were all taken away by the bandits [meaning the KMT].[91]

She neither confirmed nor denied the authenticity of the poems and the book in the forms that we know them. The long letter that Ch'ü wrote to her before his death never reached her, though a "thick envelope" was seen by her mother.[92] So the Communists are themselves in the dark regarding what Ch'ü wrote in the prison. Unless Hsiao San could produce the "original" copies of the poems and other writings in authenticated manuscripts, we would rather trust the newspaper reporters than Hsiao San. The reporters, even if we take into consideration the pressure of the "reactionary forces," could at least give eyewitness accounts, which Hsiao San cannot.

When Hsiao San was writing the protestation, he may not have seen *Superfluous Words* in any form. It was published for the first time in 1937, in the *I-ching,* as a literary "discovery." [93] I said "for the first time," for a reader wrote subsequently to the editors of the *I-ching,* expressing his gratitude for being able to gain access to an important document in modern history, though he had only known about its existence.[94] In 1937, after the Sian Incident and before the outbreak at Lukouchiao, the KMT and the Communists were working toward a united front. There was little need for the KMT, which was perhaps no longer an "enemy," to defame a Communist leader. In reprinting *Superfluous Words,* the *I-ching,* or "Fugitive Classics," a "literary and historical fortnightly," had its own repu-

---

[91] Yang Chih-hua, "In Memoriam . . . ," *Red Flags Are Flying,* VIII, 55.

[92] A man called on her mother and displayed the envelope. Yang dared not appear to claim the letter. It might have been a trap set to arrest her. *Ibid.,* p. 52.

[93] *Chan-wang (Look),* a magazine published in Hong Kong, reprinted the *Superfluous Words* in 1958 (Nov. and Dec.). Nothing is said, however, about the history of the text. Comparing the two, I presume that the *Look* version is only a reprint of the *I-ching* version, unless they are both reprints of an identical manuscript. The *Superfluous Words* is mentioned as a work by Ch'ü Ch'iu-po in *Chung-kuo wen-hua-chieh jen-wu tsung-chien (Who's Who in Chinese Cultural Circles)* (Peking, 1940), edited by a Japanese, Hashikawa Tokio. No data are given.

[94] Huang Lu-chen, "About Ch'ü Ch'iu-po," *I-ching,* Vol. II, No. 28 (Apr. 20, 1937).

tation to consider. Its editors are known for the service they rendered to the studies of modern Chinese history. Thanks to their efforts, many documents relating to the Taiping Rebellion, long unknown or thought to be lost, were rediscovered and published in the pages of the *I-ching.* It was perhaps in the same spirit as reprinting the depositions of Hung Jen-kan (Prince Kan of the Taipings) that they reprinted Ch'ü's *Superfluous Words.*[95] The good faith of the *I-ching,* it seems to me, is beyond reproof. The only regrettable fact is that we know nothing of the person, using the pen name Hsüeh-hua, who contributed the transcribed copy. He did not describe the circumstances under which he got hold of the work. Even if the whole thing was not a hoax, we do not know for sure whether or not the manuscript had been altered.

The one man who definitely saw the original manuscript and even read a part of it was Li K'e-ch'ang, probably one of the disappointing reporters mentioned in Hsiao San's article. From his account of an interview with Ch'ü in the prison, we can deduce the true nature of *Superfluous Words.* In the first place, we know that it is not in any way critical of the KMT. It does not have a "patriotic" theme, as Hsiao San might claim, for in 1935 the Communist kind of "patriotism," understood as an immediate and all-out war against Japan, was not tolerated by the KMT. If the manuscript had contained anything that might be considered subversive, inflammatory, agitating for proletarian revolution, detrimental to Sino-Japanese relations, or otherwise harmful to the KMT regime and the KMT policy, it would have been destroyed by the vigilant warden. Since the prison authorities permitted Li to take it out for a few hours, they must have thought it politically harmless.[96] When Ch'ü said that he intended to get it published so as to get "a couple of hundred dollars for pocket money," [97] he must have been sure that the book stood a chance of passing the censors. Secondly, in his own words, "It is a record of tidbits of my private thoughts. In some places, it is about the history of my life." He asked Li to read it carefully, "and then you will know better about my life and my recent thoughts and impressions." [98]

Li represents Ch'ü in prison as unruffled, unalarmed, in complete com-

---

[95] For example, in *I-ching,* Vol. I, No. 20 (Dec. 20, 1936), a discovery is reprinted entitled "Kan wang Hung Jen-kan ch'in-pi kung-tz'u."

[96] Li K'e-ch'ang, "Interview," *Kuo-wen Weekly,* Vol. XII, No. 26 (July 8, 1935), p. 6.

[97] *Ibid.,* p. 5.

[98] *Ibid.,* pp. 5–6.

mand of his faculties, and spending his time in reading, composing classical Chinese poetry, and carving seal stones. People like Mao Tun [99] might still reject this as "a fanciful fabrication of the rumor-mongers" and "a malicious aspersion of character." They might still think that their hero had been pining away defiantly in the clutches of the enemy. But this picture of calmness in prison has been accepted by one of the official biographers. Said Wen Chi-tse in 1957:

> The bandits put him in solitary imprisonment. . . . In his blue-cloth jacket and white-cloth pants, he looked in good spirits. His attitude was leisurely composure. He spent his time partly in writing poems (*shih* and *tz'u*) and off-hand essays, and partly in carving seal stones.[100]

When Li entered the cell, at eight o'clock in the morning of June 4, 1935, Ch'ü was bending over the desk, carving a stone. He was obliging enough, talking freely about his life and various other subjects, such as Lu Hsün, Ting Ling, and Hu Shih. He agreed to carve a seal for the reporter and present him with a piece of calligraphy. What he wrote down were three poems, recently composed, all very sad. One beginning with "Twenty years' floating and sinking, everything comes to nothing" [101] was probably meant as an elegy for himself. The other two, no less elegiac, centered on his wife from whom he had heard nothing since June of the preceding year. He wondered, in one of the poems, why his "amorous thoughts were still revolving around the clouded mountains" [102] after he had already attained, as he thought, a sort of nirvana. His wife, an underground agent in Shanghai, had tried to travel with him to Kiangsi, but she was ordered to stay behind. So the sentimentalist's dream of matrimonial bliss was shattered by the perversity of politics. Of course, neither husband nor wife had made any complaint. They understood their duty. But in the prison, the "thousandfold nocturnal thoughts" [103] of the poet kept flying to his mate, whose whereabouts he did not know and whose safety now mattered more to him than his own. He had lately composed more than ten poems, all affixed to the wall of the cell. Some of them may have been in a higher key with a patriotic theme, as Hsiao San so firmly believed, but Li noted

---

[99] Mao Tun, "Commemorate Comrade Ch'iu-po, Learn from Comrade Ch'iu-po," *Jen-min jih-pao,* June 18, 1955; reprinted in *Hsin-hua yüeh-pao,* July, 1955.

[100] Wen Chi-tse, "Comrade . . . ," *Red Flags Are Flying,* V, 105.

[101] The Chinese version reads: 廿載浮沉萬事空．

[102] The Chinese version reads: 何事萬緣俱寂後，偏留綺思繞雲山．

[103] The Chinese version reads: 夜思千重戀舊遊．

only these three delicate, plaintive pieces, all expressive of a lingering love for life in the face of imminent death. They are apparently the works of a man who places his personal sorrow above the fate of his country.

But to us, the interview is of greater interest than the poems, since it bears more directly upon the "thoughts and impressions" Ch'ü said he had put into *Superfluous Words*. Thus he told Li about the period when he was in charge of the party after the downfall of Li Li-san.

> I always believe that I have never rid myself of the habits of a man of letters. So I am not fit for political work. Moreover, my health was in bad shape and my nerves were extremely weak. Every year in the spring, I suffered attacks of hemorrhage from the lungs. I said to the others, "The field is to be plowed by the buffalo, not by a horse. Now you have a horse, plowing the field. I am afraid that I could show no results though I might try to use up my energy." And they said, "Until we have the buffalo, will the horse please keep on working?" Not long afterward, the buffaloes came. Ch'in Pang-hsien, Ch'en Shao-yü, Chang Wen-t'ien and others came back from Moscow. . . .[104]

The same sentiments are expressed in different metaphors in *Superfluous Words*:

> There is a saying in my native town, "to catch a crow and force him to make a nest," which means, of course, that the nest will never be made. That a mediocre man of letters, who may be even described as silly, should bear the burden of the tasks of a political leader, is indeed ridiculous, but it is a fact.[105]
>
> When a jaded, decrepit horse is pulling a cart with a several thousand *chin* load up a steep slope in staggering steps, he cannot move back, but to climb ahead is utterly beyond his power. That was exactly my feeling when I was carrying the burden of a political leader. The fatigue from the work that I wished to stop but could not became a pressure unspeakably heavy to me. Weariness in spirit made me thirst for a "sweet" repose, so much so that my nerves became numb and I ceased to think. . . .[106]

These parts of *Superfluous Words* agree essentially with the interview, the only difference being that the latter, in a casual style, lacks the intensity of utterance. What stands out in *Superfluous Words* but is not found in the interview is Ch'ü's earnest request that the "historical misunderstanding," the "farce" must be stopped. To the Communists he said that he had for long ceased at heart to be their "comrade." He would rather assign himself

---

[104] Li K'e-ch'ang, *op. cit.*, p. 3. Li Ang has this to say about Ch'ü's incompetence as a Communist leader: "Ch'ü was really a mediocre plotter who, as the saying goes, was not gifted with the talent to command, nor could he win admiration for his virtue." *Hung-se wu-t'ai* (*The Red Stage*) (Chungking: Victory Publishing Company, 1941), p. 51. "Ch'ü was indeed a blockhead (*fan-t'ung* or rice-vessel) in its fullest sense. He could never carry out any plan as he wished." *Ibid.*, p. 133.

[105] *I-ching*, Vol. II, No. 27 (Apr. 5, 1937), p. 9.

[106] *Ibid.*, Vol. II, No. 26 (Mar. 20, 1937), p. 16.

to oblivion than continue to occupy a place in history which he did not deserve. He wished that since he had spilled out everything about his unworthiness, he would not be remembered as a martyr after his death. Of his wife, his "only dear one in life," he asked forgiveness, for not even to her had he had the courage to reveal his heart. He wished that she would henceforth detest him and forget him so that his soul might rest in peace.

Nothing would disconcert historians in Communist China more than this modest request, so it is only natural that they should dismiss it as a base trick of defamation. But it would be hard for them to reject *Superfluous Words* as a whole. Evidence compels us to believe that even if the work is a forgery, the KMT did not have a hand in it, for there is a conspicuous absence of anything that might be remotely interpreted as a reconciliation with the KMT. A forger in the service of the "reactionary force" would not miss the opportunity to please his masters. It would be easy to insert a plausible statement such as, "I have come to see that the Three People's Principles are not without their good points," which would be heart-warming to the KMT and perhaps acceptable to the Communists too. But the *Superfluous Words* is devoid of such fulsome superficialities. It is an intensely personal document, and its very intensity indicates that the author, whoever he may have been, had powerful personal feelings about his subject. Besides acknowledging Ch'ü's unfitness for political work, which can be confirmed by the interview, *Superfluous Words* is also rich in penetrating self-analysis which no one but Ch'ü himself—or, if there were a forger, one gifted with exceptional intuitive and imaginative powers —could have produced. For we can describe the book as a dirge about a life misspent, a confession to cowardice, inertia, and hypocrisy which sink a man deeper into mistakes even after he has become well aware of them, and a protest, though in a feeble way, against an ironic fate which places man in the most impossible jobs and then taunts him in his naked powerlessness.

Though the work contains a great deal of material which might be used in a political biography of Ch'ü Ch'iu-po (which I have refrained from using from the same scruples as the "official" biographers), *Superfluous Words* has little to do with politics. It was written by a man to whom politics represents all that is hateful in the world: exhaustion of vitality, mortal fatigue, death in the heart, numbness of the senses, eternal lies, and destruction of natural affections. As a plaintive assertion of a weak, tired ego, the book is above politics, above class struggle, above any ideology.

It is inconceivable that a forger with political motives would have produced such a non-political or even anti-political book. I am inclined to accept *Superfluous Words* as a genuine work by Ch'ü Ch'iu-po, with only due reservations for clerical errors on the part of the transcriber. A forgery could hardly have been accepted when the real thing was written only some two years earlier. The memory of those who had seen the original was still fresh. The charges of defamation are flimsy, too, when applied to a book which makes a desperate attempt to win more sympathy and more understanding through explanation and analysis. But why should we bother to probe the motives of a forger in a case where almost certainly nothing indicates a forger was ever involved? Why do not we include the book in the author's collected body of works and reassess his position in history with the aid of the valuable material afforded?

Taken as Ch'ü's testament and confession, *Superfluous Words* does not possess much literary or humanistic value. Its strength is in the keen, relentless anatomy of a sickly ego, but its weaknesses are numerous and fatal. Its field of interest is too narrowly restricted, its focus is too constantly on the analyzed subject who has nothing but meaningless despair left, and behind all the effusions, which sometimes sound tediously redundant, there is a vacuity, a complete disregard of life's purposes, and a total unconcern with moral values. When the author declared, describing his experience in the period from early 1930 to August or September of 1934, "I did not care if the universe should collapse; I did not care if I was a revolutionary or anti-revolutionary; I only wanted to have a rest, a rest, a rest!" [107] we hear the gasp of a dying man. The "sweet repose" he enjoyed in prison was too brief for him to rebuild his strength. Before he was recovered enough to think into the future, to form a new vision of the world, to impose an order on his chaotic inner life, to find a meaning of his past experiences, all his sufferings, "farces," and "nightmares," he had been taken to the execution ground.

Though a "mediocre man of letters," as he admitted himself to be, he could still write well about himself. The passage below is rather mild; but its pathos is clear to those who have seen in the *Journey to the Land of Hunger* and *History of the Heart* how he regards a beautiful landscape as spiritual nourishment.

I am just thirty-six years of age [thirty-eight by the reckoning of the lunar calendar], but I feel I am extremely fagged out. Nothing that usually rouses the interest of a man in his prime can interest me. Not only have I become

[107] *Ibid.,* Vol. II, No. 27, p. 9.

indolently unthinking about general political problems, but any form of enjoyment, including even natural scenery, holds no meaning to me now.[108]

Another shows how he was gradually cultivating a genuine literary taste in spite of his Marxist beliefs:

In recent years, I have reread some literary classics, both Chinese and Western, and I believe that I have had some new experiences. From these works, you understand human life and society rather intimately. You understand people of differentiated characters, not in general classifications, such as "good man," "bad man," or "bureaucrat," "commoner," "worker," "rich peasant," and so forth. What are revealed before you are human beings in flesh and blood, with distinct personalities, though they are still placed in certain relations to production and in certain social classes.

This, I suppose, is the first step I have taken to advance from a mere "man of letters" to real appreciation of literature.

But is it too late? It is! [109]

The insight contained in the following can only come from a man who has really lived under the spell of Marxism:

But to say that I have given up Marxism is not correct. If you want to discuss with me any political problem, I have no approach to it except what I can deduce from my imperfect knowledge of Marxism. These deductions, as a matter of fact, perhaps contain also many elements of opportunism, i.e., viewpoints that are contrary to Marxism-Leninism. Therefore, it has become unnecessary for me to exert myself to think in vain about any problem. There is no possibility of changing my way of thinking which, ever since my youth, has been moving toward Marxism. I don't know whither this road, leading to Marxism, but intersected at many points by non-Marxist paths, will eventually take me. The principal fact is that I am tired; I cannot go any farther. I no longer have the energy to think over politics from the viewpoints of the social sciences.[110]

It is rather to be expected that he did not give up Marxism in the end. There should be no more misunderstanding about his "dual personality" after *Superfluous Words,* and he acted it out up to his last minute. Probably under the influence of liquor, he sang the "Internationale" [111] in Russian like a true martyr before he went to face the firing squad. But his final written document is a poem, a composite of four lines by three dif-

[108] *Ibid.,* Vol. II, No. 26, p. 16.
[109] *Ibid.,* Vol. II, No. 27, p. 8.
[110] *Ibid.,* Vol. II, No. 26, p. 19.
[111] According to the *Ta-kung pao,* reprinted in part in *I-ching,* Vol. II, No. 28, p. 43, Ch'ü first heard the "Internationale" in 1920 when he was joining the local Russians in celebrating the October Revolution in Harbin. *Journey, Collected Works,* I, 52. Later he translated it into Chinese, but it was still the Russian version that he sang at the time of his death.

ferent poets, a regular literary exercise for the Chinese. He was writing
this, according to the *Ta-kung pao*,[112] when, in the most dramatic manner
possible, he received the summons to the execution grounds, on the morning of June 18, 1935. The poem has a little preface:

The night of June 17, 1935, I dreamed I was walking on a mountain path.
The setting sun was glorious but was sometimes hidden, and a cold stream was
moaning nearby. It was like a fairy land. The next morning as I was reading
the T'ang poets, I came upon the line, "Setting sun, in ragged ridges, now
bright, now dim." So I made a poem impromptu, a composite of these four lines:

> Setting sun, in ragged ridges, now bright, now dim;
> Falling leaves and cold stream, in two tunes sing requiem.
> A solitary ten years have I endured,
> Ties all dissolved, my heart clinging to half a hymn.[113]

[112] Reprinted in *I-ching*, Vol. II, No. 28.

[113] The first and third lines are by Wei Ying-wu and Tu Fu, respectively, and the
remaining lines are by Lang Shih-yüan. Robert C. North, quoting another source,
gives a description of the scene different from that in the *Ta-kung pao*: "On that day
[January 18, 1935], according to a story then current, he was brought from prison
to the place of execution on a stretcher. There he drained a glass of whisky, asked
for a brush and paper, and wrote down this poem:

> The colorful splurge of the setting sun etches the mountains of Fukien.
> The rustle of the falling leaves and the sound of the running stream show
>   the winter is near.
> These are eternal.
> Ten years I have passed in worldly undertakings, and now I am prepared
>   to join heaven,
> But I leave with desires unfilled."

Moscow and the Chinese Communists (Stanford, 1953), p. 165. According to the
Ta-kung pao, he was writing the poem when he was summoned to the execution ground
and he walked "in a leisurely manner" to the place rather than being carried on a
stretcher.

THE PHENOMENON OF
CHIANG KUANG-TZ'U

I

O N October 20, 1930, the *Hung-ch'i jih-pao* (*Red Flag Daily News*), an underground Communist newspaper printed in Shanghai, published the following item:

CHIANG KUANG-CH'IH EXPELLED FROM THE CCP

Chiang Kuang-ch'ih—alias Chiang Kuang-tz'u, or Hua-hsi-li [Vassily?]—the writer who had for a long time claimed to be one of the proletarian class, was formally read out of the CCP a few days ago. This newspaper has obtained information about his case which is reported as follows.

In spite of his membership in the CCP for several years, Chiang Kuang-ch'ih was originally a student of the petit-bourgeois class. He has never engaged himself in any hard task, nor made any attempt to approach the masses. He maintains a comfortable and luxurious way of life, supposedly proper to his position as a writer. He showed vacillation in the recent upsurge of revolutionary struggles because there was at the same time an increase in white terror by the reactionary regime. As a cultural worker, he was among those who were ordered by the Central Committee, CCP, to start actual work among the masses. Having been a waverer for some time, however, he was afraid of the hard work involved in such a move. He made a request in writing to resign his membership in the party but to remain "a member of the active revolutionary masses" for the reason that the romantic, luxurious life he was accustomed to rendered him unfit for the iron discipline of the party. The party cell to which he belonged judged his case with a view to the duty of every Communist of regularly doing hard work under iron discipline—a duty which has become more demanding on the vanguard of the proletariat. Under the present circumstances in China, the reactionary government is running headlong to collapse, the revolutionary struggles have kept rising in daily surges, and the toiling masses of workers and peasants are entering the final phase of the decisive battle with the imperialists, the gentry class, and the bourgeois class. Under these circumstances, therefore, there is an urgent call for complete sacrifice, for hard work on the front line of the battles, for active leadership in the mass struggle to win the final victory of revolution. The party cell looked upon his application as the most dastardly act of a petit-bourgeois, motivated as it was by fear of sacrifice and hard work in the face of the sharpening crisis of class struggle. With a view to purging the party of opportunists and cowards and strengthening its organization, the cell reached a decision at a meeting to read him out of the party. The decision was ratified by the Kiangsu Provincial Committee.

Ever since he joined the party, Chiang never led a good organizational life within the party cell. His romantic nature as a petit-bourgeois was impervious to the injunction and education which the party never failed to give him. Last year, with the development of struggles all over the country and the intensification of the white terror, he broke with the organization and fled to Japan without authorization. The deceitful excuse for his desertion was that he had gone to Tsingtao for reasons of health. He did not then heed the final warning from the party, nor did he thoroughly acknowledge his errors. Meanwhile, he had written a novel, *The Sorrows of Lisa,* and got it published for the sake of nothing but the royalties. This book on the sorrows of the White Russians after their downfall, through a psychological analysis as reflected in purely petit-bourgeois consciousness, reads like a plea for the White Russians, who, after all their counterrevolutionary activities, are treated as if they were deserving of the readers' sympathy. It also implies a vilification of the proletarian rule of the Soviet Union. The party pointed out these errors and ordered him to stop the book from circulation. But again he paid no heed. Even then the party had had the intention to expel him. It was put into effect only recently because the necessary procedure took some time to complete.

According to sources acquainted with his private life, Chiang Kuang-ch'ih is supported by the rich monthly income from the sales of his books and leads an entirely bourgeois life. He does not have an iota of understanding of the life of the masses, since he has never come into contact with them. Besides his poor literary skill, owing to a lack of talent, few of his political notions are correct. He puts up the appearance of a learned man only because he has some knowledge of Russian, which makes plagiarism rather easy for him. The stories he wrote are extremely superficial and empty, devoid of practical significance. His vacillation and cowardice are therefore not an accident. He may still call himself "a member of the active revolutionary masses," but that is a shameless excuse and evasion. As a degenerate petit-bourgeois, he has obviously embarked upon the career of a counterrevolutionary.[1]

This piece, an exercise in defamation, does not, of course, present the case fairly. Chiang Kuang-tz'u's failure as a man, a Communist, and an author was an interesting case, significantly illustrative of the temper of his times, but his record has to be re-examined. Whatever personal reason

---

[1] *Hung-ch'i jih-pao,* Oct. 20, 1930 (Hoover Institution collection), p. 3. Chiang Kuang-ch'ih changed his name to Chiang Kuang-tz'u after the anti-Communist purge of April, 1927. *Ch'ih,* meaning "red," had too obvious a political connotation. See Yang Ts'un-jen, "The Sun Society and Chiang Kuang-tz'u," *Hsien-tai (Les Contemporains,* a monthly) (Shanghai), Vol. III, No. 4 (Aug., 1933), p. 471. Lu Hsün, never a friend of Chiang's, ridiculed his change of name by calling him Chiang Kuang-X in 1928 and Chiang Kuang-Z in 1930. *Lu Hsün ch'üan-chi (Complete Works)* (Peking, 1957), IV, 96, 171 (hereafter cited as *LH*). I shall use "Chiang Kuang-tz'u" throughout the paper, except in some quotations where "Chiang Kuang-ch'ih" is the preferred form.

prompted him to send in his resignation, Chiang probably meant simply to stay away. To sever his ties with the Chinese Communist Party did not mean that he would embark upon a "career of a counterrevolutionary." Treachery was not among his known vices. After he had made the decision to quit, there was not even much time left for him to prove, as he had wished, his worth as "a member of the active revolutionary masses." Few had believed him in 1929 when he hid away for the reason of health. However, in early 1931, a few months after his expulsion, he became noticeably sick.[2]

Among his friends, Kuo Mo-jo believed Chiang's death to be a real loss to Chinese literature:

The ancients used to say, "Le style, c'est l'homme même." Kuang-tz'u wrote in a style which was just like him. In my personal experience, I have not seen many writers who show such a striking likeness between style and personality. Those who have never met Kuang-tz'u may safely call to their minds a portrait of the man from the impression they get from his works. He was straightforward, simple, and without falsity. He had the Northerner's physique and the Southerner's nerves. A man like him, I think, is a dear. Regrettably he died young.[3] If he had lived longer, and if his frank nature had been refined

[2] In the spring of 1931, Chiang "looked extremely emaciated and panted as he spoke." Yü Ta-fu, "The Last Years of Kuang-tz'u," *Hsien-tai,* Vol. III, No. 1 (May, 1933), p. 73. Miss Wu Szu-hung noted his illness on several occasions in her *Kuang-tz'u hui-i-lu (Reminiscences of Kuang-tz'u),* serialized in *Ta-feng (Great Wind,* a semi-monthly) (Hong Kong), from September to November, 1940. After they had lived together in late 1929, Wu discovered "something wrong" in his excrements, a sight which "petrified and froze" her on the spot *(ibid.,* Sept. 20, 1940, p. 2396). He complained of stomach-ache *(ibid.,* Oct. 5, p. 2443). In reply to a girl friend of hers, she said listlessly, "He was so often sick" *(ibid.,* Oct. 20, p. 2480). There was even a hint as to why she had eventually to separate from him: "It was early summer, and the night was so warm. A breeze came in gently from the balcony. Everything was quiet. I stood alone before the standing mirror. My dress was off; there was only the undergarment on me. I looked at the person in the mirror: the long dark hair over the shoulders, a round face, large eyes, and a full bosom shimmering with a mixture of faint hues. I doubted whether the person was me. Me? What should I do? I should seek a reality much more beautiful than this. A youthful desire, the desire of a young woman, was surging within me. I clamored for satisfaction, for act, but the reality. . . . I cast a look at Kuang-tz'u sleeping in bed, motionless, not a word, not even a glance from him. His tired long body was stretched, a posture of sickness. My desire became an illusion. My existence was denied. I wondered whether the person standing before the mirror was myself. I was perhaps not myself—but a statue in plaster with living senses. Noiselessly I dropped to the other side of the bed, while tears began to wet the soft pillows and they flooded as if from a broken jar" *(ibid.,* Oct. 20, p. 2482). The summer referred to was that of 1930.

[3] By Chinese reckoning, Chiang was thirty-one when he died. Both Yang Ts'un-jen (see note 1) and Huang Yao-mien, in his "Short Biography of Chiang Kuang-tz'u," an appendix to *Chiang Kuang-tz'u hsüan-chi (Selected Works)* (hereafter cited as

by art, the question why China has produced no masterpiece might not have been raised.[4]

In the same context, Kuo noted Chiang's extraordinarily neat manuscript, not marred by a single alteration or deletion. But that was not a transcribed copy, Chiang would explain, as he showed it to his friend. It was his first and definitive draft. He would insist that his manuscript be printed the way it was written; any suggestion for changes was unacceptable to him. Such a forthrightness was embarrassing even to an indulgent friend like Kuo Mo-jo, who commented:

> Strictly speaking, Kuang-tz'u's style is actually a little too loose. Such a style might be passable in a novel, but it is not quite suitable for short stories. Therefore, his contributions to *The Deluge* [a journal published by the Creation Society] were often rejected.[5]

One may imagine the hard time Kuo had in trying to defend Chiang's "loose style" to the editorial board of *The Deluge*. What could the editors find in the pages of Chiang's clean manuscript anyway? A remarkable likeness to a personality whom most of Kuo's associates detested. Yü Ta-fu, another founding member of the Creation Society, noted how Chiang alienated people by his arrogance.[6] Kuo might have welcomed one more expression

---

Hsüan-chi) (Peking, 1951), p. xxix, gave June 30, 1931, as the date of his death. However, Fan Po-ch'ün and Tseng Hua-p'eng said the date was August 31, 1931. See the article co-authored by them, "On Chiang Kuang-ch'ih," *Wen-hsüeh p'ing-lun* (*Literary Criticism,* a bi-monthly) (Peking), Oct., 1962, p. 52. The first date seems to be more acceptable. Yang, as a close friend who attended his funeral, may have remembered correctly. He noted, "On the early morning of June 30, Kuang-tz'u passed away in the hospital, unattended by friends or relatives. . . . On the same day, he was coffined and buried. Those present at the funeral were [Ch'ien] Hsing-ts'un, [Yang] Ts'un-jen, [Lou] Chien-nan, and [Wu] Szu-hung." Yang, *op. cit.,* p. 476. *Jen-min jih-pao* in 1953 also recognized June 30 as the anniversary of his death. *Jen-min jih-pao,* June 30, 1953, p. 3.

[4] Kuo Mo-jo, *Ch'uang-tsao shih-nien hsü-p'ien* (*Ten Years of the Creation Society: A Sequel*), in *Mo-jo wen-chi* (*Collected Works*) (Peking, 1957), p. 243.

[5] *Ibid.,* p. 245.

[6] Yü Ta-fu met him in the spring of 1925. "Kuang-ch'ih's attitude and conversation were perhaps influenced by the examples of certain Western European writers. When he talked he showed an extremely high ambition, and his tone was arrogant. But at that time he had not yet published a serious work. Therefore, the younger writers at the Creation Society Publishing Department did not hide their contempt for him." Yü, *op. cit.,* p. 71. His self-confidence could on occasion win him friends. When Yang Ts'un-jen first met him in May, 1927, they were aboard a ship going from Shanghai to Wuhan, both being fugitives from the anti-Communist purge. To Yang, Chiang was "a young man with a strong character who regarded himself as marked out for something unusual." Yang, *op. cit.,* p. 470. Their friendship led to the founding of the Sun Society.

of Chiang's "frank nature," but he too was not blind to Chiang's stylistic errors. Chiang's lack of "refinement by art" would have caused despair in a friend like Kuo Mo-jo. Without refinement by art Chiang Kuang-tz'u was obviously not the man to produce a Chinese masterpiece. But to have put Chiang through a refining process seems to have been as impossible as to have prolonged his life.

Chiang's frank nature—which is truly the impression the reader obtains from his books—would have been an admirable virtue if, like Montaigne, Pascal, Rousseau, or even Yü Ta-fu, he had had a more profound self-knowledge. Frankness with him, however, seemed too often the shallowness and vanity of a bore. The *Hung-ch'i jih-pao* article used twice the term "romantic," once referring to his private life and the other time to his "nature." The term in Chinese (*lang-man*) means dissolute or even licentious in the first instance; and in the second, it summarizes the various traits of restlessness and rebelliousness, of despondency and enthusiasm, that are found in a type of personality which has been amply studied in modern European literature. We do not know whether Chiang ever tried to defend himself after his expulsion, but of those charges published, "romanticism" was one he would have proudly admitted. Not only was he perhaps by nature more romantically inclined than others, but he made a conscious effort to live up to the standard of the romantic type. He tried hard to let the world know that he was different. Both his arrogance and his quickness in converting thoughts into words were meant to show people that he did not care about such trifles as good manners or style.

Such an attitude may seem ridiculous and pathetic to readers today, but it aroused hostility among most of his acquaintances. According to Kuo Mo-jo, Chiang's "romanticism" came under heavy attack, and not only from the Communists.[7] Kuo noted, with sorrow and indignation, that the "annihilative campaign of abuse" launched against Chiang was a cause of the unhappiness which led to his death. This painful situation was largely created by Chiang himself, but it was a situation not without its sweet compensations. His logic seemed to work this way. First of all, his "romanticism" had attracted attention—a proof of his importance; secondly, if he was under attack, it meant that he was misjudged and alienated; thirdly, since every great romanticist in the past was known to have been misjudged and alienated from society in at least some period of his life, he derived comfort from the thought that he was in distinguished company.

[7] Kuo, *Ten Years* . . . , p. 244.

To prove his "romanticism" he had also to live a "romantic" life and to write about it. Thus his fame as a romantic spread wide to attract more attention and more attack, which deepened his sorrow and yet continued to flatter his ego.

There were many other romantic youths in the first generation of twentieth-century China. To mention two, both Kuo Mo-jo and Yü Ta-fu were aware, and to a degree proud, of their romanticism. But Chiang Kuang-tz'u became romanticism's loudest advocate and its most pathetic caricature, whose "frankness" was carried to the extreme of naïveté. When romanticism became a subject of discussion, Chiang would make the pronouncement with a courage that Kuo admired: "Romantic? I myself am romantic. All revolutionaries are romantic. Without being romantic, who would come to start a revolution? . . . Idealism, passion, discontent with the status quo and a desire to create something better—here you have the spirit of romanticism. A romantic is one possessed with such a spirit." Kuo liked the idea so much that he said that since he could not quote verbatim, the reader was free to take these lines as if they were Kuo's own words put into Chiang's mouth.[8]

Kuo wrote this in 1937 at a point in his career when he was about to renounce his "romantic" past. His relationship with the Communist Party had had few of the difficulties experienced by Chiang. The many years Kuo was still to live would see him as a bureaucrat remarkably adroit in his manifold service to the party. After 1949 his was a distinguished voice in the chorus of eulogies devoted to the personality cult of Mao Tse-tung. It was in the capacity of a spokesman for the party's literary policy that Kuo wrote, in 1958, about the combination of "revolutionary romanticism" with "romantic realism."[9] This brand of "romanticism" was very different from what Chiang or Kuo in his younger days had advocated.

Chiang's shorter life presented a less complicated record. He seemed to display continually a spirit of independence which Kuo, whether under pressure or out of free choice, could not maintain for long. This difference, however, did not mark Chiang out as a more admirable man or author. In both men there was some deficiency in the soul, a warped moral life, a failure to be absolutely and relentlessly honest about themselves, the world, and whatever was dear to them. Both of them failed, and their failure in some measure spelled the dilemma of modern Chinese intellectuals.

[8] *Ibid.*

[9] Kuo Mo-jo, "Romanticism and Realism," *Hung-ch'i* (*Red Flag,* a semi-monthly) (Peking), Vol. I, No. 3 (July, 1956), p. 6.

If Kuo degenerated into a flatterer, Chiang's occupation with self-flattery was no less repulsive. It was indeed a pity that for modern Chinese writers only a very narrow middle ground seemed to be left between subservience to political power and an assertion of the "romantic" self, with all its lawlessness and hollowness. To some of them communism had offered a hope for a better world and, as such, had indeed looked attractive, but when it revealed itself as a heartless bureaucratic machine and expanded into a totalitarian power that brooked nothing less than perfect conformity, even a not very intelligent Communist like Chiang Kuang-tz'u must have felt disappointment and an emptiness which was hard to bear. In Chiang's case he could only pick up, after the political crisis, the broken pieces of a "romantic" dream, dashed ambitions, and a shattered career, and with these he enlarged the cherished treasure of his petty sorrows.

Of the two men, Chiang was the poorer writer. As a stylist, Kuo has little to recommend him. Indeed, his style should also be described as "loose," with its errors of verbosity, of carelessness in diction and sentence construction, and of sentimental effusiveness. But though Kuo's writing is mediocre,[10] Chiang seemed to possess still less talent. Kuo knows how to curb his romanticism, when necessary, or, at least, how to make it more palatable to his readers. He has a larger vocabulary, a greater resourcefulness in themes and modes of expression, and a much wider interest in life and learning. Kuo, too, offends good taste and good sense, but not so consistently as Chiang. His archaeological studies are at least a proof of his amenability to scholarly discipline. In contrast, Chiang was a purer "romantic." Few things in life really interested him, and he harped on the few themes with astoundingly limited means of expression. He showed a marvelous carelessness in his handling of words and a happy unconcern about style. But at least he was true to his belief in "romanticism," for the same carelessness was manifested in his dealings with the Communist Party.

When the *Hung-ch'i jih-pao* pointed out his "lack of talent," it was not

---

[10] I agree with C. T. Hsia on Kuo Mo-jo: "Yet properly understood, his career only underscores the more dramatically the tragedy of a generation of intellectuals who began in romantic revolt and ended in subservience to a despotism which they themselves had helped to create." C. T. Hsia, *A History of Modern Chinese Fiction* (New Haven: Yale University Press, 1961), p. 94. ". . . His creative output, upon which his literary reputation must primarily rest, is of a very mediocre quality indeed. Of all the acknowledged leading writers of modern China, Kuo Mo-jo possesses least enduring merit. He must be eventually remembered as a colorful personality of his period who played a leading role in many literary and political enterprises." *Ibid.,* p. 96.

merely the opinion of those who read him out of the party. His writing is too often visibly offensive. He no doubt had his fans among the barely literate youths who did not care so much about the quality of writing as the emotions he so "frankly" expressed. Their preference for him was recorded in the sales of his books,[11] which supplied the money to support him in his "bourgeois" style of living; but he aimed at much greater things. He wanted to be known as a Byron or a Pushkin,[12] a romantic whose colorful life would be admired by posterity and whose immortal works— the "masterpieces" in Kuo Mo-jo's words—the Chinese people for centuries to come would cherish and feel proud of. Paranoiac as this desire may seem today, it was not so wild a dream to the youths brought up in the May Fourth Movement. The old literature was pronounced "dead," the new literature was yet to be born—but who would be our Dante or Chaucer? Even as sober a scholar as Hu Shih felt a thrill at the wonderful opportunity offered to the new writers of China.[13]

Among these, Chiang failed miserably, because he tried the hardest to prove his greatness. The low opinion in which his fellow writers held him was noteworthy because literary criticism in those days was not known for its strictness. If one scans the literary scene of the time, one finds no counterpart to the Scottish reviewer who, with his strict yet outmoded standard, bore down on struggling young English bards. Instead there was a general indulgence toward the nascent *pai-hua* literature produced after

---

[11] In the September, 1933, issue of *Wen-hsüeh (Literature)* (Shanghai), an advertisement of the Ya-tung (East Asia) Book Company, Shanghai, listed Chiang's *Chi-nien-pei (The Monument)* as in its ninth printing and his *Shao-nien p'iao-p'o-che (The Youthful Tramp)* as in its sixteenth printing. The publishing history of the books I have used for this study is as follows: *The Youthful Tramp:* 1st printing, Jan., 1926; 11th printing, July, 1930. *Ya-lu-chiang shang (On the Yalu,* a collection of short stories) (Ya-tung Book Company): 1st printing, Jan., 1927; 13th printing, Apr., 1949. *The Monument:* 1st printing, Nov., 1927; 10th printing, Sept., 1932. *Yeh-chi (Worship at the Unlocatable Grave)* (Shanghai, Hsien-tai Book Co.): 1st printing, Nov., 1927; 5th printing, Dec., 1929; total of the five printings, 7,500 copies. As the last figure indicates, each printing of Chiang's books probably did not exceed 2,000 copies. Yet because of his prolificness he could expect to live on the income from the royalties. Upon his expulsion from the Communist Party, he withdrew his savings from the bank, which amounted to one thousand *yüan*. Wu, *Reminiscences, Ta-feng,* Nov. 5, 1940, p. 2517.

[12] Huang in his "Short Biography" (see note 3) said, "Kuang-tz'u had an extraordinary self-esteem and used to call himself the Pushkin of China."

[13] Hu Shih in his essay, "For a Constructive Literary Revolution" (Apr., 1918), predicted that the Chinese national language would be created by China's new writers, who were expected to perform what Dante and Chaucer had done for Italy and England. Hu, *Wen-ts'un (Collected Works)* (Shanghai, 1921), 1st series, I, 79–80.

the May Fourth Movement. In the general laxity of standards, it may seem unfair that Chiang Kuang-tz'u should have been singled out as a target of contempt. He was certainly not much worse than many of his contemporaries who also laid claim to literary fame. They were pardoned or simply ignored, perhaps because they were not so serious about themselves. But Chiang's self-esteem could be insufferable. Who was he anyway? A hack who had yet to prove that he could write a simple good sentence but put on airs as if he were a great "romantic" writer whose genius should compel admiration and exonerate his atrocious manners!

Nothing, of course, could remedy the lack of talent. But Chiang Kuang-tz'u might at least have been more heedful of literary discipline. His neglect of it was partly due to the unquestionable paranoiac traits in his personality, but in a sense he was also a victim of his times. A man of his meager ability would never have become known as a writer in any other century in Chinese history than the twentieth. The movement for a new literature released his youthful energy and deluded him into overrating the importance of his "spontaneity." In the early 1920's there was prevalent among Chinese writers a strong belief in personality and a disregard of technique. Such an attitude seemed natural to those who wanted to make a clean break with the literature of the past, with its alleged suppression of personality and its rhetorical excesses. Chiang was one of the new men. He paraded his personality and observed few rules of good writing except that the author should be "frank." Yet with all his earnestness and prolificness, he only succeeded in reducing to absurdity the literary credo of the May Fourth Movement.

His failure was perhaps also due to the fact that history moved faster than he thought. At the time he began to publish, around 1925, some sort of standard for writing in the *pai-hua* was emerging. It was never clearly formulated, but it was tacitly observed by an increasing number of people who wrote. After 1927 the new *pai-hua* literature had become firmly established. More books in the new literary medium had been published, and good writing could now be more easily told from bad. Professional competence among the writers showed a remarkable improvement as a readership with a greater power of discrimination arose. Chiang's persistence in crudity made him appear a stunted growth. His incompetence was not unnoticed by the Communists. Even if he had remained obedient to the party's orders, his usefulness as a writer would not have been much esteemed. When the party decided on his expulsion, it obviously did not think it was losing an important literary asset.

Chiang's struggle to vindicate his supposed genius was pathetic. His frustration was noted by Yü Ta-fu:

I heard from a young man who was at Kuang-tz'u's deathbed that it was mental anguish more than physical disease that dealt the fatal blow. What Kuang-tz'u regretted the most in his last days was the lack of proper respect from the contemporary literary workers, for his many books attracted more contempt than admiration. In the year of his illness he was much depressed; there was not a single day of cheer. His break with the party was of course also a matter which caused him great sorrow. When his condition became critical, he could never suppress a sigh when either of the two subjects came to his mind. He complained that nobody understood him.

When I come to this point, I too feel regret. For among those who showed disrespect to Kuang-tz'u's works, I was one.[14]

His consuming desire in his last years was to redeem his literary reputation. *The Sorrows of Lisa* (1929) won no admiration, because it showed no improvement of quality, and it incurred a reprimand for its alleged anti-Bolshevik thought. The Communist Party was tightening its control, and with its increasing demand for extraliterary activities, it became for Chiang a source of irritation and a symbol of frustration. While he was in Japan, he discussed with the Japanese leftist writers the necessity for division of labor. It seemed to him that party work should be left with professional agitators and that writers could render their best service by not straying from their proper sphere of activity.[15] Such a view of the writer's independence was of course as unacceptable to the Communist Party of that time as it is now. However, he stubbornly acted on his belief. He sent in his resignation on the ground that he needed the time for writing.[16] This was

[14] Yü, *op. cit.,* p. 74.

[15] "At that time, Chiang Kuang-ch'ih and certain other literary theorists [believed] that there must be a division of labor between revolutionary writers and actual participants in revolution. Chiang Kuang-ch'ih discussed this problem with Japanese left-wing writers while he was in Tokyo. He held that it was extremely difficult to combine literary work with actual work." Fan and Tseng, *op. cit.,* p. 57. The said discussion is probably contained in Chiang's diary, *I-pang yü ku-kuo* (*Foreign Land and Native Land*), but I have not been able to find the book.

[16] "Kuang-tz'u's consideration was his health. Whatever energy was left him he wanted to use for writing. But the party at that time regarded writing alone as inadequate discharge of a member's obligations, which consisted rather in riots and underground work in the factories. Kuang-tz'u said to me, 'Since I cannot do the actual work, why must I pretend to be a Communist? If writing is supposed to be not work, I would rather quit.'" Wu, *Reminiscences, Ta-feng,* Nov. 5, 1940, p. 2516. Though Chiang's letter to the Communist Party asking to resign has perhaps never been published, there is another hint in Wu's *Reminiscences* of Chiang's displeasure at the party's intrusion upon his private life: "Kuang-tz'u wanted to finish *T'ien-yeh ti feng*

looked upon as an excuse for cowardice. In spite of his deteriorating health, he still found time to finish his last book, a novel on peasant rebellion, *Pao-hao-liao-ti t'u-ti* (*The Roaring Earth*). When his expulsion was announced, parts of that book were already available.[17] But his diligence only served as an evidence of his greed for money. Thus in ignominy and loneliness he died.

In the fluctuations of fortune within the Communist Party, individual reputation depends on the current views of the ruling clique. Since 1949, Chiang Kuang-tz'u's name has been rehabilitated.[18] This horrible man— coward, mercenary hack, comfort-loving petit-bourgeois, and counter-revolutionary, according to the party document of 1930—is spoken of with favor in the histories of modern Chinese literature published in Communist China. Ting Yi's opinion is typical of the re-estimation:

> As his novels contain analyses of the main motive forces of revolution and descriptions of important revolutionary events, they won warm approval among the younger people of those days. *The Moon Forces Its Way through the Clouds,* for instance, ran into seven editions in the first year of its publication. These big circulations spread the influence of the revolution and won many new readers to revolutionary literature. His contribution to the revolution should therefore never be forgotten.

(*The Wind over the Fields,* an alternate title for *The Roaring Earth*), so he disallowed [the party] to hold meetings at his home." *Ibid.,* Nov. 20, 1940, p. 2569.

[17] Huang Yao-mien's "Chronological Table of Chiang Kuang-tz'u's Works," in *Hsüan-chi,* p. 31, contains the following data about *The Wind over the Fields:* Chiang finished the manuscript on November 5, 1930, but the book was not published until April 30, 1932. The delay of publication is said to have been caused by the prohibition of the "reactionary government." However, the same novel, under the title *Pao-hao-liao-ti t'u ti* (*The Roaring Earth*), was serialized in *T'o-huang-che* (*The Pathfinder,* a monthly), beginning in its third issue, Mar., 1930. The publication was continued for at least three issues (Mar. through May). *The Pathfinder* was banned after its fifth issue, but the sixth issue was published under a new name, *Hai-yen* (*The Petrel*). See Chang Ching-lu, *Chung-kuo hsien-tai ch'u-pan shih-liao i-pien* (*Bibliographical and Historical Materials concerning Contemporary Chinese Publications*) (Peking, 1955), II, 48. I have not been able to find the full text of *The Roaring Earth.* What I saw was the first eight chapters in *The Pathfinder* (Hoover Institution collection), Mar., 1930, pp. 847–80, and chaps. 26–35, 42–47, reprinted in *Hsüan-chi,* pp. 193–283.

[18] The official reinstatement of Chiang Kuang-tz'u in Communist China took place in 1953 when a search was made for his remains, which, after being found, were removed to the Hung-ch'iao Cemetery in Shanghai on the eve of the twenty-second anniversary of his death. The monument on the new grave carried the legend, "Here lies Chiang Kuang-tz'u the Writer," in the calligraphy of Ch'en Yi, then mayor of Shanghai. The reburial was attended by literary and art groups of Shanghai. See the report on "The Removal to the Hung-ch'iao Cemetery of the Remains of Chiang Kuang-tz'u, Revolutionary Writer." *Jen-min jih-pao,* June 30, 1953, p. 3.

That does not mean to say that his works have no defects. As a matter of fact, practically all the defects common to the revolutionary works of his time appear in his works too. But what should be remembered is that these defects can by no means blur the lustre of his achievements. In propagating the revolutionary ideas of the proletariat, in rousing the revolutionary ardour of the masses, and in taking a lead in writing revolutionary literature Chiang Kuang-tzu [tz'u] did excellent service.[19]

Even without this "excellent service" to atone for his errors, his political crimes have become less serious in the light of history as Mao's followers conceive it. The reason is that the power that punished Chiang is held to be responsible for the condemned line of "leftist adventurism." Chiang was not guiltless, but the guilt is now regarded as shared between the offender and the offended. If Chiang was an unreformed petit-bourgeois, then the party leadership, before Mao's consolidation of power, is also said to have been tainted with the "petit-bourgeois mind." Chiang's aloofness from the masses was, as it still is, unbecoming for a Communist, but Mao did not like either the peculiar approach to the masses urged by the party leadership at that time—the organization of demonstrations, strikes, and armed rebellions to bring about a "revolutionary upsurge" with no regard to the "objective circumstances." In the current view, therefore, Chiang's apostasy was committed under extenuating circumstances because it resulted from his disagreement with an erroneous policy and an authority soon to be discredited.[20]

Time may have diluted Chiang Kuang-tz'u's political crimes and added "luster" to his "achievements," but no serious attempt has been made to revive an interest in his works. His rehabilitation has not necessarily brought

[19] Ting Yi, *A History of Modern Chinese Literature* (in English) (Peking, 1959), pp. 166–67. According to the publisher's note, Ting Yi used the materials in this book for lectures at several universities in Communist China. In 1954, he was invited to lecture on the same subject in Moscow University. His views must have been acceptable to the Chinese Communist authorities.

[20] The official Chinese Communist view of the history of that period is summarized in Ho Kan-chih, *A History of the Modern Chinese Revolution* (in English) (Peking, 1959), pp. 209–10. "In September, 1930, the Sixth Central Committee of the Party held its Third Plenary Session. Both at this session and in the course of its subsequent work the Central Committee rectified the extremely 'Left' appraisal of the revolutionary situation in China that marked the Li Li-san line. . . . But since the Third Plenary Session of the Central Committee did not undertake to thoroughly criticize the Li Li-san line, so at the session and for a time after it, the mistake of sectarianism continued in the Party and 'Left' ideas and policies still found frequent expression." Since Chiang Kuang-tz'u has been reinstated posthumously, his expulsion from the Communist Party in October, 1930, is probably regarded as an expression of those " 'Left' ideas and policies."

him many new readers. During the six years of his literary life (1925–30), he published three volumes of poetry, several novels, and a number of miscellaneous writings (essays, correspondence, etc.) but almost all of them are out of print. His works are preserved in two anthologies published in Peking. The first, published in 1951, is a selection of his prose; the second, of 1955, was probably meant to replace the earlier volume. It contains largely the same materials in prose and also a selection of his poetry. Huang Yao-mien, probably editor of both volumes,[21] recalled in the preface to the first selection:

There was a time in Shanghai when I saw him almost every day. As I am rereading his works, I feel a kind of intimacy. Often in my mind will reappear the tall build of a Northerner, a jaw slightly jutted out, the gentle smile, the flashing white teeth revealed in the smile, and the loud and properly accentuated voice of his conversation.[22]

In spite of this intimacy, Huang, like Yü Ta-fu before him, did not permit friendly feelings to cloud his critical faculty. When he said that Chiang's works should be "affirmatively evaluated," he based his judgment solely on "their positive influence under the concrete circumstances" of those days.[23] He himself was harshly critical:

Today the readers may feel wonder at the great influence he exerted on the readers of those days, in view of the fact that his characters look as if they were created out of subjective fantasy and that there is no lively portrayal in his books.[24]
Some may say that Kuang-tz'u's principal fault was his style, but I don't think this view is correct. To me his principal fault was ideological.[25]

Without making an attempt to refute the charge against Chiang's style, Huang went on with an analysis of his ideological error:

His thought was never fortified by criticism and self-criticism, and never tested by the reality of revolutionary life. His thought, therefore, never turned into something sufficiently realized, something felt in flesh and blood. It re-

[21] *Chiang Kuang-tz'u hsüan-chi* and *Chiang Kuang-tz'u shih-wen hsüan-chi* (*Selected Poetry and Prose*) (hereafter cited as *Shih-wen hsüan-chi*) (Peking, 1955) contain almost identical materials. The differences are: (a) though the "Short Biography" and "Chronological Table" are found in both selections, Huang's Preface to the *Hsüan-chi* is missing in the *Shih-wen hsüan-chi*; (b) *Hsüan-chi* does not have the poetry found in *Shih-wen hsüan-chi*; (c) *Shih-wen hsüan-chi* omits the selections from the novel *The Moon Forces Its Way through the Clouds* found in the *Hsüan-chi*.

[22] Preface to *Hsüan-chi*, p. vii.
[23] *Ibid.*, p. xvi.
[24] *Ibid.*, p. xvii.
[25] *Ibid.*, p. xviii.

mained at the level of vague ideals and the vagrant passion of an individual.

Theoretically, Kuang-tz'u believed that a revolutionary should be optimistic. But in those semi-autobiographical works of his, melancholy and depression are clearly visible. Aren't those traits the manifestations of an individualism troubled by the thought of failure to meet with proper appreciation and vitiated by pride and self-pity? [26]

So it seemed that Huang liked neither Chiang's style nor his thought. But then why the anthology? Why the bother to make a garland of rotten flowers? The preface was withdrawn from the second selection, perhaps to avoid such embarrassing questions.

The latest effort to affirm Chiang's position appeared in the journal *Wen-hsüeh p'ing-lun* (*Literary Criticism*) in 1962.[27] There his expulsion was interpreted as a "rash act" committed when the determination "to dump all literary rubbish into the historical trash can" hurt some of the "best talents" (*ching-hua*) by mistake.[28] Chiang Kuang-ch'ih (as he is called in that article) was said to be far inferior in both "thought and art" to the writers in Communist China because they were now blessed with what he did not have the chance to enjoy—the good fortune "of a political environment where they can freely and openly penetrate into the masses of the workers, peasants, and soldiers and also of the guidance of Mao Tse-tung's literary thought." [29] Even if he worked at an obvious disadvantage, Chiang's service as a "pioneer" should be commemorated:

Though Chiang Kuang-ch'ih was a revolutionary writer who received the Marxist influence at a comparatively early period, yet he remained an intellectual who failed to work out a unification with the laboring masses. A "newly arisen intellectual" like him was often caught in the revolutionary tides to display wildly his "enthusiasm," but when the revolution suffered reversals, he would easily feel vacillation and wax sentimental. Thus Chiang Kuang-ch'ih often found himself in a whirlpool of dilemmas. On the one hand, he was a leftist writer who wished to exert himself to render service to the newly arisen class, to appeal to his readers to struggle for the overthrow of the rule by imperialism and feudalism and for their own liberation. On the other hand, he remained a literatus who never struck roots into the soil of the broad masses. Nevertheless he had a very high opinion of himself, calling himself a perfect Marxist-Leninist. Improper self-esteem thus prevented him from moving one step farther towards self-reform, towards "reform through rebirth." Even so, this petit-bourgeois intellectual, this early believer in Marxism-Leninism, should be regarded as a warrior at a time when proletarian literature in China was engaged in the work of path-finding and enlightenment. The reason is

[26] *Ibid.,* p. xix.
[27] Fan and Tseng, *op. cit.*
[28] *Ibid.,* p. 42.
[29] *Ibid.,* p. 58.

that "the literary thought of the newly arisen class often takes shape through the conversion of the revolutionary petit-bourgeois class and then the new forces of the laboring masses and workers can be gradually mobilized" [a quotation from Ch'ü Ch'iu-po].[30] To the clearing of the thorny brush and to the engineering work of paving the road for proletarian literature, Chiang Kuang-ch'ih, indeed, offered his toil and sweat.[31]

To a student of Communist ideology, this article, if compared with the *Hung-ch'i jih-pao* article, reveals something interesting about the alleged roles of the bourgeoisie and the petite bourgeoisie in modern Chinese society. The 1930 document stated, "the toiling masses of workers and peasants are entering the final phase of the decisive battle with the imperialists, the gentry class, and the bourgeois class"; here reference is made to "the overthrow of imperialism and feudalism," with "the bourgeois class" significantly omitted. The earlier document attributed Chiang's various crimes to his "petit-bourgeois origin," but the present article emphasizes the contributions of the petit-bourgeois class to the "revolution" and the inevitability of the early Communists' being petit-bourgeois in origin.

The significance of this interpretation, upon which is based the reevaluation of Chiang Kuang-tz'u, goes beyond the scope of the present study. Suffice it to say that the followers of Mao have no love for either the bourgeoisie or the petite bourgeoisie. The current opinion in Communist China may indicate two things. In the first place, Mao is known for an interpretation of Chinese society in the 1920's and early 1930's different from what was held by the party leadership of those years. He plays down the role of the bourgeois class in order to justify his work in the rural villages. Secondly, the proletarian legitimacy of Mao's regime is demonstrated by calling attention to the petit-bourgeois nature of the preceding leadership of the party, and yet the continuity of party history is maintained by the acceptance of the petit-bourgeois class's "contributions to the revolution."

The petit-bourgeois intellectuals in Communist China are undergoing reform under the guidance of Mao's thought and through the machinery of *hsia-fang,* which is described in the *Wen-hsüeh p'ing-lun* article as meaning "free and open penetration into the masses of workers, peasants, and soldiers." If Chiang had lived long enough to see the establishment of the Communist regime in China, a "reform through rebirth" would have been

[30] The quotation is from Ch'ü Ch'iu-po's preface to *Lu Hsün tsa-kan hsüan-chi* (*A Selection of Lu Hsün's Occasional Essays*). Ch'ü, *Wen-chi* (*Collected Works*) (Peking: People's Literary Publications Association, 1953), II, 994.

[31] Fan and Tseng, *op. cit.,* p. 43.

awaiting him. That was what Huang Yao-mien meant when he said that Chiang had missed the test by "the reality of revolutionary life." Such a test might have strengthened Chiang's idealism, tempered his passion, and dispelled his melancholy and depression, or in a word, turned him into a better Communist. What Huang has failed to explain—and I do not think any other Communist has an explanation—is how being a better Communist may mean being a better writer.

II

Before I proceed to examine Chiang Kuang-tz'u's life and works, an apology should be made for writing at such length about an uninteresting writer. It may appear that Chiang's importance lies solely in the historic position he occupied. When literary critics in Communist China are trying to re-establish his name, they can scarcely find any enduring merit in his works. They see in him a pioneer of the so-called revolutionary literature which owed its existence to his impetus and dedicated effort. For his alleged service of rousing his readers to revolution, the Communists today profess gratitude. But something is obviously missing—something which has yet to find accommodation in Communist literary theory. To excuse him, or as was done in 1930, to condemn him on the ground of his petit-bourgeois individualism still leaves questions unanswered; it does not explain, for instance, his inferiority to other writers who come from the same class and show similar temperamental traits.

The weakness of his performance simply does not square with his exalted position in a literary movement, and this discrepancy makes the literary critics in Communist China feel uncomfortable. His slipshod style and the paucity of his imagination, confined as it was to some "formula," are there for his reader of today to see and to ponder. Did not his popularity in his lifetime constitute rather an unfavorable comment on the intellect of his readers of those days, who seemed merely excitable in temper and indiscriminate in taste? If his defects do not recommend him as a writer, they should give rise to a question as to the worth of the revolutionary literature he helped to bring forth. The question becomes all the more compelling since Ting Yi has pointed out, as an excuse, that his defects were not unique but "common to the revolutionary works of his time." Did not Chiang, by setting a bad example, deny, or at least mock, what he had created in such good earnest?

The critics in Communist China can never explain the phenomenon of Chiang Kuang-tz'u—a bad writer yet a somewhat effective propagandist—

unless they face honestly the distinction between propaganda and literature. But I do not want to press the point here, since there are already signs that Chiang's notorious neglect of art is a disturbing factor in the cultural life in Communist China. Critical attempts to excuse his bad writing by his revolutionary zeal at least indicate that he had defects. The readers who are disturbed by Chiang's crudity will carry on the hope for artistic conscience. The recognition of badness will create the need for goodness. One glaring example of inadequacy at least presupposes the existence of a standard of adequacy. For his tireless effort at literary production, Chiang stands today as a gigantic "negative lesson" to the readers of "revolutionary literature" and its would-be practitioners. So to me, Chiang's contribution was his failure, and his worth is found in his worthlessness.

So far as a reader outside Communist China can see, Chiang was a writer of mediocre ability, undistinguished except for his self-conceit and passion, and these qualities were not at all uncommon among the youths of his generation. The May Fourth Movement brought forth a number of rebellious youths who pitted their egos against society; and when they found their individual strength too puny for the contest, they extolled one class of society—the mythified proletariat, with whose interests they identified their own. Communism, of course, has manifold appeal, but in Chiang's case, he really did not have much choice. His education in Soviet Russia confirmed an early belief and determined his career.

Born to a "petit-bourgeois" family in Liu-an, Anhwei (his father was a shopkeeper), he received his first political lesson in the student movement of 1919. In 1921,[32] as a member of the Communist Youth League,[33]

---

[32] Huang in "Short Biography" does not mention the year in which Chiang departed for Soviet Russia. Fan and Tseng, *op. cit.,* p. 43, give 1921. The hero in Chiang's short story "A Nocturnal Conversation between Brothers" is said to have departed for Soviet Russia in 1920. *Hsüan-chi,* p. 345. Though the story contains obvious autobiographical materials, the reader is not certain of the accuracy of the date.

[33] Huang in "Short Biography" says, "Kuang-tz'u participated in the student movement during the May Fourth Movement. Shortly afterwards he joined the Communist Party and was sent to Soviet Russia to study." *Hsüan-chi,* p. xxiii. I suspect that what Chiang joined then was the Socialist Youth League. In Chiang K'ang-hu's report on his visit to the University of the International Toilers in July, 1921, he said, "Classes had started in its Far Eastern section. Among the students were 400 Tartars, over 20 Koreans, and over 10 Mongols. There were 35 or 36 Chinese students, all sent over and supported by the Communist Youth League." Chiang K'ang-hu, *Hsin-o yu-chi (Journey to the New Russia)* (Shanghai, 1923), p. 35. It should be noted that the Chinese Communist Youth League was known as the Chinese Socialist Youth League prior to November, 1925. Liu Shao-ch'i was in the first class at the University

he was sent to Soviet Russia, where he learned the rudiments of Marxism-Leninism and acquired a reading ability of Russian to initiate him into Russian and European literature. He returned to China in 1924, to use whatever he had learned to make a living and to propagate communism. He was appointed to teach sociology, a euphemism for Marxism-Leninism, in Shanghai College, a school with a marked political background, where were gathered, in the faculty and the student body, many agents working for the then united Kuomintang-Communist revolutionary cause.[34] Since he found teaching "boring," [35] he accepted a job as an interpreter for the Russian advisers in Marshal Feng Yü-hsiang's army in North China. He went to Peking in April, 1925, and stayed for some time in Kalgan. Thus he missed the famous May Thirtieth incident, in which the students of Shanghai College played an active part. Compared with the "dreariness" [36] of the life north of the Great Wall, Shanghai again looked attractive as a revolutionary center.

After his return to Shanghai in November, 1925, he resumed teaching at the same college but also started to apply himself diligently to writing. Shanghai indeed became an interesting place to live, with the series of riots which led to its conquest by the Northern Expeditionary Forces. However, for him, just as for other Communists, the triumph of revolution proved to be illusory. In May, 1927, he had to flee Shanghai to avoid arrest, only

---

of Toilers. His group left Shanghai in the spring of 1921 for Vladivostok and arrived in Moscow via Chita. He was then a member of the Chinese Socialist Youth League. *Jen-min jih-pao,* Dec. 9, 1961, p. 1. Chiang Kuang-tz'u was possibly a student of the same group.

[34] According to Saito Akio and Niijima Atsuyoshi, Shanghai College was founded in the autumn of 1923, following a resolution of the Chinese Communist Party for the building up of the party's cadre. Though the staff of the college was dominantly Communist, its president and vice-president were respectively Yü Yu-jen and Shao Li-tzu, both of the Kuomintang. The Kuomintang-Communist collaboration had made such an arrangement possible. After the May Thirtieth incident of 1925, the college was closed by the authorities of the International Settlement of Shanghai. It then moved from its original site at the corner of the Bubbling Well Road and Seymour Road to Ch'ing-yün Road in Chapei (North Shanghai). After the "April 12 coup" (1927), the college was closed down for good. Saito and Niijima, *Chugoku gendai kyokushi (A History of Modern Chinese Education)* (Tokyo: Kokudosha, 1962), p. 108. Another Japanese source had it that in December, 1924, "The general headquarters of the Chinese Communist Party was located in Shanghai College." Hatano Kenichi, *Chugoku Kyosanto shi (History of the Chinese Communist Party)* (Tokyo, 1961), III, 847.

[35] A letter from Chiang to Sung Jo-yü, dated April 8, 1925. *The Monument,* p. 146.

[36] His two letters dated May 5 and May 14, 1925. *Ibid.,* pp. 150, 154.

to find himself facing another anti-Communist purge in Wuhan. Again he escaped safely and returned to Shanghai, where, under the protection of the foreign settlements, he was able to live a largely unmolested life, which appeared so "comfortable" as to arouse comrades' jealousy. He spent the rest of his life in Shanghai except for the three or four months in 1929 when he was traveling in Japan.

The months in Japan (August to November of 1929) offered him the opportunity of becoming an exile. Like Kuo Mo-jo, he might have chosen to live in Japan, so as to enjoy a kind of seclusion, which might not have necessarily improved his health but which might have removed him from the political strife in China. During these months he worked hard. He wrote one novel, *The Moon Forces Its Way through the Clouds* (*Ch'ung-ch'u yün-wai-ti yüeh-liang*), and translated another, Libedinsky's *A Week*. Both were later published in Shanghai, and even his diary of this period got into print under the title *I-pang yü ku-kuo* (*Foreign Land and Native Land*). To make a living by his pen was therefore not out of the question. Japan should have looked attractive to either a coward, as the party document accused him of being, or a Byronic hero, as he often imagined himself to be. But he returned to China to face persecution not only by what was regarded as a "reactionary government" but also by his comrades. And the reason for this decision, so far as available sources indicate, was nostalgia. Nostalgia is a great lyrical theme, but I do not think Chiang's "I Should Return" will ever be classed with Wang Ts'an's "View from the City Tower" or Wang Wei's "On the Ninth Day of the Ninth Moon." Chiang's poem repeats the sentiments which he jotted down in his diary:[37]

> There, no smile will be displayed for me;
> There, sorrows are perhaps only what I can expect.
> It is indeed not so good a place as this strange land
> Where I may enjoy some degree of freedom and happiness.
>
> But I am Chinese, I am Chinese.
> My destination is sealed by my fate.
> I should return, I should return,
> Though my motherland is so bad.
>
> Thoughts have occurred to me:
> Why shouldn't I go on wandering in foreign lands?
> But I have found that it is so
> Impossible, impossible to separate myself from motherland! [38]

[37] Quoted in Huang, "Preface," *Hsüan-chi*, p. ix.
[38] *Shih-wen hsüan-chi*, p. 113.

Technically, the repetitions, "I am Chinese," "I should return," "impossible," in these stanzas mark a crude attempt at rhythm, which was still an object of experiment for the *pai-hua* poets in 1929. What incapacitated Chiang as a poet was primarily his unseeing eye. In this poem of sixty-four lines, he did not notice a single object in Japan which might speak for the "strange land's" strangeness and attractiveness. The seasonal changes from summer to early winter were roughly summarized in one statement: "The season has changed," followed by the line, "It may be said that Tokyo has better scenes than Shanghai." [39] But not a single "scene" of either Shanghai or Tokyo is shown to the reader. China, the object of love and hatred, is presented merely as a place "dark like hell" "where tigers and wolves run about" but where "the god of light" will eventually descend. From these summaries and clichés, the reader may get some idea of Chiang's troubles, but he will never be moved as he is by a good poem. This poem is a good example of Chiang's "frankness" without "refinement by art"—possession by emotions without their resolution in appropriate language. The poem's vagueness and looseness also illustrate his general loss of touch with reality and his failure to respond to life intensely as only a genuine artist can. Sorrow for China's plight, hope for her future, and a belief that she needed him are registered in many of his works. The love he felt for China was probably genuine, a love so strong as to overcome his wanderlust; but for him merely to announce to the world that he had such a love, or a love for the laboring masses and for some women in his life, did not make poetry. His love or hatred or the more complex emotion where love and hatred were mingled with other elements, for instance, his emotion for China, requires a closer scrutiny and a more forceful grasp of its contents.

"I Should Return" was written when the author felt unhappy as various forces pulled him in opposite directions: Tokyo versus Shanghai; the darkness in China as against her bright prospects; his sense of duty as against the premonition of persecution in his motherland. Though the forces at work could have been rendered more effectively, the reader can see that here is at least an inner drama inadequately enacted. Chiang did not raise his voice, since the tone here is indeed sombre. But when there was no doubt about his conviction, he had a different pitch. Then the result would be preaching mixed with outcries:

[39] *Ibid.*, p. 112.

Rise, laboring brothers of China;
We have endured the imperialist oppression to the extreme;
If we do not rise and resist,
We shall be forever sunk in the dark cavern.

To break the imperialist oppression,
 To recover the independence of the Chinese nation—
That is our own business.
Quick, quick, let us start.[40]

Or, in another example,

The nation of China,
The nation of China,
My dear nation of China!
Be quick to awake from your long dreams!
Be quick to save your fate! [41]

In both instances, Chiang Kuang-tz'u was in a state of mind where conflict was replaced by certainty, and vacillation by urgency. However, neither certainty nor urgency improved his poetical style. They choked him with emotion and made him sound like a soapbox orator at a loss for the right words but straining his voice to rouse his audience.

The quality of the verses alone should rank him far below Byron, the poet with whom he liked to compare himself. Indeed, to compare him with any known poet would be a compliment he did not deserve, since in my opinion, he could scarcely pass the test as a poet. But he was born in a difficult time when Chinese poets were supposed to start afresh, "to clear the thorny brush and pave the road." A writer with a greater care for language might have done something toward the clearing and paving. Chiang was certainly not such a writer. His respect for the Chinese language did not match his declared love for China. His kind of verse, if its influence spread, would have only added to the difficulty of clearing.

Although Chiang liked to link the name of Byron with his own, the idea of emulating Byron's poetical achievement may not have entered his mind. One even wonders how well he knew Byron's works. It was Byron's colorful "romantic" life that inspired him, as it inspired so many European youths. Byron, of course, became a legend also in Russia,[42] where Chiang

---

[40] *Ibid.*, p. 13.

[41] *Ibid.*, p. 59.

[42] "Byron penetrated deeper into Russia than into any [other] country of the world." Henry Gifford, *The Hero of His Time: A Theme in Russian Literature* (London: Ed-

took his lessons in European literature, perhaps self-taught. Chiang might have been familiar with Byron's exploits in Greece even before he went to Russia to study, since Byron's "The Isles of Greece" was then already available in Chinese.[43] Byron the poet and Byron the hero who died for Greece became indivisible in his imagination:

> In vain am I a poet;
> For my inability to protect my nation I should be ashamed to death.
> Byron felt shame for Greece;
> I am now weeping for China.[44]

My translation may not do the lines justice, but I can say that nothing in the poem is comparable to Byron's intellectual and prosodic vigor. Chiang should have felt some sorrow at his inability to give the protection due to language, an attention that China has a right to demand from her poets. When he mourned, "In vain am I a poet," he was thinking merely of the civic duty which seemed to rest more heavily on the poet than on any other Chinese citizen. *Noblesse oblige.* Being a poet, indeed, meant much more to him than the care for language. Poetry as a vocation seemed to call for certain duties and certain attitudes; and of these he was often painfully and proudly aware. Perhaps he never read Carlyle on "The Hero as Poet," but what was so obvious to him did not require a theoretical basis. The fact that he had poetical ideas and that he could put them into verse with ease would make him a poet.

So he was a poet, and Byron was a poet too, and they were equal. Byron had his Greece; he had his China, for whom he too was ready to sacrifice. There were other similarities: for instance, their "romanticism." In April, 1924, while still in Soviet Russia, he celebrated Byron's centenary by a poem, "Thoughts on Byron." This poem contains some interesting remarks about life in Soviet Russia which might have been viewed as blasphemous. I wonder why no Communist critic has called him to task on the score of these lines:

---

ward Arnold, 1950), p. 13. Gifford's book studies the hero (mostly under the Byronic influence) in the works of Pushkin, Lermontov, Herzen, Turgenev, Chernyshevsky, *et al.*

[43] "The Isles of Greece" was translated by Ma Chün-wu in 1905 and by Su Man-shu in 1907. Ah Ying (ed.), *Wan-ch'ing wen-hsüeh ts'ung-ch'ao* (*An Anthology of Late Ch'ing Literature*), Translations, I, 18, 5. Su also translated several other poems by Byron. On February 3, 1914, Hu Shih, not satisfied with either Ma's or Su's version, made another translation of the poem. Hu Shih, *Liu-hsüeh jih-chi* (*Journal of My Student Days in the U.S.*) (reprint; Taipei, 1959), I, 177–92.

[44] *Shih-wen hsüan-chi,* p. 55.

In this gloomy, dark world,
The sky is overcast with clouds; melancholy is the view on the earth.
People submit themselves to authority.
Look! Hell is everywhere.
Where indeed may I find the land of freedom!
Though motherland does not want me,
To go away and sojourn in the dreamy, golden India,
Alas, is a hope even more forlorn!
When mankind feels suffocated,
When authority intimidates,
There are only the poet's disrespectful cries:
Freedom,
Freedom,
Freedom. . . .[45]

To declare that "hell is everywhere" is the most rebellious expression Chiang ever made. He perhaps never asked himself where he should then place Soviet Russia. His refusal to grant the status of a "land of freedom" to Soviet Russia was truly Byronic in spirit, but for a Communist to air such a protest was a serious matter.

The Sorrows of Lisa, which provoked the Chinese Communists at the time of its publication, may have reflected the author's personal feelings in an oblique way. But his Byronic stance was more basically and more directly opposed to the Soviet system than were the grievances the dispossessed White Russians in Shanghai had against the Bolsheviks. To persist in this attitude, to continue his "disrespectful cries" for freedom would have disqualified him as a Communist even before his return to China. Of course he did not pursue this dangerous thought. It was not for him, a confused thinker, to be logical in his choice. His praise for the "red state of workers and peasants," a phrase found in the very poem on Byron,[46] caught the reader's eyes much oftener than his hatred for the "intimidating" quality of authority which made the Soviet system possible. A poet has the liberty to be self-contradictory in his view of the world, if the contradiction, "felt in flesh and blood," to use Huang Yao-mien's words, is turned to good use: to enhance the mystery of life and to deepen the meaning of the poet's works. However, Chiang did not seem to be bothered by the contradiction: he simply shifted, as the mood suited him, from dispraise to praise with the ease of a spontaneous writer. It was a pity that Chiang had only a dim perception of the basic incompatibility between romanticism and communism. With his habit of shallow thinking

[45] *Ibid.,* pp. 34–35.
[46] *Ibid.,* p. 37.

and careless writing, he refused to grapple with the central problem of
his life. The reader can only wish that he had been more seriously personal in his pursuit of poetical truth. He missed the chance of becoming a
better poet than he was, possibly a Yesenin or a Mayakovsky of China.

In spite of his many brilliant achievements, Byron was also known for
his inconsistency. Of the limited amount of Byronic criticism that I have
read, the following remark seems to tell profoundly of Byron's shallowness:

> The switches and reversals of mood are not so much the result of a critical
> check upon his emotion, as a flinching away from it; he hastens to a super-
> ficial kind of self-revelation, for fear of a deeper self-betrayal. Sometimes he
> seems actually frightened by a thought that has arisen in composition.[47]

Byron, of course, was a much more important poet: he was the progenitor
of a brood of lesser poets and versifiers who claimed that emotions were
their domain but who were afraid of their emotional problems. To watch
Chiang Kuang-tz'u posing before the magnificent model recalls Miss Tung
Shih's pathetic imitation of Hsi Shih:

> Ah Byron!
> You of the nineteenth century,
> and I of the twentieth . . .[48]

Chiang felt much sympathy for Byron's unhappiness:

> Wandering, calumny—
> Was this your fate,
> Or the tribute paid by society to genius? [49]

Even in 1924 when his career had barely started, he was seized with the
premonition that being a "genius" himself, he was perhaps marked out for
a wandering life and calumny. In January, 1925, he wrote to Sung Jo-yü,
the schoolteacher who would become his wife for one month before she
died of pulmonary tuberculosis in November, 1926:

> —Wandering, I may end my life in wandering.
> This is one line from my poem celebrating the New Year. I feel that my future
> will be a solitary, wandering life. But I shall not complain; nor am I afraid. I
> am a poet. Poets ancient and modern, especially those with a revolutionary na-

---

[47] W. W. Robson's paper on "Byron as Improviser" was originally published in
Proceedings of the British Academy, 1957; reprinted in Paul West (ed.), *Byron: A
Collection of Critical Essays* (New Jersey: Prentice-Hall, 1963), p. 95.

[48] *Shih-wen hsüan-chi,* p. 37.

[49] *Ibid.,* p. 35.

ture, are all known for their solitary, wandering existence. For humanity, for society, I cherish limitless hope. As for myself, I know that homelessness will be my destiny. I would rather like it to be so; otherwise I might not be able to write good poetry.

.   .   .

I feel that there is not a single one in the human sea who loves me, though I cherish infinite sympathy for the majority of the poor people or the hopeful ones. You called me your "beloved friend"—this, to be frank, I rather doubt. For I feel that no one in the world loves me.[50]

After Sung's death, he came to know quite a number of women. In the novel *Yeh-chi* (*Worship at the Unlocatable Grave*) (1927), the narrator is introduced to a woman, also a schoolteacher. The soliloquy recorded below was not necessarily taken from real life, but the reader can see how Chiang was obsessed by Byron's ghost whenever he talked of a literary career:

My spirit being high with the drink, I talked of sundry subjects. Finally I came to the fate of writers. I said that writers Eastern and Western, especially those who were great geniuses, the majority of them were failures in life: they had to suffer the calumny and jealousy of ordinary people. I said that we who engaged in literature should not entertain illusions about government offices and wealth, for government offices and wealth would harm creation. The ancient saying that the perfection of literary art comes only from a suffering author is indeed a truth. I said also that a great writer should be possessed with great rebellious spirit.[51]

The soliloquy in fiction ("writers Eastern and Western, especially those who. . . .") is echoed or even copied from the same author's correspondence ("poets ancient and modern, especially those. . . ."). Remarks about the writer's "rebellious spirit" he made at least once to Kuo Mo-jo, if not to other friends. A spontaneous writer, unless he is extraordinarily resourceful, is not only slipshod in his diction and structure but can never remember how often he has repeated himself, in the matter or manner of his writing. The things that hold deep interest for him become boring to others, because he wants to "put them over" with too much force. Either as a wanderer looking for sympathy or as a Communist propagandist shouting at the mob, Chiang always wrote as if he were anticipating an impatient audience. The irony is that the more eagerly he wanted to hold the reader's attention, the sooner he wore it out.

Communication at cross purposes is obvious in Chiang's first novel, *Shao-*

---

[50] Chiang's letter to Sung, January 11, 1925. *The Monument,* pp. 126–27.
[51] *Yeh-chi,* p. 48.

nien p'iao-p'o-che (*The Youthful Tramp*) (1926). Its very title may suggest a new type of hero in Chinese fiction; but the hero, who tells his life story in a long letter, turns out to be a pale figure. Despite his vehement language, he has more self-pity than self-confidence and appears a grumbling, incoherent sufferer rather than a disdainful, Satanic misanthrope. His purpose in writing the letter, he says, is to seek "compassion" [52] or some kind of solace which a stronger character might do without.

He is not a poet who proves his "genius" by seeking a solitary life, a Byronic rebel or a Wordsworthian recluse, but rather a victim of society interpreted according to communism. After the death of his father, a tenant farmer, at the hands of the inevitably oppressive landlord, and his mother's suicide soon thereafter,[53] the young man becomes in turn a beggar, a grocer's apprentice, a worker in a cotton mill, and an assistant at the railroad workers' union during a strike. He finally makes up his mind to join the Whampoa Military Academy in Canton, where training is provided for revolutionary youths. He meets his death, as the reader is told in the Epilogue, in action at Huichou.

Some kind of picaresque novel might have resulted from such an outline, but the narrative here is hurried, sketchy, and utterly uninteresting. Events and ideas, instead of evolving by their own logic, are summarized, and the summary is then repeated to drive home the lesson. The tedious letter-writer never misses a chance to read a lesson or two into the episodes of his life. The death of his parents, for instance, which might have won the reader's sympathy, is dispatched in a few paragraphs, which are marred by asides like these:

Mr. Wei-chia [the man to whom the letter is addressed]: I can never describe how cruel the world is or how unpredictably vicious the human heart is!
This is perhaps the utmost of the darkness and cruelty in this world!
Alas! Is there a scene more miserable than this?
This is a tragedy totally reflecting the darkness of the world.
Alas! The darkness of the world, the cruelty of humanity, the injustice of society, the destruction of reason. . . .[54]

[52] *Hsüan-chi*, p. 5.
[53] *Ibid.*, p. 17. The tramp's mother killed herself with a pair of scissors. A woman in another novel, *The Moon Forces Its Way through the Clouds*, tried to kill herself by the same means. Wu Szu-hung objected to this form of suicide as "unrealistic," since most Chinese women, so it seemed to her, would prefer drowning to stabbing if they wanted to kill themselves. *Reminiscences, Ta-feng*, Sept. 20, 1940, p. 2396. I have not seen the suicide scene in *The Moon Forces Its Way through the Clouds*, but it is interesting to note that Chiang should have conceived two such scenes in his books.
[54] *Hsüan-chi*, pp. 16–17.

Here is no doubt a suffering author, but where is the "perfection of literary art"?

Angry and mournful remarks like these confront the reader throughout the book. The author is unconcerned with characterization, tempo, color, atmosphere, climax—all the tricks usually mastered by even an illiterate farmer or nursemaid who can tell a story well. Obviously Chiang had yet to learn the fundamentals of narration. Whatever happens to the youthful tramp in this book is reduced to the one bare fact that he is suffering. And amidst his sufferings, the narrator must stop the action at the end of every two lines or so, and tell the reasons why he suffers: that the world is dark, the human heart cruel, society unjust, etc.

Chiang Kuang-tz'u had a predilection for generalizations which overpowered his imagination, while he tried very hard, almost to the point of breathlessness, to express rage and sorrow at the abstractions which seemed to have deep emotional meaning for him: "darkness," "cruelty," "society," "the world," etc. This, I think, is basically a propagandist's method. Incidents in a story written for propaganda are not interesting for their own sake but are used to illustrate abstract ideas. Ideas, indisputable and unanalyzable, dominate any kind of propaganda, but an eager propagandist like Chiang Kuang-tz'u will ignore even the art of persuasion. He would rather take pride in his "violence" (*ts'u-pao*).[55] Not a thinker himself, he forbids his reader to think. *The Youthful Tramp,* for instance, leaves many holes in the narrative, holes which are summarily stopped by "violent" ideas.

Such a defect is observable in every one of Chiang's stories. It is doubtful that he would ever have developed the talent to produce an important work, even if he had been blessed with a longer life. Most likely he would have continued to tell stories conceived in the abstract. His stories about the Sino-Japanese War, for instance, would have been sustained by the terms "fascism" and "patriotism." If he had lived long enough to undergo all the anomalies after 1949 and meanwhile had become sufficiently "reformed through rebirth," he might have been ready with more stories which impute all human sufferings to the "landlord class" during the Land Reform Movement and to "American imperialism" during the Korean War. We have seen many stories of this type. Chiang is dead, but his method has survived.

However, the kind of propaganda that Chiang carried on was looked

---

[55] *Ibid.,* p. 2.

upon with disfavor by the Communists of his time. When he was expelled from the party, it was, in a way, as if an authorized dealer had lost his franchise because he had displeased the wholesaler by taking too much liberty with the merchandise. While taking advantage of the original label, he had adulterated the material with something of his own invention. All his zeal in salesmanship was not really for the promotion of the "right product." Chang Pi-lai, a literary historian in Communist China, commented in 1955 on Chiang's "incorrect reflection of the activities of the Chinese Communist Party":

> The truth was rather that he distorted its activities. In all his publications, especially in his works of this period [up to 1928], the party's correct line was not properly reflected and its incorrect elements were not properly criticized. Instead, he extolled wanton killing and arson, blind insurrection, individual heroism, etc. These could have evil effects in actual application.[56]

Such a defect was perhaps excusable according to the 1962 article in the *Wen-hsüeh p'ing-lun,* because, as we have seen, Chiang produced these works almost independently of "the guidance of Mao's thought." In the eyes of the party leadership of 1929 and 1930, however, Chiang seemed to be a shocking example of those Communists who become their own guide in matters of ideology. Regardless of how he treated communism, it is obvious to his reader that he had two commodities to sell: communism and sentimentalism. Before the youthful tramp of that book becomes prepared to destroy his enemy, what he needs is love. Not only does he ask for the "compassion" of those who read his tedious letter, but he craves in particular for a consummation of love with the grocer's daughter, a beautiful, gentle, sensitive, and educated girl of eighteen who dies of a broken heart because of her unwillingness to be married into a rich family. Although this episode is dispatched in the same hurried and unimaginative manner as others in the same book (the girl's confession of love, emotional frustration, sickness, and death occur almost in the same instant), the reader is made aware that there are emotional problems outside the political movement.

The conflict between revolution and love was a favorite theme among the avowed revolutionary writers of Chiang's time. What helped the sales of his books (or theirs) was not revolutionary zeal, however violently portrayed, but the presentation of revolution as something bitter-sweet, and deliciously seasoned with love. Love and revolution are subjects that will

---

[56] Chang Pi-lai, *Hsin-wen-hsüeh shih-kang* (*An Outline of the History of Modern Literature*) (Peking, 1955), I, 158.

never cease to challenge the best creative minds of the world. But in China in the period concerned, both subjects and their "conflict" usually underwent a rough treatment, so clearly marked by a uniformity of purpose that it looked as if there were a "formula" for fiction-writing.[57] About the time of Chiang's death, the readers began to feel satiated. After the Mukden Incident (1931), national salvation replaced revolution as the most pressing problem for the politically sensitive youths, and China personified would absorb a great deal more sentimental love than it formerly had. Meanwhile, between 1931 and 1937, there was a remarkable showing of sophistication among independent writers. Though another formula would emerge in the anti-Japanese fiction, there would no longer be such heavy concentration on love and revolution as was exemplified by Chiang Kuang-tz'u.

What I mean by "heavy concentration" is deliberate impoverishment of imagination, an obsession with revolution and some women to the exclusion of a thousand equally interesting things of the world. There is a kind of intensity in this method, but it is the intensity of a monomaniac, or rather, a duomaniac, who has lost touch with reality. Monomaniacs are common in life, and even a normal human being may have his moments of distraction and become lost to the world. But in appropriating such personalities and such psychological lapses for his use, the novelist should maintain an awareness of the distinction between the normal and the abnormal. His story should be told so as to convey the terror of being abnormal, a terror always better suggested than stated. Where Chiang Kuang-tz'u failed was in his infatuation or identification with the monomaniac. When the "world" or "society" was severely criticized, or even cursed by the youthful tramp —the revolutionary lover—we suspect that the author was using his hero as a mouthpiece. Chiang did not achieve an artistic detachment that would permit his hero to be included as an object of criticism. He had too much "compassion" to assign a proper place in life for his hero. He could not conceive a Macbeth or a Raskolnikov; he could not even make a careful study of obsession on a small scale, as Chekhov did in *The Black Monk,* though models of this sort are not scarce in Chekhov and other Russian writers with whom Chiang must have been familiar.

This deficiency in objectivity and sense of proportion is certainly cen-

---

[57] Chang Pi-lai cited several examples from the *T'ai-yang yüeh-k'an* (*Sun Monthly*), ed. Chiang Kuang-tz'u, to show how both editor and contributors of that magazine were concerned with the problem of love and revolution. He concluded, "Not a few writers and editors of those days took it to be a matter of course that fiction should be written according to a formula." *Ibid.,* 225–26.

surable, but when the Communist critics denounce Chiang's "formularism," what they demand is often writing according to another formula—one more hollow, fantastic, and savage. Whatever Chiang's hero accomplishes or fails to accomplish is within the bounds of reason; he performs no miracles and shows no extraordinary strength of faith; he may end in defeat rather than in triumph; and by getting himself involved with the opposite sex, he shows human weakness. The new hero in the later Communist fiction will be a superman, purer in faith, less emotionally encumbered, and with greater support of the masses, a monster who evinces all "class" qualities but few human qualities. And then such a freak is demonstrated as the "norm" for all the people under Communist control to look up to.

III

Chiang was the first Chinese Communist who devoted himself to the writing of poetry and fiction.[58] But his "formula" reflected things that mattered to him as an individual: he did not invent it according to ideology. However deluded, incompetent, stupid, shallow, and confused the individual was should not concern us here, if he is to be distinguished from the more successfully depersonalized propagandists writing at the behest of the Communist Party. It is true that Chiang also tried to please the party, which, however, ended up in being offended. To confuse the political issue with love interest was not supposed to direct the readers on the undeviating road to revolution. So the label of a petit-bourgeois has stuck to him—an utterly hopeless one to the party leadership of his time but a possibly reclaimable one to the followers of Mao.

To me, the reasons for Chiang's failure are to be found in his immaturity, rather than in any class label the Communists may find for him. The romantic mind has been compared to that of an adolescent.[59] When Chiang died

---

[58] The Chinese Communists of the earliest period were all intellectuals possessed of a skill for writing. But this skill was devoted largely to political and polemical essays, though some Communists, like Ch'ü Ch'iu-po, could indulge in lyricism. Chiang Kuang-tz'u was the first Communist who established his reputation as a poet and novelist.

[59] I borrowed the idea from T. S. Eliot on Shelley: "The notes to *Queen Mab* express, it is true, only the views of an intelligent and enthusiastic schoolboy, but a schoolboy who knows how to write; and throughout his work, which is of no small bulk for a short life, he does not, I think, let us forget that he took his ideas seriously. The ideas of Shelley seem to me always to be ideas of adolescence—as there is every reason why they should be. And an enthusiasm for Shelley seems to me also to be an affair of adolescence: for most of us, Shelley has marked an intense period, but for how many does Shelley remain the companion of age?" *The Use of Poetry and the Use*

at the age of thirty, his mental age did not seem so far advanced. His one obvious weakness—the abundance of stylistic errors in his writings—should place him not among established writers but among high school students taking a course in composition. If he was not one of the brightest students of the class, he might easily be the most recalcitrant, one who would disregard the teacher's blue-pencil remarks. To assess his I.Q. would require much more data than are in a literary historian's possession, but to me he seems a young man whose mental growth was arrested after he had reached the age of nineteen. The figure I give has an historical rather than psychological significance. For in the year that he was nineteen, there arose the May Fourth Movement. This youth then had three experiences which had a lasting influence throughout his life. These experiences were so important that anything that happened afterward would find a meaning only in the mental framework formed in that year. These three experiences were:

First, he was seized with a sense of public duty—let us call it patriotism —which would continue to trouble him. I should like to consider that even his joining the Communist Party was motivated by patriotism, deluded though he certainly was in taking such a step.

Secondly, as a student agitator, he found that the pamphlets and slogans he wrote had a power over his readers. This initial success satisfied his vanity. Though not remarkable for literary talent, he was gifted with a facility in the use of language which was put to service in the excitement of a student movement where nobody cared for the quality of writing. He never lost this facility; nor did he make much improvement in the subsequent years over his youthful aptitude for scribbling.

Thirdly, he had to leave home and yet he felt deeply the need for a home. Hence his obsession with a solitary, wandering life.

Even by the end of the nineteenth century, Shanghai had begun to attract ambitious and restless youths of the neighboring provinces. After 1919, with the general loosening of family ties, Shanghai looked even more like the land of opportunity for a larger flux of migrants. With Shanghai exercising its attraction nearby, Chiang would have left home if not for any particular reason. As a member of the newly formed Communist Youth League, he perhaps received some political training in Shanghai, which was

---

of Criticism (Cambridge, Mass., 1933), pp. 79–80. Like Shelley, Chiang Kuang-tz'u was a man "humorless, pedantic, self-centered" (*ibid.,* p. 80). Abstractions, too, "would excite in him strong emotions" (*ibid.,* p. 81). But what marked Chiang below Shelley and even some modern Chinese writers of similar temperament was that he did not know how to write.

probably his port of embarkation when he took the trip to Soviet Russia.[60] Meanwhile, he had a quarrel with his family over his marriage. He was betrothed, since childhood, to a country girl who had lived under the roof of the Chiangs as an "adopted daughter-in-law." [61] Such a marriage Chiang might have tolerated in a different period of Chinese history. But under the impact of the "new ideas," he had to leave home to protest against a "marriage without love." The greatest destructive force released by the May Fourth Movement was perhaps the one which tore asunder so many marriage contracts arranged by parents. If boys and girls of those years had nothing better to fight for, they could at least fight for their own "freedom" and "happiness." An arranged marriage would summarize for them much that was bad in the old Chinese society: parental authority, deprivation of freedom, and disregard of personality. Such a fight on the child's part was often bitter, sometimes tragic, and occasionally even comic.

In one of Chiang's novels, *The Roaring Earth,* the hero was the landlord's son turned a revolutionary. He met under the most unusual circumstances the girl whom he had spurned as a would-be fiancée in a contract arranged between their parents. She was daughter to another landlord, but having received school education, she, too, became sympathetic to revolution. One day she overheard a plot to assassinate the young man. Putting aside her maidenly modesty, she rushed to warn him. So after so much opposition to an arranged marriage, boy and girl finally met, for the first time in their lives, and much to their embarrassment. But each found the other quite likable. The comic element in this episode, of course, escaped

[60] "A Nocturnal Conversation between Brothers" tells about a visit paid by the elder brother from the small town to the younger brother, a returned student from Russia who now stayed in Shanghai as a teacher at "S College." The younger man longed for his home from which he had been away for six years. He wanted especially to see his mother, whose favorite son he was. But his return to his home town would have meant the fulfillment of a marriage contract he detested. So with all his homesickness, he preferred to stay in Shanghai. *Hsüan-chi,* pp. 342–64.

[61] Wu Szu-hung recorded this: "Kuang-tz'u had a wife; that was what he told me. But she did not live with him; nor did she ever really become his wife. For that woman was brought up in his home since her childhood, a sort of adopted daughter-in-law. She was deserted for good after he had left home to study in Moscow. But it seemed that she was not altogether a weak woman. Once she raised the indignant question, 'Why shouldn't we become husband and wife in fact?' 'The reason is that you have never gone to school,' answered someone in his family [implying that she was not good enough for him]. 'Then send me to school! Why don't you allow me to study?' However, that marriage remained an 'unresolved case'!" Wu, "Notes about Kuang-tz'u," *Hsin-chung-hua* (*New China,* a semi-monthly) (Shanghai), Vol. XIII, No. 15 (Aug. 1, 1950), p. 45.

our humorless author. To strengthen the revolutionary element in his "formula," Chiang perhaps would make the landlord's son marry a peasant girl.[62]

In real life, Chiang's own "child-fiancée," having no landlord for a father to support her education, perhaps never developed a taste for revolution. Nor did she receive much "compassion" from her romantic betrothed. She probably lived a life common in Chinese provinces in those years, as half grass-widow and half spinster. She was destined never to see Chiang again after he left China in 1920.

This essay is not concerned with marriage in China after the May Fourth Movement, though in either its factual or fictional aspect it is a subject which will illustrate vividly the impact of the Western ideas on Chinese society. Instances certainly occurred where the fight for freedom in marriage brought happiness to all parties concerned. But in the case of Chiang's desertion of his fiancée, selfishness and cruelty were perpetrated in the name of freedom and happiness. This was by no means a unique case. The girl was the silent victim, but it was doubtful how much happiness Chiang was ever to experience after his release from the early matrimonial bondage. When he wrote to Sung Jo-yü, in the letter quoted above, saying "I feel that no one in the world loves me," he was perhaps once more trying to enhance a Byronic image of virility in disdainful solitude. But possibly this statement was meant as a protection for a defeatist: he simply wanted to make sure of the girl's love. The whole series of his correspondence with Miss Sung and his other works reveal him as a rather weak personality, clamoring for love, appreciation, happiness, compassion, warmth, and tenderness.

Since the mother is the usual source of feminine solace for a child or for an adolescent of retarded growth, Chiang's yearning could easily turn to his mother after he had left his home. Mother occupied an important position in both his imagination and in his thoughts of self-pity. For instance, the young man Li Chieh in *The Roaring Earth* finds his father altogether detestable, but his feelings toward his mother are different. Below is an "interior monologue" of his:

[62] From what I gather about the plot of *The Roaring Earth,* Li Chieh was in love with the peasant girl Lan-ku. But he could not obtain his parents' approval for their union. Then the girl died somehow a tragic death. Sorrow and disgust forced him to leave home and join the revolution. After his return to his native village as a revolutionary, he became enamored with Lan-ku's sister, Mao-ku. But busy with revolutionary activities, he never gave his love much expression.

I have read Turgenev's *Fathers and Sons,* said to be a classic on the conflict between two generations. But somehow I feel that such a conflict was too commonplace—how dull it was by the side of my conflict with my father! I do not know whether any writer will write down the conflict between me and my father. I wish there were such a writer.

I have no father now. I have only my enemy. It is only in the battlefield that I shall have a chance to meet my enemy, but I have heard that my mother is sick at home. . . . Mother! Please forgive your rebellious son! If filial piety, as "the foremost of one hundred virtues," was the lofty ideal of old ethics, then your son is thinking differently: there is a duty much more important, much greater than filial piety. For this duty, I am willing to take on the bad name of a rebel. Mother, you have lost your son! [63]

This rebel, however, has to face the real test when under the taunts of his fellow revolutionaries, he agrees to set fire to his own home, the Li mansion. He does not care for his father's life, but he loves his mother, a sick woman unable to leave her bed. And there is the little sister, not yet ten years old, whom he also loves. Shall they be burned to death? As a writer, Chiang is not to be trusted to deal with any emotional problem, certainly not such a problem as parricide. But in describing the hero's distress, the author comes up with a sudden flash of insight.

All the steps leading to the insight are quite dull. First there is the hero's reply to the carpenter, a firebrand among the revolutionaries:

Uncle Carpenter! If we must set fire, then the Li mansion shall not be an exception. But . . . Uncle Carpenter! My mother is sick in bed, and there is an innocent little sister. . . .[64]

Then the description of the son's mind in anguish:

Carpenter Li is going to set fire to the Li mansion. . . . the sick, bedridden mother will be probably burned to death . . . the crying, screaming little sister . . . what shall I do? [65]

Then his reply to another revolutionary:

Comrade Chin-teh! Do you think I am crazy? I am not at all crazy. A human is a human: how could I have the heart to . . . my sick mother, my innocent little sister . . . but, Comrade Chin-teh! I have to listen to Uncle Carpenter's opinion. . . .[66]

After so many repetitious statements, typical of Chiang Kuang-tz'u's method, the insight is found in the passage:

[63] *Hsüan-chi,* pp. 275–76.
[64] *Ibid.,* p. 280.
[65] *Ibid.,* p. 281.
[66] *Ibid.,* p. 282.

Alas! Comrade Chin-teh! A man after all has his sentiments. You know how distressed I am! I love my innocent, cute little sister. . . .[67]

All the marks of ellipsis in these quotations indicating hesitation or incomplete thought are found in the original. What is remarkable about the last quotation is the hero's sudden silence about his mother. In the first three quotations, both mother and sister (in that order) are mentioned as possible victims of the fire. When the hero makes his last speech, the decision has become irrevocable and the catastrophe is drawing near. Then he names only his sister. All of a sudden, mother becomes an unutterable sound. So far as I can see, this is the only spot in Chiang's works where a reader may feel touched. But is this omission a stroke of genius or is it a Freudian slip?

Shall a revolutionary permit his comrades to burn his mother and sister to death? This is the real conflict in *The Roaring Earth*. It may be called a conflict between revolution and love, but the love is that of a son and a brother. The father, being a landlord, is not to be pitied: Chiang was "revolutionary" enough to realize this. Contrary to the reader's expectation, the two girls in the book—the landlord's daughter turned revolutionary and the peasant girl in whom the landlord's son shows an earlier interest—do not figure prominently to provide a triangular situation. The theme here is quite different from what we have seen in the other novel, *The Youthful Tramp*. There the dramatic element is weaker. The tramp is frustrated in both love and revolution but dies, the reader is told, with an eternal longing.

The contrast between the two books is interesting, because it gives rise to a question: what "formula" was Chiang resorting to that could encompass the different themes? The "formula" will look even more diversified, if we take the theme of another book, *The Moon Forces Its Way through the Clouds*. There we have the story of a woman who goes through the stages of enthusiasm (when she was a revolutionary) and dejection (when she became a streetwalker after the 1927 debacle) and revived hope (when she goes to work in a factory and reunites with her lover).[68] In the last instance, love seems to aid, rather than to distract, a revolutionary. But does love always have this effect? In Chiang's first novel, at least a part of

---

[67] *Ibid.*, p. 282.

[68] I have seen only parts of *The Moon Forces Its Way through the Clouds* in the *Hsüan-chi*, pp. 285–364. My discussion here is based upon C. T. Hsia's summary. C. T. Hsia, *op. cit.*, pp. 261–62. C. T. gave the title of the book in English as *The Moon Emerging from the Clouds*.

the "darkness" of the world would be lifted and the "cruelty" of humanity would appear mollified, if the young man should win the hand of the grocer's daughter. Then he might cease to be a tramp and settle down as a grocer, or even aspire to be a social climber, like Julien Sorel. All these are interesting questions. Chiang's imagination certainly worked within a narrow range: he did have a formula, but it is the diversity rather than the uniformity of his themes that will elucidate his formula.

It seems to me that the formula of his fiction originated in a conflict in his life: the conflict between his repudiation of home and his longing for a home. His pose as a rebel required that he be tough or "violent." The ideology he professed also laid down certain rules about a revolutionary's duty being "greater than filial piety" or than love in general. But with all his Byronic bravado and his raving about "killing and burning," he was at heart a weak person. His insistence on the inclusion of "love" in his books about revolution was to satisfy his own emotional needs. What he longed for was the kind of affection and warmth which most "petit-bourgeois" (excuse my borrowing the term) families seemed to enjoy but which seemed to be denied to him. It was one of the reasons for his self-pity. He himself also wanted to know why he was so unhappy. The easiest explanation was the example of Byron. Perhaps he too was a genius and a "genius with a rebellious nature," and therefore homelessness and unhappiness were his destiny. But unfavorable opinions about his works did not seem to justify his claims for genius. A real genius or a madman might not have cared about his reputation. Chiang, being neither, did. While self-esteem prevented him from confessing to his weakness, his suppressed desire for a home, for warmth and affection, a desire quite unbecoming for a Communist, gave shape to the plots of his stories, which may be described as the daydreams of a frustrated man.

His comrades, not supposed to have an interest in personal problems, felt dismay at the "distortion of revolution" which he presented. If burning one's mother and sister to death was the cost of joining the revolution, Chiang's writings, in their view, would certainly have evil effects. Such a consideration for the party's image perhaps did not enter the author's mind, which was engrossed in the problems of revolution versus home (or revolution versus love). In spite of the admonitions from the party, he had to tell his story in his own way, or according to his "formula," since storytelling became one of the few outlets for his suppressed desire. *The Roaring Earth* ends on an optimistic note, showing the revolutionaries, with the burned houses behind them, moving to Mount Diamond (Chin-kang-shan), which was interpreted in 1962 as an allusion to Ching-kang-shan, Mao Tse-tung's first guerrilla base.[69] But the echoes of the "Internationale" can hardly fill up the emptiness in the heart of Li Chieh, whose last feeble protest is, "A man after all has his sentiments."

The Sorrows of Lisa made another feeble cry for sentiments. In this novel about a White Russian prostitute in Shanghai, the elements of Chiang's formula are still there, though instead of revolution versus home, the variation here is counterrevolution versus home. Lisa's husband, once a colonel, fled with his wife to Shanghai, after his units under General Kolchak had been defeated by the Bolsheviks in the Russian civil war. Within two years, he became a human wreck, having squandered his fortune and used up his energy. Lisa, once "a delicate white flower among the aristocratic Russian women," has now to sell her honor to support herself. Amidst her shame, the following thoughts run through her mind:

> Now I often ask myself this. If in those years I had loved Carpenter Ivan, the one with curly hair, and married him, what would have become of my condition? Isn't being wife to a toiling carpenter better than being a prostitute? Carpenter Ivan had a low social position—but nowadays carpenters in Russia do enjoy an extremely high position! If he could support his family with his strength, love his wife with his sincere love, and protect her from such shameful things as I do, then would he not deserve higher respect than the bunch of execrable aristocrats? Which choice was better, that I should have accepted the honest Ivan with curly hair and lived a toilsome and yet pure, independent life on the Volga? Or that I should have followed the ex-nobleman Bergen [Pai-ken in the original] to Shanghai, to the strange land where my body is being played with and trampled upon every day? . . . Oh, my God! How I wish I were a carpenter's wife! How I wish I were a carpenter's wife! [70]

This passage might be cited to answer the charges about the anti-Bolshevism in the book, since Lisa's thoughts were obviously not altogether in favor of the Tsarist nobleman. But the political views contained in these lines do not really matter. What interested Chiang and aroused his pity was the woman's right to a decent home, to a "toilsome and yet pure, independent life," which was denied her because of an earlier wrong choice. Lisa was no doubt an unloved, solitary, wandering figure, another self-pitying tramp. Chiang found such a life as hers unendurable. In the earlier book the youthful tramp was killed in battle, and Chiang had to send Lisa to her death too. She commits suicide.

[69] Fan and Tseng, *op. cit.,* p. 55. I have not seen the section of *The Roaring Earth* alluding to Mount Diamond.

[70] *Li-so-ti ai-yüan* (*The Sorrows of Lisa*) (1st printing of a new edition; Shanghai: Hsin-tung Book Company, 1940), p. 98.

Lisa belongs with Wang Chung (the youthful tramp), Man-ying (the woman in the *Moon*), Li Chieh (the landlord's son) and a group of other characters who won the author's sympathy and stirred his imagination. They all have strong likes and dislikes which seem to coincide with his own likes and dislikes. Though they are troubled by active consciences, they are hampered by small minds. Since the author was not concerned with the smallness of their minds, their meaning of life is put within the narrow limit of his imagination—or in his formula. There were in the world only two things which seemed to him as worth enjoying: revolutionary activities and family life. The restlessness of his characters is directed toward either of the two aims or both. Lisa will not participate in revolution, but she can still wish for a decent family life. The youthful tramp joins the revolution, but he has no family and he is unhappy. Li Chieh joins the revolution but he loses his old home, and he is unhappy too. Man-ying is the happiest because in the end she enjoys both blessings: revolution and a husband's love.

The weakness in the plot of *Lisa* is inadequate motivation. That pitiable woman has been in her line of business for some time: there is no immediate, impelling reason for her to kill herself. The real terror in the situation of a seasoned prostitute like Lisa, so far as I can see, is her possible hedonism and apathy. She might feel some kind of morbid pleasure, or she might become indifferent to her own fate and the fate of the world. The story of such a woman, treated as a study of death in the soul, should be more terrible to read. But death in the soul, as well as many subtle psychological situations, did not find a place in Chiang's formula. When Man-ying in the *Moon* became a streetwalker, she was filled with a desire to take revenge upon her patrons.[71] Lisa is pitiable because she is burning with a sense of shame. While Man-ying remained at heart a revolutionary, Lisa is always a decent woman of the family type. Beyond such two types of characters, Chiang's imagination simply ceased to function.

His abhorrence of prostitution is expressed also in the short story "One Night at a Hotel in Hsüchou" (date of composition: September 3, 1926). The hero of the story, who stops in Hsüchou on his way to Kaifeng to visit his sick lover, could be Chiang himself. (His lover Sung Jo-yü taught school in Kaifeng.) The manager of the hotel turns out to be a pimp who tries to impose a call girl upon him and he is horrified:

[71] C. T. Hsia, *op. cit.,* p. 262.

How could I do such a thing? My own lover is sick in bed and expecting me. Where would be my good conscience if I did such a thing as sleep with a call girl? How could that be? And to buy somebody's flesh with money—and still call myself a socialist? Should not I rather be a bastard? No, that won't do! I have never visited a brothel—should I lose my innocence tonight? No, that won't do! That manager is a bastard, a real dirty bastard! [72]

Before he can stop her, however, the girl sneaks in. The unwanted visitor somehow arouses his pity. So he begins to listen to her story. She happens to be a "child-fiancée" whose betrothed husband has been away for five years without sending home a word since he left home to join the army. There is no way to support herself and her mother-in-law, who rather encourages her to call at hotel rooms. The manager is in fact a kind person who helps in making contacts because of his friendship with her deceased father-in-law. And here is the hero's reaction:

Ah, what a horrible world! Horrible! Very horrible! Chieh-sheng felt he was trembling all over. Mournfully the girl repeated once more:
"Woe is me. . . ."
"Alas! Woe! Are you the only person that is woeful?" [73]

He permits the girl to share the bed with him, though he never touches her. In the morning, he gives her seven silver dollars and bids her go. Then he heaves a sigh: "Miserable China! The miserable Chinese!" [74]

The reader is not supposed to know that the author of this story had left behind a "child-fiancée" at his home. Though the structure of the story does not call for this knowledge, such an emotional element is interesting to the biographer. However, the reader does notice that whatever moral problems the episode gives rise to (for instance, the girl's calling the manager "a kind person") are dismissed once the name of China is invoked. China is large enough to absorb the fate of the poor girl. Even the burden of compassion can be picked up later since as a "socialist" he can deceive himself with the thought of his eventual usefulness to the girl. Meanwhile, he may devote himself to his sick lover who is expecting his visit. The sigh which Chieh-sheng utters while waiting for the train to Kaifeng is a sigh of relief.

Such a comment on the nature of pity is not implied in Chiang's story on the night in a hotel. He took a peek into the horrors of life, but when China appeared to obstruct his view, he stopped looking further. His preoccupation with China or with her need for revolution, indeed, is one of the

[72] *On the Yalu,* p. 91.
[73] *Ibid.,* p. 92.
[74] *Ibid.,* p. 99.

important factors that made him such a superficial writer. There is an episode in his novel *Tsui-hou-ti wei-hsiao* (*The Last Smile*) (1928), whose possible meaning or meanings are dismissed in a similar manner. The hero of the novel is a nineteen-year-old worker who is fired from the factory because of his revolutionary activities. Finally, he becomes a killer and takes his revenge upon the foreman. (That is what Chang Pi-lai had in mind when he said that Chiang "extolled wanton killing.") However, before he steals a pistol and pursues his enemy, he has a dream. He finds himself in a teahouse where much prostitution is going on. He watches a man over fifty years of age fondling a girl of about fourteen or fifteen. The fondling is given in rather "naturalistic" details, which the dreamer watches with horror. Then he suddenly discovers that the girl is none other than his own little sister:

> The round eyes, the round dimples while she smiles, and the cherry-like mouth, all this . . . this is Ah-yung. This is Ah-kuei's little sister! [75]

Previously, the reader is told that the young man loves his sister, who is only five or six years old:

> Ah-kuei saw his little sister coming to him. He took her to his bosom, and stroked her pigtails. Ah-kuei loved his sister very much. When he returned home from the factory, the first thing he used to do was to show his affection by giving her either a hug or a kiss.[76]

Now his fears about the dissolution of his family owing to his unemployment lead him to the dream where his sister is turned into a young prostitute. He awakes from the dream in a panic and tries to drown her in a pond before a fate worse than death snatches her away. This temporary madness is stopped by the mother. Such an episode, left in the bare outline, raises perhaps more questions than the author could answer. But he must dispel the mystery by putting into Ah-kuei's mouth a sentence which he has learned from the Communists:

> Girls from poor families are destined to be insulted by rich men! [77]

In order to strengthen the "revolutionary" element of his formula, this sentence is repeated no less than three times.

Ah-kuei's love for his sister may recall the incident in *The Roaring Earth* in which both mother and sister are threatened with death by fire.

---

[75] *Tsui-hou-ti wei-hsiao* (*The Last Smile*) (1st printing of a new edition; Shanghai: Hsin-tung Book Company, 1940), p. 54.

[76] *Ibid.*, p. 48.

[77] *Ibid.*, pp. 54, 55.

Some kind of abnormal sex psychology may be involved here as there. However, I hesitate to tread on unfamiliar ground. Sister, like mother, could be an object of repressed sexual desire, but she may be also simply a woman to whom the man of the family feels strong attachment. Obviously, Chiang's interest was in the conflict between a person's natural feelings toward his family and a violent revolutionary passion. Ah-kuei's revolutionary activities cost him his job and finally cost him his family. Since the latter loss is harder to bear than the former, he excites himself into a state of frenzy before he can afford to lose his natural sentiments.

How much autobiographical element is found in that episode in *The Last Smile* is hard to determine. We do not know anything about the author's sister, or even whether he had one.[78] But being a revolutionary himself, and quite an active one during the years 1926–28, he had moments when a woman's love was badly needed. It was a kind of love no prostitute could give; prostitutes might arouse in him either the thought of broken families, thus sinking him deeper into self-pity, or the thought of the need for revolution, a thought from which he now and then would rather take a vacation. Perhaps what he missed was affection rather than sexual love. If he had had a sister, his thoughts might have turned to her. But he had a mother, and mother, as I have said, occupied an important position in his thought and imagination.

In the story "A Nocturnal Conversation between Brothers" (composed July 4, 1926), a returned student from Russia is found moping in Shanghai. He utters this agonized soliloquy under emotional stress:

> But my mother! Is it that I do not like to come home and visit you? Is it that I forget you? Is it that I do not understand your feelings toward your son? But, but . . . my poor mother! I have my painful reasons for not coming home! Do you know this? Alas! Alas! . . . [79]

In *Worship at the Unlocatable Grave,* the narrator records his feelings when the landlord's daughter admonishes him for his excessive drinking:

> When she gave me this advice, so many layers of deep feelings were hidden in her heart! I felt deeply grateful: except my mother, not a single person so far had taken so much care of me. Rarely indeed had a person like me, leading habitually a wandering life, received such sincere advice.[80]

---

[78] "I am not clear about his childhood. I learned from him only that as a little boy, he was often obliged to hold his baby brother (or perhaps a sister or a nephew)." Wu, "Notes about Kuang-tz'u" (cited in note 61), p. 22.

[79] *Hsüan-chi,* p. 349.

[80] *Yeh-chi,* p. 52.

His feelings as a son were evinced with the least disguise in the long autobiographical poem completed in October, 1927: *K'u-su* (*An Appeal in Tears*), which was later renamed *Hsieh-kei mu-ch'ing* (*Written for Mother.*)[81] In giving his mother a part in the dramatic dialogue on his sorrows over the Communist debacle of 1927, Chiang displayed an amazing "frankness" about his immaturity:

> Ah Mother!
> I would really become crazy!
> I would really become crazy!
> My little tender soul—
> How could it sustain so much damage?
> Oftentimes I said to myself:
> Better follow the dead and die—
> I could no longer endure the man-eating demons.[82]

I do not think that his real mother would have responded to this appeal. Mother in this poem is rather an ideal woman whose love, no less than the revolutionary ideal, was an object of pursuit throughout Chiang's life. I think this is the essence of Chiang's "romanticism." Since both aims were elusive, if not unobtainable, he indulged in fantasies disguised as fiction. Nevertheless, his mind was active enough to attack the problem of revolution versus love from as many angles as he could. What he found was that revolution and love were generally incompatible. *The Moon Forces Its Way through the Clouds* promises a happy union of the two, though how lasting the union will be the reader is left to guess.

Of all his books, only in *Tuan-k'u-tang* (*Des Sans-culottes*—the title in French was suggested by the author himself) (1927) are there men and women who find happiness in both revolution and love. In this story about the riot in Shanghai before the Northern Expeditionary Forces entered the city in 1927, one of the Communist leaders, Yang Chih-fu, is described as being sick in bed, but he has a loving wife whose sole duty, upon the party's order, is to nurse him back to health.[83] Another leader, Shih Chao-yen, is also a tubercular. He collapses after overexerting himself, but there comes along a schoolteacher, a "lovely, lively, passionate"

---

[81] Fan and Tseng, *op. cit.*, p. 49. I have seen only a few lines of *An Appeal in Tears* quoted in Fan and Tseng's article.

[82] *Ibid.*, p. 50.

[83] Yang Chih-fu, a character in *Des Sans-culottes,* is said to have been drawn after the model of Ch'ü Ch'iu-po. *Ibid.*, p. 48.

young woman[84] who is willing to give all the care and love that he needs. Then there are the two workers, a husband and his wife, who spend an affectionate night together before they meet their deaths the next day. Amidst all the bloodshed, carnage, and slogans, Chiang at least succeeded in creating a "pastoral" where man and woman love and die as revolutionaries. Not a blemish can be found in either love or death.

Such a kind of pastoral love amidst violence represents his absurd formula in its full operation and his "romantic" imagination at its most exuberant. However, *Des Sans-culottes,* with the perfect state of love and revolution as its theme, is not so interesting to read as his other works, where there are at least some hints at the true human condition, i.e., imperfection. His own life was an example of frustration, there being little happiness found in either love or revolution. The Communist Party denounced his "romantic," luxurious way of life, but the women in his life, including his mother, might have complained that he was too much involved in politics to pay them sufficient attention. With his dual aim, he was not always sure what he was after. The formula in *Des Sans-culottes* may suggest that the ideal woman for a man like him should have been a Communist. But nothing is on the record to indicate that he ever had an affair with a female comrade in his party.

In *Worship at the Unlocatable Grave,* the narrator, an inactive Communist but a boastful writer, teaching at a college, might well be a self-portrait of the author. There a puzzling situation is presented. The landlord's daughter is young, intelligent, not pretty but at moments quite attractive, serious in purpose, zealous in the cause of revolution, and what is more important, solicitous about the young man's welfare and ready for his courtship. The reason the narrator could not love her until it was too late, until she had been arrested and executed, was perhaps that she reminded him of his mother, as the passage quoted above indicates. But then the girl might have been too vivacious to suit his taste. For there is another piece of evidence, more reliable biographical information, which suggests that the woman he was looking for was rather an old-fashioned housewife, one who should bear a closer resemblance to his mother than did the revolutionary type. Here is what Wu Szu-hung, the last woman in his life, told Yü Ta-fu:

---

[84] *Hsüan-chi,* pp. 162–66. The character Shih Chao-yen is perhaps meant to be identified with Chao Shih-yen, a Communist leader in the Shanghai uprising of 1927.

According to Miss Wu, Kuang-tz'u's personality, unlike his ideology, was quite old-fashioned. His ideal woman was one who possessed the qualities of a model wife and model mother—a good housekeeper who would stay indoors all day to keep him company while he was writing. "However," said Miss Wu, "this was impossible for me. That is why in his last days we found ourselves often in disagreement." [85]

Yü Ta-fu noted also that he had heard much "adverse criticism" about Miss Wu but that he, for one, was ready to forgive her.[86] What these critical opinions were Yü did not specify. In 1940, about ten years after Chiang's death, Miss Wu published a long memoir of the time she had spent with him, a record of his private life since late 1929 after he had returned from Tokyo.[87] In 1950, she shortened and revised the article, omitting everything that might have sounded, as in the earlier version, critical of the Communist Party.[88] Both articles commemorated their love, but there were also allusions to the facts which might have given rise to rumors: First, Wu had been separated from Chiang by late 1930. When she returned from Hangchow, he had become critically ill. Though Chiang had consented to the separation, his friends might have blamed her for her neglect of him. Second, according to the earlier version, Wu was quite a potent influence in Chiang's decision to quit the Communist Party. His "comrades" might have thought ill of her as a *femme fatale* who had led the "good boy" astray from the "right path of revolution."

As a student of art, Wu was vivacious and versatile: she performed on the stage, she painted, and she also dabbled in creative writing.[89] But she regarded herself as a Bohemian. Indeed, she registered her feelings in these lines when she decided to live with him and move to his flat which, by the way, though middle-class by the American standard, looked quite "luxurious" to her:[90]

[85] Yü, *op. cit.*, p. 74.

[86] *Ibid.*

[87] About Wu's *Reminiscences of Kuang-tz'u,* see note 2.

[88] About Wu's "Notes about Kuang-tz'u," see note 61.

[89] Wu featured in several plays produced by T'ien Han. See T'ien Han *et al.* (eds.), *Chung-kuo hua-chü yün-tung wu-shih-nien shih-liao-chi* (*Historical Materials concerning the Spoken Drama Movement in China during the Past Fifty Years*) (Peking, 1948), I, 131, 134, 137. From her *Reminiscences,* the reader will find that she was a student of painting and that she also wrote poetry and fiction. A pencil sketch of Chiang by Wu is found in *Ta-feng,* Nov. 5, 1940, p. 2516. A short story by Wu, "Huan-hsiang-chi" ("Native Village Revisited") was published in *Nan-kuo yüeh-k'an* (Shanghai), Nos. 5 and 6 (a combined issue), 1930.

[90] Chiang's residence on Seward Road (?), East Shanghai, was a flat on the second floor. When Wu moved in, she noticed that in the square-shaped living room, which

> You are a Bolshevik, a political figure;
> I am an art student, a Bohemian,
> But who says that we cannot live together? [91]

Her wild nature was perhaps what appealed to the "tramp" in Chiang. Though her age was not revealed, he was only twenty-eight or twenty-nine when they first met. However, before any disagreement occurred between them, they seemed to be both aware of their discrepancy in age. Chiang, in his habitual boastful talk, compared himself to Dostoevsky, and now it seemed that their similarity would become even more striking since he, too, would have a young wife to help him to literary fame. On Wu's part, there was a reluctance to grow up. One day after they had lived together, Chiang suggested that she should do her hair into a chignon. But she did not want to give up her pigtails and said, "I would like to remain a child forever." Sitting on his knee, she called him "Papa." [92]

Whatever psychological factor was involved, it was apparent that Miss Wu was not the mother type. She was perhaps a willful girl. On May Day, 1930, after Chiang left home to participate in a demonstration, Wu, having nothing better to do, went to spend her time in a cinema, where she cried a great deal. He looked extremely tired at the time he returned home. He explained, "I cannot stand it." Wu wrote in her memoir:

> I stood by him, stupefied. Then he continued:
> "They [his comrades in the Party and the League — Wu's note] think that revolution means to go with them to smash glass windows and to stage riots. But I am a writer! I can only struggle with literary means — literature is my revolutionary tool."
> "Then why must you go? If I were you, I should go if I would; I should not go if I would not!" I said.
> "This is not a question whether you would or you would not, you don't understand." When he said this, his whole face looked as if it were going to explode. [93]

But under her influence, he made a decision. He had to give up his dual aim. He believed that he could still write about revolution, but active participation was too strenuous and perhaps too dangerous for him. He would now be contented as a family man, to have a pigtailed girl as his

---

served also as his study, there were two upholstered chairs, a leather sofa, a writing desk, a dining table, and two bookshelves filled with Russian books. The bedroom was behind this and there was a small bedroom for the maidservant, who happened to be an old woman. *Ta-feng*, Sept. 20, 1940, p. 2395.

[91] *Ibid.*

[92] *Ta-feng*, Oct. 20, 1940, pp. 2482–83.

[93] *Ibid.*, p. 2480.

companion, while he would work hard as a writer to emulate Dostoevsky. He sent in the resignation to the Communist Party. And then some time later, Wu moved out.

Before he lived with Miss Wu, there was Miss Sung Jo-yü who was his wife for one month. In 1925 he wrote to her:

> Yü my sister [referring to her name Jo-yü]! Let us be poets together. Let us get lost in the world of poesie. Let us live a poetical life together. Let everything about us become poetized. Yü my sister, you are my muse, my guardian angel, my most precious. . . .[94]

In almost the same month, his tone changed:

> Have you made up your mind to share fortune or misfortune with me? I have said to you several times that I am a revolutionary poet, that I am a rebel, and that my life in the future will most probably be that of a wanderer, a tramp. If you do not realize this, you will feel disappointed in the future.[95]

If Miss Sung had taken these words seriously, she might have felt bewildered. Chiang Kuang-tz'u, the dreamer in a world of poesie, and Chiang Kuang-tz'u, the self-conscious rebel, was a phenomenon of his times, though by no means a unique phenomenon. If we feel pity for him today, it is because with all his literary effort, he has not left behind a "monument" [96] to either his escapism or his commitment. He should have been an ideal person to write about the phenomenon, with its aspirations and frustrations, its momentary ecstasies and long-lasting woes, its stresses and conflicts, and the strenuous efforts to seek release from the tension, either in political or personal life, but he failed his readers completely. Who will read Chiang Kuang-tz'u?

---

[94] Letter to Sung, dated June 18, 1925 (The date should be perhaps May 18, 1925, if the chronological order of the letters is to be accepted.) *The Monument,* p. 160.

[95] Letter to Sung, dated May 25, 1925. *Ibid.,* p. 170.

[96] *Chi-nien-pei (The Monument)* was the title Chiang gave to the collection of correspondence between him and Miss Sung. Unfortunately, the collection has more biographical than literary interest. His love for Sung Jo-yü perhaps deserved a better monument.

LU HSÜN AND THE DISSOLUTION OF
THE LEAGUE OF LEFTIST WRITERS

"When a great man is recognized as great, he has already become a puppet or a fossil."

Lu Hsün, 1926. *Ch'üan-chi*, III, 240.

I THE DUBIOUS LEADERSHIP

THE Chinese League of Leftist Writers was an organization of revolutionaries, formed in 1930, with the avowed purpose of "promoting and engaging in the production of proletarian art." But art was not their sole, or even their major, concern. Their works were dedicated to class struggle, to the "bloody," "death or victory" battle, to the "complete liberation of mankind." [1] Their political objectives therefore coincided with those of the Communist Party. But that was not a mere coincidence. In the words of Feng Hsüeh-feng, an underground Communist worker in Shanghai from November, 1928, to the end of 1933, "The Leftist League was of course directly led and supported by our party." [2] While actual fighting was raging in Kiangsi and elsewhere to determine the fate of the Soviet government in China, the "guerrilla warfare" [3] conducted by the writers in Shanghai must have had more than diversionary effects on the outcome of what turned out to be the most important struggle for power in modern China. They were fighting the war

---

[1] "The Theoretical Principles of the Leftist League," *Meng-ya yüeh-k'an* (*The Sprout Monthly*), No. 4; reprinted in Wang Yao, *Chung-kuo hsin-wen-hsüeh shih-kao* (*History of New Chinese Literature, A Draft*) (2 vols.; Peking: Kaiming Book Company, 1951), I, 155–56.

[2] Feng Hsüeh-feng, *Hui-i Lu Hsün* (*Reminiscences about Lu Hsün*) (Peking: People's Literary Publications Association, 1952), p. 50.

[3] The words are Agnes Smedley's. See her *Battle Hymn of China* (New York: Knopf, 1943), pp. 69–98.

on the literary, artistic, and ideological fronts. Their influence never failed to reach, through their writings, a large number of readers, in spite of the much accursed censorship of the Kuomintang government. If they were not drawing new recruits for the Communist Party, they were at least winning sympathy for it and beating down whatever ideological opposition might stand in its way.

Lu Hsün was the most dauntless fighter among them, the most biting critic, the most formidable polemic, and the most prolific and energetic journalist in the campaign to undermine public confidence in the Kuomintang government and the nonpartisan liberals, fire the revolutionary spirit, and arouse admiration for the Soviet Union. Despite the achievements of such leftist writers as Mao Tun and Ting Ling, Lu Hsün was the towering figure of the group. At one time a professor of Chinese literature, he was probably as learned in his field as any scholar of his time; with his knowledge of Japanese and German, he had more than a nodding acquaintance with Western literature. He introduced in his essays and stories a new style of Chinese prose—terse, forceful, and condensed in thought but capable of flights of fancy, and stirring in a dry and sardonic way—a solid proof that the *pai-hua* was not necessarily sloppy, loose, or vulgarly sentimental. He enjoyed immense prestige both at home and abroad. And now he was using this prestige to push forward the literary movement for the proletariat, devoting his talent, learning, and energy almost entirely to what he believed to be true and good. In describing this writer, who was to be canonized by the Communists after his death, Mao Tse-tung said in his essay *On New Democracy* (1940):

> Lu Hsün was the greatest and the most militant standard-bearer of this new cultural force. . . . Lu Hsün had the most unyielding backbone. . . . Lu Hsün, representing the great majority of the people, was an unprecedented national hero on the cultural front, the most correct, the bravest, the firmest, the most loyal and most zealous hero who stormed and broke up the enemy's front. . . . [4]

It is conceivable that the literary historians in Communist China, anxious to adhere to the "most correct" party line, would take their cue from Mao and ascribe to Lu Hsün every heroic quality. Wang Yao and Liu Shou-sung, for instance, exaggerate the importance of Lu Hsün's leadership in the Leftist League.[5] The leadership was, in fact, divided. Lu Hsün, as a

---

[4] *Selected Works of Mao Tse-tung* (Bombay: People's Publishing House, 1954), III, 144.

[5] Wang Yao, *Draft*; Liu Shou-sung, *Chung-kuo hsin-wen-hsüeh-shih ch'u-kao* (*History of New Chinese Literature, First Draft*) (2 vols.; Peking: Writers Publish-

prominent writer and dedicated fighter, commanded respect as few other fellow-traveling writers did, but he led no political party, imposed no discipline, and issued no dogma. In sacrificing his own comfort he was apparently not seeking personal power or position, but he willingly lent his name to the service of the Communist Party. The other leadership, on all evidence the true one, was composed of Communist agents who, tough, disciplined, and unscrupulous, resorted to methods quite unacceptable to an individualistic sympathizer of revolution like Lu Hsün. Working under the so-called white terrorism in Shanghai, the Communists were facing great difficulties. They were running the daily risk of arrest and bodily harm, and their organizations, of destruction. They had to use the fellow travelers to camouflage any open activities, and the illustrious name of Lu Hsün met that need very well. He himself may not have feared violent death, but that he could continue to live safely in Shanghai indicates that the Kuomintang authorities, stupid as they seemed, did make a distinction between fellow travelers and Communists. The five leftist writers arrested and executed in Shanghai in 1931 were all members of the party actively engaged in agitation and subversion.[6] But Lu Hsün lived on, fearless and defiant, and gave as much aid and comfort to the Communist Party as he liked. Upon his death in 1936 from a natural cause, Wang Ming made the following remark:

When the Chinese Communist Party was greatly handicapped by lack of funds, Lu Hsün more than once made donations and loans with what he laboriously earned from his writing. When some comrades of the Chinese Communist Party were being hunted by the reactionary police force, Lu Hsün defied all danger to secure the safety of these revolutionary fighters. For example, Comrade Ch'ü Ch'iu-po, with his help, was able to hide in Shanghai for several months.[7]

So he was not only the League's star writer, but also for a time its guardian angel and the symbol of its survival. "So long as Lu Hsün lived, the League would not die. So long as he stood, the League would not collapse." [8] But since he did not participate in the regular party functions, and since his meetings with the party members were only personal and casual, he might

---

ing Association, 1956). Wang borrowed heavily from both Hu Feng and Feng Hsüeh-feng; and Liu, from Feng Hsüeh-feng, on matters of theory and criticism. Both books contain other heresies which cannot be tolerated today by the Communist Party. That is perhaps the reason why the authors call their books mere "drafts." The party line is hard to follow indeed.

[6] Wang Yao, *Draft,* I, 141–42. Liu Shou-sung, *First Draft,* I, 285–305.

[7] Wang Yao, *Draft,* I, 188, reprinted from *Chiu-kuo* (Paris).

[8] Feng, *Reminiscences,* p. 53.

not have had a complete knowledge of the party's policies, activities, and intrigues, save for its alleged far-reaching aims, of which he completely approved. Under such circumstances misunderstandings and disagreements might arise between Lu Hsün and the party, and, as it turned out, they did. In Wang's and Liu's books, much is said about Lu Hsün, though not always correctly, but very little about the other leadership backed by the organized strength of the party. It is perhaps because the party in Shanghai was then not under Mao's control; if credit could not go to Mao for the success of the League, had it not better be given to the man for whom Mao had the highest praise?

The leaderships worked harmoniously together for a time. The success was due as much to Lu Hsün's personal friendship with Ch'ü Ch'iu-po and Feng Hsüeh-feng and the latter's tactfulness in humoring the older man as to Lu's enthusiasm for Communist revolution. But after their departure for Juichin, then the Red capital (Feng arrived there in December, 1933, and Ch'ü in January or February, 1934),[9] it seemed that not a single Communist agent left in Shanghai was able, or cared, to maintain good relations with the irritable and suspicious Lu Hsün. The two leaderships began to drift apart.

Lu Hsün, with his undying faith in communism, remained nevertheless an artist; he lost none of the artist's sensibility, idiosyncrasies, or propensity for independent action or independent inaction, even after years of association with Communists. His revolutionary views did not help him to live happily with the revolutionaries. His qualities as a writer and a man, his bitterness, his relentlessness, his demoniac delight in picking a fight, and his courage in defending his position are well known to the readers of his polemic and satirical essays, and it was these qualities that made him such a stubborn egotist and difficult comrade. Most adept in exposing the shams and hypocrisies of the old Chinese society, he was subject to moods of despondency, caused, no doubt, by his dark thoughts about human nature. Though he was saved from pessimism by his faith in the future of humanity, a conclusion he drew from his study of the theory of evolution even before he embraced Marxism, he never became a "true believer" as defined by Eric Hoffer.[10] He clung to his personal habits of thinking and put the dictates of his own conscience before the orders of any authority. He was perhaps a bit too sincere, too honest, and too pure in his idealism to become a good member of any political party. That kind of egotism—his

[9] *Ibid.,* p. 141.
[10] *The True Believer* (New York: Harper, 1951).

consciousness of being in the right and his mistrust of the people about him—produced in him a sense of loneliness that drove him to seek comradeship among people with a similar outlook. But such comrades were not easy to find. He was rather an example of Czeslaw Milosz's "alienated intellectual" whose great longing it is to "belong to the masses." [11]

Unfortunately for him, there was almost no mass movement for him to join at that time in Shanghai, the Communist Party not being strong enough to launch any. So instead of surrendering himself to a mass meeting, to "crowds, red faces, mouths open in a shout, marches, arms brandishing sticks," [12] as Wen I-to and other so-called democratic leaders were later able to do, Lu Hsün could do no better than forge, usually after midnight and in the seclusion of his bedroom, the only weapons known to him, his cold, cutting, brilliant essays and his blunt and cumbersome translations from German or Japanese. The company of Communist workers and fellow travelers in his own League, with only a few exceptions, especially after the departure of Ch'ü and Feng, tended to enhance, rather than dispel, his sense of isolation. The life he led in Shanghai, though not without frequent relief in parties and movies (as his diary shows),[13] was not such as to cheer a mind originally saturnine or to remove the psychological barriers he had erected to guard himself against suspected or actual enemies, or to free him of a persecution mania whose symptoms are manifest throughout his writings.

Financially he was well off; he was amply paid for his books and con-

<hr />

[11] Czeslaw Milosz, *The Captive Mind* (New York: Vintage Books, 1955), p. 7. Cf. Lu Hsün's 1932 preface to *Lu Hsün tzu-hsüan-chi (An Anthology of Lu Hsün's Works, Selected by the Author)*: "After the group of contributors to *La Jeunesse* broke up. . . . I became a straggling soldier. I could not march in a formation. . . . Where were the new comrades-in-arms to be found? . . . I collected eleven short stories written at that time and gave them a title: *P'ang-huang (Hesitation)*. I wish I should never have the same experience again." *Lu Hsün ch'üan-chi* (Complete Works of Lu Hsün) (Shanghai: Lu Hsün ch'üan-chi ch'u-pan she, 1946), V, 50–51. [This edition is cited hereafter in this essay as *Ch'üan-chi*. In the other essays in this volume it is the Peking 1957 edition that is referred to, abbreviated *LH*.]

[12] Milosz, *op. cit.*, p. 8.

[13] *Lu Hsün jih-chi (Lu Hsün's Diary,* in facsimile) (24 vols. in 2 boxes; Shanghai Publishing Company, 1951). Though Lu Hsün was a regular diarist, his diaries, except those sketches in the form of a diary written for publication, for example, "Ma-shang jih-chi," in *Hua-kai-chi hsü-pien, Ch'üan-chi,* Vol. III, have no literary value, being too brief and fragmentary. He did not even care to write a complete sentence. He simply jotted down notes about the weather, the books bought, the letters received and mailed, the people he saw, and so forth. He seldom, if ever, revealed his heart in the *Diary* as he did in his *Correspondence,* compiled by Hsü Kuang-p'ing (Shanghai: Lu Hsün hsien-sheng chi-nien wei-yüan-hui, 1946).

tributions to magazines and newspapers. But his health was weak. His chronic tuberculosis, worsened by hard work and lack of sleep, perhaps also had a bad effect on his moods, which became terribly gloomy in 1935 when his relations with the League reached a breaking point. Then, in the debate over the slogan "National Defense Literature" in 1936, which resulted in his leading a splinter group of revolutionary writers and marked an open split between the old comrades, his temper flared up and his anger with some of his co-workers, long suppressed, found a vent at last. He died on October 19 of the same year.

So when Liu Shou-sung writes, "In 1936, under Lu Hsün's leadership, the Leftist League voluntarily suspended its activities . . . ," his overemphasis on Lu Hsün's leadership in the League is quite without basis.[14] Although Lu Hsün's leadership was a major factor in the formation of the League and in supporting it for three years at least, he did not give his approval of its dissolution or reorganization. The fact was that he had lost much of his interest in the League and had been sorely disappointed in it at times, when the shift of Communist policy required that it be reorganized along the lines of the "united front." To this change, Lu Hsün was never entirely reconciled; and because of his stubbornness and his eminent position, the erstwhile leader became a source of embarrassment to the party workers eager to produce results for the newly hatched literary movement which apparently had nothing to do with class struggle or the proletariat.

Lu Hsün may have been deluded about the true nature of communism, but he remained to the last a man of principle. He was not fickle, and his mind did not have the training to see that the united front would afford the much debilitated Communist Party its only chance for a breathing space, for resurgence, regrouping, expansion, and final victory. Bewildered, he nevertheless retained his faith in the party. It was perhaps not the party that was wrong but its commissars, with whom he would not now hesitate to differ. He was to choose his own company and fight for his own convictions, while the party asserted its authority and enforced its discipline. Though the united front was finally effected among literary workers and —after the Sian incident—between the Kuomintang and the Chinese Communist Party at large, the controversy over two slogans, one advanced by the pro-party writers and the other upheld by Lu Hsün, caused a split among the writers once united under the banner of class struggle. Its re-

[14] Liu Shou-sung, *First Draft*, I, 231.

verberations, together with the clash of personalities, were still audible in the purges in mainland China in 1955 and 1957, when the names of Hu Feng, Feng Hsüeh-feng, and Hsü Mou-yung became identified with treachery, capitalist ideology, and anti-party activities, and their deeds or misdeeds in 1936 were judged anew by the current orthodox party line and by the men who now interpreted it. One of the interpreters or accusers, and a very important one at that, happened to be Chou Yang, the doughty fighter for orthodoxy in the 1936 debate.

The true story of Lu Hsün's unhappy situation in the later phase of the League and in the debate will perhaps never be told by the Communist historians. He is long dead, and his position as a "hero" is sanctioned by Mao Tse-tung. It will remain unchallenged unless Mao himself undergoes the same fate as Stalin, and is exposed and re-examined after his death. Until then, Lu Hsün will remain the "most correct" hero who ever fought for the Communist cause.

Dr. Hu Shih is perhaps the only historian on record who has made a conjecture about the possible fate of Lu Hsün amidst the uproars of witch-hunting after the Communist conquest of the mainland. He was watching closely, out of personal as well as scholarly interest, the series of events which began with the attacks on Yü P'ing-po's *Studies on the Hung-lou-meng* and were climaxed by the vilification of Hu Shih. When a part of the attacking force was directed against the official literary organ, *Wen-i pao,* then under the editorship of Feng Hsüeh-feng, for its unwarranted praise of Yü's book, a theoretician and poet by the name of Hu Feng made the fatal blunder of extending his criticism to the general sphere of the party control of literature and demanded a greater freedom for expression and thought.[15] Immediately, all over the mainland of China a tide of angry protests arose, and Hu Feng was condemned from all sides. For several months in 1955, the *Hsin-hua yüeh-pao* ran in its *Index of Periodical Literature* department long lists of articles denouncing Hu Shih and Hu Feng.[16] That Hu Feng should share his distinction as the archenemy of the people must have been intriguing to Dr. Hu Shih. So he made a study

---

[15] For a brief, though not entirely reliable, summary of the case, see the two articles by Chao Ts'ung in the *Tsu-kuo* (*China Weekly*) (Hong Kong): "Chung-kung wen-i ta-cheng-su," Vol. IX, No. 3 (Jan. 17, 1955); "Hu-feng pao-cha-hsia-ti huo-hua," Vol. X, No. 12 (June 20, 1955).

[16] In the June issue, for instance, about fifty titles concern Hu Shih, and sixteen concern Hu Feng and his clique. In the July issue, Hu Shih dwindled in importance and became the topic of some twenty titles, while about sixty titles were attacks on Hu Feng himself and forty on his clique.

of the case, and his findings were summarized in a letter published in the
Free China Fortnightly, Taipei:

> I have collected much material about Hu Feng's case and I discover that the
> rustic from Hupeh, a man whom I have never met in my life, is really a faith-
> ful devotee of the Renaissance Movement in China. The battles he fought were
> fought bravely and desperately on the literary front of the Movement. It was
> not an accident that Hu Feng became a martyr during the powerful campaign
> "in liquidation of Hu Shih." If you can get in Taipei *Lu Hsün's Correspondence,*
> you will find from his letter No. 4 to Hu Feng (September 12, 1935, pp. 946–
> 48) that if Lu Hsün had not been already dead, he also would have been be-
> headed.[17]

Hu Feng stood out as a rare specimen of moral courage who rebelled
against Mao's dogmas about literature, which he contemptuously regarded
as the "totem." [18] He is known to have long been engaged in quarrels,
mostly over matters of principle, with the commissars in charge of the
rectification of thought, whom he called "princelings" and "mandarins."
That evil fate should not have descended upon him until 1955 was due to
his silence which he had prudently kept since 1949. The *Wen-i pao* case
was described by the author of the *China Weekly* article as a trap, and he
foolishly fell into it. He threw caution to the winds and submitted to the
party authorities a memorial of about 300,000 characters, criticizing every
literary and ideological phenomenon in Communist China. The sum of the
accusations brought against him was that he was not only ideologically an
enemy of the party and of socialism, but also an active spy in the service
of Chiang Kai-shek and the American imperialists. The latter charge was
of course based on very flimsy evidence. Hu Feng has not been heard of
since a recommendation was made by the Presidium (whose Chairman is
Kuo Mo-jo) of the All-China Association of Literature and Arts, to refer
his case to the People's Supreme Attorney.[19] He may not have been beheaded (Dr. Hu was apparently using a hyperbole in his letter), but the
deprivation of life may not be the worst punishment that the Communists
can inflict on an "enemy of the people."

Feng Hsüeh-feng, as one of the party's leading theoreticians, curiously
did not join the mob in throwing stones at the "dog struggling in the
water." [20] Instead of coming out as a defender of the correct party line in

[17] "A Letter from Dr. Hu Shih," to Lei Chen, Vol. XIV, No. 8 (Apr. 16, 1956).

[18] "Totem," "princelings," and "mandarins" appeared in Hu Feng's private letters,
later published as evidence of his crimes. *Hsin-hua yüeh-pao,* June, 1955, pp. 2–37.

[19] *Ibid.,* p. 39.

[20] "To strike a drowning dog" was approved by Lu Hsün. See his essay, "No Time
for 'Fair Play' " (1925), in his *Ch'üan-chi,* I, 249–59.

refutation of Hu Feng's heresy, as he was expected to do, he made a little speech in a session of the Presidium of the All-China Association of Literature and Arts. His mood was reminiscent rather than indignant. He recalled the years when Hu Feng was a member of the Leftist League:

> Hu Feng began to sneak into the camp of revolutionaries around 1933, when he participated in the activities of the Leftist League. I was then in Shanghai too, but I did not detect his treachery. . . . Upon my return to my duty in Shanghai in the early summer of 1936, it seems to me now that Hu Feng apparently had been engaged in dividing the ranks of revolutionary literature. . . .
>
> Hu Feng wanted to drive a wedge not only between Mr. Lu Hsün and Comrade Chou Yang, Comrade Hsia Yen, etc., but also between Mr. Lu Hsün and myself. It was because these people, including myself, were all party members.[21]

Though these facts are interesting to us, they did not satisfy the men in power. In 1957, when Feng himself became a victim of the purge, though he had been under attack since the *Hung-lou-meng* case, his failure to display a more hostile attitude toward Hu Feng was seized upon gleefully by one of his enemies:

> At the time of the liquidation of Hu Feng, we were all expecting Hsüeh-feng to write something. He himself realized that it was not good for him not to write. He collected much material and pondered over this and over that. He tore and wrote, wrote and tore, but never could he overcome the difficulty of writing about Hu Feng.[22]

Chou Yang, whose rise from an active party member in the League to his present position as an arbiter of all literary matters on the mainland has been phenomenal indeed, seems to have had a better memory. His version of the story, though it confirms Hu Feng's evil doings, did not place Hsüeh-feng in a better position:

> Feng Hsüeh-feng did some work for the revolution. But his strong individualist and anarchist thought has come regularly into conflict with the collectivist thought of the labor class and with the organizational and disciplinary nature of the party. . . . He came to Shanghai in 1936 from Northern Shensi, then the revolutionary base. With the airs of an Inspector-General, he, on the one hand, accepted Hu Feng as his comrade, and on the other, launched the vilest sectarianistic attacks on the party's underground organization in Shanghai. . . .[23]

[21] "Some Facts about Hu Feng's Anti-Revolutionary Activities," *Wen-i pao*, No. 12, June 30, 1955.

[22] "Literary Teahouse," *Wen-i pao*, No. 21, Sept. 1, 1957. See also Lin Mo-han's speech on August 6, condensed in *Wen-i pao*, No. 20, Aug. 18, 1957.

[23] Chou Yang, "A Great Debate on the Literary Front," *Wen-i pao*, No. 5, Mar. 11, 1958. In the article on Hu Feng in *China Weekly* (Hong Kong), Vol. X, No. 12

The *Jen-min jih-pao* put the case more explicitly:

Feng Hsüeh-feng came to Shanghai in 1936 from Northern Shensi. He did not trust the party's underground organization then operating in Shanghai. Instead, he introduced into the party Hu Feng, who had been working against the party and who was thus enabled to remain in the party for a while. His sectarianistic activities served a function in splitting the revolutionary literary work led by the party.[24]

From these quotations, we can see that those who represented the Chinese Communist Party orthodoxy admitted that the Leftist League had undergone a split in 1936, which allegedly originated in Hu Feng's treachery and widened under Feng Hsüeh-feng's influence. It strikes me as strange, as it did Dr. Hu Shih, that Lu Hsün's name was kept inviolate amidst all these denunciations.[25] Hu and Feng may have disagreed on many points with the responsible cadres in Shanghai, but without Lu Hsün's help and encouragement and "leadership," their chance of success would have been much smaller and they could not, left to themselves, have caused such a wound in the once united body of leftist writers which kept festering even after a lapse of so many years. Evidently Lu Hsün was the major culprit in the crisis of 1936 which threatened to disrupt the literary front formed to promote Communist policy and ideology, and which still rankled with the Communist leaders in the late fifties.

Lu Hsün's friendship with Feng Hsüeh-feng began in December, 1928, but he did not know then that the young man was a Chinese Communist Party member.[26] A few quotations from his *Diary* will show how intimate they were:

JULY 19 [1929].   Went out for cold drinks with Hsüeh-feng, Jou Shih, . . . and Kuang-p'ing [Mrs. Lu Hsün].
JULY 20.   Hsüeh-feng came. Lent him $30 as an advance.
AUGUST 15.   Hsüeh-feng came tonight. Returned $30.

(June 20, 1955), there is the statement: "The real boss of the League of Leftist Writers was its Secretary-General Chou Yang who represented the Communist Party." But I need confirmation on this.

[24] Reprinted in *Wen-i pao*, No. 21, Sept. 1, 1957.

[25] Mrs. Lu Hsün wrote in *Wen-i pao*, No. 20, 1957, commenting on the cases of Ting Ling and Feng Hsüeh-feng: "What angers me is that there are still malicious people who are using Lu Hsün's name to attack comrade Chou Yang. . . . There are people today who will ascribe so many things to Lu Hsün. The rightists suggest that if Hu Feng's memorial in 300,000 characters had been sponsored by Lu Hsün, then it would not have caused so much trouble. This is, of course, the opinion of the reactionaries." It seems that rumors and conjectures of that kind were circulating in Communist China in 1957.

[26] "The Party Imparted Strength to Lu Hsün," in Feng Hsüeh-feng, *Collected Essays* (Peking: People's Literary Publications Association, 1952), I, 244.

Lu Hsün could see that Feng was in need of money. He tried to help him, and here we have a little human drama.

OCTOBER 12 [1929]. Finished the translation of *On Art* [by A. Lunacharski] tonight.

OCTOBER 13. Afternoon, mailed a letter to Hsüeh-feng and a copy of *On Art* in manuscript.

OCTOBER 14. Paid Hsüeh-feng $50 for his editing [of the manuscript].

OCTOBER 15. Afternoon, a letter from Hsüeh-feng. $50 returned. Night, gave the same money to Hsüeh-feng.

Here is another entry which shows the warm feelings Lu Hsün had for the young man.

JANUARY 25 [1933]. Chinese New Year's Eve. Prepared some dishes and invited Hsüeh-feng to dinner.[27]

How the two men worked together as comrades is described in Feng's *Reminiscences about Lu Hsün* and *Collected Essays,* Volume I. Mrs. Lu Hsün has also handed down a record of the man whom she calls Mr. F.: how he bothered Lu Hsün with every minor detail about the publications of the League, drove him to write on assigned subjects, never gave an inch in argument until the old man was convinced, and deprived him of sleep and rest which he badly needed. But Lu Hsün liked him and approved of his ways.[28]

Feng's departure for Juichin seemed to have left a void in Lu Hsün's life which was not to be filled until 1934 and 1935, when his friendship with Hu Feng began to develop. Like Feng Hsüeh-feng, Hu Feng was well versed in Marxist theory and took a strong interest in the leftist literary movement. Unlike Feng, he did not belong to the party. But he received a much worse treatment than a common fellow traveler would have at the hands of Communist cadres looking for help from outside. Kuo Mo-jo, who had known him in Japan, wrote about him in 1936 as "a young man, rather intelligent and somewhat intransigently ambitious." [29] These qualities will perhaps explain his predilection for independent thinking, though with a Marxist coloring, and his unpopularity in the League. The feud between Hu Feng and Chou Yang probably began with their debate in 1935 over

[27] According to the Chinese custom, only the closest friends were invited to the dinner on Chinese New Year's Eve, which was meant for the reunion of the family.

[28] "Lu Hsün and the Young People," an appendix to Hsiao Hung, *Hui-i Lu Hsün hsien-sheng (Recollections of Mr. Lu Hsün)* (3d ed.; Shanghai: Sheng Huo Book Company, 1948), pp. 100–101

[29] "An Inspection of the Military Exercise," reprinted in the *Chinese Literary Yearbook for 1936,* ed. Yang Chin-hao (Shanghai: Pei Hsin Book Company, 1937), p. 315.

typical characters in literature, and by 1936 it was already common knowl-edge in literary circles.[30] The price Hu was to pay for his unpopularity and all the flaws in his character was very high indeed.

Though he may have alienated himself from many of his fellow writers, he more than compensated for the loss with the sympathy and support of Lu Hsün.[31] His name hardly appeared in Lu Hsün's *Diary* for 1933, and not more than ten times for 1934. In that year, however, there are two interesting entries related to Hu Feng. One is about a looking glass which Lu Hsün received as a gift and gave to Hu Feng's wife (October 25). On December 18, Lu Hsün personally went to Liang Yüan, a Honanese res-taurant, to make a reservation. Then the next day, he noted that Hu Feng and his wife failed to appear at the banquet. (He had written to them on the seventeenth; apparently an invitation was enclosed in the letter.) In 1935, letters were exchanged quite often between the master and the dis-ciple, for Hu Feng was known as Lu Hsün's "disciple" or "first disciple." [32] But the collection of Lu Hsün's correspondence mentioned in Dr. Hu's letter contains only four. The rest are perhaps lost forever. But these four letters show what confidence had been established between the two men and how Lu Hsün might easily have imparted to a confidant his anger and irritation at the Communist leadership in the League—feelings he would have suppressed in writing for the public.

I shall quote from the fourth letter, the one Dr. Hu believes would have brought Lu Hsün to the executioner. Here are the two most significant pas-sages:

> About San Lang, I can without hesitation state my opinion: better not join at present. What happened in the beginning would make a long story, so I

[30] Articles by both critics on typical characters are reprinted in Hu Feng, *Mi-yün-ch'i feng-hsi hsiao-chi* (*Records of a Stormy Period*) (Hankow: Hai-yen shu-tien, 1938). The *Chinese Literary Yearbook for 1936*, pp. 231–57, reprinted a "Table-Talk" of nineteen novelists, who all seemed to be keenly aware of the feud between Hu Feng and Chou Yang. One of them even suggested that their magazine *Hsiao-shuo-chia* (*The Storyteller*) should reject any contribution from Hu Feng, for fear that it might lead to the conjecture that they represented Hu Feng's interests. The suggestion was not accepted.

[31] In "Lu Hsün and the Young People," Mrs. Lu Hsün also told about a Mr. X who was back from Japan. Lu Hsün had a very high regard for him in spite of the man's unpopularity. An appendix to Hsiao Hung, *Recollections of Mr. Lu Hsün,* p. 102. That man can be no other than Hu Feng. Hu Feng was deported from Japan in 1933. Hu Feng, *Essays* (Shanghai: Chun Ming Book Company, 1948), p. 76.

[32] In Hu Feng's own words, "After Mr. Lu Hsün's death, certain tabloid journalists maliciously call me Lu Hsün's 'disciple' or 'chief disciple.' " *Essays,* p. 141. The nick-name seemed to meet with general acceptance.

won't talk about it. In view of the happenings in recent years, I feel it would be better to have a few new writers appear among the people who do not belong; they may show something fresh. Once a man has joined, he will be forever involved in petty squabbles and cannot make his voice heard. Take myself as an example, I always feel that I am bound in an iron chain while a foreman is whipping me on the back. No matter how hard I work, the whip will fall. When I turn my head and ask what are really my faults, the man will clasp his hands and politely shake them and say that I am doing an extremely fine job; that he and I are surely the best of friends; and what a fine day, ha, ha, ha. . . . That so often disconcerts me. I dare not speak to the outsiders about ourselves; to the foreigners, I simply avoid the subject. If I have to speak, I only lie. You see what a predicament I am in.

This opinion of mine, in the eyes of the field marshal, must be incriminating against me (though he and I are surely still the best of friends), but I think I am right. . . . Now the field marshal is strengthening his relations with the "confessors" (that's why their words carry such weight among us), and a new offensive is under way. I really don't know when we can see light again.[33]

The name of San Lang does not concern us so much as the identity of the field marshal. San Lang may have been just another young writer who aspired to membership in the League; but the field marshal was the man who had real power in the League. Was he Chou Yang or Hsia Yen? (These were, according to Feng Hsüeh-feng, the men whom Hu Feng wanted to estrange from Lu Hsün.) Or was it somebody else? As for the "confessors," they were the writers who, after being arrested by the Kuomintang authorities, confessed to their crimes. We shall hear more about them. Meanwhile, there is another complaint about the field marshal, in the second letter (June 28, 1935):

. . . I think that to concentrate our attack on the enemy is of primary importance, but this view seems hardly to meet with support. It appears that the literary world will be unified if only a few people are knocked down. . . .

I used to go around quite often, but as I know of late that our field marshal keeps himself indoors and orders others about, I think I had rather sit in my home. I remember what Tolstoy said in a story. A foot soldier is generally forgetful about his danger but the bullet-proof iron plate in front of the general reminds him of his own safety, and thus his heart beats so violently that he dares not move ahead. But if the field marshal thinks the value of human life is not equal in every case, then I shall have nothing to say. I am only ready for the floggings (*chün-kun*).[34]

Another of Lu Hsün's confidants was Yang Chi-yün, the compiler of his *Uncollected Works* (*Chi-wai-chi*) and, in collaboration with Mrs. Lu

[33] *Lu Hsün's Correspondence,* Letter No. 4, pp. 946–48.
[34] *Correspondence,* Letter No. 2, p. 944. According to *Lu Hsün's Diary,* the date should have been June 29 instead of June 28.

Hsün, of his *Correspondence*. To Yang he wrote the letter from which the following excerpt is taken:

The lap dogs are not to be feared. The real threat is the so-called "comrades-in-arms" who do not say what they think. I cannot be vigilant enough to guard against them. For instance, men like Shao-po, even now I do not know what his real intention is. To protect myself from the rear, I have to stand slantwise. Thus I cannot stand facing the enemy. And it requires much more energy to watch simultaneously forward and backward. My poor health is due to age and has nothing to do with them. But sometimes I feel angry indeed; the energy spent on them could be better used for better results. [December 12, 1934.] [35]

Shao-po was a pseudonym of the leftist dramatist T'ien Han,[36] who wrote under that name a gossipy article on the thesis that the Chinese are the race most ready to reconcile. He cited, as an example (but that was the real sting of the article) the appearance of both Lu Hsün and Yang Ts'un-jen in the same number of a magazine. Yang was an ex-Communist, one of the self-styled "third group" of writers, who tried to rise above the political struggle between the Kuomintang and the Communists. Lu Hsün had detested the man and said that he had a "pshaw" for him.[37] Did it not mean that Lu Hsün was reconciled to a turncoat and an enemy by contributing to the magazine in which also appeared Yang's "Return from the Red Areas"? The tone was sarcastic but quite mild, at least so it appears to me. A man with a more generous cast of mind would have dismissed such frivolous writing with a smile; a man with more important matters to look after would have simply ignored it. But Lu Hsün was a man of neither kind. It threw him into a fury. In his "Letter to the Editors of the *Drama Weekly*," after a discussion of the adaptation of his *True Story of Ah Q* for the stage, he concluded with a vehement protest:

. . . Several months ago I wrote a letter to a friend in answer to his questions about the "popular language." That letter was published in the *Social Monthly;* in the end of that issue was an article by Mr. Yang Ts'un-jen. A certain Mr. Shao-po commented on this in the *Torch* (literary supplement of the *Ta-wan-pao*), alleging that I have reached a reconciliation with Mr. Yang and deploring with a deep sigh that the Chinese are simply too good at reconciliation. . . . I beg to state in this connection that I do not have the power to prevent people

[35] *Correspondence*, p. 695. The lap dog is Lu Hsün's favorite expression to designate the type of man who works obsequiously for the government. He first introduced it probably in "No Time for 'Fair Play,'" *Ch'üan-chi*, I, 249–59. It appears also in his "Letter to the Editors of the *Drama Weekly*," *ibid.*, VI, 148–49; and in his letter to Yang Ts'un-jen, *ibid.*, V, 221–32.

[36] "Notes to *Ch'ieh-chieh-t'ing tsa wen*" (1934), *Ch'üan-chi*, VI, 215.

[37] "An Open Letter in Reply to Mr. Yang Ts'un-jen's Open Letter" (1933), *Ch'üan-chi,* V, 221–32.

from publishing my private letters; that I cannot know beforehand in whose company my letter will appear; that therefore there is no question of reconciliation or irreconciliation at all when two such contributions are placed together; but that my hatred and contempt for the man of my own camp, who, in disguise, stabs me in the back, are much greater than for an obvious enemy.[38]

His open letters, the one just quoted being an example, are often at a much higher pitch, showing much more consciousness of rhetorical effects than his easygoing and spontaneous private correspondence. Anyhow T'ien Han was one of the editors of the *Drama Weekly,* to whom the open letter was addressed, and T'ien Han also happened to be Shao-po. Lu Hsün knew who Shao-po was when he wrote the rejoinder; but he did not reveal the identity of the rascal until the letter was reprinted in a new volume of his essays. And then in the Notes, which he wrote about one month later than the open letter, he told the whole story of the incident and explained why the complaint should have been directed against the editors of the *Drama Weekly.*

T'ien Han's "stab in the back" was only one of those minor incidents which showed the unpleasant feelings that were separating Lu Hsün from some powerful members of the Leftist League. How Hu Feng played upon his weakness to widen the rift and sow the seeds of dissension, as his accusers attested, is yet to be proved. But from Lu Hsün's correspondence and essays, it is manifest that he was morbidly sensitive to stings and pricks, which he would magnify into stabs, cutting deep and inflicted out of sheer malevolence. He was quick to see hostility and accept a challenge. He would never hesitate to enter the lists, upon the smallest provocation, if the adversary was a "gentleman" like Ch'en Yüan or Liang Shih-ch'iu,[39] or a "third man" like Yang Ts'un-jen, or, in a word, an enemy. But a jeer from a comrade-in-arms like T'ien Han was different. He had to keep in mind the solidarity of his own camp. Besides, to beat down an "enemy," he not only indulged in the satisfaction of personal revenge but served a higher moral cause. His personal enemy was also the enemy of the revolution. But to seek revenge upon an offending comrade, for whom his hatred

[38] *Ch'üan-chi,* VI, 148–49.

[39] Ch'en Yüan (pseudonym, Hsi-ying, 1895–   ), a Chinese delegate to UNESCO. He will perhaps be long remembered for Lu Hsün's scurrilous attacks on him. See especially Lu Hsün's collection of essays *Hua-kai-chi* (1925), *Ch'üan-chi,* Vol. III. As a contributor to *Hsin-yüeh* (*The Crescent Moon*), Liang Shih-ch'iu (1902–   ), professor of English literature at Taiwan Provincial Normal University, used to hold debates with the leftists on literary theories. Lu Hsün took him more seriously than he took Ch'en. See his reply to Liang's criticisms: "On 'Stiff Translation' and the 'Class in Literature' " (1930), *Ch'üan-chi,* IV, 202–26.

and contempt might be even greater than for a real enemy, would only expose him as a self-indulgent and peevish person in the eyes of the people, whose high regard for him he wished to keep. Pain naturally consumes one's energy, and it must have been doubly painful for Lu Hsün to have to hide his pain from the public.

As a leader of the League, he must have been beset, at times, with a more painful sense of loneliness than when he was writing the poems-in-prose collected in *The Wild Grass* and the stories that were to bear the title *Hesitation*. Then he was unashamedly a solitary fighter; he could, to use his own image, hurl his spear at will at any single enemy or the combination of all enemies.[40] He could look deeper into his own loneliness, and the results of this search, though without a social message, could reveal more truths about human nature. But the straggler had to join the ranks before he could develop to a much higher degree his *esprit de corps* or his tolerance of affronts and offenses. Still it would be only natural for Lu Hsün to be angry with "men like Shao-po."

I only regret that he showed no sign that his life had become richer because of his new experiences with the revolutionaries. He failed to seek, as he might have, to understand the role of an artist in a revolution and the inherent contradiction, as well as the necessary interdependence, between an individual and the organization to which he belongs. He failed to sublimate his anger, frustration, and disappointment or to direct his pent-up emotions to a new creative effort. He did not benefit from the tension, from the hostility he felt in his own camp, from the necessity to "watch simultaneously forward and backward," from the feeling of energy being thus wasted. All this should have made him a much wiser man, and such wisdom is the foundation on which greater works of art can be built. But the revolutionary zeal was so strong in him that it blinded him to certain aspects of revolution which, fortunately or unfortunately for him, he did not live long enough to witness or to fight against. He had to die a grumbling, unforgiving, narrow-minded man, the most loyal hero of communism, and an egregious case of great talent most stupidly wasted.

That so many letters were left behind him, telling about his unhappy situation in the League, is surely a blessing to his biographer, but they also show his weakness: how badly he was in need of a sympathetic listener to whom he could pour out his woe. In this correspondence, if read side by side with his other writings, we can get a clear picture of the man—the

---

[40] "This Kind of Fighting Man," in *The Wild Grass, Ch'üan-chi*, I, 525–27.

sensitive nerves behind a stern appearance, the tender heart palpitating so close to an "unyielding backbone." Some of those addressed to the couple Hsiao Chün and Hsiao Hung are particularly warm, frank, and enlivened with a beguiling touch of naïve humor. He gave instructions to his young friends, refugee writers recently arrived from the Northeast (Manchuria), about the streets of the strange metropolis of Shanghai, made fun of their names, and invited them to dinner with brief notes of playful elegance.

Hsiao Hung has left for us a very intimate portrait of Lu Hsün, evincing great feminine perception in describing his home, his parties, his working habits, and his illness.[41] A little episode strikes me particularly not only for its poignancy but also for the symbolism that might be in it if we think of how lightly his sufferings were taken by the ones most dear to him. It was in 1936, when Lu Hsün was critically ill (we shall come to it in the second part of the essay). His seven-year-old son was displaying to his little playmates the empty, amber-tinted ampules he had collected from the sickroom and said proudly, "These are daddy's medicine. You don't have them, do you?" [42]

Hsiao Hung herself died in 1942 in Hong Kong. Her husband, Hsiao Chün, in 1948 became a forerunner of Hu Feng and Feng Hsüeh-feng as an anti-party and anti-socialist element, when, as editor of a newspaper in Harbin sponsored by the Communist Party, he became unreservedly critical of the Communists, both Chinese and Russian.[43] But in the thirties neither he nor his wife seemed to have been directly involved in the literary quarrels in Shanghai. To them, of course, Lu Hsün had a great deal to say about the subject:

> The enemy is not to be feared. The real threat is the vermin in our own camp. So often have they brought defeat to us, which sometimes causes within me a sense of loneliness. But I will persist in doing the things I used to do, though my physical strength is no longer what it was. Because of the limitations of my learning, I cannot satisfy the thirsty longing of the younger generation. But to shrink back is not for me. [December 6, 1934.]

[41] Hsiao Hung (Chang Nai-ying, 1911–1942), *Recollections*. Her first novel *Sheng ssu ch'ang* (*Field of Life and Death*) (1935) was prefaced by Lu Hsün. For her life and works, see Jos. Schyns *et al.*, "Short Biographies of Authors," *1500 Modern Chinese Novels and Plays* (Peiping: Catholic University Press, 1948), p. 7.

[42] Hsiao Hung, *Recollections*, p. 49.

[43] Wang Yao, *Draft*, II, 244–47; Liu Shou-sung, *First Draft*, II, 221–25. A short biographical sketch of Hsiao Chün can be found in Edgar Snow's introduction to the English version of his *Village in August* (New York: Smith & Durrell, 1942), a widely praised novel, prefaced by Lu Hsün. He was born in Manchuria in 1908, and came to Shanghai in 1934. Fifty-four of Lu Hsün's letters to either Hsiao Chün or the couple are in *Correspondence*.

The enemy is not to be feared. What chills and depresses me the most are the cowardly arrows shot by allies from behind and the smiles of gratification on the faces of the men of my own camp after I am wounded. So whenever I received a wound, I would hide myself in the depth of the forest, lick the blood dry, and dress it with my own hands. No one is ever to know of it. I believe such a situation is terrible. I am not exactly despairing: I can always stand up after a little rest. But the effect somehow still shows, not only in my writings, but also in my moods. I can myself feel that most of the time I am "chilly." [April 23, 1935.]

It would be very hard to write for that magazine, though I once promised to contribute. But an open letter was published in its pages; it was an attack on me by my comrades. The names they used were some real and some fictitious. They even invented a name, Kuo Ping-jo, trying to mislead the reader into believing that it was a typographical error meant to read Kuo Mo-jo. I protested, but the only answers I could get were evasive and equivocal. I felt as if I were seeing a ghost; I was frightened. Incidents like this happened again twice, and my heart has not been warmed ever since. Now people will say, at times when they think they should say, that I am "better." But that is a rumor: I am only worse. [April 28, 1935.][44]

The case of the abusive letter is interesting, but I cannot find any allusion to it in the *Complete Works*. No trace seems to have been left of it, except in this letter, after Lu Hsün had dressed his wound in the darkness of the forest and had once again taken up his post.[45] The two subsequent incidents

[44] *Correspondence,* pp. 775, 807, 809.

[45] Hu Feng in his essay "In Memoriam, Tung-p'ing" recalled that in 1932 the young writer Ch'iu Tung-p'ing, out of a motive quite free from malice, joined others and signed an open letter protesting against Lu Hsün's "conciliatory" attitude toward the neutral writers. Hu, *Essays,* p. 75. The magazine in which the letter appeared was probably the *Wen-hsüeh yüeh-pao,* for according to Hu Feng, Ch'iu had contributed to it a short story in the same year. In December of that year, Lu Hsün wrote an open letter to the editors of the *Wen-hsüeh yüeh-pao,* bearing the title "Insults and Threats Do Not Constitute the Battle." It was mainly about a revolutionary poem, filled with insults and threats, which Lu Hsün regarded as poor literature and harmful to the revolutionary cause. Then, in conclusion, he came up with the following passage which might allude to something other than the poem: "Of course, the common practices of the Chinese men of letters for a long time have been libel, scandal, threats, and insults. Take up any large volume of history, and you will come across writings of that kind. They are still in use, and have become even worse than before. This heritage, I think, had better pass to the lap dog writers. If our own writers did not do their best to cast it off, they would become no better than those people." *Ch'üan-chi,* V, 47–48. He said "our own writers," for the monthly was edited by two members of the League, Yao P'eng-tzu and Chou Yang, then known as Chou Ch'i-ying. Schyns, *op. cit.,* p. 109 (see note 41). Though Lu Hsün could bear, in 1935, a grudge against an incident that happened in 1932, the greatest objection to that theory is that the *Wen-hsüeh yüeh-pao* did not have such a long life. Most periodicals put out by the leftist writers had only an ephemeral existence. The *Wen-hsüeh yüeh-pao* was not listed in the *Chinese Literary Year Book for 1935* (Shanghai: Pei Hsin Book Company, 1936). It probably had by then ceased publication.

will also remain a mystery, though he mentioned several such happenings in his important open letter to Hsü Mou-yung. Perhaps no one can say definitely today which incidents he was alluding to in the letter just quoted. Of one thing we are sure: they were unpleasant.

Anyhow, chilliness, wounds licked in private, awareness of his failing strength, resentment at the field marshal and some comrades-in-arms, smoldering anger, bewilderment at people who should have known how to act more wisely and behave more respectfully, and a growing disaffection for the group to which he still belonged—such was Lu Hsün's relation with the League for the latter part of 1934 and all of 1935. These wounds and grumblings, significant as they were, he might have carried to his grave without attracting much public notice if he had not broken his silence in 1936 and dealt several stunning blows to the comrades-in-arms whom he detested. This was the debate over the two slogans. Then the crack in the hitherto seemingly solid body of the Leftist League became visible to any-one who cared to read about leftist literature in that year. Lu Hsün died a fighter, but it was an irony of fate that he used much of his waning strength in his last year on earth to battle against men formerly of his own camp. He could hardly justify himself in the separatist movement he led, judging from the damage he inflicted on the "cause." I do not know whether his-tory will justify him, but Mao and the scholars of Communist China will. Indeed, they have already made it clear that everything he did or said must be right.

II TWO SLOGANS

The leftist writers, in late 1935 and early 1936, were confronted with a new situation and a new set of problems. The Communist Party, after the adoption of the popular front as its over-all policy, was riding high on the waves of the nationwide anti-Japanese sentiment. After so many recent setbacks—the loss of the base in Kiangsi, the terrible casualties suffered in the Long March, and the defection, arrest, and execution of the cadres in the cities, the party found that it could now hope to enlarge its hold on the masses and win the support not only of the proletariat and intellectuals but of people of every class, the nation as a whole, if it could succeed in establishing itself in the popular imagination as the party of patriots. What opened endless vistas of a triumphant future to the leaders in Yenan was that the mass movement, which had almost completely stopped in the "white areas" after 1927 for lack of a "hot" issue rather than because of Chiang Kai-shek's suppression, was now reviving.

The students' anti-Japanese demonstrations in Peiping on December 9, 1935, electrified the nation in a manner that could be compared only with the May Fourth (1919) or the May Thirtieth (1925) movements.[46] Here was a political and psychological situation that the Communists could exploit to their best advantage. Patriotism again provided a climate beneficial to the spread of agitation and propaganda and the promoting of the growth of political organization. By supporting and infiltrating a mass movement, the Communists stood the best chance of leading it and turning it to serve their own purpose. The popular demand was for resistance against Japanese aggression, and that seemed to coincide exactly with the policy of the Communist Party. The Chinese Soviet Republic had declared war on Japan as early as in February, 1932,[47] while the Kuomintang Government had been allowing the Japanese imperialists to occupy one Chinese province after another. But it was no time to blame the Kuomintang either; the nation could be saved only through united national effort. The paramount duty of every patriotic Chinese was to see that the civil war (what Chiang Kai-shek called the bandit-suppressing war) was stopped and that an All-China United People's Government of National Defense and an All-China Anti-Japanese Defense National Army were formed.

These were the points that Wang Ming stressed in the Seventh World Congress of the Comintern in July, 1935,[48] and they gained further publicity as slogans after the Chinese Communist Party published its *Letter to Fellow Countrymen* (August 1, 1935).[49] To take the place of class struggle there was the war of resistance against the Japanese; to take the place of the proletariat there was the united front of the people of every class. At such a reversal of policy, a deep-grained Marxist would no doubt be bewildered. But that was the line of the party, and the party no doubt spoke in the best interest of the proletariat.

The main problem that faced the leftist writers in Shanghai was how leftist they should remain. Or at least that was the problem that troubled

[46] For student movements on and after December 9, 1935, and the related movements (e.g., The National Salvation Movement in Shanghai) see the contemporary accounts in the book *Yi-erh-chiu yün-tung* (*The December Ninth Movement*) (edited and published by the People's Publication Association, distributed by the Hsin Hua Book Company, Peking, 1954).

[47] Benjamin I. Schwartz, *Chinese Communism and the Rise of Mao* (Cambridge, Mass.: Harvard University Press, 1951), p. 208.

[48] Harold R. Isaacs, *The Tragedy of the Chinese Revolution* (London: Secker and Warburg, 1938), pp. 438–39.

[49] Wang Yao, *Draft*, I, 178.

Lu Hsün, for to some other leftists, "revolutionary literature" might easily pass into "yes-men's literature" [50]—they could always obey the command or follow the fashion. The League of Leftist Writers seemed to have served its function, for leftist principles and leftist slogans were to be discouraged, at least temporarily, for the sake of the united front. The League had been inaugurated with a ceremony on March 2, 1930, and Lu Hsün's address on that occasion is one of his most quoted writings.[51] But now there was no ceremony to mark its closing, no speech to praise its achievements on its final day. There was perhaps not even a final day in the career of the League. It simply evaporated together with the enthusiasm for the so-called leftist literature. According to Feng Hsüeh-feng, whose friendship with Lu Hsün had been resumed after Feng came back to Shanghai in April, 1936, as an "inspector-general" from Yenan to re-establish the broken connection between the party's underground organizations in Shanghai and its headquarters then recently set up in Yenan, Lu Hsün quite often revealed to him his "inner conflict" regarding the dissolution of the League.

At the time (in the beginning of 1936) when the Leftist League was dissolved, there was not even an adequate discussion among the members themselves. It was especially a great mistake that the comrades of my party did not make a serious study of the case together with a man like Lu Hsün who stood in such intimate relations to the League. Instead, they only summarily sought his opinion. Lu Hsün did not deny, in his conversation, that he had agreed to its dissolution, since persecution had made it impossible to perform any task. But on several other occasions, he would say in a reproachful tone, "To be dissolved like that! Not to regard it as a battle line at all! . . ." [52]

The tone was not only reproachful but also pained. A battle line—but to fight against what? To the orthodox Communists, their only enemies were now the Japanese and the Chinese collaborating with the Japanese (and also Hitler and Mussolini, perhaps). Chiang Kai-shek was the man to be appealed to, won over, and united with. But that was a bitter pill for Lu Hsün to swallow with his "extremely deep class hatred" of Chiang and

[50] One of Lu Hsün's five lectures delivered in Peiping in November, 1932, was on "Revolutionary Literature and Yes-men's Literature" but it has not been collected in his *Ch'üan-chi.* Only the title is left. *Ch'üan-chi,* VII, 557.

[51] "Opinions about the League of Leftist Writers," *Ch'üan-chi,* IV, 236–42. There was an entry in his *Diary* for March 2, 1930: "Attended the inaugural meeting of the League of Leftist Writers at I-shu University." A more detailed account of that event is found in the article by Han T'o-fu, "Mr. Lu Hsün as Seen by a Communist," in *Hui-i wei-ta-ti Lu Hsün hsien-sheng (Recollections of the Great Lu Hsün)* (Shanghai: New Literature Publication Association, 1958).

[52] Feng, *Reminiscences,* pp. 156–57.

his reactionary regime.[53] "To unite with the Kuomintang—that would be the most welcome news to the traitors who have gone over to the enemy." [54] By traitors he meant Yang Ts'un-jen and the other so-called confessors who had betrayed the leftist movement.[55] To readmit them into the united front was as dreadful to think of as joining forces with Chiang Kai-shek. But to reject them would be contradictory to the policy of the united front advocated by the top Communist leaders. Such was Lu Hsün's dilemma; such were his doubts and apprehensions. I believe Feng Hsüeh-feng gave a faithful account of his impressions of Lu Hsün in April and May, 1935, for in his own writings there is ample evidence of his struggle to accept the new policy, or rather to abandon the principle in favor of the policy. He was no less patriotic than any other Chinese,[56] but he was also a leftist writer. To reconcile the two positions was particularly difficult at a time when so many of his comrades seemed to be ready to jettison the leftist ideals along with their "class hatred." The mass movement was rising in one city after another, and the whole nation was buzzing with patriotic fervor, but Lu Hsün found himself again in the unenviable position of a straggler. He craved to join the ranks no less than ever, but he could not join them until he decided how far he should go in revising his attitude as a leftist.

Wang Yao, a literary historian in Communist China, criticized Feng's *Reminiscences* during the 1957 purge for its egotistic traits: "From his book, we get the impression that Lu Hsün was great, but Feng was greater; at least that without him, Lu Hsün could not have accomplished his greatness." [57] This piece of condemnation, it seems to me, contains para-

---

[53] *Ibid.,* p. 156.

[54] *Ibid.,* p. 155.

[55] Besides Yang, these names also appeared in Lu Hsün's works: Mu Shih-ying, Han Shih-heng, and Mu Mu-t'ien. He had little to say against Ting Ling and Yao P'eng-tzu, who after their arrest probably also made some sort of "confession."

[56] Lu Hsün had several Japanese friends when he was in Shanghai. Some were very close (especially Uchiyama Kanzo, the bookseller). Both Cheng Hsüeh-chia, author of *Lu Hsün cheng-chuan* (*True Story of Lu Hsün*) (Hong Kong: Asia Press, 1953), and Miss Su Hsüeh-lin, in her letter to Dr. Ts'ai Yüan-p'ei, which is summarized in Ts'ao Chü-jen, *Lu Hsün p'ing chuan* (*A Critical Biography of Lu Hsün*) (Hong Kong: New Culture Publishing Company, 1956), suspected Lu Hsün of underhand pro-Japanese activities; but their theory was not based upon factual evidence. Lu Hsün's anti-Japanese sentiments pervaded many of his writings after 1934. His personal relationships with the Japanese should not be confused with his feelings against Japan as an aggressor.

[57] Wang Yao, "Concerning the Understanding of Certain Important Problems in the History of Contemporary Literature," *Wen-i pao,* No. 1, 1958.

doxically a certain degree of truth so far as the cheer and comfort that the old friend had brought from Yenan were concerned. No one could so vividly and convincingly describe to Lu Hsün the strength of the party as a comrade who had survived the Long March; no one could so resolve his doubts as an old friend who placed implicit faith in the leadership of Mao Tse-tung. At the end of 1935, Lu Hsün and Mao Tun sent a telegram to Yenan congratulating the party on its success in establishing a new base. "The future of China and mankind rests on you," the message said.[58] But Lu Hsün knew little about the new leadership of the party. The overtures of peace to the Kuomintang and the concessions the Communist Party was ready to make in exchange for the formation of the National Defense Government were puzzling to a mind haunted by the bloody memory of Chiang Kai-shek's betrayal of the "revolution" in 1927. But nothing of the sort would ever happen again, Feng was assuring him. The mistakes committed by Ch'en Tu-hsiu in 1924–27 would not be repeated because of the strength of the party and the Red Army, and also because of the reassuring instances of "the genius-like triumphs scored by Mao in his revolutionary leadership." Talks of this kind must have gone on at great length, for Feng stayed in Lu Hsün's house for more than two weeks, and his presence there was noted by both Smedley and Hsiao Hung.[59] Lu Hsün must have thus received a few very useful lessons in high politics while he was entertaining his guest.

But whatever the powers of persuasion that Feng used to convince Lu Hsün, he himself could not avoid being involved in the strife in the lower echelons, the squabbles and jealousies among the writers themselves. When he left Shanghai at the end of 1933, the Leftist League, under the joint leadership of Ch'ü Ch'iu-po and Lu Hsün symbolizing the harmonious union of the Communists and the fellow travelers, had been in much better shape. True, some personal animosity had carried over from the 1928 debate between Lu Hsün and Mao Tun on one side and the Creation Society and the Sun Society on the other. In 1932, for instance, Lu Hsün's description of the Creation Society as a group of "wits plus vagabonds" [60] had incensed Kuo Mo-jo, who wrote the book *Ten Years of the Creation Society* as a reply.[61] Nevertheless, the League had been able to put up a

[58] Wang Yao, *Draft*, I, 178; Feng, *Reminiscences*, p. 144.

[59] Agnes Smedley, *Battle Hymn of China*, p. 133. Hsiao Hung, *Recollections*, pp. 9–10.

[60] "A Glimpse of Literature in Shanghai," in *Ch'üan-chi*, IV, 276–92.

[61] *Ch'uang-tsao shih-nien* (*Ten Years of the Creation Society*) (Shanghai: Kuang Hua Book Company, 1932).

show of solidarity, or at least there had been few incidents that Lu Hsün would consider signs of disunity. But now Feng returned to a different scene. He found Lu Hsün not at all happy when they met for the first time in more than two years. "With a melancholy air he took my hand which was held out enthusiastically. . . . The first words he said were, 'About what has happened in these two years, I'll talk to you later.' " [62]

What he had to say must have been largely about the neglect, the back-biting, and the wounds he had suffered, grievances he had been airing in his correspondence and perhaps other matters too delicate or complicated to be fairly treated in a letter. His complaints did not at first make a deep impression on the guest, who was too full of stories of his own about the Red areas, the Long March, and Mao Tse-tung's wonderful leadership to be a good listener. But one or two weeks after his arrival, when he had got over the excitement of seeing old friends and old places and had made contact with the underground organizations, he realized that "the literary circles in Shanghai were in an even greater complexity and confusion than they had been a few years before." One cause of all this he discovered to be "sectarianism."

> The sectarianisms held by various members of the League were intermingled with the sectarianisms held by the various progressive writers outside the League. That made a bad picture indeed, but in addition to that, the enemy, both from inside and from outside, was further applying the tactics of splitting and dividing. That resulted in the quarrels, disunity, and confusion among the revolutionary and progressive writers. [63]

The situation was all the more serious if we consider the difficulty of the task facing the representative from Yenan: to implement the policy of the united front and to help to reunify the writers. After the dissolution of the League, perhaps even before that, his comrades in Shanghai (e.g., Chou Yang and Hsia Yen) had been actively preparing for a new organization that would stand as a typical example of how a united front should be formed, how old differences could be buried, how the basis of formation could be widened, and how members old and new could work harmoniously and effectively under the slogan "National Defense Literature"—the counterpart in the literary sphere of "National Defense Government." [64] The

---

[62] Feng Hsüeh-feng, *Reminiscences,* pp. 144–45.

[63] *Ibid.,* p. 151.

[64] "The birth of the slogan [National Defense Literature] took place earlier than the North China crisis. The name was proposed two years ago in certain progressive periodicals but it did not then meet with wide response, owing no doubt to the politi-

success of their work would evidently depend upon the number of writers they could "unite," especially those whose names alone would lend an immense propaganda value to the new body. Here Feng's service might have been helpful. Although he could not have cured every writer of his sectarianism, he might have tried at least to win over Lu Hsün.

What he did in that regard is not on record; we have only seen how he himself was accused of sectarianism during the 1957 purge. Instead of working as a unifying influence, or even standing aloof from factious squabbles, he took a side—not the side of the party's underground workers but the side of Lu Hsün and Hu Feng. Had he come under Lu Hsün's influence as much as Lu Hsün had come under his? Was it that while the imagination of the one was stretching to the caves built in yellow-earth mounds in Shensi, and particularly to one of them in which sat the great leader Mao, pondering, planning, and beaming with confidence, the other was reconstructing in his mind the whipping, the back-stabbing, and sniping in Shanghai that inflicted so much pain on his friend who, in a sense, was also a leader? Since communications between Shanghai and Yenan were then difficult and since Lu Hsün stood very high in the opinion of the men at Yenan (his first instructions were to get in touch with the party workers through Lu Hsün),[65] Feng Hsüeh-feng was not far wrong when he used his discretion to support Lu Hsün when he had to take a side. But he would soon have ample reason to regret this choice.[66]

---

cal situation. After the North China crisis [became a national problem], two slogans were proposed by the progressive periodicals to speak for the anti-Japanese and National Salvation Literature. One was National Self-Defense Literature and the other, National Defense Literature. But since the formation of the united front and the rise of the National Salvation Movement, National Defense Literature has become, together with National Defense Music, National Defense Drama, National Defense Movies, one of the central slogans for workers in literature and arts." Hsü Mou-yung, "Facts Outside of Theory," in *Lun hsien-tsai wo-men-ti wen-hsüeh yün-tung (On Our Current Literary Movement)*, ed. Teng T'ai (Shanghai: Chang Chiang Book Company, 1936), p. 209.

[65] Feng, *Reminiscences,* p. 144. Lu Hsün had previously served as a relay station for the Communist Party. The Students' Union of Peiping after the December Ninth Movement also communicated with the Party Headquarters via Lu Hsün. See Tsou Lu-feng, "The Party's Dearest Friend in Battle," in *Recollections of the Great Lu Hsün,* pp. 168–174.

[66] After the outbreak of the Anti-Japanese War in 1937, Feng retired from politics and led the life of a recluse for a time in his native province of Chekiang. (Chou Yang, "A Great Debate on the Literary Front," *Wen-i pao,* No. 5, 1958.) This strange behavior, it seems to me, was caused by the probable fact that he had fallen out of favor. His mismanagement in Shanghai had perhaps been censured by the party.

Lu Hsün's mood and physical condition in early 1936 were described in a letter to Wang Yeh-ch'iu:

Some of the heroes here criticize me that I do not work. Actually I have never stopped writing and translating for a single day, so much so that I have almost deprived myself of the pleasure of living. I sometimes cannot but become really angry if, even so, I am to receive such irresponsible criticism. Sometimes I think that it would be better to stop working completely; if I were doing nothing, there would at least be nothing to blame me for. In the beginning of March I suddenly had attacks of asthma owing to fatigue and a cold. When I thought I was going to die, I felt peace. But after I received several injections from a doctor, the paroxysms gradually subsided. I was laid up for many days, but when I could sit up, I had to return to work, if only a little. Now I may be said to have recovered, but work still fatigues me. I am not sure whether I shall suffer from another attack.

I think that in our ———, too many people are supervising, but too few are really working. If everyone wants to become the "foreman," the task assigned to the common worker must be even heavier than usual. Now this Wing [the Left Wing] has been dissolved; another what-d'ye-call Association will take its place. I'll never join again. But the work that I have been doing regularly will, of course, continue as usual. [April 5, 1936.] [67]

Another letter addressed to the same man is dated May 4, 1936. He wrote this after he had had the long talks with Feng Hsüeh-feng. Whatever he thought of the general political situation was not discussed here, but he showed no sign of relenting toward the "heroes."

Every year I want to take a rest, but day after day I only see the piling up of official business, private affairs, and irritations. I cannot find time to rest, to read, or even to write a letter. I am completely recovered now, but still I feel weak—or not strong enough to handle all such sundry affairs. My memory is also failing. But the blows from the heroes continue to fall on me. These days they are busy about the Writers' Association, yelling the slogan National Defense Literature. I have taken warning from my past experience; so I do not join them. The heroes consider this a crime inimical to the national interest; they go so far as to denounce me in a public meeting. It is indeed time for me to retire; if I did nothing, I could at least be clear of the guilt of commission. But China is after all not their private property; I have every right to stay where I am. So I have packed a counterblow in two of my essays. But these people are no better than empty shells; probably they will soon become silent and vanish for good. Men like them we have seen before in plenty.[68]

[67] *Correspondence*, pp. 969–70. Wang Yeh-ch'iu is the author of the biography *Min-yüan-ch'ien-ti Lu Hsün hsien-sheng* (*Lu Hsün before 1912*) (Shanghai: O-Mei Publishing Company, 1947).

[68] *Correspondence*, p. 971. The letter to Yang Chi-yün (*Correspondence*, p. 710) revealed that he was considering taking a trip for a change of climate. Elsewhere in the *Correspondence*, he also discussed with friends the possibilities of travel, especially with Shen Ming-fu (possibly another name for Mao Tun). He wanted to revisit Japan, but he hesitated because his wife did not speak Japanese. Mu-kan-shan,

Lu Hsün's refusal to join the Writers' Association (a tentative name soon to be revised) marked his open rift with some of his former comrades. He had his reasons, and the reasons, as contained in his formal reply to the invitation, were considered by one of the "heroes," Hsü Mou-yung, to be "just." [69] That document has perhaps never been reprinted. The letter just quoted, however, also provides a clue to his skeptical attitude toward the Association formed by people of whose evil nature he had had a firsthand knowledge. He said that he had taken "warning from . . . past experience," and in another letter he showed how much he had learned. The letter was addressed to Shih Tai, probably a young writer seeking his advice on the new organization.

The Writers' Association has changed its name to the Association of Literature and Arts, and the founders are composed of various sorts. I do not think any of them has great selfish designs. Some want their names to be known, some others may want to have theirs cleaned of their stains [referring to the betrayers who now rejoined], still others may lend theirs just in good grace to save somebody's face. For it would constitute a serious crime to turn down a request, made in the name of the public interest, for the use of one's name as a founder of a worthy enterprise. I am the guilty one who has so declined. You know that most people in Shanghai are clever. If the use of their names is requested, they will oblige, for they know their signatures signify nothing: they are not thus bound to any duty.

I think you had better join. A young man with little worldly experience might be driven to insanity. But once you have joined, there won't be much trouble. What you'll have to do is only to support the so-called "directors" in attacking this or praising that. Tasks, more or less laborious, may fall on you, and there will be rumors for your ears. As to the serious works of National Defense Literature, there will be none. Their sole interest is in denouncing the crimes of those who are opposed to National Defense Literature. They will entangle themselves in such trifles, until they themselves become bored and the readers become bored too. And then their association will fold without having made any noise or leaving any trace. But if oppression comes from somewhere before they have lost interest in it, then the heroic directors will be the first to hide themselves or to declare that they have quit. The small members will be left to their own fate. [May 25, 1936.] [70]

---

in Chekiang, was close to Shanghai but it seemed to him too crowded and small. (*Correspondence,* pp. 1006–7.) There was also an invitation for him to visit Russia. See Mao Tun, *Chi-nien Lu Hsün hsien-sheng (In Memoriam, Mr. Lu Hsün),* quoted in Wang Shih-ching, *Lu Hsün chuan (Life of Lu Hsün)* (Shanghai: Hsin Chih Book Company, 1948), pp. 489–90.

The two essays referred to may possibly be "The Foreign Settlement in March" (dated April 16) and " 'The Pass' in 'Out of the Pass' " (dated April 30), *Ch'üan-chi,* VI, 516–26. But they pricked with barbs rather than were packed with power.

[69] Hsü Mou-yung, "Facts Outside of Theory," in *On Our Current Literary Movement,* p. 213.

[70] *Correspondence,* pp. 1001–2.

In predicting the future of the Association, he was drawing a caricature of the League in the past. The slogan had changed from proletarian literature to National Defense Literature, but in his opinion the same bunch of people, driven by the same base motives, would only continue to play the same old game. The name of Shih Tai is not found in the list of the members of the Association published in the *Chinese Literary Yearbook for 1936*. Possibly he did not join.

In reading the quotation above, I cannot help feeling what a fine satirical story Lu Hsün might have written about the cowardice, pettiness, and vainglory of the leftist writers as he knew them, qualities that characterized the intellectuals of modern Shanghai to no less a degree than the peasants and gentry in his native prefecture of Shaohsing. These characters would have gained profundity, as well as universality, if they had been held up as fictitious figures to ridicule and pity. But he was now too much involved in the bickerings and squabbles himself to keep a clear head about his own small world.

About the larger world, his vision was even more dimmed and warped by the revolutionary zeal that had kept burning in him after the period of *Hesitation,* or 1926, the year which, according to William Schultz,[71] marks the end of Lu Hsün's creative life. The world, cut and served and even predigested on the platter of Marxist theory, had become too simple to stimulate any deep thinking or to challenge his creative imagination. Never again would he, with his acceptance of the ready-made theory, be able to see the multiple sides of a situation or probe deeply into a crisis, personal or national. It seemed that the older he grew, the more shallow and gross his mind became. He dissipated his energy and complained of his heavy load of work.

In this final year of his life, he was busy with what he called his "regular work": the compilation of Ch'ü Ch'iu-po's works, the translation of Gogol's *Dead Souls,* the reprinting of woodcuts and engravings, and miscellaneous writings.[72] Not that these works are trifling, but they could

---

[71] William R. Schultz, "Lu Hsün, the Creative Years" (Ph.D. dissertation, University of Washington, Seattle).

[72] Ch'ü was executed in Fukien on June 18, 1935 (Liu Shou-sung, *First Draft,* I, 285). Lu Hsün's compilation of Ch'ü's works began in October, 1935. They came out in two volumes under the title *Hai-shang Shu-lin.* Lu Hsün as usual took meticulous care with proofreading, printing, binding, cover design, and so forth. He, together with some friends, used their own money to make the publication possible.

Dead Souls, Part 1, was translated in 1935. He did three chapters of Part 2 in

have been done as well by men of lesser genius. It was a loss to Lu Hsün himself and to Chinese literature that his inspiration should have withered so soon. Although he maintained his control of the language in the form-lessness, brevity, and extemporaneousness of the genre called the *tsa-kan* (*feuilleton* was Ch'ü Ch'iu-po's translation of the term),[73] his irony could never convey such richness and profundity of meaning as is found in the earlier works, since his view of the meaning of life had already become simplified according to the formula in which he believed. His personal ex-periences with the so-called revolutionary writers, so madly exasperating but so comically incongruous with his ideals and beliefs, might have reopened his eyes. But they did not; they only sent him down to a blind fury and meaningless despair until his death.

The dissolution of the Leftist League was a crisis, the last one, alas, in his life. Not only had he to redefine his own position, but Marxism, the sustenance of his spiritual life for so many years, was at stake. To meet this crisis, he displayed neither perception nor subtlety of mind nor self-criticism, but only a narrowness and a stubbornness that stood for him as moral strength. He knew what to avoid. He was unable to cooperate with, or work under, the mock "heroes" for the emotional reasons that we have seen. But there was a positive step he had to take.

He would not give up the fight for the ideals summarized in the "Theo-retical Principles of the Leftist League." The Association of Literature and Arts to him was not "an organization meant for battle," [74] and its slogan National Defense Literature was vague and subject to misinterpretation.[75] He was therefore working out a substitute slogan which would not suggest the termination of leftist literature but rather an extension of it, and which would incorporate the new policy of the Communist Party into the tradition of the proletariat. The slogan he decided upon, after consulting

---

1936 (February to May). Then work was suspended owing to illness. In October he believed he was recovered enough to do the editing of the manuscripts. They were published, after revision, in the *I Wen*. (*Ch'üan-chi*, XX, 606.) In 1936 he also translated several short stories by Chekhov. He edited two art books in 1936: (1) *A Selection of Käthe Kollwitz's Engravings* (private publication by Lu Hsün under the name of San Hsien Book Company), and (2) *A Selection of Soviet Engravings* (Liang Yu Book Company).

[73] "Lu Hsün's *tsa-kan* is indeed a kind of social criticism—the *feuilleton* for battle." Ch'ü Ch'iu-po (ed.), Editor's Preface, *An Anthology of Lu Hsün's Tsa-kan* (first printed, Shanghai, 1933; reprinted, Shanghai Publishing Company, 1950), p. 2.

[74] Feng, *Reminiscences,* p. 157.

[75] See the subsequent paragraphs in the text dealing with Lu Hsün's "Talks to an Interviewer" and his "Reply" to Hsü Mou-yung.

Mao Tun and others, was "Mass Literature of National Revolutionary War." [76] The problem that had troubled him, and perhaps some of his friends too, was solved at last: he knew how much he would concede to the new demands of the party; he found how he could remain a leftist without doing harm to the united front. Since his leadership was still something to be reckoned with, he could at least do something to offset the influence of the "heroes," who apparently had only their own self-interest in mind when supporting National Defense Literature.

He did not foresee that instead of showing the right direction to the writers, the new slogan would only add to the general confusion; that if, as he predicted, there could be no serious works of National Defense Literature, the chances were no better for the production of serious works in the line of Mass Literature of National Revolutionary War when the writers of both camps came to be locked in a "sectarianistic fight." Neither could he foresee that some of his friends, and also, ironically, the enemy who took the most terrible beating from him, would be dragged to a tribunal in Peking some twenty years later to be judged anew for, among other things, what they did or said during the contention between the two slogans in 1936.

In his letter to Wang Yeh-ch'iu just quoted, he said he was apprehensive of another attack of asthma. On May 15 he was ill again. [77] Then in the month of June his condition became much worse. There was no entry in his journal after the fifth. On June 30 he wrote down a summary of his physical condition for the remainder of the month and noted that he might have died. For an invalid so badly in need of rest, June was unfortunately a very busy month. A great debate was touched off by Hu Feng's article "What Do the Masses Demand of Literature?" (and the answer was Mass Literature of National Revolutionary War). [78] He was immediately engaged by the champions of National Defense Literature, Chou Yang and Hsü Mou-yung. And thus started the Battle of Two Slogans. Since so

---

[76] "A Letter in Reply to Hsü Mou-yung and on the Anti-Japanese United Front," *Ch'üan-chi,* VI, 538.

[77] "May 15—Again Fell Ill." *Lu Hsün hsien-sheng nien-p'u (A Chronological Outline of Lu Hsün's Life), Ch'üan-chi,* XX, 633. In the *Diary* he noted that under that date the Japanese doctor diagnosed his disease to be in the stomach. So it seems he was worn out by a variety of diseases—asthma, stomach trouble, pleurisy, and pulmonary tuberculosis.

[78] Hu Feng wrote this upon the request of Lu Hsün. See Lu Hsün's "Reply" to Hsü Mou-yung, cited in note 76. Lu Hsün said that the idea did not belong to him alone either.

many people participated in the debate, including Mao Tun (supporting Lu Hsün) and Kuo Mo-jo (supporting National Defense Literature), it is impossible to do them all justice within the scope of an essay primarily concerned with Lu Hsün.[79] But not all the participants were good debaters: issues were confused, arguments mixed with personalities, statements repeated rather than developed, and the charge of sectarianism was bandied back and forth between the two camps.

The main arguments, so far as I can see, may be boiled down to these points:

(1) *Against Mass Literature of National Revolutionary War:* (a) It was a malicious attempt to supplant a slogan that already had a wide circulation. The suspicion was confirmed by the fact that Hu Feng did not even mention the term National Defense Literature in his article; (b) It was "leftist," and had an alarming effect on the non-leftist writers who would thus hesitate to join the united front. (2) *Against National Defense Literature:* (a) It was vague and subject to misinterpretation; (b) It neglected the proletariat; (c) After Chou Yang had made the following definitions of National Defense Literature: "The theme of National Defense must be the most central subject matter of the productions of every writer but the nation's traitors" and "The creation of National Defense Literature must

---

[79] The sources I used were: Li Ho-lin, *Chin erh-shih-nien Chung-kuo wen-i szu-ch'ao lun* (*Chinese Literary Thought of the Last Twenty Years*) (3rd ed.; Chungking: Sheng Huo Book Company, 1946); Teng T'ai (ed.), *On Our Current Literary Movement,* written by Lu Hsün *et al.* (note 64); the *Chinese Literary Yearbook for 1936* —useful for tracing the periodicals published in that year, but it does not give the dates for the Association of Literature and Arts or the *Chung-kou wen-i kung-tso-che hsüan-yen* (*Manifesto of Chinese Literary Workers*). Hu Feng's article "What Do the Masses Demand of Literature?" can be found in any of the three. We see from *Correspondence,* pp. 1001–2, that the Association had been in existence on May 25. According to Liu Shou-sung (*First Draft,* I, 233) it was formally inaugurated on June 7 as the base of those who advocated National Defense Literature. A Declaration was issued. The *Manifesto of Chinese Literary Workers* was probably published also in June, said to be "immediately after" the inauguration of the Association. (Wang Yao, *Draft,* I, 181.) Sixty-seven "literary workers" signed, and the list was headed by Lu Hsün. They, however, did not form into an organization.

It is interesting to compare the two documents (the Declaration of the Association and the *Manifesto*). The Declaration, speaking for a current policy (National Defense Literature), stressed the new situation. The phrase "ever since last December" appeared three times. But the *Manifesto,* speaking for the principle, stressed the tradition of the revolution. It said that foreign aggression did not begin only yesterday and that the signatories did not discover only today the importance of fighting for the freedom of the nation. These two documents, it seems to me, summarized the two attitudes.

be done by adopting the method of progressive realism," [80] he was accused by Lu Hsün, Mao Tun, and Feng Hsüeh-feng of being dictatorial and shutting the door of the united front upon those who might not conform to either the subject matter or the method as assigned, but who might still remain good, honest Chinese writers.

Such arguments were brought forth in a much more dramatic manner in the letters exchanged between Hsü Mou-yung and Lu Hsün, and the debate can be said to have closed with Lu Hsün's reply to Hsü.

Meanwhile, during his illness in the month of June, Lu Hsün, as the champion of the new slogan, could not remain silent. He was too ill to write, but he still could publish what he dictated. The policy he advocated, or the justification for Mass Literature of National Revolutionary War, as explained in the three articles published in that period, amounted to an eclecticism of Trotskyism and the current line of the Communist Party. This was perhaps the only compromise he could make to satisfy the demands of Mao Tse-tung and Stalin without sacrificing the principle of class struggle. The united front he recognized to be necessary, since Japanese aggression was the primary concern of the Chinese people. But struggle on the home front should never be allowed to relax. He openly rebuffed the Trotskyite policy of proletarian revolution as against the national interest.[81] But while the Trotskyites failed to realize that "the nationalist standing was the true standing for the [proletarian] class," some of his own comrades displayed an "equal stolidity" by losing their identity in the united

[80] These statements appeared in Chou Yang's article "On National Defense Literature," in Teng T'ai (ed.), *On Our Current Literary Movement,* p. 189. Chou Yang was refuting Hsü Hsing's ultra-leftist theory, which consisted of a complete denial of the united front. Hsü Hsing took an attitude independent of the two groups, though his first article also appeared in May. He was entirely for the proletariat, and called patriotism a "cesspool," which occasioned Kuo Mo-jo's article "National Defense—Cesspool—Purgatory." See Li Ho-lin, *Chinese Literary Thought of the Last Twenty Years.*

"After the publication of Chou Yang's and Kuo Mo-jo's articles on liquidation of mechanism, Hsü Hsing never made any reply. Was it not that he admitted defeat?" Li Ho-lin, *op. cit.,* p. 463. But Cheng Hsüeh-chia suggested that the man was possibly silenced by assassination (Cheng, *op. cit.,* p. 96). Hsü Mou-yung wrote in his letter to Lu Hsün about the difficulty of "dealing with them effectively" ("them" referring to Hu Feng and others), and Lu Hsün retorted in his "Open Reply," "And what is the meaning of 'dealing effectively'? To exile them, or to behead them?" *Ch'üan-chi,* VI, 545. Since Hsü Mou-yung did not give an explanation, I, too, am puzzled by the phrase "dealing effectively."

[81] "A Letter in Reply to the Trotskyites," dictation taken by O. V. (Feng Hsüeh-feng), *Ch'üan-chi,* VI, 584–88.

front and abandoning the leading position due the proletariat in the National Revolutionary War. The "bloody battles" against fascism, against reactionaries of all sorts, should never be discontinued under the new slogan, which only meant that all these battles were now merged into the main current of the fight against the Japanese and the nation's traitors.[82] Any slight neglect of this strategic principle might cause the total loss of the fight itself.[83]

Perhaps naïve is the word for these views, so painfully thought out and so painfully enunciated. Only an impractical fellow traveler like Lu Hsün, full of good intentions, could be troubled by the fear that a true Communist might ever abandon his principles, though the slogan he used might indicate that he had.

In the year 1936, when much would depend upon the nation's acceptance of the Communist Party as a patriotic organization, with no ill feelings against any other Chinese but the traitors, Lu Hsün's openly declared loyalty to the revolutionary principles, though it had once been a help, was now embarrassing. War cries should of course still be made, but not for "bloody battles against reactionaries of all sorts." By insisting upon his own line, Lu Hsün was simply undoing what the underground Communists in Shanghai had been diligently building up. To ignore a man of such eminence would have been impossible; to denounce him in the public press would have been tantamount to an open admission of the failure of the united front. But something had to be done. Perhaps this man could still be saved if he were properly remonstrated with. And remonstrance might better come in the form of a friendly letter.

I do not know for sure whether the man who wrote the letter, Hsü Mou-yung, was at that time a member of the Communist Party.[84] Any-

---

[82] "On Our Current Literary Movement, Talks to an Interviewer during My Illness," dictation taken by O. V., *ibid.*, pp. 589–91.

[83] "On Several Important Problems," an interview with the reporter from the *Chiu-wang ch'ing-pao (National Salvation Bulletin)*, in *Supplement to Lu Hsün's Ch'üan-chi*, ed. T'ang T'ao (2d ed.; Shanghai Publishing Company, 1948).

[84] Hsü Mou-yung is said to have already been a member of the Communist Party when he was in Shanghai. Chang Ta-chün (ed.), *Chung-kung jen-ming tien (Who's Who in Communist China)* (Hong Kong: Liberty Publishing Corporation, 1956). Ts'ao Chü-jen, a close associate of Hsü in Shanghai, thus describes their relationship: "At that time [when Hsü wrote the letter to Lu Hsün], Hsü and I were living under the same roof. There was nothing to hide between us—but of course, he would not talk about the secrets of the party." *A Critical Biography of Lu Hsün*, I, 140. It suggests that Hsü belonged to a "party," if not the Communist Party. But according to one Communist publication (*Wen-i pao*, No. 35, Dec. 8, 1957),

how, he was then very close to the group of writers represented by Chou Yang, and his letter, as we shall see, did speak for "the majority." He was the right person to do the job because of his intimacy with Lu Hsün. At the time Lu Hsün wrote the preface to a collection of Hsü's essays, *Ta-tsa-chi* (March, 1935), and praised their "pertinence to the current situation," their "liveliness and force," and their "beneficial effects" on the mores and morals of China, Hsü had Lu Hsün's high regard and friendship no less than Hu Feng or Huang Yüan, editor of the magazine *I Wen* (*Translations*).[85] Pa Chin (the novelist) had never attained such an intimate relationship with Lu Hsün.[86] Forty-three letters addressed to Hsü, dating from November 15, 1933, to February 21, 1936, were collected in Lu Hsün's *Correspondence,* and his name appeared very often in the *Diary* for that period too.[87]

It was apparently on the strength of this friendship that Hsü took the liberty of writing the letter of admonition. And in it, he was mindful that he was writing to an elder. The polite form "sir" rather than the pronoun "you" was used throughout the letter. (It is impossible to render this polite style into English.) He was not ironic, either. His explanation of the "basic policy" and his warning against the evil company of Hu Feng and

---

Hsü, although a member of the Leftist League in Shanghai, did not join the Communist Party until he went to Yenan. I have observed one significant fact that may suggest that Hsü was not a party member in 1936. Hsü's name is found in the membership list of the Association of Literature and Arts in the *Chinese Literary Yearbook for 1936,* p. 228, but not the names of Chou Yang (or Chou Ch'i-ying), T'ien Han, Hsia Yen (or Shen Tuan-hsien), P'an Han-nien, or any known Communist. Perhaps it was the party's policy that in order to give the Association a "harmless" look, the members of the party should operate behind the scenes. Hsü, as an active fellow traveler, was available as a cat's-paw.

[85] "Preface to Hsü Mou-yung's *Ta-tsa-chi,*" *Ch'üan-chi,* VI, 289–93. Lu Hsün also helped in editing. *Ch'üan-chi,* XX, 639. Huang Yüan's own account of the publication of the *I Wen* is reported in Wang Shih-ching, *Life of Lu Hsün,* pp. 448–53. Lu Hsün edited the first three issues (Sept.–Nov., 1934) and was responsible for its success.

[86] Pa Chin was a known anarchist; his pseudonym was a composite of Bakunin and Kropotkin. He himself said that he had seen Lu Hsün only about a dozen times. "Mr. Lu Hsün as I Knew Him," in *Recollections of the Great Lu Hsün,* pp. 107–11. His name appeared only a few times in Lu Hsün's *Diary.* As to his life in mainland China after 1949, see the article, written by Chao Ts'ung, "Pa Chin Destined for the Trials in Purgatory," *The China Weekly* (Hong Kong), Vol. XXIV, No. 7 (Nov. 17, 1958).

[87] Some letters are apparently left out. On March 27, 1936, Lu Hsün noted in his *Diary* that a letter was received from Hsü Mou-yung, and he immediately replied. On May 5 and June 3 he again noted letters from Hsü, but probably they were not answered. If those letters were available, we could have a fuller knowledge of the circumstances that led to the quarrel in August.

others, though blunt, sounded sincere. It was perhaps his hope that Lu Hsün could be finally won over to the united front, as he and his colleagues understood it, after everything was clarified. While his pen was dripping with venom when he came to attack Hu Feng and others, he displayed no ill feelings against Lu Hsün personally. Apparently he did not mean the letter to be provocative; he did not expect it to be a firebrand bringing upon his own head a torrent of abuses from an unforgiving, wrathful man.

The opening paragraph began thus:

Have you fully recovered from your indisposition? Your health, sir, is certainly a cause of anxiety to me. But it often saddens me, too, to think how much I have missed your guidance and instructions because of the unhappy state of affairs existing among the writers since you were afflicted with illness.

His explanation of the literary situation suffering under "the vicious tendencies" formed the main body of the letter:

I cannot at present get rid of the feeling that your views and actions of the recent six months are unwittingly strengthening the vicious tendencies. Before you have studied carefully the characters of certain men, such as Hu Feng with his treachery or Huang Yüan with his flattery, you have allowed yourself to fall into their possession, to be used as their private property. They are availing themselves of you, sir, as an idol to delude the people. It is because of your name, sir, that the separatist movement, born of their ambitions, cannot be checked once it gets started. The behavior of men like Hu Feng is motivated apparently by nothing but self-interest and extreme sectarianism. Their theories are self-contradictory and full of mistakes. For instance, the slogan "Mass Literature of National Revolutionary War" was first proposed by Hu Feng to vie with "National Defense Literature." Then it was interpreted that one was primary, and the other was secondary. Then the first one was again defined as the slogan for the left-wing literature since the movement had evolved to a new stage. The interpretations are marked by such uncertainty and vagueness that even you, sir, cannot give them full justification. It would not be difficult to belabor them for what they have said or done, but, alas, they are protected behind your name as a shield. Is there anyone among us who does not love you, sir? Hence the great difficulty in dealing with them effectively or engaging them in debate.

Your considerations, sir, I believe I understand quite well. For fear lest the left-wing comrades-in-arms should relinquish their original standing after joining the united front, you have shown preference for men like Hu Feng who seem to you so attractive for their leftism. But I ask leave to remind you, sir, that you seem to be unacquainted with the current basic policy. The present united front—whether in China or all the world over—is of course formed with the proletariat as its main force; but the proletariat owes its dominance not to its name, nor to its special position or history, but to its correct handling of the reality and its great fighting strength. Therefore, in its objective existence, the proletariat is the main force, but in its relation to itself, the proletariat should not wear a distinct badge and thus scare off the comrades of the other classes. It should demand leadership not simply because it is the proletariat but rather on account of the work it is ready to perform. To introduce a left-wing slogan into the united front under the present circumstances is, therefore, a mistake and harmful to the cause. The statements in your recently published *To an Interviewer during My Illness* that "Mass Literature of National Revolutionary War" is a new development of proletarian literature and that this slogan should become the main slogan for the united front, are both mistaken.

Furthermore, the "comrades" who have joined the Association of Literature and Arts are not every one of them as rightist or decadent as you may suspect and fear. Cannot they individually stand comparison with Pa Chin and Huang Yüan? And you have allowed them to be collected around you and numbered as your "comrades." From what I have read in the newspapers, the anarchists in France and Spain are no less reactionary and bent on disrupting the united front than the Trotskyites. The anarchists in China play an even worse game with their meanness. As for Huang Yüan, the man is a clod completely devoid of intellect, a parasite who manages to make a living by fawning on celebrities. The obsequious looks he wore in the days when he was running around at the doors of Fu and Cheng were not different from today, when he is all respect and love toward you.[88] That you should choose, sir, to keep their company, but think it beneath you to associate with the majority puzzles me indeed.

The letter was dated August 1. The entry under August 2 in Lu Hsün's *Diary* contained this dispassionate little phrase, "Received a letter from Hsü Mou-yung." Then under August 5, he noted, "Tonight, finished the reply to Hsü Mou-yung." The reply was published in the August issue of the *Writers Monthly* and Hsü's letter was also reprinted.[89] The effect was stunning, for Lu Hsün had never been so overpowered with passion.

The reply was very long (about six thousand characters).[90] His tone was anger undisguised, unrestrained, almost shrill anger. There were few signs of his usual cleverness, wit, and understatement, no attempt to turn out learned allusions, no trace of the tongue-in-cheek slyness that distinguishes so many of his best satirical writings. For Lu Hsün's intention in this instance was certainly not satire. The reader will look in vain for the subtle

[88] Fu was probably Fu Tung-hua (1895–   ), translator of Homer, Aristotle, Dante, Cervantes, and also Kathleen Winsor and Margaret Mitchell. He was editor of the influential magazine *Wen-hsüeh* (Sheng Huo Book Company) where many of the best works of the period were published. Cheng was probably Cheng Chen-to (1897–1958), literary historian. As editor of *Wen-hsüeh chi-k'an* (*The Literary Quarterly*) (Peiping, 1934) and then *Shih-chieh wen-k'u* (*World Classics*) (Shanghai, 1935) he was also an influential literary figure at that time.

[89] *Writers Monthly,* Vol. I, No. 5. The monthly was edited by Meng Shih-huan; but according to *Literature in China* (by Y. H. Su, P.O. Box 5271, Hong Kong, 1959) its co-publishers were Hu Feng and Feng Hsüeh-feng. The magazine first appeared in April. It was suppressed after eight issues.

[90] Kuo Mo-jo called it a "ten-thousand-character-letter," but according to my count, it runs to about six thousand characters. See Kuo's "An Inspection of the Military Exercise."

touch of the surgeon's scalpel. In the long article he no longer killed with the flashing thrust of a dagger or a spear, by which he had once disposed of the enemy at one stroke and with apparently little effort.[91] It can be said that many of his essays and some of his stories were motivated by anger at personal affront or social injustice. But it had been an anger so inseparable from sardonic humor and expressed with such economy that it appeared that his temper, though fearful, was well under control; that his delight in the art of killing, his pleasure in dealing a swift, neat, telling blow could get the upper hand of his passion; and that his hatred could be deepened by art or couched in a style that was forbiddingly cool. But in this open letter words rushed out, and he sustained himself in the heat of anger for several pages—a rare feat for the master of brevity. None of his enemies, Ch'en Yüan, Liang Shih-ch'iu, or others, had received, in one treatment, such a liberal amount of verbal lashings. On no other occasion had he allowed his wrath to run on in such a terrible eloquence. His protests had been much shorter against, for instance, the massacre of students in Peking on March 18, 1926, or against the secret execution of the five leftist writers in Shanghai in 1931.[92] The latter incident called forth a poem in the old style, with the memorable couplet which is typical of the way he dealt with his passions:

> Restraining myself, I watch my friends turning to new ghosts;
> Anger drives me to seek little poems in the bayonet grove.[93]

"Little poems" were what he sought to celebrate the martyrs or to condemn the Kuomintang government, and he knew how to restrain himself. Was Hsü Mou-yung, the cause of this heated diatribe, a more hateful person to Lu Hsün than all his enemies who had, in one way or another, irritated his sensitive nerves or aroused his indignation? Ambitious, narrow and muddleheaded the young man might be, but he was after all a fellow leftist writer and once a personal friend. But Lu Hsün did not treat him merely as an offending individual but rather as the representative of a group.

[91] Lu Hsün said in "The Crisis of the Essay" that the kind of essay that met the demands of the time should be like a dagger or a spear. *Ch'üan-chi*, V, 170.

[92] See the essays he wrote after March 18, 1926. *Ch'üan-chi*, III, 247 ff.; and "Proletarian Revolutionary Literature in China and the Blood of the Pioneers," *Ch'üan-chi*, IV, 267–69.

[93] Written in 1931, the text was found in the *Diary* under July 11, 1932. (He noted that it was a poem written a year ago.) Hsü Shou-ch'ang said the poem as he knew it had "tao-pien" instead of "tao-ts'ung." *Wang-yu Lu Hsün yin-hsiang chi (Impressions of My Deceased Friend, Lu Hsün)* (Shanghai: O-Mei Publishing Company, 1947, p. 81; reprinted by People's Literary Publications Association, 1953).

His violent reaction came indeed as an outburst of his long-suppressed anger with those leftist writers who, though he would never admit it, perhaps ranked with the Japanese imperialists, the Kuomintang or non-Kuomintang reactionaries, and the turncoats as his worst enemies. The first three were, in a certain sense, completely at his mercy. He could draw his pen against them whenever he liked. But how often he must have regretted that with all his polemic genius and his proficiency in the vitriolic style, he could never have a chance to come into the open with those people, heroes or cowards or whatever they might be called. Of course he had had his scruples which had restrained him.

Now Hsü Mou-yung's letter came at a time when perhaps his self-control had deteriorated along with his physical condition, and he had become even more irritable and suspicious than ever. When he composed this masterpiece of vituperation, he was living under the shadow of death. He suspected Hsü and his group of a baser motive. He had a feeling that the purpose of Hsü's provocation was to hasten him to death! On August 28, three weeks after he had written the "Open Reply," he explained in a letter to a worrying friend, Yang Chi-yün, why he had not been able to take the matter more lightly:

It is true that literary work does not agree with this disease of mine. This year I am well aware of my weak health, so I have written very little. I want to free myself from all obligations and to take a rest for a considerable period of time. Translations alone would be enough as a means of subsistence. But my health has not improved. And because I did not join the Association, the "immortals" have formed themselves into a battle array and are closing in upon me. Hsü Mou-yung was the first to come to my door and to bravely give his challenge, though he knows quite well that only a little time ago I was critically ill and almost died.

His change is not surprising. A little while ago, he was himself running against "nails," [94] so he felt that my personality was "good." Now he is a director of the Association of Literature and Arts and editor of the *Wen-hsüeh-chieh*,[95] so he has the power to "deal effectively." He is not only holding

[94] "Running against nails"—literal translation of *p'eng-ting-tzu*. There was a time when Hsü was under attack and he was hard put to defend himself. Lu Hsün advised him, on June 21, 1934, to take the criticisms lightly: "From what I have read of your recent writings (e.g., the article in the *Jen-chien-shih* [*Human World*]), you are fighting a defensive war. You'll suffer much from it. It seems to me you should completely ignore the criticisms but do your own reading and writing. . . . If more criticisms should come forth and you have to answer all of them, then your life would be spent in vain. You would do neither yourself nor the community any good." *Correspondence,* p. 610.

[95] *Wen-hsüeh-chieh* (*The Literary World,* a monthly), first issue June, suspended after four issues. The organ of National Defense Literature, it was nominally under the editorship of Chou Yüan—"a collective pseudonym" (*1936 Yearbook,* p. 5).

the nails in his own hand now, but the nails may turn out to be the nails of somebody's coffin. As "one's position affects the air, and nourishment transforms one's body," so it is not surprising that he now finds me "mistaken," "ridiculous," "promoting the vicious tendencies," and "as an idol."

To tell you the truth, though the letter is signed by one man, he is representing a group. If you read it carefully and study its style, you can see that. That's why I deem it necessary to write an open reply. If this affair were only a private matter having no relevance to the general situation but concerning only two of us, why should I have taken so much trouble to speak out in a magazine? You think that it was only "a waste of energy," but that's not true, sir. The beam of light I have shed may reveal the ugly faces of all the goblins gathered under the standard. . . .

P.S. The doctor forbids me to see interviewers or talk too much. If I get a little better, I may take a rest out of town. . . .[96]

The three opening paragraphs of the "Open Reply" will suffice to demonstrate the fiery style so rare in Lu Hsün (if I have not lost too much in the translation):

The above is a letter from Hsü Mou-yung which I am publishing in these pages without his consent. The publication of such a letter, containing nothing but lectures to myself and strictures on others, will not be detrimental to his dignity. It is probably a work which he expects me to publish. But it goes without saying that the reader will thus find that the writer himself is a rather "vicious" youth.

I'll make a plea, however, and hope that none of the three, Messrs. Pa Chin, Huang Yüan, and Hu Feng, will follow Hsü's example. They would only fall into a trap if they, minding what is written about them, should return tit for tat. Cannot we identify Hsü and his like with the people who, at this time of national peril, vaunt lofty ideals and high-sounding principles in daytime but, in the darkness, are occupied in splitting, dividing, and instigating disunity and dissension? There is a plan behind the letter: it is their new challenge to those who have stayed aside from the Association of Literature and Arts. If you accept the challenge, you will be accused of "disrupting the united front." You will be stigmatized as traitors. But we shall not. The points of our pens shall not be turned against a certain few individuals. We are not those who place "pacification at home" above "resistance against aggression." [97] That is simply not our policy.

But I have here a few remarks to make. First, my attitude toward the anti-Japanese united front. On several occasions I have already clarified my position. But it seems that Hsü and his like simply refuse to look at the printed word. Instead, they hold on with sheer persistence to where their teeth are planted in my flesh. Perversely they stick to the charge that I am "disrupting" the united front, and keep on admonishing me, on the ground that I do not

[96] *Correspondence*, p. 710. About his plans of travel, see note 68.

[97] A satirical allusion to Chiang Kai-shek's policy of first exterminating the Communists before launching an all-out resistance against Japanese aggression. *Tsung-ts'ai yen-lun* (*The Speeches of the Director-General*) (4 vols.; Chungking: China Cultural Service, 1939), IV, 82.

"understand the current basic policy." I cannot see what basic policy men like
Hsü Mou-yung can possibly possess. (Isn't it their fundamental policy simply to
bite at me?) But I have seen the anti-Japanese policy of the united front advocated by the revolutionary party in China at present, and I have been giving
it my full support. Unconditionally I have joined that front. The reason is
that I am not only a writer but also a Chinese. The policy to me is perfectly
right. Even after I have joined, the weapon I am to wield is of course still the
pen, and the tasks I have assigned myself are still writing and translation.
When the time comes that the pen will give way to weapons of other kinds,
I don't think I shall be in any way inferior to people like Hsü in the plying of
them!

Then he goes on to defend his attitude toward the united front in the
literary circles, his relation with the slogan "Mass Literature of National
Revolutionary War," his personal life, and his relations with Hu Feng, Pa
Chin, and Huang Yüan.

He said he was absolutely in favor of the unity under an "anti-Japanese
slogan" of all Chinese writers, irrespective of their creeds and schools. As
regards the formation of such a unified body, he had offered his opinion,
but "naturally" his opinion was only to be suppressed by the so-called directors. (That episode calls to the reader's mind Feng Hsüeh-feng's remarks about the dissolution of the Leftist League.) It was because of this
that he did not become a member of the Association of Literature and Arts.
For he was suspicious. He wanted to wait and see, to watch what the "directors" and young men like Hsü were "up to" before he would commit
himself. Experience had warned him that those who wore the looks of revolutionaries but fell readily to the practice of name-calling, throwing about
the charges of "treachery," "anti-revolution," "Trotskyism," and even "high
treason," were mostly unreliable. They were only weakening the strength of
revolution or using the revolution to seek their selfish interest. He indicated
that he was not himself above "smelling a rat" in his own camp. "To be
frank," he said, "I have sometimes even suspected that the name-callers
are themselves spies of the enemy." Anyhow, to avoid them was to avoid
a group which, if not actually dangerous, would simply do no good. It
would be better not to "obey their command." The truth about them, he
believed, would be only revealed by facts in the future.

About the Association of Literature and Arts, he said, "Don't think that
the united front has already been accomplished with the formation of that
Association. Far from it. It has not yet included writers of every school.
The reason for the failure is that the Association is still marked with a
strong tendency to sectarianism and the features of a guild or a gang. . . .
On the theoretical side, the articles on 'unity' and 'national defense litera-

ture' in the first issue of the *Wen-hsüeh-chieh* are basically sectarianistic."

Here the blow was directed against Chou Yang, though the name was not given. "There was an author who in explaining National Defense Literature said that a correct method was a prerequisite for the creation of National Defense Literature and again that if literature today was not for National Defense, it must be Literature of the Traitors. Before he unites the writers under his slogan, the man has prepared a term Literature of the Traitors, to be used against those whom he will some day censure. A splendid piece of sectarianism indeed!" Though Chou Yang, whose words we have seen above, was not so explicit about his authoritarianism, perhaps the intention was there. For the Communist criterion of criticism is only a choice between two extremes: either revolutionary or reactionary, proletarian or bourgeois, materialist or idealist, National Defense or "Traitors." To allow for a literature standing above or beyond the dichotomy is inconceivable to the party theoreticians. The Debate over the Two Slogans at least revealed one significant fact, that Lu Hsün, Mao Tun, and also, what is exceptional for a Communist, Feng Hsüeh-feng, all attacked Chou Yang and fought for a greater freedom of creation. Lu Hsün's words should have a special significance today if we substitute "literature of the workers, peasants, and soldiers" (orthodox party line since Mao Tse-tung's *Talks at the Yenan Forum* in 1942) for "National Defense Literature," and "bourgeois literature" for "Literature of the Traitors." He said, "National Defense Literature is not co-extensive with literature. For outside of National Defense Literature and Literature of the Traitors, there is a literature which is neither the one nor the other."

As to the slogan advanced by Hu Feng, Lu Hsün said that the idea was not Hu's. Surely he had written the paper that started the controversy, but he wrote it upon the request of Lu Hsün. It was not Lu Hsün's innovation. The slogan was a conclusion reached after a conference with several people, Mr. Mao Tun being one. Kuo Mo-jo was not consulted because communication with him was so difficult. He was in Japan and under police surveillance. "The only regrettable fact was that our consultation did not extend to Hsü Mou-yung and his like," remarked Lu Hsün sarcastically. The new slogan was necessary, for it was to supplement the thought content of the rather obscure term National Defense Literature and to correct certain erroneous ideas that had been injected into the old one. But he never regarded the two slogans as in opposition to each other. Here again he expressed his distaste for "monopoly" in literature: "I believe that any contribution to the strength of the anti-Japanese battle front should be welcome, that free expression of new literary ideas should be permitted, and that there is nothing reprehensible in either innovation or difference of opinion." No doubt National Defense Literature preceded Mass Literature of National Revolutionary War, but precedence does not mean monopoly.

> But you have never registered your patent right with the Nanking Government or the "Soviet" Government. Now it seems that there are two houses of writers under two different signs. For this division, men like Hsü Mou-yung should be responsible. As can be seen from my "Talks to an Interviewer during My Illness," I personally have never acknowledged that there are two such opposing houses.

As to his personal life in the recent half year, he had printed, published, and translated something, and he had been ill for three months. He had signed a document.[98] But he had never visited "the cat-house or the joint," nor had he attended any meeting. Therefore, he retorted indignantly, "I really don't know how I have been able to strengthen any vicious tendencies or what vicious tendencies I have been strengthening. Is it that my illness is to be blamed? Unless they hate me because I have been ill but have refused to die, there is only one possible answer. I have been ill; therefore I have not been able to fight the vicious tendencies represented by men like Hsü Mou-yung." That seemed to him to be his only fault.

There was nothing seriously wrong to be found in his friends Hu Feng, Pa Chin, and Huang Yüan, either. Huang Yüan to him was a hard-working, serious translator; Pa Chin, though known as an anarchist, was a passionate writer with progressive ideas, one of the very few "really fine" writers. If they wished to join the united front (since they had signed the *Manifesto*), they were of course welcome. What "meanness" was indeed in them? About Hu Feng, he had more to say. Hu Feng was "tactless and blunt" and therefore made enemies easily. He was nervous and finical about details, he was apt to be overtheoretical, and he did not like to write in a popular style. "But he is a promising young man. He has never associated himself with any movement that is opposed to the anti-Japanese movement or the united front. Such a fact men like Hsü Mou-yung can never deny, with all their cunning and schemes." Lu Hsün also related an incident which should be of particular interest if read in the context of the Communist purges of 1955.

> One day last year I was invited to have a talk with a famous person. When I arrived, there also came an automobile. Out of the automobile briskly jumped four huskies: T'ien Han, Chou Ch'i-ying [Chou Yang], and two others. They

---

[98] Lu Hsün was here glossing over the main issue. His leading a group of writers to publish a *Manifesto* (see note 79) was the greatest blow to the Association. The left-wing front was then unmistakably divided.

were all dressed up in the Western fashion and looked very smart indeed. They said that they came on the special mission of giving me the information that Hu Feng was a traitor, an agent from the government. When I inquired about evidence, they said that they had learned it from Mu Mu-t'ien, a man who had already changed his side.[99] Was I not stunned at the fact that the words of a turncoat should have carried such weight within the Leftist League! After putting them through a catechism, I said: Your evidence is extremely weak; I simply cannot believe it! Then we parted company; none of us was pleased.[100]

Was "the famous person" the "field marshal" who was described in Lu Hsün's letter to Hu Feng as one who "kept himself indoors but ordered others about"? [101] Anyhow it is only surprising, after we have read this anecdote, that the official charges against Hu Feng as a traitor and agent should have been brought out as late as 1955.

Lu Hsün's long letter elicited a very feeble response from Hsü Mou-yung. Hsü no longer insisted on the accusations of "vicious tendencies," "treachery," and so forth. He seemed to have been dissatisfied with Hu Feng, Pa Chin, and Huang Yüan, principally because they had not replied to the invitations to join the Association.[102] After Lu Hsün's death, he sent a little gift, a couplet in his own handwriting to be hung at the funeral service. It read:

> Am I an enemy or a friend? I have only to ask myself.
> Did you forgive me or did you not? Alas, you cannot speak.[103]

This couplet was not put on display. After the outbreak of the war in 1937, Hsü went to Yenan with Chou Yang. While the latter became the Commissioner of Education for the Northern Shensi Special District, Hsü, ironi-

---

[99] Mu Mu-t'ien, a poet of the Creation Society (Wang Yao, *Draft,* I, 79–80). On July 30, 1934, Lu Hsün noted in the *Diary:* "Heard about the arrest of Mu-t'ien." On August 5, 1934, he wrote to Cheng Chen-to: "Mu Mu-t'ien was arrested; I don't know why." On January 8, 1935, he wrote to the same person: "Mr. Mu Mu-t'ien has also changed his side. He and three others have signed a report to the authorities, doing their best in their attempt to destroy the Left Wing. What a change from his former attitude." *Correspondence,* pp. 566–81.

[100] *Ch'üan-chi,* VI, 541.

[101] *Correspondence,* p. 944. That famous person could possibly be Mme. Sun Yat-sen.

[102] Hsü's reply was published in the *Chin-tai-wen-i* (a monthly), a "little-known" magazine, according to Li Ho-lin. The letter is quoted in an abbreviated form in Li Ho-lin, *op. cit.,* p. 530.

[103] The couplet is found in a little essay in Fan Ch'eng (ed.), *Lu Hsün hsien-sheng-ti kai-kuan lun-ting* (*The Final Judgment on Mr. Lu Hsün*) (Shanghai: All World Book Company, 1939), p. 38. In the same essay, Hsü did not show that he had changed his attitude. He said that Lu Hsün could have made mistakes, especially in choosing his friends. About the episode of his couplet not being hung up, see *op. cit.,* p. 182.

cally, taught at a school dedicated to Lu Hsün, the Lu Hsün Institute of Arts. In 1957, when so many of our old friends in this story fell as victims to the purges, Hsü did not have a better fate. He was also purged. One of the charges against him was:

> In 1936, when the party's organizations and the left-wing cultural bodies in Shanghai were in utter difficulty, Hsü Mou-yung, out of his own ill will, wrote a letter to attack Mr. Lu Hsün, to disrupt the relations between Lu Hsün and the party (and also the League). Then he refused to take the party's good advice, and continued his attack.[104]

If at that time he had again raised the question about whether he was forgiven, Lu Hsün perhaps would have answered in the Red Elysium, "Yes, you are."

A few more details about 1936. Lu Hsün's sheer force of eloquence silenced the debaters. It was compared to an "iron broomstick sweeping away all his babbling and chattering opponents." [105] Only Kuo Mo-jo in Japan, still defending National Defense Literature, made the remark, "Those friends who have read Lu Hsün's article, especially the younger ones, are all indignant. Many have manifested even greater pessimism than before and said that the situation had become more serious." [106] That mood of indignation and pessimism at the serious split of the leftist writers was perhaps also felt by Kuo's friends in Shanghai, though it was scarcely expressed.[107]

The composition of the long letter, and the passion that went into it, must have been quite an ordeal for an invalid like Lu Hsün, who had been snatched back only a month before from the brink of death. On August

[104] A report on Hsü's case is found in *Wen-i pao*, No. 35, Dec. 8, 1957. Besides Hu Feng and Feng Hsüeh-feng, these men also fell: Huang Yüan—charged with forming an "anti-party clique in Chekiang." *Ibid.*, No. 34, Dec. 1, 1957. Mu Mu-t'ien —"Twenty years ago that man was already a renegade from revolution. So Lu Hsün called him a turncoat." *Ibid.*, No. 37, Dec. 22, 1957. P'an Han-nien—I have mentioned his name only in note 84—was one of the active party workers in Shanghai in the thirties, having been one of the pioneers of proletarian literature (Creation Society) in the twenties. The post he occupied about that time in Shanghai was Secretary, Committee on Literary Works, Shanghai Special District, Chinese Communist Party. In 1955 he was purged with Hu Feng. *Ibid.*, Vol. XI, No. 4, July 25, 1955.
[105] Li Ho-lin, *op. cit.*, p. 474.
[106] *1936 Yearbook*, p. 315.
[107] An interesting episode is related in Cheng Hsüeh-chia's *True Story*, p. 112. When Lu Hsün's body was moved to the funeral service, handbills were passed in the street by the Communist workers, attacking the mistakes committed by the man before his death. Since Cheng did not say that it was an eye-witness account, the veracity of the episode has to be checked.

1, one day before he received Hsü's "challenge," he noted in his *Diary* that he weighed 38.7 kg. (85.8 lbs.) and that he was troubled with pleurisy. The next day after he finished the reply (August 7), two hundred grams of "water" (exudation) were extracted from his pleurae. Another week later (August 13), he noted that blood first appeared in his sputum. But he did not take much rest. On October 17 he caught a cold. On October 19 he died.

ASPECTS OF THE POWER
OF DARKNESS IN LU HSÜN

As the legend goes, the reign of Sui Yang-ti was a great heroic age. The heroes were destined to fight either on the side of or against the great emperor to come, T'ang T'ai-tsung. Before the fall of Sui, however, Sui Yang-ti summoned all the rebels to Yangchow for a tournament. The champion was to win the title of the Supreme Rebel, to whom would be accorded the honors due a king. The plot was to let the rebels kill each other with their own hands, and the survivors would then be killed by mines set off soon after the contest was over. If there were still some survivors left, a gate which weighed one thousand *chin* would be lowered into the city wall to block their retreat so that a massacre might be carried out by the imperial troops. But since Sui Yang-ti was to lose the mandate of heaven, his plot did not work. An insufficient number of rebels were killed in the arena, and the mines did not explode as planned, thanks to the happy intervention of an ancient fox who had to save the life of the true dragon, T'ang T'ai-tsung, among all the rebels. When the gate was lowered, it was caught by a Herculean bandit who supported it long enough to let the eighteen princes and the lesser rebels from all over China escape to safety. But the gate proved too great a burden even for such a giant, and he was crushed to death.[1]

The heroic episode of the bandit who supported the lowering gate had a special significance for Lu Hsün, who had loved this sort of legend as a child, long before he took a scholarly interest in the history of Chinese fiction. When he wrote the following passage in an essay in 1919, five months after the Fourth of May, I strongly suspect that he had this legend in mind:

Let the awakened man burden himself with the weight of tradition and shoulder up the gate of darkness. Let him give unimpeded passage to the chil-

---

[1] *Shuo T'ang (The T'ang Saga)*, chap. 41.

dren so that they may rush to the bright, wide-open spaces and lead happy lives henceforward as rational human beings.[2]

From these sentences alone, it may seem that the children are little innocents who need protection. But the allusion to the gate of darkness implies that the children and the burden-bearing giant have something in common: they are all rebels.

During the May Fourth period the Chinese language itself took on the melodramatic colorings of the battle between new and old. Conscious rebelliousness developed the rebels' prose, and Lu Hsün was one of its chief architects. He loathed the old and hailed the new with too much vehemence to allow his argument to be contained within an entirely rational framework. The power of his rhetoric has much to do with violent contrast between light and darkness, sleep and awakening, between the man who refuses to be eaten and the man who eats men, the human being and the ghost, the single fighter and the hostile forces around him, the contrast between everything the rebel identifies with and everything that oppresses and crushes him.

Allusion remains an important feature of this rhetoric. Although the decay of classical education was to make the allusive literary language (*wen-yen*) obsolete, any writer aware of the literary or cultural heritage he shares with his audience inevitably makes some use of allusion, the symbolic reference to a literary work or to a historical or legendary episode. Hu Shih, the first theorist of the *pai-hua* (vernacular) movement, spoke unfavorably of the use of allusions. But as a popular writer he often made felicitous references to episodes in popular fiction such as *Hsi-yu-chi* (*A Pilgrimage to the West*) and *San-hsia wu-i* (*Three Knights-Errant and Five Chivalrous Men*), or to well-known lines of T'ang poetry. Allusion certainly does not serve pedantry alone; from the hand of an artist it fuses memories with emotions and imagination, superimposes the ancient on the modern, and projects reality into a richer context of history, myth, and poetry. Lu Hsün is remarkable for his gift of bringing out fresh and vivid allusions to illustrate what an inexhaustible source of images China's long cultural tradition provides for the Chinese language.

In some kinds of literary images, therefore, the past lives in the present and the irrational threatens the rule of reason. To us, this should seem only natural; but it was a source of irritation to Lu Hsün, who was committed

---

[2] *What Is Required of Us As Fathers Today,* in *Lu Hsün ch'üan-chi* (*Complete Works*) (hereafter cited as *LH*) (Peking, 1957), I, 246.

to progress, to science, and to a denial of the backward, superstitious, cruel, and shameful old China. Poor old China seemed to own little else except its shame. He was irritated because as a pioneer of enlightenment he would have liked to be consistent in his logic, to practice earnestly what he preached. But as a literary artist he could not shake off the past. He admitted that for his style and diction, and even for his thought, he was very much under the influence of the old *wen-yen* books. But then he said:

I feel very unhappy about the ancient ghosts that I carry on my back. I cannot shake them off. So often do I feel a heavy weight that depresses me.[3]

Hence the image of the "gate of darkness" that the giant shouldered up.

His irritation found expression in his contempt for literary art. In 1925, he was approached by a newspaper to recommend a reading list for Chinese youth. Here is his answer:

I have never studied this problem; so I cannot answer.

But I want to take this opportunity to say something of my own experience for the benefit of the readers.

Whenever I read Chinese books, I feel that I quiet down, that I am being separated from life. When I read foreign books—Indian books excepted—I feel often a closer contact with life. I feel an urge to do something.

There are indeed Chinese books which speak for taking an active part in life, but that is only the optimism of a vampire. Foreign books may also inspire dejection and pessimism, but that is the dejection and pessimism of living human beings.

My advice is therefore not to read any Chinese books, or to read as few as you can. But read more foreign books.

If you do not read Chinese books, you will end up in being unable to write. But what modern youth needs is not to write, but to act. If you remain a living human being, it does not really matter if you cannot write.[4]

Although this is not among Lu Hsün's best pieces, the contrast here between the vampire and the living human is another instance of the rhetoric of melodrama, a malediction of the past which he wished to see buried and forgotten. According to Lu Hsün, the proof of a living human being is in his ability to act, but there is not much action in his own life to be remembered today. His fame rests on his literary works, of which, paradoxically, he had a rather low opinion. His disapproval of a literary career sounded pathetic when it was aired on another occasion. A few months before his death, he left a testament to his son: "Do not become a good-for-nothing writer or artist." [5] If this was not meant as an admission of his own failure

---

[3] *Postscript to the Grave, LH,* I, 363.

[4] *A Reading List for the Youth, LH,* III, 9.

[5] *Death, LH,* VI, 496.

as a man, his conviction remained firm that there were better things for a man to do than write.

So Lu Hsün became a writer, and a voluminous one at that, almost by accident. He cultivated the craft of writing against his own wishes. Much as he depended on the vocabulary and rhetorical devices of the *wen-yen* for his compositions in *pai-hua* prose, it is his poetry that carries most significantly the paradox of his historical position. Lu Hsün's poetical production was intermittent and never large in quantity, but the excellence of the poems that he wrote in the old style is undeniable. They at least equal his best *pai-hua* prose in terseness, bitterness, sardonic humor, and the strange beauty of "frozen flames" and the "intricate red lines forming patterns like coral beneath the surface of bluish-white ice." [6] But these poems are also traditional literary exercises couched in a language too learned for readers not conversant with classical culture, exercises that served a dubious public function but deflected the energy of both author and reader from "action." In these private compositions, intended to be read by at most only a few friends, he was more than satisfying a whim: he was writing poetry in the manner used by the poets before him; he was indulging in the "vampire's optimism," or, sometimes, pessimism, in a "dead language." Though he was obviously neglecting his public duty, he did not necessarily feel more lonely when he was sending an epistle to a friend than when he was addressing the anonymous masses. Much sophistry, attitudinizing, and oratory could be left out when there was no question of a public for him to instruct, to insult, to ridicule, to cheer up, or to shock out of its complacency. In spite of his extreme position in the rejection of old China and old Chinese books, he could at times submit himself completely to old Chinese poetry, with all its obscurity and weight of tradition. He could adapt himself to the culture of the traditional elite and derive whatever comfort it might still afford in an age of violent social changes and political revolution.

In contrast with Lu Hsün's accomplishment as a poet in the traditional style, his contribution to *pai-hua* poetry was meager and indifferent. It is true that his urge for poetical creation was never sufficiently strong to call forth that supreme effort of creation: to bring "the language of the masses" to a state of purity and versatility which should at least equal the perfection found in traditional poetry. But when now and then his creative urge took a poetical turn, he simply resorted to *wen-yen,* a handy vehicle for a man with his cultural upbringing. He was not entirely unhappy within the

[6] *Dead Fire, LH,* II, 116.

restriction of the traditional poetical form, which became for him rather a fulfillment and a challenge. As a literary craftsman, he delighted in the *mot juste* and neat phrasing, in excision and compression, in making subtle allusions, in giving surprise by contrast and juxtaposition, and in regulating his emotions according to rhyme, rhythm, and form; he might also have felt the secret gratification of seeing a job well done, a pride in his successful emulation of the masters whom he knew by heart. Meanwhile, he quarreled with tradition *in toto*. How dismayed he must have been when he found that there was no escape from tradition if he wanted to practice the craft of writing. It was therefore hard for him to reconcile his taste to the historical movement. But the historical movement was obviously not Lu Hsün's sole concern. There was at least another side to his problem, which was the integrity of art and the artist in the modern age, an integrity to be upheld against the current of history or at the cost of enlightenment, if necessary. Needless to say, this is a side which Lu Hsün seldom tried to defend, nor has it attracted much attention from other modern Chinese writers.

Lu Hsün left behind a book of unique interest: *Yeh-ts'ao* (*The Wild Grass*). Of the twenty-four pieces included, only one reads like a formal *pai-hua* poem, "A Lament for My Disappointed Love";[7] but it is a burlesque, not a very clever burlesque either, of the current love poems which Lu Hsün disdained for their cheap facile sentiments and jingling notes. The presence of doggerel among serious poems-in-prose in *The Wild Grass* implies a comment on the sorry condition of *pai-hua* poetry as Lu Hsün saw it. The rest of the book is genuine poetry in embryo: images imbued with strong emotional intensity, flowing and stopping in darkly glowing but oddly shaped lines, like molten metal failing to find a mold. In a typical piece, "The Farewell of the Shadow," the Shadow says:

> I am only a shadow, now bidding you farewell before sinking into darkness. Yet darkness will engulf me; yet I might cease to exist in the light.
> Yet I do not like to wander between the light and darkness. I had better lose myself in darkness.[8]

The series of "yet's" (*jan-erh*) makes the lines uncomfortably jagged and jerky: it breaks the rules of elegant composition in either *wen-yen* or *pai-hua*. But that is an effect probably intended by the author. To be confronted with the Doppelgänger and to hear him talk is an unsettling experience; to be on the verge of losing one's own Shadow is even more terrifying. Lu

---

[7] *LH*, II, 164.
[8] *LH*, II, 160.

Hsün's dream world is extremely bare, being composed of nothing but light and darkness and the colorless, half-awake nonentity who helplessly listens to what is said to him and watches things happen to him. This is an experience which requires much greater poetical talent than Lu Hsün possessed to bring out its full meaning. Troubled by dreams like that, Lu Hsün might have carried Chinese poetry, even in its classical form, into a new realm, to give formal rendering to a kind of terror and anxiety, an experience which we might call modern, since it is hardly found among the themes of traditional Chinese poetry, rich as its contents are. Instead, he wrote in prose, but in a style which, highly personal in its jerky rhythm and stark images, had a salutary effect on the *pai-hua*. For he took the *pai-hua* away from the paths guided by the ideals of democratism. It is when the writer is profoundly concerned with his private thoughts that he begins to feel the inadequacy of his means of expression. In the intensity of his introspection, he is forgetting about addressing the audience; but his creative process will eventually lead towards the transformation and enrichment of *their* language. Lu Hsün's rhetorical devices may degenerate into mannerisms, at the hands of his imitators as well as at his own hands, in less felicitous moments; but he let *pai-hua* do things that it had never done before—things not even the best classical writers had ever thought of doing in *wen-yen*. In this sense, Lu Hsün was a truly modern writer.

In another piece, the dreamer is reading a tombstone which, in its dilapidated condition, reveals the following fragments of inscription:

. . . Once there was a lost soul who was metamorphosed into a snake with venomous fangs. He did not bite other creatures; but he gnawed into his own body until he succumbed . . .
. . . Stay away! . . .

Then, on the reverse side of the worn-out mossy stone:

. . . He plucked out his own heart and ate it; he wanted to find out its original taste. The pain was severe; how could he find out its original taste?
. . . The agony subsided and now he could enjoy the repast with more leisure. But the heart became already stale; how could its original taste be known?
. . . Answer me. Or, stay away! . . .[9]

The epitaph in dignified *wen-yen* interspersed with the command in *pai-hua* ("Stay away!") places the past and the present on the same plane. It mingles sight (reading) with hearing; it also vividly suggests the possibility that the command was coming from the dead. The theme is a variation on that of cannibalism in the *Diary of a Madman*, which is often read as an in-

9 "The Inscription on the Tombstone," *LH*, II, 191.

dictment of the "man-eating old social system." But the imagined fear of the *Diary* is here turned into the quasi-reality of a nightmare. The conflict between the oppressive social force and its deluded victim of the short story is here reduced to a simple, but no less terrible, act of self-destruction. This short piece calls attention to the truth that it is not only society which oppresses and destroys, but that a lost soul can turn into a snake and eat itself, trying to find the "taste of his own heart." This truth is important, though it is often ignored in the general enthusiasm for social reform.

Those who admire Lu Hsün as a great realist should be reminded of the dimensions of his realism. He began several pieces in *The Wild Grass* with the statement, "I had a dream . . ." and those dreams have such a bizarre beauty and delirious terror that they are really nightmares. Even pieces not marked out as dreams have that nightmarish quality of inconsequence and the shock of misplaced reality. In *The Wild Grass,* therefore, Lu Hsün glanced into the unconscious. He wrote these pieces mostly in 1924 and 1925, in the middle of the decade of *The Waste Land* and *Ulysses* and *The Sound and the Fury.* His failure to produce a masterpiece using his knowledge of the unconscious mind was probably due to his fear. He was too much occupied with the struggle to shake off the dreams. His beliefs in enlightenment did not really dispel the darkness; but they served as a shield from the dangerous attraction that darkness exercised. Hope, however illusory, looked lovelier, and it was preferred to the dreams of night.

So it may be said that the gate of darkness for Lu Hsün owes its weight to two forces: one is traditional Chinese literature and culture, the other the writer's troubled psyche. These two forces, oppressive, penetrating, yet unavoidable, were keenly felt by Lu Hsün. One may not agree with his contention that a younger generation could be raised to lead a life free of them, but he uttered the cries of hope in desperation. His heroic stance implies defeat, and the position he chose for himself was almost tragic. The very allusion to the legendary hero who was crushed to death suggests Lu Hsün's sense of powerlessness against darkness and his acceptance of sacrifice. It is this sense that gives his body of writings a sadness which marks his genius.

If there is anything that has the mysterious oppressive power of the gate of darkness, which acts irrevocably and threatens to shut off light completely, it is death. Death is something too ponderous for any single man or even for the entire human race to bear. It spares neither reactionaries nor progressives. Happy is he who, like Spinoza, can keep his thoughts off this awesome subject. But Lu Hsün, even as a pioneer of modernism in China, was conscious of this terrible burden.

Hope and aspiration, indeed, are offset by the sombre aspects of his writings. Lu Hsün seemed to be an expert in depicting death's ugliness, not only in his poems-in-prose, but also in his short stories. Many living creatures in his fiction have such a pallid hue, stony stare, and slow, still movements that they seem like corpses even before death finally catches up with them. Funeral rites, graves, executions, especially by beheading, and even sickness are the themes that repeatedly engage his creative imagination. The shadows of death creep over his works in various shapes, ranging from a subtle menace, as in the madman's imaginary fear of death in the *Diary of a Madman,* through the quiet disappearance of Hsiang-lin-sao in *Benediction,* to the real terror: the beheaded martyr and the tuberculosis patient in *Medicine,* the old scholar who ran after the illusory white light only to drown himself in the lake in *The White Light,* and the corpse with a grim smile on its face in *The Solitary.* The "happy ending" of *Ah Q* perhaps has its happy side when death comes to the ignorant villager.

But there was one thing Lu Hsün certainly abhorred—the old China with her "putrid morals and death-stiff language." [10] In his public utterances and creative writings, Lu Hsün did not seem to be so much horrified by death itself as by death as the symbol of a bygone age. Here arises an interesting question: Which did he hold in greater abhorrence, old China or death? If we see him as a leading intellectual of the May Fourth Movement, it should be the former. But if we view him as a morbid genius, it was perhaps the latter. And his enthusiasm for revolution only gave him strength to endure the ghosts that he carried on his back.

Lu Hsün actually studied the question of immortality of the soul. In *Benediction,* the pathetic figure Hsiang-lin-sao asks the first-person narrator: Is there life after death? The answer is noncommittal. In 1936, several months before his own death, Lu Hsün wrote: "Thirty years ago when I was a student of medicine, I studied the problem of soul. What I found was that I did not know." [11] Such an admission sounds much like Confucius; it was at least an honest statement from a spokesman for science. But the question of whether the soul is immortal remained unanswered throughout Lu Hsün's life. The great void that lies beyond was not penetrated by medical science. It remained a mystery. And it acted upon him in a way it never did on Confucius, or on his own brother, Chou Tso-jen.[12]

[10] *Random Thoughts* (57), *LH,* I, 420.

[11] *Death, LH,* VI, 494.

[12] Chou Tso-jen said that he did not believe in the immortality of the soul. See his "On Gossiping about the Ghosts," in the volume of essays, *Kua-tou-chi* (*Melons and Beans*) (Shanghai, 1937), p. 21.

So death, like old China an object of revulsion, has also its fascination. Lu Hsün never made up his mind about the attitude he should adopt toward these two objects of revulsion. His extreme position on the issues of the day, his militant advocacy of progress, of science and enlightenment, is well known. But this does not make up the whole of his personality, nor does it account for his genius unless we take into consideration his curiosity, his secret longing and love for what he hated. To take Lu Hsün as merely an angel who sounded the trumpet for daybreak is to overlook one of the more profound souls of modern Chinese history, and a morbid soul, too. Some trumpet he did sound; but the music he made was sombre and sardonic, expressive of despair as well as hope, a mingling of heavenly and infernal notes.

There are some aspects of Lu Hsün's style which indeed suggest a trumpet. The instrument, called *Mu-lien hao-t'ung,* is described vividly in his essay on *Wu-ch'ang,* or *The Infernal Agent,* which he wrote in 1926. On the stage of *Mu-lien-hsi* (about which more will be said), before the Infernal Agent appeared to arrest the Bad Man on the orders of Yen Wang (King Yama), you would hear the *hao-t'ung:*

> The instrument is like a trumpet, very slender and about seven to eight feet long. The music it made was perhaps loved by the ghosts, for the trumpet was never used on occasions unrelated to ghosts. When it was blown, it emitted the notes: nhatu, nhatu, nhatututu.[13]

Then appeared Wu-ch'ang, whose first act was to make one hundred and eight sneezes to indicate, perhaps, that the human stench of this world does not agree with his sensitive nostrils. All the audience would laugh at his antics. He was dressed completely in white, with an extinguisher-like tall hat on his head. His knitted eyebrows were black as pitch and from his face you would not know whether he was crying or laughing. His face was very white, and his lips very red. But jocularly, Lu Hsün used a familiar phrase to describe this sharp contrast in colors, a phrase usually reserved for a beautiful woman: *fen-mien chu-ch'un* (powdered face and rouged lips).

In 1936 Lu Hsün wrote about another ghostly figure from the *Mu-lien-hsi: Nü-tiao,* or the *Ghost of the Hanged Woman.*[14] Wu-ch'ang, he said, represented a "helplessness" and "casualness" toward death, but Nü-tiao was "more beautiful and stronger than all other ghosts" because she carried with her a somewhat "revengeful nature." However, the revenge motive is imputed by Lu Hsün, for in the actual performance as he remembered

---

[13] *Wu-ch'ang, LH,* II, 248.
[14] *Nü-tiao, LH,* VI, 498.

it, the female ghost, after a recounting, in mournful tones accompanied by terrible gesticulation, of her miserable life which terminated in suicide, showed "tremendous surprise and joy" when she heard the cry of another woman who was about to commit suicide. In the belief of the superstitious Chinese, who flocked to the "ghost festival" in the seventh moon of the lunar year, the ghost of a suicide was under a curse: she was forbidden to re-enter the cycle of transmigration of souls until she found a "substitute," or somebody who had committed suicide in the same manner as the ghost had done (by hanging, in this instance). Nü-tiao may have expressed, amidst her complaints, a wish to take revenge on those who had wronged her in her lifetime; but the moment she was assured of the presence of a "substitute" who would afford her the opportunity of returning to human life, self-interest prevailed over justice. She was eager to take the life of another innocent but would spare that of the wrongdoer.[15]

Lu Hsün tried to read a moral into the episode of Nü-tiao in the *Mu-lien-hsi,* but he did not really dwell upon the motive of revenge. The style of this essay shows the same kind of pleasant raillery and high spirits found in the piece on Wu-ch'ang. This is how the female ghost is introduced:

> At first there was of course the melancholy trumpet; a little while later, the flap in the backdrop was lifted and there she entered: in a vermilion blouse and a long, black sleeveless garment, her long hair streaming down and two strings of joss-money hanging from her neck. Her head lowered and her arms dangling, she walked zigzag all over the stage. . . .
> She shook back her long sheet of hair and a face as white as limestone was revealed; her thick eyebrows were pitch black, with dark shades around her eyes and her lips were scarlet. . . . If an apparition like this, with powdered face and rouged lips, should appear in dim light after midnight, even a person such as I am now would have been attracted to take a closer look, though, of course, I don't think that I should have fallen to the temptation to hang myself.[16]

Lu Hsün no doubt carried some ghosts on his back. But they are not so hateful as his polemical essays suggest. For some of them he could even harbor a secret love. His attitude towards the ghostly figures in the *Mu-lien-hsi* was that of doting fondness. Few authors are able to discuss a macabre subject with so much zest. These two essays are especially precious since they are from Lu Hsün, a social reformer surprisingly sympathetic

[15] The scripts of the Wu-ch'ang and Nü-tiao episodes from the *Mu-lien-hsi* are printed in *Chü-pen* (*Plays,* a monthly) (Peking), Dec., 1961, pp. 80–84. One is never sure what liberty the performers in Communist China have taken with the original play. The latest version of the *Ghost of the Hanged Woman* does put her revenge into effect, but according to a comment by Tai Pu-fan, "in the original version, her act is to seek a substitute." *Ibid.,* p. 89.

[16] *LH,* VI, 501–2.

to popular superstitions. Whereas Chou Tso-jen wrote a number of witty but rather dispassionate studies of Chinese folklore, Lu Hsün's interest was not purely scholarly. He took a fascinated look at and then made fun of the ghosts' horrible looks. He let his fancy run freely over the subject, and, in good humor, he tried to find if there were some reason that we should all love these ghosts. With his vivid imagination he called them back to life, as it were, and affectionately showed them around to his readers.

The *Mu-lien-hsi,* or *Cycle of the Legends of Saint Mu-lien,* was, according to Chou Tso-jen, the only extant religious drama in China around the year 1900.[17] The earliest evidence of the transplant of the Indian legend into Chinese folk literature was found in the Tun-huang manuscript, *Ta-mu-ch'ien-lien ming-chien chiu-mu pien-wen (The Popularized Story of Maudgalyāyana's Rescue of His Mother in Hell).*[18] In its dramatic form it was a very long play. It could run continuously for more than a week in the Sung dynasty, from the eighth to the fifteenth night of the seventh moon, according to *Tung-ching meng-hua-lu (Reminiscences of Kaifeng).*[19] In Hsin-ch'ang, a town about forty-five miles southeast of Lu Hsün's native city of Shaohsing, the play used to last also seven afternoons and nights (totaling thirty to forty hours of performance) as it was presented annually until its suspension in the year 1943 or 1944.[20] But as Lu Hsün saw it as a child, the play began at dusk and ended at dawn of the next day. Even in this shortened version, it seemed to contain a large variety of elements:

[17] "On the Miracle Play of Mu-lien," in Chou Tso-jen, *T'an-lung-chi (The Dragon Essays)* (Shanghai, 1927), p. 140.

[18] In Wang Chung-min, *et al.* (eds.), *Tun-huang pien-wen chi (A Collection of Popularized Literature from the Tun-huang Caves)* (Peking, 1957), there are two other texts on the same subject: *Mu-lien yüan-ch'i (The Original Story of Mu-lien),* pp. 701–13, and *Mu-lien pien-wen (The Popularized Story of Mu-lien),* pp. 756–60. But *Ta-mu-ch'ien-lien ming-chien chiu-mu pien-wen,* pp. 714–55, contains the richest material.

[19] Meng Yüan-lao, *Tung-ching meng-hua-lu* (1147), reprinted in one volume with four other books on the capitals of the Sung: Kaifeng and Hangchow (Shanghai, 1956), p. 49. More information about the *Mu-lien-hsi* can be found in Chao Ching-shen, "The Development of the Legend of Mu-lien," in a volume of his studies on Chinese vernacular literature, *Yin-tzu-chi (Silver Characters)* (Shanghai, 1946), pp. 149–77

[20] During the "hundred flowers" movement in October, 1956, and on the occasion of the twentieth anniversary of Lu Hsün's death, an amateur theatrical troupe of forty-two actors from Hsin-ch'ang, composed of farmers, masons, tailors, workers in bamboo, and so forth, put on a performance of the *Mu-lien-hsi* in Shanghai. According to a report, "for 13 years no such performance has been given in the countryside of Hsin-ch'ang." More information about the *Mu-lien-hsi* and the performance can be obtained in the report. *Jen-min jih-pao* (Peking), Nov. 22–23, 1956, p. 8.

singing, dancing, acrobatics, satire, and sheer nonsense, obscenity and lessons in retribution, horrible superstitions, and beliefs in salvation. Its main plot concerns the descent into hell of the Saint, one of Lord Buddha's disciples, to rescue his mother who is there receiving punishment for her sins. But the terrors of hell were mingled with many humorous interludes, scenes also witnessed by the Saint, so that it amused while it shocked. What made this kind of miracle play all the more interesting was that most of the actors were amateurs: the local butcher, carpenter, nightwatchman, etc., in their shabby costumes, were delightfully recognizable, particularly to the children in the audience.[21] It left a lasting impression both on Lu Hsün and on his more even-tempered brother, Chou Tso-jen.

There were no doubt many influences in Lu Hsün's literary life, the impact of history and his wide readings being the most often noticed. But I should like to call attention to the resemblance between the world of fiction that he created and the world of the *Mu-lien-hsi,* with its horror and humor and the final hope for salvation. It is perhaps not too farfetched to suggest that for Lu Hsün, the mother to be saved was Mother China whose shame and sin her son must bear and cleanse, whether he was cast in the role of a heroic bandit, a Nietzschean superman, or a Buddhist saint on his journey through hell. Some episodes of the play, enacted by rustics and villagers, had such a naïve charm and absurd simplicity that they might well have fitted into Lu Hsün's world of fiction. Of the many ghosts assembled on the stage during the scene of almsgiving, there are a group of "examination-hall ghosts" who, having fallen to their deaths in the midst of literary examinations, now walk in airy, tottering steps, still holding writing-brushes in their hands.[22] The reader can perhaps see their likenesses in Lu Hsün's K'ung I-chi and the pathetic hero of *The White Light.* Chou Tso-jen recalls a scene where a man is reading the inscription on a scroll hung on the wall of a parlor:

> The sun rises red in the East
> And the bride is taking a bath.
> Her father-in-law is peeping.
> Oh, father-in-law, please don't!
> Mother-in-law is watching!

---

[21] Chou Tso-jen mentioned the amateur actors in his essay, "On the Miracle Play of Mu-lien" (see note 17). How a child recognized the characters is described in another essay, "The Theatrical Troupe in the Village," Chou, *K'an-yün-chi* (*Looking at the Clouds*) (Shanghai, 1932), pp. 260–62.

[22] *Jen-min jih-pao,* Nov. 22, 1956, p. 8. Lu Hsün also mentioned the "examination hall ghosts" in *Wu-ch'ang, LH,* II, 245, and in *Nü-tiao, LH,* VI, 500.

Then, connoisseur-like, the man remarks, "Signed by T'ang Po-hu. Aha, truly a masterpiece!" [23] The coarse humor here suggests the more subtle insinuation in Lu Hsün's *Soap.* Chou Tso-jen recalls also a fool of a mason who is so much absorbed in his work that he finally seals himself in the wall. In another scene, a water-carrier complains: "The wage, as agreed upon, was supposed to be sixteen cash for one carrying, but by some mistake it has become one cash for sixteen carryings. So after working for a whole day I have earned only three cash." Yet another scene is known as "Chang Man Beats His Father," where the father says, "In former days when we beat our father, we would stop if father ran away. But now, even if he runs away, the son will pursue him and never stop beating." Mishaps and pleasantries like these could happen, if not to any other character created by Lu Hsün, at least to Ah Q, the very apotheosis of the absurd in Chinese life.

Outstanding among the characters of the *Mu-lien-hsi* were Wu-ch'ang and Nü-tiao, whose horrible looks exercised a fascination over Lu Hsün throughout his life. They became subjects of two whimsical essays into which Lu Hsün put the best of his literary skill. But to relate them to Lu Hsün's body of creative writings, one can see that the ghosts supplied more than occasions for him to display his scholarly curiosity and superior wit, or to register his nostalgia. They represented something with a deeper significance: the terror and beauty of death and the mystery of life peeping through the heavily powdered and rouged masks. Lu Hsün did not accomplish much in the exploration of this mystery; he was far more pronounced in his angry protest against social evils. But what set him apart from his contemporaries was that he acknowledged the mystery and that he never denied its power. He could even be spellbound by the dark forces in life; he had feelings for individuals in moments of isolation from their social environment, as several of his best short stories, the poems-in-prose of *The Wild Grass,* and some other occasional essays attest. These works are perhaps what will continue to be read after the issue of social reform in China has changed its nature. Indeed, Lu Hsün was not a true representative of the May Fourth Movement insofar as that term is understood to mean a popular movement with positive aims to discard the old and adopt the new. He embodied rather the conflict between the old and the new and some deeper conflicts, too, that transcend history. He never attained that state of serenity enjoyed by his contemporaries Hu Shih and Chou Tso-jen, but he was probably a greater genius than either of them.

[23] This and other episodes are described in Chou Tso-jen, "On the Miracle Play of Mu-lien" (see note 17).

A truer representative of the May Fourth Movement was Hu Shih, whose commitment to progress appeared to be unequivocal and consistent and over whose life shone the steady, serene light of optimism. Ghosts, indeed, became powerless in his world of enlightenment. In 1927, after his visit to Paris, he was asked why he had spent sixteen days with the Tun-huang Manuscripts but neglected the Louis Pasteur Institute. Here is his reply:

Let me rip open my heart and explain to the world: it is only because I believe perfectly well that in the "piles of rotten paper" are numberless old ghosts who can eat people and cast a spell over people. For the harm they can do, they are much more deadly than the germs discovered by Pasteur. But it is also because I believe that though I am powerless against the germs, I take pride in my ability to "chain the demons and subdue the ghosts." [24]

His boast is of course not to be taken seriously. But if one examines his facetious tone, one wonders whether Hu Shih sincerely believed that "the old ghosts can eat people and cast a spell." Compared with what possessed Lu Hsün, these are poor harmless ghosts who can be chained and subdued by a scholar working in the library.

I have mentioned that Chou Tso-jen is author of a number of learned essays on Chinese folklore, but the ghosts have also a symbolical meaning for him. Chou Tso-jen's name as a reactionary or a conservative, so commonly accepted today, cannot be established without serious reservations. As a writer emerging from the May Fourth Movement, he too showed little sympathy for the evils of old China. He retreated from the avant-garde position when China after 1919 took a shape which did not justify his initial hopes. He disliked modern China not so much because he preferred old China as because the two Chinas looked so much alike in their ugliness. In the present he saw the ghost of the past. In 1925 when the nation was in the tide of a wave of anti-imperialism known as the May Thirtieth Movement, he remarked bitterly that this was no time for "a Chinese Renaissance" (in contradiction to Hu Shih)[25] but that China of the 1920's struck him as a copy of China at the end of the Ming dynasty in the 1640's. And his pessimism found a symbol in Ibsen's *Ghosts*:

Sun Yat-sen may not have been a reincarnation of Ch'ug-chen [the last Ming emperor] to seek revenge on the Manchus, but I find that among the people of all sorts today there is no lack of avatars of the Chi Society [an organization of literati of the late Ming], the Fu Society [another organization of agitating literati], Kao Chieh and Tso Liang-yü [warlords], Li Tzu-ch'eng

[24] Hu Shih, "Sinological Research and Subduing the Ghosts," in *Hu Shih wen-ts'un*, Third Series (Shanghai, 1930), II, 211.
[25] Hu Shih, *The Chinese Renaissance* (in English) (Chicago, 1934).

[bandit], Wu San-kuei [the general who led the Manchus into China], etc. When Mrs. Alving discovers that her son is flirting with the maid in the same manner as his father, she cries, "Ghosts!" Should we not be similarly shocked and horrified when we look at the present situation? [26]

In 1927 he commented on the applause by Wu Chih-hui, once regarded as a leading intellectual, of the execution of the radical youths:

> In this man we can see the ghosts of the tyrants, Yung-lo and Ch'ien-lung.[27]

Echoes of both Hu Shih's optimism and Chou Tso-jen's pessimism can be found in Lu Hsün, who shared their dissatisfaction with the present. What distinguishes him is that he embraced a great deal more. The future, as bright as it appeared to the radicals and also to moderates like Hu Shih, could not always hide its dark spots under his scrutiny. When Chou Tso-jen, Lin Yutang, and others were trying to rediscover a serene, more lovable traditional China, the past remained accursed to Lu Hsün, yet it was attractive with all its hideousness. His problems were more complicated and more oppressive than those faced by many of his contemporaries; in this sense he was more truly representative of the issues, conflicts, and anxieties of his times. To identify him with one movement, to assign him one role, or to put him in one direction is to extol historical abstractions at the expense of individual genius. Anyway, what was the nature of Lu Hsün's times, even if they are treated as merely a period of transition? It can never fully be comprehended by means of such contrasting metaphors as light and darkness, because there was such an interesting variety of shades of grey. The twilight hours hold ghostly shapes, shadowy whispers and other wonders, and phantasmata which are apt to be dismissed in the impatient waiting for the dawn. As a chronicler of those hours, Lu Hsün wrote with fine perception and a subtlety and profundity of feeling, qualities which were usually lost to him when he spoke as a conscious rebel. His treatment of the darker themes is particularly important since no one really knows how long the twilight hours will last, if not on the surface of the earth, at least in the heart of man.

Lu Hsün's sensitivity as an individual in the difficult times is not fully appreciated by his followers and interpreters in China who, as lesser rebels, perhaps do believe that they owe whatever sunshine they enjoy to his gigantic effort in shouldering up the gate of darkness. There is one side to Lu Hsün's genius which can be dazzling in its effect: his scintillating wit, flashes of insight, and brilliant play with words. This side has attracted a great

---

[26] Chou, "A Letter," in *T'an-hu-chi* (*The Tiger Essays*) (Shanghai, 1929), pp. 172–73.

[27] "A Random Thought," *ibid.*, p. 277.

amount of attention from his readers. As I have pointed out, Lu Hsün was a principal maker of the rebel's prose, which exalts and condemns too readily and too categorically to be fair in attitude or truthful in content. For the lesser rebels, this rhetoric, a combination of sophistication, oversimplification, and emotional bias, has become a reliable means of interpreting life in China. I wonder how much of the "people's speech" was ever seriously studied in the vernacular movement after 1919; the voice often heard is that of a clever but angry man. On the strength of Lu Hsün's success as a stylist, both cleverness and anger are so securely built into the rhetoric of *pai-hua* that it has become very hard for subsequent writers in that medium to avoid them. For this reliance on wit and on the vocabulary of hatred and contempt in the development of *pai-hua* prose, for this actual narrowing down of the possibilities of the Chinese language, Lu Hsün was largely responsible. But Lu Hsün was great enough to enjoy freedom within his own rhetoric which frequently had only restrictive influence on his imitators. He could do anything with the hateful darkness and ghosts; he could even draw them close to him and fondle them as his moods suited him. His imitators, however, would be taken aback by the repulsiveness of the metaphors and would refuse to give them a second look or hearing.

Lu Hsün, indeed, was a man of moods. He could be alternately gloomy or cheerful, whimsical or angry, lighthearted or relentless. In the current image of him, his sarcastic or prophetic sides have perhaps been overemphasized. It would have been easy for me to play up some other aspects of Lu Hsün's genius so as to present a more or less balanced portrait of the man, or to elicit an even larger number of illustrations than are assembled here to demonstrate the morbidity of his genius, to make him look more like a contemporary of Kafka than of Hugo. But to do that is only part of my intention. I think that it would be as futile to follow Lu Hsün in the shifts of his moods as it is deplorable for him to have dissipated his ideas and feelings in occasional essays, brilliantly executed as they often are. What he might have done is to bring these moods into a greater "fusion" which should reflect richly, and in a larger symbolic unity, the world as he saw it. He might have given more serious thoughts to the conflicts in him, conflicts obvious to his readers but left unresolved within the structure of art. As a rhetorician, he was never anything less than clever in grinding out paradoxes. But the paradox of his personal life and modern Chinese life, the conflict between hope and despair, and something more subtle than the conflict—the almost unaccountable fading of light into darkness and vice versa, the dilemma of the shadow whose existence is threatened by both the light and the darkness

—have not found in his works a perfect symbolic equivalent, except in *The True Life of Ah Q,* which has shortcomings in structure.

A puzzle of modern Chinese literature was Lu Hsün's career as a writer of fiction, which he did not keep up after a very promising start. It is not for me to offer any explanation of that subject in this study. But in the absence of a major masterpiece, his minor masterpieces are his short stories which are studies of the darker side of life. In addition, there are his poems-in-prose and several of his essays (especially those collected in the volume *Morning Flowers Collected in the Evening*) which are likewise dominated by nostalgia, compassion soured by a sense of helplessness, forebodings of defeat in a solitary struggle, and the landscape of desolation and ruin. Hope appears in the form of flowers atop a martyr's grave (in *Medicine*) or Ah Q's boast about "twenty years later" in his ride to the execution ground or the Ghost of the Hanged Woman who forgets to carry out her revenge in her pursuit of self-interest. No anthology of Lu Hsün's works, I believe, can exclude these and other ghosts. Lu Hsün told us in the essay on Nü-tiao that as a boy he used to participate in a ritual of invocation as an opening of the festival which would feature the *Mu-lien-hsi.* An actor in a scaly costume, his face painted blue, was supposed to be the Prince of Ghosts. About a dozen boys, Lu Hsün among them, all volunteers, their faces cursorily painted, became his ghostly cohorts. At sunset they would ride on horseback to the country until they reached the place where the nameless graveyards were. They would make three circuits on horseback and then dismounting would emit terrible yells and throw the javelins with forked heads at the graves. Quickly pulling the javelins back, they would remount and gallop home. They would throw the javelins into the boards of the stage. In this way the ghosts were thought to have arrived on invitation and the *Mu-lien-hsi* would start. Lu Hsün, of course, never saw the ghosts he brought home on his javelin. But with the pen, he has recreated them, and they have lived a charmed life ever since.

ENIGMA OF THE FIVE MARTYRS

Trust!—Trust we have a good conscience! . . . For it does not appear that the sermon is printed, or ever likely to be.

Laurence Sterne, *Tristram Shandy*

PREFACE

The present study is an essay in the literature and politics of modern China. In the lives of the so-called five martyrs who were executed in early 1931, I am trying to discover the character and spirit of an age. The subjects of my study—Hu Yeh-p'in, Jou Shih, Feng K'eng, Yin Fu, and Li Wei-sen—were writers of small talent. Indeed, no judicious critic would commend their literary effort without reservation. If a justification is needed for an elaborate thesis on some mediocre writers, it is that their failure was not an isolated case. In ways I shall try to define, both their naïve view of life and their imperfect understanding of literature were symptoms of an age of revolution.

Revolution was glorified in China even before its dubious success in 1911. The failure of the republican government in Peking to maintain order only brought home the truth of the "unaccomplished task of revolution." While the revolutionary spirit found a louder expression in the mass movements, especially those of 1919 (May 4) and 1925 (May 30), the First Popular Front of the Kuomintang and the Communist Party (1923–27) exercised over the youth of the nation a profound influence, the significance of which is yet to be studied.

It was in such a cultural environment that the five youths of my study were brought up. They did not have the genius to transcend their time, nor the perception to see the relativity of human values; but they did not stand aloof. They were fully committed at the time of their death.

To analyze the historical forces suggested above is impossible in a paper of this size. But a biographical study may bring out, though in a limited scope, the problems, whether cultural, political, or emotional, that troubled the brief and misdirected existence of the "five martyrs." That they turned to communism for a solution to these problems was particularly significant.

There are two questions I shall try to answer: Why did they become Communist? What happened to them after they turned Communist? Since these questions cannot be completely answered, this paper is appropriately titled "Enigma of the Five Martyrs." The discovery of additional materials will illuminate many of the dark spots in the narrative. But there will always remain an eternal aspect to the case of the "five martyrs" which should be of interest to philosophers and religious thinkers. Loaded with political themes though my paper is, I have barely succeeded in resisting the temptation to lift the case out of its historical context and to study it as if it were an *exemplum*. If religious musings were permitted in a historical study, my theme might well be the defeat of the human spirit by human fallibility.

The power struggle within the Chinese Communist Party in the period under study has been expertly summarized by Professor Tso-liang Hsiao in his *Power Relations within the Chinese Communist Movement, 1930–1934* (Seattle: University of Washington Press, 1961). I was unable to consult Professor Hsiao's book while I was working on this paper. Now I can gratefully include some of his findings in my footnotes.

ON the night of February 7, 1931, twenty-three Communists were executed in Lunghwa, a suburban town south of Shanghai famous for its pagoda and peach blossoms, but also known to be the site of the fearful Shanghai-Woosung Garrison Command. Viewed in a longer perspective, their death was perhaps not so much a loss as a gain to the Communist Party. The party did not have much difficulty in replacing the dead with people equally brave and dedicated; but it was seeking sympathy while it was weak, and popularity while its own good name was stained with the blood of landlords and "reactionaries" killed in its unsuccessful insurrections. The case of the twenty-three provided an image of heroism and persecuted innocence with which the party could identify itself, while its enemy, the Kuomintang government, became, in the eyes of the well-meaning people of the world, synonymous with tyrannical oppression. The twenty-three are remembered as victims of the White Terror which, beginning with the "massacre of workers" in April, 1927 (Li Ta-chao was hanged in the same month), accounted for lives that must have run into the thousands. If a general description could be made of such a large group, it might be said that they were all courageous and earnest, determined in their struggle for a better world and ready for sacrifice. The same qualities could indeed be found in the character of the martyrs who died for the Kuomintang in its long history, but it was the heroic death of these Communists, rather than their surreptitious existence, that spread the fame of the revolution and won for it a continued supply of new blood to make up for what had been lost.

The year 1931 is so close to our own time that it is hard for us to avoid an affective state of mind in any discussion of so painful a subject. Since the struggle between the Kuomintang and the Communists has never really ceased, in spite of a brief truce after the Sian incident, we, even from a non-partisan stand, feel still very much involved in the issues of thirty years ago. Human sympathy naturally goes to the weak and the persecuted. Furthermore, there are certain matters in which a detached attitude is simply impossible, and brutal killing is one of them. One cannot but shudder at the spectacle of prisoners being tied together in manacles while facing the firing squad and the possibility of some being buried even before they were quite dead. For such was the cruelty the twenty-three victims suffered, as was evidenced by the condition of the bodies exhumed after the Communist occupation of Shanghai in 1949.[1] After the remains were located and rediscovered, they were moved to the Martyrs' Cemetery in Tach'ang on the north of Shanghai, a burial ground more suited for their posthumous honor. But whether their souls now rest in peace seems still open to question.

Revolution can be as careless about human life as war, and like war, it has always its Nameless Soldier. A man was killed, a body was found— but who was he? A nobody while alive, now he receives homage from generals and the heads of state; a mere corpse, he now animates millions of

---

[1] Feng Hsüeh-feng, "First Page of History Recorded in Fresh Blood," in *Lun-wen-chi (Essays)* (Peking: People's Literary Publications Association, 1952), I, 222. Feng reports that twenty-three bodies were discovered. Previous estimates put them at either twenty-four or twenty-five.

living souls. He becomes an idol, but not quite a legend, for he has no name and nothing is known about his life. He is absolutely secure in his fame, for he has no personal enemies to settle an old score, no valets to recall his little unheroic foibles; and no sceptic can doubt his one virtue—the only important event in his life—that he died. It seems that immortality may be attained simply by dying anonymously.

Who were these wretches? The Kuomintang authorities have never published a name-list; nor, to our knowledge, have the mourning comrades ever given a full account of the identity and history of these martyrs. Six names we do know for sure; the others, except for a few possible guesses,[2] are nameless. The usefulness of these nameless revolutionaries for the historian is therefore limited to a symbol, a grim reminder of the White Terror. They represent a group image rather than individual images. They can only be studied in general terms, for our knowledge does not exceed the obvious fact that their hard struggle was defeated by their hard times.

The most distinguished of the six, in view of his record of service, was probably Ho Meng-hsiung, whose career is summarized in a footnote in Mao Tse-tung's *Selected Works:*

> Member of the Chinese Communist Party, one of the early organizers of the trade union movement in North China, and the founder of the Railwaymen's Union on the Peking-Suiyuan Line. After the Kuomintang's betrayal of the revolution in 1927, Comrade Ho Meng-hsiung worked in Shanghai and served as a member of the Party's Kiangsu Provincial Committee and as secretary of its Peasant Department. In 1931 he was arrested by Chiang Kai-shek's bandit gang and died a martyr at Lunghwa.[3]

This man Ho seems to have been a veteran organizer and agitator, a professional revolutionary. The other five were amateurs, for writing was supposed to be their main occupation, but their creative life was lamentably cut short in its prime. Their biographical sketches were published in the *New Masses,* an organ of the Communist Party of the U.S.A., which also printed, in the same issue, "An Appeal from the Writers of China," which called for "immediate and determined help against the White Terror in China."

[2] For Lin Yü-nan see note 92. Wei Chin-chih said that he saw on the stone monument in the Ta-ch'ang Cemetery the name of Lung Ta-tao, a native of Yunnan, a student of the work-study group in France, and a trade-unionist in the Chinese Communist Party. Wei, "Time Spent in the Company of Jou Shih," *Wen-i yüeh-pao* (*Literary Monthly*) (Shanghai), Mar. 5, 1957, p. 44.

[3] Mao Tse-tung, *Hsüan-chi* (*Selected Works*) (Peking: People's Publication Association, 1953), III, 1000; Mao Tse-tung, *Selected Works* (in English) (New York: International Publishers, 1956), IV, 341.

Hu Yeh-p'in—Born in 1905 of a middle-class family of Foochow, Fukien. Worked his way through Peking National University. His first poems and short stories appeared in 1925. Wrote *Go to Moscow!* in 1929. Chairman of the Board of Correspondence with workers, peasants, and soldiers. Arrested by British police January 17; shot February 7 in Shanghai.

Jou-Shih—Born in 1901, Chekiang Province. Teacher, short story writer. Founded the Ninghai School. Translated literature of North and Eastern Europe. One of the founders of the *Leftist Writers League.* Arrested January 17; shot February 7, 1931.

Feng K'eng—Born in 1907, Kwangtung Province. Appeared as a writer at the age of 15. Represented students organizations of Chaochow and Swatow. Joined the Leftist Writers in 1930 and was in the Propaganda Committee at All-China Soviet Congress. Shot February 7 at Shanghai.

Li Wei-sen—Born 1903 in Hupei Province. Directed student movement of the Wuhan area. Studied in Soviet Russia 1925–26. Edited *Young Vanguard* of Canton. Was in the Canton Commune 1927. Editor of *Shanghai Pao* in 1928. Translated books and pamphlets from the Russian. Arrested January 17 and buried alive with five others a few days afterwards.

Yin Fu—Born in a village of Chekiang Province in 1909. Student at Tung Chi University, Shanghai. Arrested in Silk Workers Strike in 1929. Poet, contributor to *Lenin Youth,* secret weekly. Member of the Leftist Writers and contributor to many workers' papers. Shot at midnight of February 7 at Shanghai.[4]

The open letter met with the expected response. Undoubtedly, the Chinese League of Leftist Writers, in whose name the letter was published, had its international connections, but the tragic incident had in itself an appeal not only to the political left but to all who cared about the worth of human life. Of the protests from various parts of the world,[5] Malcolm Cowley's article in *The New Republic,* "Twenty-four Youngsters," was perhaps most representative of the shock, dismay, and indignation which many others must have felt at the senseless killing of creative young people. Wrote Mr. Cowley, after making an introductory statement about Hu Yeh-p'in as a typical revolutionary Chinese youth:

Hu Yeh-pin had become a Communist. He began to associate with writers like himself, undernourished young men with faces grave beyond their years, who translated books from the German, Russian, or English, and planned

[4] *New Masses,* June, 1931, pp. 14–15. The same article also commemorates the death of Tsung Hui, a leftist dramatist, who was shot in the autumn of 1930. Since that was a separate case, his name does not come up in this article.

[5] Feng Hsüeh-feng lists these names: Michael Gold of the U.S.A., Ludwig Ling (?) of Germany, Hans Meyer (?) of Austria, Harold Hyslop (?) of England, and Nagada Hiroshi (?) of Japan. Feng, *Essays,* I, 227. The International League of Revolutionary Writers also issued a protest, with many more signatures.

ambitious novels in the intervals between fleeing from the police and organizing strikes among the factory workers of the Yangtze Valley. They took themselves seriously; on their shoulders they felt the whole burden of creating a new China. On January 17 they held a secret meeting at the Eastern Hotel in the International Settlement of Shanghai. Twenty-four Communists were present; five of them, including Hu, were writers. There was Li Wei-sen, an essayist and biographer who had spent two years in Moscow; there were two novelists and a talented poet; there was Feng Keng, a woman writer of talent and obstinate courage whose character suggests that of Mary Wollstonecraft or Mary Shelley. The oldest of the five was twenty-nine, the youngest twenty-one. They were, in a sense, the flower of their generation. All were arrested by the British police and turned over to the Chinese military authorities for trial and execution.

.   .   .

That was five months ago, but the campaign of extermination against Chinese writers still continues. A vigorous and hopeful generation is being butchered off . . .[6]

The five, because of their youth and promise as writers, excite profound sympathy. But neither sorrow nor anger should be allowed to obscure the fact that the young writers were executed in the company of their non-literary comrade, Ho Meng-hsiung. What is disturbing is the mysterious circumstances said to be attendant upon *his* arrest. It was impossible for Mr. Cowley or any other sympathizer to have suspected in 1931, when information was scant, that the Kuomintang could be as guilty of stupidity as of brutality and that it could play into the hands of one Communist clique which was trying to destroy another. But we have now Harold Isaacs' word, and his authority is not easily dismissed. In spite of his personal involvement in the policies of the Chinese Communist Party, he must be credited with the eminent research that he has done, as well as the valuable information he gathered first-hand. Thanks to his pioneering work and studies by other scholars, we know much more today about the intra-party strife centering around the Li Li-san line and the anti-Li-Li-sanists.

One of the worst crises that the Chinese Communist Party has survived occurred in late 1930 and early 1931 when the powerful Li Li-san was dismissed from office, and abject confessions to mistakes were made by Li himself, Ch'ü Ch'iu-po, and Chou En-lai. The coveted leadership was won by the so-called Returned Students Clique headed by Wang Ming, a group of upstarts whose sole strength seemed to be derived from the sup-

[6] Malcolm Cowley, "Twenty-four Youngsters," *New Republic*, July 8, 1931, pp. 205–6.

port of Pavel Mif, representative of the Comintern. What then happened, according to Mr. Isaacs, was the tragedy that concerns us here.

The young men so abruptly enthroned as "leaders" of the Communist Party had all been students in Moscow during the years of the revolution and had won their spurs conducting witch-hunts against Trotskyist sympathizers among the students at Sun Yat-sen University. To give them control Mif shouldered aside the group of old militants who had served, not without opposition, under the leadership of Li Li-san. A group of these older Party members and trade unionists, and some younger men, led by the veteran, Ho Mung-shung [sic], met at a Shanghai hotel on the night of January 17 to consider the new situation with which they were confronted. In circumstances which are still a whispered scandal in the Party ranks, that meeting was betrayed to the British Police of the International Settlement. Ho Mung-shung and twenty-four others were arrested, handed over to the Kuomintang authorities and executed at Lunghua on February 7. Mif's docile young men became the undisputed leaders of the Party.[7]

This was in the 1938 edition of Isaacs' *Tragedy of the Chinese Revolution*. More than a decade later, two American scholars also suggested the possibility of treachery. Said Benjamin Schwartz:

Thus we find that the Ho Meng-hsiung, Lo Chang-lung faction simply refused to accept the decisions of the Fourth Plenum or the authority of the new Central Committee even though this leadership was directly imposed by Moscow itself. Instead of bowing to party discipline, Ho Meng-hsiung, Lo Chang-lung, Wang K'o-ch'üan, Hsü Hsi-ken, and others formed an "Emergency Committee" to consider further steps . . . On January 17 a meeting of the committee was discovered by the British police. The members of the committee present were all arrested and on February 7, Ho Meng-hsiung and twenty-four others were executed by the Kuomintang. Hostile sources have strongly intimated that Wang Ming was implicated in this event; that the Emergency Committee represented such a danger to the authority of the new Central Committee that its existence could not be tolerated.[8]

And Robert North:

With Comintern authority, Mif was able to establish the new hierarchy, and the greater part of Communist leadership accepted discipline. But Ho Meng-hsiung and some of his supporters broke away. On January 17 this faction's newly constituted Central Committee was apprehended in session by the British police in Shanghai and placed under arrest. Three weeks later Ho Meng-hsiung and twenty-four others were executed by the Kuomintang. According to Li Ang

[7] Harold R. Isaacs, *The Tragedy of the Chinese Revolution* (London: Secker and Warburg, 1938), p. 407.
[8] Benjamin I. Schwartz, *Chinese Communism and the Rise of Mao* (Cambridge: Harvard University Press, 1952), p. 166.

and other sources, the British police had been informed by Wang Ming. In any case, the Returned Students had fewer opponents to worry about.[9]

The names of the five writers do not appear in the above accounts; for the purposes of a political history, their importance in the party was negligible. The indisputable fact is that they shared the fate of Ho and other Communist men whose death is shrouded in a mystery which, until there is access to the secret files of both the Kuomintang and the Communist Party, it is almost impossible to penetrate. However, even from the limited materials available, the case should provoke deeper feelings than mere revulsion at the notorious White Terror. What distinguishes a tragedy from a tragic melodrama is that in the latter victims always become "good guys" because they are in the end bound to be killed by the bad guys; but the former relentlessly and bewilderingly pits the victims against some unsuspected, dark forces as well as against their open enemy. History, often too complicated to be dramatic, is certainly not composed of a sequence of bloody scenes, with good and evil clearly demarcated and in perpetual conflict. The temptation to treat the story of the twenty-three as one of such melodramatic episodes is great, since the "bad guy," the sadistic persecutor, the brutal killer, is so easy to nail down. But if it can be illustrated that the "good guys" could hate each other with a vehemence which should have been reserved for their common enemy, our study will perhaps reveal a tragic irony which is closer to historical truth.

MAO TUN, TING LING, AND HU YEH-P'IN

There is no way of telling how many of the twenty-three were natives of Shanghai. The five writers all came from the provinces: two from Chekiang, the other three from Fukien, Kwangtung, and Hupeh. Ho Meng-hsiung was probably born in Hsiangt'an, Hunan.[10] From these samplings, we may say that most of the twenty-three were provincials who somehow had drifted to the metropolis, known then as "the Paris of the Orient, the home of the homeless, the haven of undesirables, and the paradise of adven-

---

[9] Robert C. North, *Moscow and Chinese Communists* (Stanford: Stanford University Press, 1953), p. 150.

[10] See "My Impressions of Ho Meng-hsiung" in the gossipy paper, *She-hui hsin-wen* (*Society Mercury*) (Shanghai), Mar. 30, 1933, available at the University of Washington Library. Another source gives Ling-hsien, Hunan. *Hsien-tai shih-liao* (*Materials on Current Chinese History*) (2d printing; Shanghai: Hsin-kuang Book Company, 1935), I, 246.

turers." [11] The sobriquet stood as appropriate to its Chinese as to its foreign population in those hectic and crowded days when the International Settlement and the French Concession attracted, and generously accommodated, the refugees from civil war and famine, the fugitives from law, peasants who had lost their land, ambitious young men who came to make their fortunes, and retired officials to spend theirs. Shanghai, as a center of revolutionary movements, held a position in modern Chinese history unequalled even by Canton or Peking. It was here that Chiang Kai-shek served his revolutionary apprenticeship; Mao Tse-tung helped to establish the Chinese Communist Party; and Sun Yat-sen lectured on the Three People's Principles. After 1927, the Central Committee of the CCP was seated in Shanghai, assisted in its activities by the Kiangsu Provincial Committee, the seven district committees on the city level,[12] trade unions, and numerous front organizations. Few other places would qualify so well as a "hotbed of rebellion." Though Shanghai was seldom touched by civil war, the "extermination campaign" was fought as bitterly here as in Kiangsi. It was Chiang Kai-shek's successes in this area of operation, owing partly to the White Terror, that drove Wang Ming and other Communist leaders to the interior. How that helped the rise of Mao as supreme leader of the party has already been a subject of extensive research—for example, in Schwartz's *Chinese Communism and the Rise of Mao.*

This study will be concerned primarily with the year 1930, which saw the fall of Li Li-san and the ensuing scramble for power in the CCP. These incidents scarcely appeared in the headlines; indeed, one wonders whether they were reported by any except the Japanese newspapers.[13] The event of the year, which had the most profound effects, was the world-wide depression. As the economic crisis drove people to despair, the radical philosophies of communism and of its declared opponent, fascism, began as never before to gather a following. In China, the impact was felt, but in a manner pe-

[11] G. E. Miller (pseudonym), *Shanghai, the Paradise of Adventurers* (New York: Orsay Publishing House, 1937), p. 254. The adventurers here are foreigners.

[12] "The C.P. has divided Shanghai into seven districts: Central, Northern, Western, Eastern, French Concession and Nantao, Woosung, and Pootung." *North China Herald* (Shanghai), Apr. 15, 1930, p. 92.

[13] Titles of contemporary articles on the CCP published in the Japanese *Shanhai nippo* (*Shanghai Daily News*), *Mantetsu nippo* (*Southern Manchuria Railway Daily News*), *Shanhai shuho* (*Shanghai Weekly*), etc., are found in Hatano Kenichi, *Chugoku Kyosanto shi* (*History of the Chinese Communist Party*) (Tokyo, 1961), I, 650–57.

culiar to Chinese society. To a superficial observer, the major events in China reflected little of the acuteness of the world economic situation: some seemed almost like anachronisms that could have taken place in any other year or century. A northern coalition of Feng Yü-hsiang and Yen Hsi-shan challenged Nanking's hegemony, resulting in another "sport of generals" which was costly in human lives. The disturbances staged by the Communists in Shanghai turned out to be ridiculously unimpressive, demonstrating nothing but the futility of Li Li-san's grandiose plans; they led to arrests and executions, thus further weakening the party, which was already plagued by internal dissension. The Red Army departed from its guerrilla tactics and became a respectable fighting force with the capture of Changsha. This ill-advised military adventure, however, ended in fiasco, brought sharp criticism on the leadership of Li Li-san, and hastened his downfall. Communist-led riots, on a less ambitious scale, broke out in some provinces. Their significance was yet to be appreciated. Meanwhile the Red Army in Kiangsi once again showed prowess in a successful countermovement against the First Extermination Campaign.[14]

About the social conditions, much can be learned from Mao Tun's *Tzu-yeh (Midnight)*, which bore in its original edition a subtitle in English, "The Twilight, A Romance of China in 1930,"[15] with the scenes mostly laid in Shanghai. A work of fiction purporting to illustrate the Stalinist thesis "How Chinese industrialists, groaning under foreign economic aggression, were hindered on the one hand by the feudal forces and threat-

---

[14] General Chang Hui-tsan, commander of Nanking's eighteenth division, was killed after being taken prisoner in spite of his plea for mercy. See Liu Ya-lou, "The First Great Step," in *Jen-min jih-pao,* July 4, 1961, p. 7. ". . . General Chang was badly tortured. After he was shot to death, he was beheaded, and the head, tied to a wood plank, was floated down the river to Kian." Ku Kuan-chiao, *San-shih-nien-lai-ti chung-kung (The Chinese Communist Party in the Last Thirty Years)* (Hong Kong: Asia Publishing House, 1955), p. 54. Another gory incident occurred in December, 1930: "During the sanguine Fut'ien Incident of December, 1930, Mao struck out against a party faction which had been formed in opposition to his growing power over the countryside. According to Chang Kuo-t'ao, '. . . Mao arrested and executed hundreds of anti-Mao Communists who were dubbed members of the A-B (Anti-Bolshevik) Corps.'" North, *op. cit.,* p. 173. For details compiled from Communist sources, see Tso-liang Hsiao, *Power Relations within the Chinese Communist Movement, 1930–1934* (Seattle: University of Washington Press, 1961), pp. 98–113.

[15] A facsimile of the frontispiece of the first edition of *Tzu-yeh* is reprinted in *Mao Tun wen-chi (Works of Mao Tun)* (Peking: People's Literary Publications Association, 1958), Vol. III. For the plot and a critical appraisal of *Tzu-yeh,* see C. T. Hsia, *A History of Modern Chinese Fiction* (New Haven: Yale University Press, 1961), pp. 155–60.

ened on the other by the control of the money market by compradore-capitalists," [16] it nevertheless gave satisfaction to readers who had been brought up on the fare of the naturalistic school. *Tzu-yeh* means "Midnight," which is now the title of the authorized English version, but the earlier suggested title "Twilight," meaning "gathering darkness," may stress even more the gloom that our romancer found in Shanghai. Mao Tun's attempt was to "interweave three strands, represented by compradore-capitalists, reactionary industrial capitalists, and the revolutionaries and the working masses," [17] and he regretted his inability "to portray the revolutionaries as the principal characters," [18] a failure he attributed to difficulties with the censorship. But his romance about darkness was a much more honest attempt at realism than the prevalent revolutionary literature of his time. The latter's vision of a dawn was at best prophetic, but more often simply hallucinatory. Economic theory notwithstanding, Mao Tun seemed to be fascinated by the very things he cursed—bourgeois life with its parlors and boudoirs, its business offices and stock exchanges. He scarcely concealed his admiration for the hero he created, the industrialist capitalist, Wu Sun-fu, who, even in his collapse, fell like a giant.

As one of the better novels of modern China, *Tzu-yeh* actually places the revolutionaries in a proper perspective. The author's apology for not giving them bigger roles sounds insincere and unjustified, unless it was meant to please the Communist Party. The capitalists then did hold the stage (time: 1930; scene: Shanghai), fighting, intriguing, and making love with as much importance as was presented in the book. Doomed though they might be, the catastrophe was yet to come. Someone was digging their graves perhaps, but the digging was only remotely heard.

But our admiration for this major novelist prompts us to ask how Mao Tun, with his omniscient realistic methods and tragic sense, would have treated the Communists in Shanghai in 1930. They were in rather bad shape, and to write about them truthfully would have been very embarrassing for a Communist sympathizer. The plot would have had to do with an over-zealous, boastful, and high-handed leadership, causing demoralization and dissidence among the cadres who could hardly win over the cowed or otherwise unenthusiastic masses. The hero of such a story would have been an idealist, a type with which Mao Tun must have been familiar. Occupying

---

[16] Mao Tun, Author's Preface, *Midnight* (in English) (Peking: Foreign Languages Press, 1957).

[17] *Ibid.*

[18] *Ibid.*

a position similar to that of the industrialist-capitalist, the idealist-revolutionary, to imitate Mao Tun's phraseology, "groaning under the pressure from the Comintern, was hindered on the one hand by the White Terror, and threatened on the other by the stupidity and inhumanity of the party leadership." The conflict between Communists could be, of course, as fierce and fascinating as the struggle of Communist against capitalist. Here was a theme full of dramatic potentialities, but one which Mao Tun, to the loss of his readers, never exploited. Only a few hints are given in *Tzu-yeh* about the revolutionary situation, but even these little revelations set the author apart from his fellow left-wing writers, few of whom, indeed, ever attained his breadth of mind.

Even in their minor roles, the revolutionaries in *Tzu-yeh* were at least an assorted lot. Writing from hindsight (the work was composed in late 1931 and 1932), Mao Tun could tell the difference between the incorrect Communists and the correct ones, or between the Li Li-sanists and the non-Li-Li-sanists. Besides, there was a Trotskyist and a member of the Wang Ching-wei faction or the so-called left-wing Kuomintang. Both could pass for revolutionaries at the time in question, as Ch'en Tu-hsiu, the Trotskyist leader in China, and Wang Ching-wei did command a following among the Chinese youth.[19] Mao Tun was too much occupied with the charms and complexities of bourgeois life to pay such people sufficient attention; and besides, he had to keep the narrative interest in mind. To expose the false prophets with cogency would have required the intrusion of polemics, which could be very boring. But Mao Tun had at least the historical sense to allow the Li Li-sanist, the Trotskyist, and the Wang Ching-weist to appear in his story, though he only hurried to dismiss them with contempt.

Miss Ting Ling's *Shanghai, Spring 1930,*[20] which covers about the same

[19] Of 571 students at the National Peking University who answered a questionnaire put out as part of celebrations commemorating the thirty–first anniversary of the University (December, 1929), "ninety-seven expressed open admiration for Wang Ching-wei, and no other Chinese statesman got anywhere near the number of votes . . . 'Who is the contemporary thinker in China whom you admire most?' Ch'en Tu-hsiu (almost unknown abroad) received more votes than any other. He is now a fugitive from justice." "Potted Wisdom from Peking," *North China Herald,* Jan. 21, 1930, p. 96.

[20] Ting Ling, *I-chiu-san-ling-nien ch'un shang-hai (Shanghai, Spring 1930),* serialized in *Hsiao-shuo yüeh-pao (Short Story Magazine)* (Shanghai), Sept., Nov., Dec., 1930. Ting Ling did not join the Left League until the summer of 1931. See Li Ho-lin *et al., Chung-kuo hsin-wen-hsüeh-shih yen-chiu (Studies in the History of Modern Chinese Literature)* (Peking: New Construction Magazine Association, 1951), p. 81. **She**

period as *Tzu-yeh,* does portray "revolutionaries as principal characters."
But they were of only two types: those who had found their faith and those
who had not yet. It was the former who, setting an example by their joyous
outlook and self-assured views, gave encouragement and guidance to the
latter—the petty-bourgeois intellectuals who were finally enabled to rise
above their private worries to join wholeheartedly the mass movement. Such
a differentiation sounds crude, but any nicer distinction did not seem to interest Ting Ling. What mattered to her and many other intellectuals was the
line separating the revolutionary from the nonrevolutionary. From biographical information, we know that by the middle of 1930 Ting Ling was about to
cross that line, though not without misgivings. She was aware that a literary
career demanded as much sacrifice and devotion as a revolutionary one and
that by accepting the one, she had to neglect the other. But revolution proved
to have a stronger pull.

Shanghai, Spring 1930 is a novelette in two disconnected parts, or rather
a combination of two independent stories. They serve to illustrate one idea,
as the second part only repeats the thematic pattern of the first. The idea is
simple: how intellectuals discover the meaning of their lives in a mass movement. In the way Ting Ling treats them the intellectuals do not appear capable of much thinking. The only intelligent problem discussed is that of the
nascent proletarian literature, whose truth, however, seems to be self-evident
and whose opponents never have anything serious to say. Petty-bourgeois re-
spectability and security, as in the first part, and sex, as in the second, are
recognized as evils that can lead one away from the true life. How the revolutionaries fortify their souls against the temptations forms the main narrative
interest of the story. Mei-lin, heroine of the first part, is a woman of some
literary training who is induced by her friends to join first a "literary study
group" (obviously a Communist organization) and then a street demonstration. Before she takes the plunge, she writes to bid farewell to her husband,
who remains incurably a petty bourgeois in his ways of life and his views of
literature. How she fares in her encounter with the police is not told, but
Wang-wei, hero of the second part, is shown being dragged into a police van
when a mob riot is suppressed. He, too, has had his weakness to overcome,
for it is not easy for him to sever relations with his mistress, a ghostlike

---

said in "Life of a Real Person" (cited in note 21), pp. 17–18: "To me, the choice was
then either to look for my old friends [Ch'ü Ch'iu-po and others] and occupy myself
entirely with underground work, or to write. I could not see clearly the relation
between revolution and literature. Individual heroism also disposed me to regard
revolution as meaning non-literary work."

woman who has found her way back from his unrevolutionary past to haunt him amidst his meaningful activities.

A slender work within a limited range, Ting Ling's story may be disappointing to the reader who is led by the title to expect more of the energy, tension, and complexity of the life in Shanghai. But her deliberate choice of subject matter reveals an interesting view of history. These sketchy studies of ennui, eroticism, and revolutionary zeal, these little episodes about discontented intellectuals who do not actually suffer from material want, these vignettes filled with self-pity—do they contain some of the most significant events at the time and place referred to? Only in the eyes of a few of her contemporaries; but these few were not entirely wrong. If the importance of an event is to be judged by its consequences, then the handful of young people, who broke away from their families and lovers to participate in street demonstrations foredoomed to failure, were harbingers of bigger events to come. It was young intellectuals not unlike the characters in Ting Ling's story who kept replenishing the ranks of revolutionaries. It was they who carried on and spread the revolution in its most difficult time. Their emergence and continuing growth in number therefore merit serious attention. While Mao Tun was gloating over the body of the old feudalistic society and diagnosing the diseases that were killing the monster of "national capitalism" in its infancy, Ting Ling turned her eyes from the putrid grotesqueness and poured out her love for those people whose fate belonged rather to the future. The future, of course, was then only a vision, but what a vision!

There was no doubt where Ting Ling would show her love, for her husband, Hu Yeh-p'in, was one of such young intellectuals. His life has been written, lovingly, by Ting Ling,[21] and, with friendly understanding, by Shen Ts'ung-wen.[22] Malcolm Cowley, in the article previously cited, described him as "typical of the new generation of writers in China." But unlike the other four martyrs, he was never an active revolutionary until the last few months of his short life. Of the three passions that consumed his life—passion for art, for his wife, and for revolution—the last was a poor third, though it turned out to possess the most destructive power. His revolutionary beliefs he had acquired from books, and what he did had been no more than to propagate these beliefs until he joined the League of Leftist Writers some-

---

[21] Ting Ling's "The Life of a Real Person" is printed as an introduction to *Hu Yeh-p'in hsüan-chi* (*Hu Yeh-p'in: Selected Works*) (Peking: Kaiming Book Store, 1951). These selected works are hereafter cited as *HYP*.

[22] Shen Ts'ung-wen, *Chi Hu Yeh-p'in* (Shanghai: Kuanghua Book Company, 1932). Hu also appears in Shen's *Chi Ting Ling* (Shanghai: Liang-yu Company, 1934).

time around May, 1930. After years of wandering and literary ventures (he and Ting Ling were married in 1924 in Peking), he had a bizarre experience in the spring of 1930 when he taught high school in Tsinan, Shantung. The incident is remarkable as an indication of the political unrest and the feebleness of the Communist Party at that time. An inexperienced teacher, he found himself immensely popular. He was loved and revered as a sort of leader. What little he learned from Plekhanov and Lunacharsky (through the translations by Lu Hsün and Feng Hsüeh-feng) created such a stir among the young minds that the whole school was talking about proletarian literature. Even the principal and the proctor, under the pressure of the students, changed the tone of their lectures. A "literary study club" was formed, with a membership of over four hundred. On May 4, when the annual celebration was held, the students were so excited that they almost rioted. Hu was worried, for in the unwitting role of a Pied Piper, he was incapable of leading the crowds whom his magic had gathered. By definition, only the Communist Party should assume the leadership, but in Tsinan, no one seemed to know where the party was. Was it not in Shanghai? He was about to make the journey to look for it when the rumor came that the agitation at the school had attracted the notice of the authorities and Hu would be in trouble soon. So he fled to Shanghai.[23]

In Shanghai he joined the newly formed League of Leftist Writers, an "open" organization under the control of the Communists. Ting Ling, debating within herself the advisability of a revolutionary career, did not take immediate interest in the League's political activities. She was still trying to remain primarily a writer, though the direction of her sympathies is clearly illustrated in *Shanghai, Spring 1930*. In addition, her pregnant condition also prevented her from overwork. But whatever mental reservations she may have had, nothing seemed to deter her husband, who plunged into his new life with zest and abandon. A more passionate nature, combined, perhaps, with a mistrust of his own artistic talent, drove Hu Yeh-p'in to accept responsibilities which were only so many distractions from literary creation. He taught at a summer school, presumably for workers, and was elected a member of the Executive Committee of the League, chairman of its Board of Correspondence with Workers, Peasants, and Soldiers, and a member of the delegation to the Soviet Congress to be convened in Kiangsi. One new duty led to another, until in the end he was almost accepted by the Communists as one of them. To apply for party membership was now inevitable,

[23] *HYP*, p. 21.

which he did in November, 1930, and was soon approved. Ting Ling gave birth to a boy at about the same time. To celebrate that happy event, or even before the baby was born, he wrote a story,[24] in which the father, very busy with clandestine meetings, could be a self-portrait. The fictitious young man allowed an abortion to be procured for his young wife. His son was killed in imagination, at the risk of his wife's life, only three months before he himself met death.

Hu, in this story, held a view about childbirth similar to that of Feng K'eng (original name Feng Ling-mei), the girl from Kwangtung. *The Outpost,*[25] a secret publication dedicated to the five martyrs, printed the following eulogy about her:

> Her looks were like a man's with thick brows and big eyes and with her distaste for makeup. Usually she cohabited with comrades, but she made a vow never to be troubled with pregnancy. She employed all means of contraception lest her revolutionary work should be hindered. She was successful in this even unto the last days of her life.[26]

In Hu Yeh-p'in's story, there is a passage:

> "Don't feel sorry," she took his hand and said. "We do love each other. You are not to be blamed; you have already exercised enough self-control. I am now with child, and I am responsible for it. Of course, if the circumstances were other than they are, the child should be brought up. But now, even though we could afford to bring it up, we should not allow it to see the light. Once there is a baby, our work will be hindered. We cannot have the baby." [27]

This was a statement Ting Ling in real life might have made, but perhaps never did. She not only cherished private dreams about a writer's life, but remained sufficiently feminine to become a mother. But her husband, burning with a purer fire of revolutionary spirit, thought differently. It was not that he did not love their boy; he even felt proud as a father should. After his arrest, he sent a short note from the prison, addressing Ting Ling as "Young Mama" and concluding with the signature "Young Papa." [28] But to him, nothing was more important than the *work,* for which everything else should be sacrificed. The story he wrote has an apposite title: "Sacrifice."

---

[24] "Sacrifice," *Short Story Magazine,* Dec., 1930, pp. 1713–22. The author used a name, Hu I-p'ing. The name Hsiao-p'ing was given to his son. *HYP,* p. 22.

[25] *The Outpost* (Shanghai), Vol. I, No. 1 (Apr. 25, 1931). This rare item is found in the collection of the Hoover Library, Stanford University.

[26] *Ibid.,* p. 10.

[27] *Short Story Magazine,* Dec., 1930, p. 1716.

[28] *HYP,* pp. 29–30.

Later, Lu Hsün selected Käthe Kollwitz's woodcut "The Sacrifice," showing a sorrowful mother giving up her son, as most expressive of his feelings at the death of Jou Shih, another of the five.[29]

At meetings and in other activities, Hu Yeh-p'in came to know the other four young writers, though nothing on record indicates that friendship existed between him and any of them. His best friend, and also Ting Ling's, was still Shen Ts'ung-wen, a non-leftist writer who was perhaps caricatured in *Shanghai, Spring 1930* as the sullen opponent of proletarian literature. In spite of their visions and aspirations, not all of the leftist writers were able to cut off their ties with the old society. The most eminent example was Lu Hsün, who, under the patronage of Ts'ai Yüan-p'ei, continued to receive from the Nanking government $300 a month, which went into the building of his private collection of books.[30] Neither Ting Ling nor Hu Yeh-p'in had a patron. Living by their pens, they were at the mercy of publishers whose interest in money-making was surpassed only by their fear of getting involved in subversive activities. Books on socialism or written from a socialist point of view were published in 1930 in large numbers,[31] for there was a demand

[29] *Lu Hsün ch'üan-chi* (*Complete Works*) (Peking: People's Literary Publications Association, 1957), IV, 374 (hereafter cited as *LH*).

[30] "From the time he came to Shanghai (October, 1927), he was appointed by Ts'ai Yüan-p'ei, through the recommendation of Hsü Shou-ch'ang, as Special Editor of the Ta Hsüeh Yüan [Grand Academy] (later the Ministry of Education), a post which he occupied until the reorganization of the National Government after the Battle of Shanghai (January 28, 1932). So for five years he was in a sense an employee of the Ministry of Education under the National Government." Ts'ao Chü-jen, *Lu Hsün p'ing-chuan* (*A Critical Biography of Lu Hsün*) (Hong Kong: New Culture Publications Association, 1956), p. 101. See the entries, for instance, in Lu Hsün's *Diary* for 1930, under 1/27, 2/28, 3/26, 4/29, 5/27, 6/30, 9/8 (for July), 10/3 ("Received from the Ministry of Education editorial fee $300 for August"), 12/15 (for September); and also 1/8/1931 (for October, 1930), 3/7 (for November, 1930), 4/5 (for December, 1930). Lu Hsün, *Jih-chi* (*Diary*) (Peking: People's Literary Publications Association, 1959).

[31] Hu Ch'iu-yüan, commenting on a list of translated books on social sciences published in 1929, says, "About 140 titles were translated that year. . . . Nine-tenths of them were of a Marxist, socialist, or Communist nature. . . . If each book sold 3,000 copies, the total should amount to 400,000 copies—their influence on the contemporary youth must have been tremendous." *Min-chu-ch'ao* (*Current Democracy*) (Taipei), Sept. 16, 1960. The said list, originally published in 1930, is reprinted in Chang Ching-lu, *Chung-kuo hsien-tai ch'u-pan shih-liao* (*Bibliographical and Historical Materials concerning Contemporary Chinese Publications*) (Shanghai: Chung Hwa Book Company, 1955), II, 7–18. A comparable list is found in K'o Po-nien, *Tsen-yang yen-chiu hsin-hsing she-hui k'o-hsüeh* (*How to Study the New Social Sciences*) (Shanghai: Nan Ch'iang Book Company, 1930). T'ao Hsi-sheng made an interesting remark in 1931: "No one can deny the leftist inclination of the youth, which is

in the market, but proletarian literature, making no pretense of scholarship and containing passages too obviously offensive, was regarded as dangerous. As Hu Yeh-p'in grew more outspoken about his personal beliefs, he found fewer buyers for his manuscripts. Recommendation by Shen Ts'ung-wen used to help, because of his better relations with editors and eminent writers such as Hu Shih and Hsü Chih-mo, but now he could do nothing about the rejection slips. This seemed to bother Hu less than it did his friend, since he was ready for even greater sacrifices. Anyway, both Hu and Ting Ling could still get their works published, although her market too was affected by the changed outlook in her stories.

His *magnum opus, Light Is Ahead of Us,* a novel of about two hundred pages, was not rejected. But according to Shen, the magazine that printed it was fined, and consequently suspended publication.[32] This and a shorter and earlier work, *Go to Moscow!,* mentioned in the *New Masses,* were Hu's major contributions to proletarian literature; but strangely, Ting Ling did not like them. After commenting on Shen's hobnobbing with the "gentlemen class," she said, ". . . but neither did I like Yeh-p'in's works after his conversion. I used to say to Yeh-p'in that he was a case of leftist infantilism." [33] Without going into the arcana of Leninist terminology, she perhaps meant, in plain language, that they were immature in spite of their tendentiousness. This is to be expected since our author never had a chance to achieve maturity.

If by maturity is meant the ability in a writer to see things from more than one side, to weigh ideals against experience, and to recognize human weaknesses even in the midst of the noblest deeds, then such a quality is missing in Hu Yeh-p'in. But neither did Ting Ling possess it to a remarkable degree. The greatest difficulty with revolutionary writers is their passion for the revolution. They believe so strongly in its supreme goodness that they cannot ask questions about it. Motives are always too pure to need analysis, and one's faculty of reason seems out of place in the ecstatic moments of a strike, a demonstration, or a riot. Slogans shouted by the mob in a novel are echoed by its author, and he can hardly control his excitement. For Hu

---

reflected in the leftist tendency of the publishing business. There is no denying, too, that the current publications are mostly socialist in nature. . . . It is the leftist inclination of the youth that causes such a flood of leftist publications; and it is not the books that cause the leftist inclination among the youth." T'ao, *Chung-kuo she-hui hsien-hsiang shih-ling (Gleanings of Chinese Social Phenomena)* (Shanghai: New Life Book Company, 1931), p. 285.

[32] The magazine was published in Wuchang. Shen, *Chi Hu Yeh-p'in,* p. 72.

[33] *HYP,* p. 17.

Yeh-p'in and many of his contemporaries, including his critical wife, Ting Ling, revolution was something to rave about, a natural solution to the personal problems of the intellectuals, an endless source of fiery poetical phrases, and the *grand finale* to conclude a work of fiction with a chorus of slogans and a tableau of heroic gestures. Professedly realistic, they wrote about revolution as if it existed in their heated brains rather than in reality. The strong beam in their eyes (*Light Is Ahead of Us*) blinds them to certain basic facts about revolutions and the men who make them. But these facts are important, if not for the sake of truthfulness, at least as a setting to show in relief the meaning of such heroism as was exemplified by the five young writers.

Comparatively speaking, Mao Tun is the most mature of all the leftist writers. Even though it was written under political dictates, *Midnight* contains insights which are not found in Ting Ling and others. Here are a few lines of dialogue between Wu Sun-fu, owner of the factory, and Tu Wei-yüeh, its able and cynical manager bent on breaking a strike:

Wu Sun-fu listened with his brows drawn together in a frown. His lips were pressed tightly together and his keen glance darted all round. Suddenly, he broke in with impatience, "Do you think they'd dare smash the machines? Or set fire to the premises? Or start a riot?"

"They're like a lot of raving lunatics at the moment, and I wouldn't put anything past them. Though it can't last long; once the crowd is dispersed they'll quiet down again." [34]

This is not a defamation of revolution or a desecration of the masses. On the contrary, the latter's fickleness, frantic outbursts, and easy retreat into inaction are the very realities which a professional revolutionary has to cope with but which a revolutionary writer, in his or her idealism, is apt to ignore. Contrast the lines above with a few from Hu Yeh-p'in's *Light Is Ahead of Us:*

"General strike!" This was a strong electric current.

"General strike!" At once, the current electrified the earth, electrified the people on the earth—setting fire to their hearts and their passions.[35]

And the lines from a poem by Yin Fu:

> Suddenly,
> The Red Angel throws the Fire of Revolution
> Onto the Earth!

[34] *Mao Tun wen-chi*, III, 400; *Midnight*, pp. 363–64.
[35] *HYP*, pp. 262–63.

This is not an accident,
This is not an accident! [36]

These last quotations show how the passion for revolution could be set above the revolution itself. For an "electrified" moment at least, revolution enters the realm of mysticism. The lines above, though they seem only a jumble of clichés, carry personal conviction. Such images as earth in the broadest sense, fire, light, and the people of the world indicate an expansion of the soul which is often felt in the midst of an excited crowd. The thrilling sensation may be exactly what the bored intellectuals in Ting Ling's *Shanghai, Spring 1930* were seeking. But to invest a local riot with cosmic significance is only to dismiss its special problems and ignore its actual operation. By magnifying it the writer is only generalizing and simplifying it. He will overlook the actual struggle; he will take little notice of all that makes an organized mass movement work: scheming, timing, maintenance of discipline, calculated sacrifice of human lives, inflammation and exploitation of public sentiments, tactical moves and countermoves. If a writer fails to notice these things, he is unaware of the circumstances under which human nature is at once ennobled and debased—shamelessly manipulated and mocked while it is supposed to glory in true heroism. Revolution is after all made by man and not a gift from some angel. The horror, falsehood, and ludicrousness that characterize its operation are as human as the ideals that motivate it. If the former depresses and irritates, one can always derive cheer and comfort from the latter. This is what Mao Tun did. But to ignore the former is to blink at catastrophe and to misunderstand history and human nature. For his incapacity to comprehend revolution in its wholeness, Hu Yeh-p'in was at worst an "infantile" writer. But if he engaged in political struggle without raising his mentality above the puerile level, the consequences could be disastrous.

It is hard to say how much Ting Ling disapproved of Hu's treatment of revolution, a difficult subject anyway, one too ponderous even for her flimsy genius to support. What she could perceive, and what should be obvious to his readers, is the inadequacy in his rendering of Chinese society. Ting Ling was allowed by her reservations to see at least the charms, problems, and meanings of a nonrevolutionary life. The occasional psychological subtleties, the little tremors of a sensitive mind that enliven her writings are absent in his. His eagerness for revolution made it im-

[36] Yin Fu, "The Metabolism of the Ages," in *Hai-erh t'a* (*Pagoda for the Infants*) (Peking: People's Literary Publications Association, 1959), p. 103.

possible for him to dwell on such trivialities or on anything or any person that was doomed to be swept away by the surging tides of history. The characters belonging to the "old society" could never win the author's love unless they too would see the light. He tolerated their appearance only with impatience. If he could not yet eliminate them from society, he could at least limit their role in his books. His *Go to Moscow!* is another variation of the Nora theme, but here the wife not only walks out on her husband but travels to Moscow with a new life in prospect.[37] While Ting Ling employs the same theme in the first part of *Shanghai, Spring 1930,* Hu's approach is much bolder. In Ting Ling's work, the husband is still a human being, whose unlovableness is due to his insensitivity to his wife's darker moods and his refusal to keep abreast of the "march of time." Hu, on the other hand, complicates the plot of his story by giving the woman a Communist lover who is killed by her beastlike husband who happens to be a government official. Class struggle is thus put neatly within the framework of the eternal triangle—a rather unwarranted application of the Marxist theory. *Light Is Ahead of Us* concerns three sets of stereotyped characters: Communists, writers of the "art for art's sake school," and anarchists identified with "utopian socialists." As "light" is finally seen by the exponents of the last two schools of thought, they join the mass movement led by the true revolutionaries. The happy ending shows the Communist boy and the girl converted from anarchism making strides into the "bright sunshine."

In spite of its optimistic tones and fiery images, one can detect in *Light Is Ahead of Us* a note of nostalgia. Written in 1930, the story is about the May Thirtieth movement of 1925. The author, then in Peking, was now in Shanghai. The great mass movement was tastelessly exaggerated, as the author simply tried to recapture a grandeur that belonged to the past. Another mass movement on the scale of 1925, one that could win so much public support, did not seem likely in 1930 and Hu was destined never to witness one. He could not help being fascinated by the events of only a few years

---

[37] *Go to Moscow!* and *Light Is Ahead of Us* form the main body of *HYP*. Two works by Hu not discussed in the paper are: (a) "Cohabitation," a short sketch about married life in the Soviet areas, reprinted in *The Outpost*, pp. 25–28; (b) "The Bricklayer's Family," a one-act play which presents the bricklayer as an alcoholic, his wife as a mahjongg addict, and their daughter as a victim of their tyranny. The play is an interesting example of his "humanitarianism" before he embraced Marxism. It was reprinted in Hung Shen, *Chung-kuo hsin-wen-hsüeh ta-hsi* (*A Comprehensive Anthology of Modern Chinese Literature*) (Shanghai: Liang-yu Company, 1935–36), IX, 310–17.

earlier, which yet looked so remote. He was now ready for "fight," but the fires of 1925 had been all but extinguished. He realized how much he had missed in life. In 1925, he might have been one of the demonstrators in the streets; he might have written leaflets and slogans denouncing the imperialists. But it was also possible that he made no contribution whatsoever. For his life in the years after his marriage was marked, according to Shen Ts'ung-wen, by pastoral quietness in a cottage in the hills west of Peking;[38] and, according to Ting Ling, by a regrettable seclusion from human affairs. Said Ting Ling:

> My thought at that time was in utter confusion. I had extremely rebellious sentiments, having once blindly favored social revolution. But because of my petty-bourgeois illusions, I had estranged myself from the ranks of revolutionaries and taken the solitary path of moroseness, vain struggles, and suffering. Neither my eccentricity nor my pride could of course exercise any salutary influence over Yeh-p'in. He contracted the diseases of melancholy and nihilism. The poems he wrote at that time were filled with such deplorable emotions. For quite some time we lived in solitude. Meanwhile, the great revolutionary movement in China was raging in all its fury in the South, but we lived like hermits, doing nothing in Peking. Day and night Yeh-p'in buried himself in his poetry, and I passed each day in ennui. Reflecting on this now, I can only say what a pity indeed it was! [39]

Hu Yeh-p'in's poetry was described by Ting Ling as either "an imprecation on life," or "a hymn for love." It was only natural for him to speak unkindly of life, since life was not particularly kind to him. His rebellious nature was formed when he served as a goldsmith's apprentice. His school education was erratic, though he entered a naval academy and, later, Peking University. As a writer struggling hard for a living, he did not get along well in the world. The surprising fact was that after so much hardship, sublimation in the form of poetry was still possible for him. As for love, it was sexual love. How love troubled a whole generation of Chinese youth liberated from the old marriage system is too large a subject to be treated here. Suffice it to say that many ardent revolutionaries began as ardent lovers. Amorous passion, indeed, can enlarge into passion for revolution, as Yü Ta-fu points out in his postscript (1926) to Kuo Mo-jo's *The Bottle,* a cycle of love poems:

> We who have read his "Essays on Literature" probably all know that Mo-jo's thought has radically changed [for proletarian literature].

> Here are forty-two poems written only last year which he did not want to publish. It is we who put them in print.

---

[38] Shen, *Chi Hu Yeh-p'in,* pp. 17 ff.
[39] *HYP,* pp. 15–16.

I think it would not really matter if poets were socialized. A truly revolutionary poem is not one which rattles with pistols and grenades or contains
the word "revolution" repeated hundreds of times. But speak out your genuine
sentiments under no disguise, emit your passion as if it were lava from a volcano
—this is the paramount duty of a poet. The emergence of a revolutionary
career is possible only for that little passion, the cultivation of which is inseparable from the tender and pure love of a woman. That passion, if extended,
is ardent enough to burn down the palaces of a despot and powerful enough
to destroy the Bastille . . .[40]

Yü Ta-fu, known to be a decadent, "extended" his passion only for a short
time: he became disillusioned with the conditions in Canton even before
the Northern Expedition. His theory, so naïvely put, was applicable not
only to himself and Kuo Mo-jo but also to Hu Yeh-p'in and others. It was
of course another example of immature thinking that revolution should be
regarded as a purely individual affair.

FROM LYRICISM TO REVOLUTION

It was no accident that Hu Yeh-p'in once wrote poetry. An investigation
of the careers of Jou Shih, Feng K'eng, and Yin Fu reveals also an early
propensity for lyricism. These four should be counted among the hundreds
of Chinese youth who found their poetical voice after the May Fourth
Movement of 1919. A new poetical culture came into being in almost every
high school, where boys and girls, encouraged by the "experiments" of
professors and scholars, began to publish their immature works. Endless
strains floated into the air which sang of young love or mother's affection,
teardrops and sweet smiles, little flowers, blue sky, and white clouds. Nothing profound or abstruse was said: poetry was then an easy vehicle for
communication. As to the form, a facile but regular rhyme pattern was
generally followed though the "shackles of the old verse" were broken.
"Little poems" in two or three irregular lines, in the manner of Tagore,
were the boldest attempt at free verse. The old tradition was carried on in
spite of the theorists, since one had still to look into the treasure of the
classical poets for phrases to arrest a melancholy mood or to dress up a
beautiful landscape. The youthful poets had a sense of beauty which permitted a continuity of the tradition. Indeed, they were not so much conscious linguistic or literary reformers as conscious voices of self-expression.
Their works were to register a mood, to convey an emotion, and to seek
sympathy. ("To strike an echoing chord" was one of the favorite phrases

[40] *Mo-jo wen-chi* (*Collected Works*) (Hong Kong: San Lien Book Company, 1957),
I, 271.

of the time.) Poetry gave them their first lessons in literary composition, awakened them to a sense of power over language, and sharpened their reaction to the little sorrows in life. If they did not produce a masterpiece, the moods and the styles they somehow shared were a notable cultural phenomenon. Adolescents are always notorious for their creative urge, but at this particular juncture of Chinese history, their versified moans and rhymed sighs won recognition as a new departure for literature.

This silver age of lyricism lasted only a few years; so it has not sufficiently caught the attention of historians. And the poems, mimeographed on flimsy paper or printed in pamphlets which never enjoyed a large circulation, are hard to find today. Those that were posted on walls or copied in diaries and correspondence will perhaps be lost forever. Few of the juvenile poets lived up to their promise. It was not that they began to write worse poetry after they had passed the age of twenty; they simply ceased to be poets. As they grew up, they became engrossed in more practical affairs, and when and if they published again, their works were more likely to be prose. The political events after 1925 worked so violently on the minds of the Chinese youth that lyricism was almost killed in shock. Tears that used to be shed in a solitary mood or at the parting of a dear friend were now held back. Sadness on such occasions was perhaps no longer felt, as a greater sorrow for the oppressed condition of China and the oppressed masses of the world overpowered the poet's growing sensibility. Sorrow soon passed into anger, and anger into action. Poetry, of course, could still be written on momentous subjects, but the tone was definitely changed. The sweet little songbirds became hoarse, and battle cries deafened the ear for melodies. The dilemma that troubled Ting Ling was experienced by many. Those who chose the revolutionary career would hardly pick up poetry again; they hated to think that they could once have been "prisoners in the ivory tower."

A typical case is found in Hu Yeh-p'in's *Light Is Ahead of Us*. Here is a poetess who creates a beautiful impression at her first appearance:

> The thought suddenly comes to him that this girl friend of his, pretty as a rose, is only a poet shut up in the ivory tower. Her poetry has attracted some attention in literary circles, but she is only capable of such pieces as "Beautiful dreams are no more" or "Please kiss me again." [41]

Later the same girl is aroused to anger at the news of the massacre in Shanghai:

[41] *HYP*, p. 125.

She, apparently so much like a rose, now becomes a red day lily (*hsüan*) and emits hot-red flames.[42]

Finally, she and her good-looking fiancé, an "ivory tower" novelist, decide to publish a magazine called the *Blood Flower Weekly*.

The images may make one smile today. Because they embody the essence, they look like exaggeration, or even parody. Hu is certainly crude in handling the psychological development of his heroine. But since such a transition was the most important fact in his own life, he saw with exceptional clarity the three stages in the evolution of a revolutionary. In his florid manner he summarizes the progress from beauty to violence, from imagination to action, and from Eros to Thanatos. At first a rose whose pricks do not diminish its loveliness; second, a lily that spits fire, but still a flower; and third, a blood flower, which may mean a flower that gets its nourishment from blood.

Then the three stages are projected into society as three attitudes toward life. Implied in the theme of Hu's book is the tripartite division of writers. To the first group belong those who deal with trivialities; the second, those for whom the revolution exists only on paper or in imagination; and the third, those who take action, which begins with meetings and demonstrations and ends with the acceptance of the rigors of life in a factory or rural villages or, what was so hard to avoid in those days, violent death. Writing as a profession is not worth serious consideration, for from the writer's early experience, he knows that a life dedicated to writing is a life wasted. Words are still useful if they advance the cause of revolution, but deeds are infinitely more important.

The climacteric change for a writer in the middle or later 1920's was a swing from passive sentimentality to revolutionary frenzy. His emotional instability tended to carry him to extremes, but a prevalent misconception of literature also limited his field of choice. Writing some years after 1919, he was still in a sense a pioneer. Only a few beaten tracks lay ahead of him, the other possibilities for literature being unknown. He used to be familiar with one kind of writing, whose rhetorical devices he had begun to learn as a schoolboy. But this he was taught to despise as useless. His writings were now not to satisfy himself but rather the demands politics made on him. Literature became a means to an end; and if there were better means to serve that end, he had to employ them.

The soul-searching by a character in *Shanghai, Spring 1930* is partic-

[42] *HYP*, p. 210.

ularly revealing. In a long passage this character indicates that he does not know that there are other alternatives to revolutionary literature than mere maudlin or driveling insipidness. He believes he should give up writing entirely and never explains why. This does not seem to bother Mei-lin who listens approvingly and responds not so much by changing her style as by revolutionizing her life. The man says:

> About literary composition, I sometimes feel that it would not be a serious loss if we gave it up entirely. We write, and the people read. Time passes, and no influence whatsoever. Then what is the meaning of all this, except that we get paid for it? It is of course possible that some readers are touched by a turn in the plot or by certain passages of writing—but who are these readers? Students of the petty-bourgeois class above the high school level, who have just reached adolescence and are subject to melancholy. . . . But the consequences, I now understand, are harmful. We do them a great wrong by leading them to the paths that we ourselves have trodden: sentimentalism, individualism, grumblings or sorrows for finding no way out. . . . Where is the way out indeed? They will sink deeper and deeper in their moroseness, not seeing the relation between society and their sufferings. Even if they could improve their language and produce essays and poems that win praise from some old writers, what good, I ask you, is that to them? And what good to society? Therefore, personally, I am willing to give up writing. To my fellow writers, I hope they will heed this: they should change their direction even by a little. At present, no masterpiece is possible. But their attempt will be not without significance in the literary history of the future.[43]

Though this is a point which wins from his listener only wide-eyed admiration, the tone of superiority is irritating. By giving up writing, this man can concentrate on the good that he will bring to society. He is going to make history, while his friends, who may still need the money paid for their writings, can at best try to write something along the same lines as history in general is taking. Dare they follow his example and make sacrifices? This is the real challenge.

The challenge, in the case of our five young writers, was accepted. How, after that, they could still squeeze out time for writing when "fleeing from the police or organizing strikes" was a wonder, and indicated, at the least, uncommon energy. Judging from their works available though, they do not impress us as being talents of the first order. They have been discussed as a group, for psychologically they were in many ways alike. In addition they had something in common with many of their contemporaries and even characters in contemporary fiction. Their meeting in Shanghai from various provinces almost coincided with the convergence of their careers in the

---

[43] *Short Story Magazine,* Sept., 1930, p. 1299.

Communist Party where, under strict discipline, sensitive individuals usually lose both their sensitivity and individuality. But the Communist Party at that time was not a homogeneous body of revolutionaries; rather it was a deeply split party. This was something that had never occurred to them in the wildest visions caused by the "light" in their eyes. Their mental state before joining the Communist Party—their sentimentality, moroseness, and aspirations—is familiar to readers of contemporary literature; their reaction to the fight among the comrades has been unluckily a neglected subject. Their story does not end with their union with the party, just as matrimonial problems begin only after the consummation of a love affair. That is the cruel reality, even though much modern Chinese fiction with a revolutionary theme ends in a happy chorus.

JOU SHIH, LU HSÜN, FENG K'ENG, AND YIN FU

Jou Shih (pseudonym of Chao P'ing-fu), the oldest of the five, seems also to have been the soberest. His photographs, published in the *New Masses, The Outpost,* and in two posthumous volumes,[44] show him to have had an emaciated face, a high brow with long curly hair waving behind his head, and stony eyes staring out of round glasses. Though he was not so handsome as the other three young men, who all had his lean, intelligent looks, he too had shown an early interest in literature and took to poetry while studying at the First Normal School in Hangchow. One poem of this period has been preserved and it opens thus:

> Autumn wind comes from the west,
>   Listen, how the reeds are rustling;
> Autumn wind comes from the west,
>   Look, how the falling leaves are dancing.[45]

He must have written a great deal more as a member of the Morning Light Society (1921–22).[46] This literary club, formed by students of his school under the tutorship of their teachers, Chu Tzu-ch'ing and Yeh Sheng-t'ao,

---

[44] The contents of these two selections are almost identical: *Jou Shih hsüan-chi (Jou Shih: Selected Works)* (Peking: Kaiming, 1951). *Jou Shih hsiao-shuo hsüan-chi (Fiction by Jou Shih, A Selection)* (Peking: People's Literary Publications Association, 1954).

[45] Facsimile of a manuscript reprinted in either of the two selections.

[46] For a short history of the Ch'en-kuang-she (Morning Light Society) see Feng Hsüeh-feng's Preface to *Ying Hsiu-jen P'an Mu-hua hsüan-chi (Selected Works of Ying Hsiu-jen and P'an Mu-hua)* (Peking: People's Literary Publications Association, 1957).

is particularly relevant to our study of the progress from lyricism to revolution. At least two other members turned Communist.[47] One, P'an Mu-hua, was arrested in 1933 in Tientsin as Commissar for Propaganda, Tientsin Municipal Committee, CCP, and died one year later of starvation in a protest against the bad treatment of the prisoners. The other, Feng Hsüeh-feng, survived his friends to participate in the Long March of 1934, only to be purged, together with Ting Ling, as a rightist in 1957. Both are presented in the *Comprehensive Anthology of Modern Chinese Literature* (1935–36) as "specializing in love poems." Chu Tzu-ch'ing, editor of the volume of poetry, remarked: ". . . at that time they were almost living in poetry. P'an Mu-hua was the saddest, with his extremely moaning tones. Feng Hsüeh-feng was more bright and gay, but there were also tears in his laughter." [48] Jou Shih, who was not selected, perhaps did not equal them in poetical achievement in the opinion of his teacher. His poetical drama *The Human Comedy* (1924) has never been published.[49]

Jou Shih became a schoolteacher after graduation from the normal school in 1923. The lectures he attended at the National Peking University in 1925 as a poverty-stricken, unregistered student did not quite satisfy his hunger for learning, but since he had a family to support, he went back to his native province to resume teaching after less than a year's stay at Peking. In 1927 he was promoted from his position as teacher in the Ninghai Middle School to director of education of his native town, Ninghai *hsien*. That was the year when the "old order" was broken by the victorious Northern Expedition, and positions left vacant by old bureaucrats were filled by young men with revolutionary zeal. Their good days, however, were about over. A purge had started in Shanghai and Wuhan. Those who had shouted leftist slogans were under suspicion if they had not yet come to grief. Much has been written about the terrorism of the Nanking Government, but the equally significant fact that many youths took official positions at the expense of their revolutionary ideals is not so well known. The Kuomintang leaders were apparently not devoid of the

[47] A biographical sketch of P'an Mu-hua is found in his selected works (see above). Another member of the Morning Light Society, Wei Chin-chih, was probably also a Communist in the early thirties. We shall learn more from him about the case of the five martyrs. The "hat of rightism" was lifted off the head of Feng Hsüeh-feng in December, 1961, together with some three hundred other one-time dissidents. Ting Ling's name, however, does not appear in the partial list published in the *Jen-min jih-pao*, Dec. 17, 1961, p. 1.

[48] *A Comprehensive Anthology of Modern Chinese Literature*, VIII, 4.

[49] The title is found in his biographical sketch, *Fiction by Jou Shih*, p. 2.

cynical knowledge that the lure of offices and rewards would succeed where terror alone might fail. Being from the favored province of Chekiang, and having already made a good start as director of education on the *hsien* level, Jou Shih might have enjoyed security and power in the Kuomintang bureaucracy which was then being built if he had been more cooperative. Instead he became somehow involved in a local riot in April, 1928, and as a consequence not only lost his position but had to escape to Shanghai. His family was left behind.[50]

In Shanghai, chance threw him into the company of Lu Hsün, who did not at first remember that this student had attended his lectures in Peking. Now they were close neighbors in the Ching-yün Li on Paoshan Road. Lu Hsün had a small house of his own in the network of alleys; Jou Shih occupied a flat on the second floor in a house in the front row. Another house in the front was taken by Chou Chien-jen, a biologist, Lu Hsün's youngest brother, who, through the recommendation of Jou Shih, sublet a "pavilion room" (room above the kitchen) between the second and third floors to Feng Hsüeh-feng, then an underground Communist agent. These intellectuals, all from Chekiang and sharing radical views to a certain extent, met frequently, and friendship grew fast between Lu Hsün and Jou Shih.[51]

The two men formed a most cordial master-disciple relationship; the one, elderly, brilliant, suspicious, opinionated, meticulous, self-conscious about his rebelliousness but also taking pride in his worldly wisdom; the other, young, earnest, diligent, trustworthy, unobtrusive, stolid in his myopic way, full of good will, and ready to serve and learn from his

---

[50] *Ibid.,* pp. 1, 3.

[51] Some sources about the life of the literary group: (a) Lu Hsün, "Perhaps I Had Better Forget," in *LH,* IV, 366–76; (b) Feng Hsüeh-feng, *Hui-i Lu Hsün* (*My Recollections of Lu Hsün*) (Peking: People's Literary Publications Association, 1957; a somewhat shortened version of the 1952 edition which has gone out of print); (c) Wei Chin-chih, "Time Spent in the Company of Jou Shih," *Wen-i yüeh-pao,* Mar. 5, 1957. Mao Tun was another neighbor, but he had little intercourse with the group until the spring of 1930: "The first time I saw Lu Hsün was in October, 1927, when we had just returned to Shanghai, he from Canton and I from Wuhan. The house he rented happened to be located in the same alley as mine. He and his third brother (Chou Chien-jen) paid me a call. But since my freedom of movement was then restricted, I never went to his house, which, I understood, often received too many strangers for my convenience. So probably we never saw each other until the spring of 1930. From that time on, I made a stop of my travels and began a longer stay in Shanghai. We met more frequently." Mao Tun, "In Memoriam, Mr. Lu Hsün," in *I Lu Hsün* (*Reminiscences about Lu Hsün*) (Peking: People's Literary Publications Association, 1956), p. 62.

elder. According to Feng Hsüeh-feng, Jou Shih adored Lu Hsün with something like filial piety, which surely gratified the master.[52] A professor now deprived of his chair, Lu Hsün did not get over his habit of lecturing, and his talks must have been fascinating. An entry in Jou Shih's diary recounts:

> Several times I felt unusual discomfort in my heart and I don't know why. But whenever I had a meal at Mr. Chou's [Lu Hsün] home, I felt much better. His brother has a scientific outlook and mind which put me to shame because of my nameless hypochondriac sorrow: his strong character, clarity of thought, learning, and reasoning all disconcerted me. But Mr. Lu Hsün's kind heart, his humorous gibes at society, and his profound critical opinions not only gave me pleasure but also improved my learning.[53]

Lu Hsün, then busy with various publishing enterprises, was pleased to find in Jou Shih a willing assistant and errand boy. Together with Yü Ta-fu he continued in charge of *Pen-liu* (*The Torrent,* monthly, June, 1928–December, 1929), a serious literary magazine, in which translations of Russian literary theory appeared.[54] But the editorial duties of *Yü-ssu* (*Threads of Talk,* a weekly of essays and satire, banned by the Peking government in November, 1927, and revived in Shanghai in February, 1928) he gradually passed over to Jou Shih, who succeeded him as editor in December, 1928.[55] In January, 1929, a publishing house, Chao-hua She (Morning Flower Society), was established with Jou Shih in charge under Lu Hsün's sponsorship. In the pages of *Chao-hua* (published weekly for twenty issues, and three times a month for twelve issues) and of *I-yüan chao-hua* (*Morning Flowers of the Garden of Art,* published irregularly for five issues) were printed, respectively, translations from Scandinavian and Russian literature and reprints of Japanese and Western engravings.[56] By the end of 1929, all these magazines had folded because of financial difficulties. In January, 1930, they started another magazine, *Meng-ya* (*The Sprout,* monthly) with Feng Hsüeh-feng as co-editor. After March of that year it became an organ of the Left League and was banned after five issues.[57]

[52] Lu Hsün did not have a son of his own until September 27, 1929. See *Diary* under that date.

[53] Jou Shih's *Diary* is now preserved in the Lu Hsün Museum of Peking. This particular entry is quoted in Wang Shih-ching, *Lu Hsün* (Peking: China Youth Publications Association, 1958), pp. 159–60.

[54] Lu Hsün, *LH,* IV, 519.

[55] Lu Hsün, "My Relations with *Yü-ssu*," *LH,* IV, 136.

[56] *Fiction by Jou Shih,* p. 1; *LH,* IV, 369.

[57] *LH,* p. 519.

The magazines supported by Lu Hsün in the 1928–30 period represented a peculiar stand in the proletarian literary movement. With all his sympathies for revolution, Lu Hsün still stood for common sense, good taste, and truthfulness in the depiction of life. He hardly concealed his scorn for the sentimental effusions that seemed to flow so easily from the pens of the so-called revolutionary writers. On September 17, 1930, his fiftieth birthday, at a celebration sponsored by the Left League, he talked about his own work and the future of proletarian literature in China. A summary of the talk is found in Agnes Smedley's *Battle Hymn of China*:

> In later years, he had studied German and Russian and translated a number of Russian novels and essays. His purpose, he said, was to lay before Chinese youth the best of modern social literature. He had also begun to collect Western classical and modern paintings and specimens of the graphic arts, and had published a number of volumes for young artists. He was now asked, he said, to lead a movement of proletarian literature, and some of his young friends were urging him to become a proletarian writer. It would be childish to pretend that he was a proletarian writer. His roots were in the village, in peasant and scholarly life. Nor did he believe that Chinese intellectual youth, with no experience of the life, hopes, and sufferings of workers and peasants, could—as yet—produce proletarian literature. Creative writing must spring from experience, not theory.[58]

Lu Hsün, like Ting Ling, never succeeded in reconciling politics with literature. While Ting Ling reluctantly submitted to politics, Lu Hsün maintained his artistic conscience by refusing to admit that he was a proletarian writer. His remarks about the works by "intellectual youth" were tantamount to a denial of the existence—as yet—of proletarian literature, which deflated the pretensions of the whole movement. But not all his advice was sound. His stress on "experience" and his belief that "whatever a revolutionary person produced must be revolutionary literature" [59] do not pass the test of history. Too much trash has been written by "revolutionary persons" not wanting in experience. In 1930 he was perhaps too old to acquire the necessary experience, and therefore he ceased to create. His heart was then lifted by hope of the kind that animated Hu Yeh-p'in, but which not even a man of his genius knew how to manage. Politically he had grown, but artistically he had not. He remained dry and sardonic in his essays, being wary of the infantilism that debased so many of the current works. He limited his attacks to the

---

[58] Agnes Smedley, *Battle Hymn of China* (New York: Knopf, 1943), p. 80.
[59] "Revolutionary Literature," an essay in Lu Hsün, *Lun wen-hsüeh* (*On Literature*) (Peking: People's Literary Publications Association, 1959); see also *LH*, IV, 79.

enemy whom he could handle, for instance, the "gentlemen" of the Crescent Moon Society; he seldom bothered about the overthrow of the regime or revolution on the cosmic scale. No peddler of cheap optimism, he believed that his more solid and enduring wares were translations which he brought out with great labor as models for Chinese writers. "Accumulate experience and study the models before you create" was advice hard to swallow by youth impatient for results. To them his method seemed slow and his approach timid; his whole attitude had a rather dampening effect. No applause greeted his talk at the birthday party; it only elicited the remark "disappointing," as noted by Smedley.[60] While everyone seemed to agree on the necessity of getting acquainted with the life of peasants and workers—for therein lay the beginning of revolutionary work—many were planning, to use Malcolm Cowley's phrase, "ambitious novels." If these were not to come from Lu Hsün, somebody else would have to write them.

That Jou Shih, his loyal follower, should also harbor the ambition to write a "great novel" came as a surprise to Lu Hsün. Probably he doubted the young man's abilities, but, as we have seen, he was also opposed to the idea as a matter of principle. Any such attempt was premature for a writer who still had much to learn. Only after Jou Shih's death did he painfully realize that while his own laziness hindered him from serious creative work, he was jealous of the ambition of others. "I am not actually a better man than those hypersensitive literary youths with a touchy ego whom I always prefer to avoid," [61] he confessed with admirable candor.

Jou Shih had scarcely the time to complete, or even to start, his ambitious project.[62] Under the direction of Lu Hsün, he translated *Faust and the City* by Lunacharsky, *The Artamonovs' Business* by Gorky, a volume of Danish short stories, and several Russian short stories (including "The Old Rat" by Zoshchenko).[63] His creative writings, which Lu Hsün also blue-penciled, are remarkable for their restraint and sobriety. The contrast with Hu Yeh-p'in is therefore great. Here is a writer who is chary of clichés and moderate in his emotions. But while he shuns excesses, he does not move with a strong power of imagination either. In his case a plain flawless style is used to cover a small talent. Caution only results

---

[60] Smedley, *op. cit.,* p. 81.

[61] *LH,* IV, 371.

[62] *The Outpost,* p. 8, reports that among Jou Shih's papers was discovered an outline for a novel, *Ch'ang-kung Ah-ho (Ah-ho, the Farm Laborer).*

[63] *Shu-ch'in (The Harp),* a collection of ten short stories by Russian fellow-traveling writers in Chinese translation, ed. Lu Hsün (Shanghai: Liang-yu Company, 1933). Lu Hsün's preface to the volume is reprinted in *LH,* IV, 330–33.

in lack of brilliance and of power. The short story, "The Mother Who Is a Slave," [64] about a furrier who, like the Mayor of Casterbridge, sells his wife to a gentleman to be his concubine, contains good descriptions of village life, but nothing happens after a promising start except for sentimental scenes between the woman and her former husband and son. The theme apparently involved more moral problems than the author cared to investigate. A longer work by Jou Shih is the novel *February* ("This is only February, not yet spring" [65]), which revolves around a psychological malaise without ever getting to its core. The hero, Mr. Hsiao, is a good man but weak, moody but with no clear purpose in life, a Rudin without his philosophy, a shirker who unwittingly becomes a scoundrel. The young man, a graduate of the First Normal School in Hangchow like the author, finds, after six years of wandering life, a teaching job in a small town, whose atmosphere is not so chilly as the title suggests. He comes on the invitation of an old classmate, now principal of the school, and he might have become a social success except for his unhappy experience with women. He wins the love of a schoolmistress, an intelligent pretty young woman who happens to be also the principal's sister. But he steps out of his way to help another woman, a young widow with two children, to whom the schoolmistress also shows sympathy. He could marry either of the two women, but he says that he wants no woman's love (though children appeal to him) and that he is too "melancholic" to have a family. When he has made up his mind to marry the widow, out of pity rather than love, and also as an expedient to silence the gossip, it is too late. She has hanged herself. Then full of remorse he leaves for Shanghai, where the strong-willed schoolmistress is determined to pursue him. Will spring then catch up with February?

The man's recoil from life puzzles Lu Hsün, who says in the preface, "Mr. Hsiao's decision to run away is perhaps a performance of abstinence caused by a weak stomach, though I am ignorant of the antecedents. I do not know whether that is in the man's nature or only a momentary symptom of weariness after the battles." [66] So much is left untold in the story that the young man serves only the dramatic function of disturbing the peace of the small town life until he is rejected. He seems to have a mysterious past, having spent years in Hankow, Canton, and Peking, but few references are made to it in the story. He behaves not at all like a

[64] This and *February* form the main body of both selections mentioned in note 44.
[65] Jou Shih, *Selected Works,* p. 66.
[66] *LH,* IV, 118–19.

revolutionary, but then he may eventually become one if he has not already been one. (What does Lu Hsün mean by "the battles"?). The incidents are supposed to have taken place before the Northern Expeditionary Forces reached Chekiang (the widow's husband was an officer of the Whampoa Military Academy killed in action at Huichou, Kwangtung), but it did not appear that the small town was going to experience political upheavals. Here Jou Shih was not so much interested in history as in the case of a "superfluous man." Mr. Hsiao was probably meant as a type of Chinese intellectual whose capacity for action was inhibited and whose futile good will could be tragic in its consequences. As inaction breeds self-contempt, violence might be another form of overcompensation for a life given to scruples. The notorious futility of Chinese intellectuals has its cultural reasons, and its transmutation in a time of crisis should become a fascinating study, but Jou Shih was not the man to do it. His hero is a small mystery, who is often too dull to be enigmatic. Jou Shih was not Turgenev, any more than Hu Yeh-p'in's study of young revolutionaries made him a Dostoevsky. They were dimly aware of the sickness of the age but did not have the genius to bring out its artistic and human significance. Only their lives and deaths are remembered as some of its symptoms.

Jou Shih's understanding of human nature was not adequate. Innocence, indeed, was his chief virtue and weakness. "His earlier works," said Lu Hsün, "may convey the impression of pessimism; but that is not true: he actually believed in the good nature of human beings. Sometimes I would talk to him about how men would deceive one another, how friends would be betrayed and their blood sucked. He would then protest, his forehead glistening and his nearsighted eyes opening wide in astonishment and disbelief, and mutter 'But how could that be? It is not likely, is it?' " [67] According to Lu Hsün again, he was so tactless and inflexible that he rather erred on the side of incorruptibility. (The word used to characterize him is yü—pedantic.) A good man, in his association with people not so good, could even look comic. One anecdote, narrated by Jou Shih's son, was about a present he received when he was director of education. A job-seeker brought him a ham, which he would not accept. So he followed the visitor out of the door and kept thrusting the ham back into the man's hands. He had to walk over half a mile before he could convince the gift-bearer of his seriousness. [68]

He was survived by his mother, wife, two sons, and a daughter, whom

[67] *LH,* IV, 370.
[68] Chao Ti-chiang, "My Father," reprinted in Jou Shih, *Selected Works.*

he loved with the natural affection of a Chinese. As a friend he was loyal too. "Whether for the reasons of the old ethics or for those of the new, he would pick up and place upon his shoulders anything beneficial to others but harmful to himself." [69] He was not of the complaining sort, but self-sacrifice, even for such a good man, had a limit. A few weeks before his arrest, he grew angry at his "friends" who took him to task for having stayed too long with his mother in his home town during the Chinese New Year. The old woman had lost her eyesight, and not knowing what her son had been doing (the news of his death was later withheld from her), wished selfishly to keep him for a few days more. But he had belonged to the Communist Party since May, 1930, and now his "friends" grudged him the holiday from the "new ethics" to enjoy a little indulgence in the "old." [70]

The force that threatened to alienate him from his small world was embodied in the person of Miss Feng K'eng, a passionate woman whose ardent nature seemed to shine forth through her plain looks. She is more interesting as a person than as a writer. Though she was known to the readers of the *New Masses* as "one of the most brilliant and hopeful young women writers that China has produced," [71] her literary remains consist of only a dozen short lyrics which form the appendix to the biography *Feng K'eng, the Martyr,*[72] and some excerpts from the diary of a woman soldier, probably fictitious.[73] While the former are as neat as a schoolgirl's composition could be, the latter retains all the slipshod workmanship of a diarist. Neither the bulk nor the quality of her works seems to justify her being ranked with the story writers Hu Yeh-p'in and Jou Shih or the poet Yin Fu. She became a Communist in May, 1929, one year earlier than Jou Shih, and after the latter's initiation they were ordered to live as husband and wife as a camouflage, since a married couple stood a

[69] *LH,* IV, 371.

[70] *LH,* IV, 374.

[71] *New Masses,* June, 1931, p. 15.

[72] Hsü Mei-hsün, *Feng K'eng lieh-shih* (*Feng K'eng, the Martyr*) (Canton: Kwang-tung People's Publications Association, 1957). This book is hereafter referred to as *Feng K'eng.*

[73] *Hung-ti jih-chi* (*The Red Diary*), reprinted in *The Outpost,* pp. 18–24, was allegedly based on what the author heard from the delegates of the Red Army who came to attend a meeting in Shanghai. *Feng K'eng,* p. 70. Another short story, "The Loss of the Paradise," deals with a young schoolmistress who, after her school has been turned into barracks by the government troops, declares, "We shall unite, we shall organize before we resist." *T'o-huang-che* (*The Pioneer*) (Shanghai), Vol. I, No. 2 (Feb., 1930). Available on microfilm, Hoover Library, Stanford University.

better chance of averting the suspicion of snooping neighbors than a single person. Miss Feng was "married off" to other comrades on other occasions, but she maintained a household with Jou Shih. From what we know about Jou Shih, it was at first almost a cruel practical joke. The affair must have begun in a very awkward manner. He was not only married and devoted to his family, but so shy that, according to Lu Hsün, he used to keep himself at a distance of three or four feet from any female companion whom he could not shake off in the street.[74] But one's scruples can be overcome by one's sense of duty, and she was after all not an utterly unlovable woman. He still kept his bachelor apartment, where he was regarded as a writer and editor. The secret documents entrusted to him were put away at the new address known to only a few comrades. Playing his dual role and divided between two homes, not counting the third one in Chekiang, Jou Shih was moving away from Lu Hsün's influence and entering deeper into Feng K'eng's magic circle, with all that she represented: illicit love, conspiracy, and proletarian literature. It was she who gave the eulogy at Lu Hsün's birthday party and offered him the laurels of proletarian literature, and we have seen how she was rebuffed.[75] Did Lu Hsün mean this as a last effort to break the spell that Feng K'eng cast over the poor Jou Shih? For he suspected that she was behind Jou Shih's decision to develop a new style of writing. His old style, though undistinguished, was at least lucid and had been groomed by Lu Hsün at great pains. This, he said, he would now give up. But what would the new style look like? An example is found in a poem reprinted in *The Outpost,* "The Blood Is Boiling":

> The blood is boiling!
> The heart is burning!

---

[74] *LH,* IV, 370. For how Feng K'eng was used as a wife for hire, see *Feng K'eng,* p. 72. Wei Chin-chih noted that Jou Shih and Feng K'eng were "in love" (see his "Time Spent in the Company of Jou Shih," *Literary Monthly,* Mar. 5, 1957). See the quotation below (note 109) for their "secret office."

[75] "A short heavy-set young woman with bobbed hair began to tell of the need for developing proletarian literature. She ended her address by appealing to Lu Hsün to become the protector and 'master' of the new League of Left Writers, etc." Smedley, *op. cit.,* p. 79. The woman was said to be Ting Ling (*Wen-i-pao,* Dec. 15, 1956, p. 8), which could not be true, since Ting Ling was not then a member of the League. Shen P'eng-nien, an eminent researcher on Lu Hsün, has rightly identified her as Feng K'eng in "Concerning Lu Hsün's Fiftieth Birthday Celebration Party," *Jenmin jih-pao,* Sept. 27, 1961, p. 8.

> The earth is shaking!
> The volcano is erupting! [76]

The same revolutionary rhetoric that characterizes so much inferior work of that time—the same intoxicant that few writers with revolutionary inclinations could resist is illustrated here. It is small wonder that Jou Shih should have unlearned so fast all the lessons about good writing. Judging from this performance (dated October, 1930), we would say that in the last phase of his life his promise as a writer had diminished.

Feng K'eng's promiscuity in Shanghai may serve as an ironic footnote to Jou Shih's short story "The Mother Who Is a Slave." When this story was written, Jou Shih did not foresee that he himself would be obliged to take a mistress who was somebody else's wife. "Wife" is perhaps not the right word, since Feng K'eng was not legally married. But she and Mr. Hsü Ngo had begun to "cohabit" in 1926, when she was a girl of nineteen before her graduation from the high school in Swatow.[77] He was probably a schoolmate who did not meet with her parents' approval. Their unlawful marriage was therefore a union of love in defiance of parental authority and social conventions. After much adventure in Kwangtung, then torn by revolution and counterrevolution, the young couple came to Shanghai in the spring of 1929. Mr. Hsü joined the Communist Party in the same month as she did. After that, they surrendered what little they had. For a man to sell his wife was not an evil peculiar to the old society; the new ethics had its abnormalities too.

Of the lyrics she wrote in 1925, some were probably meant for Mr. Hsü, for example:

White Candle

> You give me a candle, white and pure.
> Your meaning I think I understand.
> Each night I used to shed my tears alone.
> Now I have some one to shed tears with me.[78]

The candle with its idle tears did not keep her company for long. It was to be snuffed out by the storm of political events gathering in the very year when poetically she was most productive.[79] She was to emerge out

---

[76] This poem, more than a hundred lines in length, commemorates the death of a "young Hunanese comrade." *The Outpost,* pp. 14–18.

[77] *Feng K'eng,* p. 38.

[78] *Ibid.,* p. 93.

[79] All the eleven poems reprinted in *Feng K'eng* were written in 1925.

of her solitary nights to mingle with people and work feverishly to advance the cause of revolution. She never became a mother, but a slave she surely was to her own passions—but, as it appeared, to fanaticism rather than lust. There is nothing to indicate that she enjoyed her promiscuity, which should rather be interpreted as a sacrifice in the same sense as Jou Shih's farewell to his sightless mother.

During the strikes in the May Thirtieth movement, she wrote and directed a play in which she also performed the leading part. Never as beautiful as a rose (her nickname at home was Crab, and in school, Yaksha),[80] she gave notwithstanding a stirring performance, declaiming lines such as, "Are you willing to see your wives and children starved to death by the imperialists? Are you willing to see your husbands, sons, and fathers beaten to death?" With untiring energy, she edited the students' paper and was active in the literary societies outside the school. By March, 1925, she had been exposed to Communist influence when her home town, Ch'aochou, and its neighboring areas in the East River valley, including Swatow, were liberated from the Cantonese warlord, Ch'en Chiung-ming. With the victorious Kuomintang army came the Communist agents who were busy organizing the Peasants' Union, Labor Union, and Women's Liberation Association. Fraternization of students with soldiers and political commissars was, of course, not calculated to calm the general excitement. After the revolutionary forces' withdrawal in June to suppress the Yunnan and Kwangsi cliques then occupying Canton, the East River valley was once again lost to the generals supporting Ch'en. Under the hostile government, Feng K'eng, with unabated fervor, continued to write, shout slogans, and organize the students. All such activities received great stimulus in November when the Second Eastern Expedition was won by the Kuomintang army with heavy casualties. (Among them was the fictitious officer in Jou Shih's *February*.) The Communist agents were back, or again came into the open. The celebration of the October Revolution held in Swatow, presided over by Chou En-lai and General Galen, was one of the most memorable events in her life. Later she met P'eng P'ai, the famous peasant organizer. Her association with Communists was so close that during the 1927 purge she had to go into hiding in the villages for several months. Her activities during the seven days in October, 1927, when Ch'aochou and Swatow were occupied by the Communists under Ho Lung and Yeh T'ing, only put her in a more difficult situation after their retreat. When it was safe for her to come out to resume teaching, life became too dull

[80] *Feng K'eng,* pp. 2, 10.

for her. So together with her lover, she went to Shanghai, where she expected to meet comrades of the old days.

It is significant that Feng K'eng, with all her experience of peasant life, did not follow, nor did she later seek, the guerrillas under Ho Lung and Yeh T'ing. Perhaps it did not occur to her that the future of the Communist Party would lie in the rural villages. To her, as to many others, Shanghai was then the Moscow of the Orient.[81] In its native habitat, the Communist Party was trying to rebuild its strength on the support of the proletariat.

One of the builders, or active labor agitators, was Yin Fu (pseudonym of Hsü Pai), also known as Pai Mang, the youngest of the five and politically even more precocious than Feng K'eng. When he died at the age of twenty-two, he left behind a remarkable career. It is not on record when he joined the Communist Party, but he may have succumbed to its influence as early as 1925 as a high school student in Shanghai. He went to jail in April, 1927, as a Communist suspect and was detained for three months. After he had been released, he entered T'ung Chi University where he received a sound training in German. That was his second foreign language, since the schools he attended (first Min-li, and then Pootung Middle School) had already equipped him with a competency in English. He also manifested an interest in chemistry which might have become his career. Talented but restless, however, he quit school in 1929 to devote himself to the labor movement, probably on the orders of the Communist Party. In September of that year he was arrested again, this time for some role he played in the strike of a silk factory. But again he was set free.

The man who twice bailed him out of prison was his elder brother, Hsü P'ei-ken, a soldier who was rising rapidly in the hierarchy of the Kuomintang Army. By 1934 he was head of the administration of the Chinese Air Force.[82] It was most embarrassing for a man in his position

[81] *Ibid.*, p. 63.

[82] The family background of Yin Fu is described in Chiang Fu-sen, "Lu Hsün and Pai Mang," *Ta-feng pan-yüeh-k'an* (*The Great Wind Fortnightly*) (Hong Kong), Nov. 25, 1939. See also Lu Hsün's preface to the *Pagoda for the Infants, LH,* IV, 401. The career of General Hsü P'ei-ken (1898–   ) is summarized in *Gendai chugoku jinmyo jiten* (*Who's Who in Contemporary China*), ed. Ajiakyoku Gaimusho (Asia Bureau, Ministry of Foreign Affairs of Japan) (Tokyo, 1957):

1938–39	Head of Second Bureau, Committee of Military Affairs
1941	Chinese Military Attaché in Washington
1943–50	Commandant of the Cadre School
1951–54	Deputy Chief of General Staff (Taiwan)
1954 —	President of National Defense College (Taiwan)

and with such high prospects to be loaded with a Communist brother. Their father having died early, Hsü P'ei-ken did not appear to fail in either brotherly love or brotherly duty. While there were so many positive ways he could share his success with his family, the best service he could do his younger brother turned out to be intercession with the government authorities to obtain his release from prison. Unless the young man was reformed, Hsü was aware that the day would surely come when not even his influence could protect him. So he tried desperately to stop his younger brother from following his road to perdition. He remonstrated; he threatened; he promised to send him to Germany to study; and he put him under house arrest, using his brotherly authority instead of that of the government.[83] All this, however, only whetted Yin Fu's appetite for fight and fed his self-importance. With his flair for self-dramatization, Yin Fu looked upon his own family as if it were an arena for class struggle, with the good brother standing for the "exploiting class." Reconciliation became thus out of the question. He saw nothing but heroism in his own perversity. When he repudiated his brother's help, he was prepared for the consequences. Why should he be afraid of going to jail once again if that only flattered his ego?

His poem "Good-bye, Brother," dated April 12, 1929,[84] is remarkably lucid in stating his own position. Evidently he did not say good-bye without a troubled heart; but the conviction comes out so clearly that the total effect is a terrible calm. He gives his best account of himself when he says, "Truth and anger make me strong." The opening stanzas, in paraphrase, read as follows:

> Good-bye, my dearest brother,
> Your letter has made up my mind.
> 'Tis a pity that I cannot for the last time hold your hand
> Before I take, independently, my strides ahead.
>
> Twenty years of brotherly love and fondness,
> Twenty years of protection and bringing up,
> Please take them back in this last teardrop;
> Take them back, as if they were only a nightmare.

And then other forces overcame these sentiments:

---

[83] See Ah Ying, "On Rereading Yin Fu's 'Reply to a Brother,' " *Jen-min jih-pao*, Feb. 7, 1961, p. 8. Ah Ying is also the author of a biographical sketch of Yin Fu appended to *Yin Fu hsüan-chi* (*Yin Fu: Selected Works*) (Peking: Kaiming, 1951).

[84] Yin Fu, *Pagoda for the Infants*, pp. 80–83.

But your brother is hungering and thirsting,
Hungering and thirsting after the eternal truth.
Neither honor nor offices he desires;
He is striving on a pilgrimage to the Kingdom of Truth.

Therefore the moans of machines disturb him in his sweet dream;
And the cries of the toiling masses shake his spirit.
He is aggrieved day and night,
Wishing to bring light to humanity like Prometheus.

Truth and anger make him strong;
Never again will he fear the wrath of God.
He is ready to sacrifice his life.
Not for him the top hat made of paper.

The poem bears a subtitle, "Let this be a farewell to a *class* [original in English]" and ends:

The only chance for us to meet again
Is when battle fire is exchanged between us and your class.

The same theme is repeated in prose, "Reply to a Brother" (dated March 11, 1930),[85] which does not seem to have the simple beauty of the poem. The tone is arrogant, and the syntax often clumsy. But the following lines still show that they are from a poet whose mind, though perverse and perhaps insane, is nevertheless original in its search for the simplest truth:

Of course you have never treated me as cruelly as I have treated you. That is because to you I am your brother; but to me you are the enemy class.

In spite of his paranoiac comparison to Prometheus, he had the honesty to admit that he had only a "thin arm":

I have taken my position in the ranks whose size is unequaled in the world's history, and my thin arm is linked with muscles as tough as steel.

With such emotional intensity, Yin Fu was not an amiable person to meet. After some unpleasant personal experiences, Lu Hsün characterized him as a typical "hypersensitive literary youth with a touchy ego." [86] But Yin Fu's works still make interesting reading today, while the works by other sensitive youths, which were never distinguished in their own days, seem even more mediocre with the lapse of time. As a poet he held an advantage over storytellers like Hu Yeh-p'in and Jou Shih. He did not have to understand the old society, or anything he did not like, in order

[85] See Ah Ying's article, *Jen-min jih-pao,* Feb. 7, 1961, p. 8.
[86] *LH,* IV, 367.

to write about it. When emotional truth takes precedence over objective truth, even ignorance can become a power and perversity an attraction. Yin Fu was sincere like so many others of his generation; but his strength lies in his preserving his naïveté and sincerity against the onslaught of the prevalent bad taste of his time. Though his themes were familiar, his approach was original, and that bespeaks a talent rarely equaled by his fellow writers. The poem earlier quoted about the Red Angel and the Fire of Revolution is a bad one; it would be worse if he went on glorifying the revolution in cosmic terms. The poem is saved by these two lines, addressed to the "enemy class":

> Today
> You may crawl under the table!

Instead of threats, he points out a place where the enemy may hide himself, i.e., under the table. Such a thought can occur only to a child or to one who thinks as a child. Nothing is more refreshing than the intrusion of naïveté into a context of grandiloquence. The incongruity is an almost pathetic evidence of the poet's sincerity: he does not conceal his mental age, even though he is talking about the most serious business of revolution.

He introduced slogans into his verse that described a modicum of the good life, which, ironically, must be as remote as Paradise to the commune dwellers today:

> Let's celebrate the May Day, the Labor Day!
> Eight hours for work!
> Eight hours for education!
> Eight hours for rest! [87]

But his better poems such as "Good-bye, Brother" show a poised control of tension, an avoidance of gushing sentiments, and an honesty about facts as he perceives them. His keen sense of physical reality delightfully redeems some of his inferior works. In the same poem about May Day, a desolate scene of the early morning precedes the gathering of the crowds:

> Tick, tock, tick, tock, to the beat of my heart,
> My shoes make sound on the pavement.

The description is so true to the poet's feeling that the reader may still ponder over his loneliness even amidst the slogans and demonstrations that are to follow. Before he loses himself in the crowds, there are moments

---

[87] Yin Fu, *Pagoda for the Infants,* p. 86.

when the streets are deserted and the poet hears nothing but his own footsteps in the shadows cast by the "weary plane-trees." But then only a true poet, his political beliefs notwithstanding, would see the significance of desolation on a riotous day like May 1. In a different way, the closing lines of "Resolutions" (November, 1929) are touchingly human:

> Tomorrow, that will be a day different,
> We shall shout!
> We shall leap!
> But it is also important to go to bed early tonight.[88]

The surprise is great, for one is apt to forget that conspirators need sleep too. Such a simple thought, coming at the end of a clandestine meeting under an oil lamp and amidst human stench, is a mark of great honesty. By reverting to such basic physical facts of human life, Yin Fu, in spite of the ranting gibberish that he also produced, rose above politics. Here is a poet who, because of his better linguistic training and unusual honesty about his thoughts, perceptions, and physical wants, could be really original.

THE LI LI-SAN LINE

In one way or another, Hu Yeh-p'in, Jou Shih, Feng K'eng, and Yin Fu left the imprint of their immaturity on the contemporary literary scene. Thirty years have elapsed since their death, and many of their writings have yet to be rediscovered. Those still available are of uneven quality. It is hard to say that they have produced, among them, a masterpiece on which their literary fame can securely rest. Of the four, Yin Fu seems to be the only one who may yield some useful lessons for the writers of today, but it is his misfortune that his craftsmanship and unstudied charm are lost to those who respond simply to his political message. When Lu Hsün was asked to write a preface to a posthumous collection of Yin Fu's poems, he explained his importance by a string of metaphors:

> They [his poems] are the faint gleams in the east, the "signal arrow" in the forest, the sprouts coming out at the end of the winter, the first steps of a military march. They are a banner celebrating the love of the vanguard and a monument dedicated to the hatred for the destroyers. They bear no affinity with any work characterized by adroitness or terseness, sublimity or subtlety; for these poems belong to a different world.[89]

In a word, Yin Fu's literary qualities should not be taken seriously. If his flaws are excusable, his beauty is negligible. He served a historical

[88] *Ibid.,* p. 101.
[89] *LH,* VI, 402.

function, which would have been important enough without his having ever written a single readable line. The dawn would break, and he heralded it; the outlaws would descend from the forest, and he announced it. What he did therefore was no more and no less than the service performed by Hu Yeh-p'in, Jou Shih, Feng K'eng, and many others who all proclaimed the future. Personal differentiation between them, ever so slight, was submerged in the mass movement for the creation of a new world. Their individual styles and talents, their family problems, and their literary ambitions—what were these if not trifles in the onrush of historical events?

These four were writers who turned Communist. Self-expression had been at one time or another irresistible for them before they attained the Communist virtue of self-denial. But Li Wei-sen, the fifth member of the group, was a Communist who took up writing merely as a sideline. His literary works include a critical biography of Dostoevsky and a volume of essays; whatever he produced in the line of creative writing—poetry or fiction—is not on record.[90] As editor of *Shao-nien hsien-feng* (*Young Vanguard;* co-editor: Hsiao Ch'u-nü) in 1926 and then of *Shanghai pao* in 1928, he must have written a number of articles which were not literary in nature. On the other hand, his political career was long and distinguished. Before he went to study in Soviet Russia (1925–26), he had been a student leader in Wuhan during the May Fourth period (when he was sixteen) and an organizer of the strike on the Peking-Hankow Railway (the "February 7 Strike" of 1923). After the 1927 purge the task of reorganizing the labor movement in Shanghai fell on his shoulders. He participated in and survived the Canton Commune. In all, his record is comparable to Ho Meng-hsiung's, surpassing in its importance and professional character the sum total of revolutionary experiences of the four writers combined. To treat him as primarily a writer is unfair to this record. *The Outpost* introduced him under another name: Ch'iu-shih. And the name of Li Ch'iu-shih appears in the "Resolution on Some Questions in the History of Our Party," which is reprinted in Mao Tse-tung's *Selected Works.* A footnote to that document tells more of the man:

Member of the Chinese Communist Party, Comrade Li Ch'iu-shih served in 1928 as a member of the Central Committee of the Chinese Communist Youth League, as head of its Propaganda Department, and chief editor of *Chinese Youth,* organ of the C.C. of the C.C.Y.L. In 1931 he was arrested by Chiang Kai-shek's bandit gang while working in the Propaganda Department of the Chinese Communist Party, and died a martyr at Lunghwa.[91]

[90] The works by the five writers are listed in *The Outpost.*
[91] Mao, *Hsüan-chi,* III, 1000. *Selected Works,* III, 340–41.

Li Wei-sen, or Li Ch'iu-shih, occupied an important position in the "right wing" of the Communist Party; so important, indeed, that his name is printed above that of Ho Meng-hsiung in the current official version of the history of the party's struggle against the "right deviation." How the four amateurish revolutionaries, Hu Yeh-p'in and the others, came to be involved in that struggle is not yet clear, but Li and Ho, as two of the "twenty-odd important cadres," are said to have sustained "blows" from the Ch'en Shao-yü (alias Wang Ming) leadership in January, 1931. Thus spoke Mao Tse-tung in post mortem:

Owing to the pressure applied from all directions by the doctrinaire sectarians with Comrade Ch'en Shao-yü at their head, and to the concessions and support accorded them by some comrades in the Central Committee who were victims of empiricism, the Central Committee of the Party held another plenary session (the fourth since the Sixth National Congress) in January 1931. This session, accomplishing nothing positive or constructive, accepted the new "Left" line, which triumphed in the central leading body; thus began, for the third time during the Agrarian Revolutionary War, the domination of a "Left" line in the Party. . . . Although to all appearances it raised the banner of combating Li Li-san's line and the "line of conciliation," yet in essence its main political programme consisted in "combating the Right deviation." . . . On the basis of this programme both that plenary session and the Central Committee after it promoted "Left" doctrinaire-sectarian comrades to leading posts on the one hand, and, on the other, dealt excessively severe blows at comrades who had committed mistakes along Li Li-san's line, misdirected blows at comrades headed by Ch'u Ch'iu-pai who had supposedly committed "mistakes along the line of conciliation" and, immediately after the session, misdirected blows at most comrades of the so-called "Right wing." As a matter of fact, the so-called "Rightists" at that time mainly emerged from the sectarian fight "against the Right deviation" at this session. Of course there were among them the few splitters headed by Lo Chang-lung, who later formed a real Right wing, degenerated into counter-revolutionaries and were expelled permanently from the Party, and who beyond any doubt should be resolutely opposed because their establishment and maintenance of a dual Party organization was absolutely incompatible with Party discipline. But as to the twenty-odd important cadres of the Party, including Lin Yu-nan, Li Ch'iu-shih and Ho Meng-hsiung, they did much useful work for the Party and the people, maintained excellent connection with the masses and, when arrested shortly afterwards, stood up firm to the enemy and became noble martyrs.[92]

The fourth Plenary Session of the Sixth Central Committee of the Chinese Communist Party was held on January 8, 1931.[93] What were

---

[92] Mao, *Hsüan-chi*, III, 966. *Selected Works*, IV, 182–83.

[93] Other sources may give January 7. Our authority is Hatano, *op. cit.*, I, 552–53. The Plenum lasted only fifteen hours. *Ibid.*, p. 562.

the blows, then, that fell on the "twenty-odd" comrades *en masse* in the nine days from that date to January 17 when they were arrested? The blows, which could be mild but were more often "excessively severe," were not what the young writers expected from their own comrades when they joined the party. They had believed, to use Yin Fu's words, that their thin arms were "linked with muscles as tough as steel." What a shock it would have been to them to discover that the "tough muscles," instead of being applied solely to the enemy class, could bear down on them and that they, of all people, could be marked out as the "right wing." Whether Ch'en Shao-yü was the villain who betrayed the young writers is not the point here. Betrayal, if it could be proved, would have been only the last stab; the damage had already been done. The severest blow to them fell at the moment when they discovered in the last days of their life that "revolution is a bitter thing, mixed with filth and blood, not as lovely or perfect as poets think." [94] Finally, they saw the other side of revolution; but it was too late for them to tell the tragic truth to the world.

It was Lu Hsün who made the remark that "revolution is a bitter thing . . . ," but the full implications of this statement need a clarification not found in his works. In the first place, as power corrupts, the struggle for it within a revolutionary party entails filth and sometimes also blood. Secondly, when the party decides how its dubious interest may be served, it may demand the lives of its members—not necessarily the lives of the "deviationists" but of the loyal, trustworthy followers as well.

Some Communist leaders have testified to the treacherous, brutal acts perpetrated against their comrades during the years when our young writers saw nothing but the pure fire of revolution around the image of the Communist Party.

Pavel Mif quotes a delegate from Hunan in 1928:

"If certain comrades committed some mistakes, their superiors did not correct them. Instead, they killed them; they shot them to death. I can cite some facts. In February 1928, after the failure of the great insurrection, a woman member of the Communist Party from a landlord's family was shot to death. She was a Communist, a true comrade, who had done long and useful service after the Northern Expedition—an excellent Communist who was shot to death simply because she had belonged to a landlord's family." The same peasant from Hunan reported that he once received an order from

---

[94] *LH,* IV, 182–83. An English version of "Thoughts on the League of Left-wing Writers" is found in *Chinese Literature Monthly* (Peking), Sept., 1961.

the District Committee to shoot two members of the Party to death. He did not obey and the secretary of the Committee said, "Why are you afraid of shooting people? If you are afraid, then you yourself are an opportunist." [95]

Mif recommended that "the Party should never allow bodily destruction to be inflicted on comrades who have committed unintentional mistakes or insisted on independent views on controversial issues." [96]

In December, 1930, a session was held by the Presidium of the Executive Committee, Communist International, to review the errors of the Li Li-san line in China. One member brought to light an episode which probably occurred during the June–September period in 1930 when Li Li-san, as dictator of the party, established an Action Committee to prepare for a large-scale uprising. Thirty Communists were arrested in Nanking by the Kuomintang authorities and handed over to a unit of KMT troops, which happened to be under the control of undercover Communists. The CP's Nanking Municipal Committee wanted the release of the prisoners at all costs. The troops concerned were to move out of the city of Nanking and declare themselves to be a part of the Red Army. But the more power-ful Kiangsu Provincial Action Committee preferred to keep the troops in the Kuomintang uniform. They could better serve the Communist Party this way, even though that would mean that they had to execute the thirty comrades. "So these comrades were put to death by our own hands," said the high-ranking official of the Comintern. He made a further remark: "It is indeed a special feature of some Party branches that comrades could be destroyed with such great ease." [97]

Readers of Li Ang's *Red Stage* will remember how Li Li-san removed his political rival Yün Tai-ying by transferring him to the District Com-mittee of Eastern Shanghai, where it was calculated that he would fall into the hands of the police. Working as uncomplainingly and selflessly as ever in spite of his disgrace, Yün was arrested in May, 1930, and executed in 1931 after his identity was discovered. The Kuomintang authorities could not at first believe that they had bagged such an important Com-

[95] An article by Mif originally published in the *Communist International,* Nos. 39–40 (a combined issue?), Oct. 9, 1928. The Chinese version is included in Mif, *Chung-kuo ko-ming (On Revolution in China)* (Moscow: Wai-kuo kung-jen ch'u-pan-she [Foreign Workers' Publishing House], 1933), p. 247.

[96] *Ibid.*

[97] The Russian's name in Chinese transliteration is K'u-ch'iu-mu-fu. *Pu-erh-sai-wei-k'o (Bolshevik),* May, 1931, pp. 17 ff. (Hoover Library). A summary of "Remarks by Kuchumov" is found in Hsiao, *Power Relations,* pp. 80–82.

munist leader! [98] Because of its scurrilous style, Li Ang's book has never won much respect, and this episode has been treated as slightly better than gossip. The surprise was great when twenty-five years after Yün's death, Li Li-san himself confirmed Li Ang's account. This, of course, does not altogether establish the credibility of *Red Stage*—the information contained therein needs to be examined at every point—but Li Li-san's account of a "criminal act against revolution" should have been revealing to our revolutionary writers. Said Li, at the Eighth National Congress of the Chinese Communist Party on September 23, 1956:

> This kind of subjectivism, which went rampant, manifested itself in organization as violent sectarianism. Not only I was incapable of listening with a cool head to the opinion of others, but those comrades who held views different from mine were arbitrarily accused of being opportunists or conciliationists. They were repudiated and came under blows, thus resulting in an extremely abnormal state in the Party and even the sacrifice of some of the best cadres that we had. The sacrifice of Comrade Yün Tai-ying, for instance, has always been a source of pain to me whenever I think of it. Comrade Yün Tai-ying had been working in the Central Propaganda Department, and had on several occasions expressed disapproval of the adventurist course. Now denounced as a conciliationist, he was dismissed from the central organizations to be secretary of the Eastern Shanghai District Committee. He was then a quarry hunted by the enemy; he was not familiar with the conditions in Eastern Shanghai; and he was extremely myopic. So he was arrested during a routine police check-up. Later he was betrayed as a traitor and sacrificed. This proves that a cadre policy based on sectarianism not only constitutes a grave political mistake, but can also lead to criminal acts against revolution.[99]

In December, 1930, Li Li-san said in another confession:

> Ever since the Sixth National Congress (July–September 1928) the organizational line of the Party Central has been closely related to my mistakes. Our understanding of the Party discipline has been mechanical. We forbid self-criticism; we forbid free criticism of political problems . . . The mistakes have persisted to the present day.[100]

Of our five young writers, four learned their political lessons under the Li Li-san leadership. Only Li Wei-sen had longer experience in the Com-

---

[98] Li Ang, *Hung-se wu-t'ai* (*Red Stage*) (Taipei: Victory Publishing Company, 1954), pp. 68–70. (First edition published in Chungking, 1942.) More information about Yün Tai-ying can be found in a special issue of *Chung-kuo ch'ing-nien* (*China Youth Fortnightly*) (Peking), May 6, 1950, No. 38, commemorating the nineteenth anniversary of his death.

[99] *Chung-kung ti-pa-tz'u ch'üan-kuo-tai-piao-ta-hui wen-hsien* (*Documents of the Eighth National Congress, CCP*) (Peking: People's Publishing Association, 1957), pp. 409–10.

[100] *Pu-erh-sai-wei-k'o*, May, 1931, p. 9.

munist Party. The characteristic of the Li Li-san line, as Li himself later admitted, was "revolutionary fanaticism" [101] which permeated the policy of the party in mounting intensity. Fanaticism is supposed to be rooted in "petty-bourgeois ideology," but the wrong attitude became inexcusable only after it failed to produce the results it promised. After the 1927 debacle, the Trotskyists favored a retreat in China; but the Stalinists, out of spite if for nothing else, insisted on keeping up the offensive. The issue of the debate was to be decided by the results of the action taken by the Chinese Communists. Li Li-san believed that he could deliver what was ordered by Moscow. He was fired because he could not.[102]

The catchword of the Li Li-san era was "revolutionary high-tide," which Lu Hsün, upon hearing it repeated once too often, dismissed with a laugh.[103] Mao Tun ridiculed this kind of boastful talk in his *Tzu-yeh:*

As Tsai Chen looked at it, the question was simple enough: "The workers' spirit of struggle was running high" because the "high tide of revolution" was at this moment sweeping the country! Since March there had been strikes by the bus and tram drivers in the International Settlement and by workers in the powerhouse in the French Concession. The "spontaneous struggle" of the workers had been kept up without a break in factories all over Shanghai, and every

[101] *Documents of the Eighth National Congress, CCP,* p. 409.

[102] Li Li-san was aware of the Comintern's dislike for him. He admitted, "If we could take Wuhan, then we could assume a different tone in our talks with the Comintern." Quoted in the Comintern's letter to the CC of CCP, received November 16, 1930. The document is found in the Ch'en Ch'eng Collection, microfilm reel 12; reprinted in *Ch'ih-fei fan-tung wen-chien hui-pien* (*A Collection of the Red Bandits' Counterrevolutionary Documents*), II, 446. This collection was probably published in Nanking, 1935; reprinted in Taipei, date unknown. A version in Japanese is available. Hatano, *op. cit.,* I, 537–46. Li's admission is on p. 546. The Ch'en Ch'eng Collection is available on microfilm at the Hoover Library, Stanford University, and the Center for Chinese Studies, Berkeley.

[103] "At that time (1928–29), other comrades of our party had already come into contact with him [Lu Hsün], mainly through the Revolutionary Mutual Aid Society. I remember that one day when I went to see him, he was just seeing a visitor off. He began to talk about the visitor, '. . . from the Revolutionary Mutual Aid Society, has been here three times. Rather naive. Each time he lectures to me on the revolutionary high-tide.' After saying that, he laughed heartily, revealing his love for that comrade under his benevolent sarcasm." Feng Hsüeh-feng, *Essays,* I, 244. The said Society was known under the name of China Relief Society until December, 1929. Chronological Table in Hatano, *op. cit.,* I, 644. The Society, established in January, 1926 (*Jen-min jih-pao,* Dec. 12, 1961, p. 6), was allegedly a charity organization for aiding the families of the Communists imprisoned or killed by the government. Since it accepted donations from sympathizers, it could maintain broader relations with the public. The Sixth National Congress of the CCP (July–September, 1928) passed a resolution "to promote the Relief Society movement." Hatano, *op. cit.,* I, 244.

"economic struggle" had a way of turning instantly into a "political struggle" with the result that "the revolution had now reached high tide." Tsai Chen had heard all this time and again and had adopted it as her own formula for thinking.

This "formula" sounded simple, clear and "reasonable," and, along with a lot of other jargon, had been firmly memorized by Chen Yueh-ngo and through her instilled into the minds of Chang Ah-hsin and Ho Hsiu-mei, whose simple minds and warm hearts were just the right sort of fertile soil for "formulas" of this kind.[104]

Mao Tun wrote the above from hindsight, when it was safe and "correct" to criticize the Li Li-san line. What interests us, however, is his insight into human weakness, an insight which distinguishes him as a novelist in spite of his effort to fit his book into an ideological mold. Who are these "simple minds and warm hearts" who are particularly vulnerable to this or any other "formula" that satisfies intellectually for its simplicity and clarity and emotionally for its reassurance of victory? In *Tzu-yeh,* they are factory workers. But from what we know about the immaturity and enthusiasm of Mao Tun's fellow writers, we suspect that they too can be placed in the same category.

We shall never find out how unpopular the Li Li-san line really was in its heyday, since few critics dared to speak out until Li was repudiated by the Comintern. According to Li himself, the only serious criticism he ever encountered came from Ho Meng-hsiung.[105] But there was also Yün Tai-ying, and possibly others. Perhaps his critics were better theoreticians in matters such as the interpretation of the "uneven development of revolution." As was revealed after Li's downfall, those cadres who "maintained excellent connection with the masses" did not like to see the small strength of the party pitted against the Kuomintang government in a series of desperate, almost suicidal, challenges. The workers were ordered to go on "political strike"; the Red Army was sent to capture the cities; and urban intellectuals were rallied to expose themselves in street demonstrations. "One time after another, blood covered our head after our clash (with the enemy); but we did not turn back. Desperately and obstinately we charged ahead, only to cause immense losses to the strength of the revolution," said Li Li-san in 1956.[106]

The League of Leftist Writers, as a front organization, was not spared by the "adventurist" policy of the Communist Party. A member of the League, if he obeyed the orders, could only neglect his writing which,

[104] *Mao Tun wen-chi,* III, 391. *Midnight,* pp. 355–56.
[105] *Pu-erh-sai-wei-k'o,* May, 1931, p. 8.
[106] *Documents of the Eighth National Congress, CCP,* p. 409.

presumably, was his proper business. How the League might have been more wisely used to advance the Communist cause is indicated in Feng Hsüeh-feng's lament:

At that time, we, the younger members of the Party as well as the Party Central in Shanghai, regarded the Left League as principally a revolutionary body to be used in direct political struggle. What should be emphasized—its special character and function in the struggle on literary and ideological fronts and the accomplishment of its mission of the political struggle through literary and ideological means—was utterly disregarded.

Next, we treated the League as if it were a quasi-political party; therefore, organizationally, it could not avoid the mistaken path of shut-door-ism. At the same time, in our tactics of struggle, little estimate was made of the unprece- dented conditions under which oppression was then brought by the fascist KMT on revolutionary struggle and revolutionary cultural movement. We attempted futilely to break through the oppression with the very insignificant strength we possessed—a sad example of subjectivism. We abandoned almost entirely the effort to win an open, "legitimate" or "semi-legitimate" status and to adjust our methods and forms of struggle accordingly. The League was therefore compelled to seek its growth underground: its semi-secret existence was to become entirely secret. Our activities were in fact gradually curtailed until the League was supported by none but a few writers and party members who were not yet arrested or killed.[107]

The activities of the League were curtailed when the Communist Party in the so-called "white areas" was already very much weakened. But under Li Li-san's leadership, the party was showing its strength by sending its members and sympathizers into the streets to shout slogans and distribute handbills. Wei Chin-chih, a schoolmate of Jou Shih and Feng Hsüeh-feng, recalls:

I remember that parading in the streets and distributing handbills were very common in those days. Sometimes we were scattered around to distribute hand- bills; at other times we handed out leaflets when we were parading in forma- tion. Many of us were thus arrested at first; so later we changed this to "flying meetings" (*fei-hsing chi-hui*),[108] which means that our people were stationed around a prearranged spot, posing as pedestrians or shoppers. When a signal was sounded, we clustered together, shouting slogans and distributing handbills. When the police arrived, we left the scene separately, again as pedestrians or shoppers.[109]

[107] Feng, *My Recollection of Lu Hsün*, pp. 22–23.
[108] *Fei-hsing chi-ho* is listed as a method of demonstration in a document on the Organization of the Grand Demonstrations on August 1 (1930). Hatano, *op. cit.*, I, 508.
[109] Wei Chin-chih, "Miscellaneous Reminiscences about the 'Left League,'" *Wen- hsüeh p'ing-lun* (*Literary Criticism*) (Peking), Apr., 1960, p. 81.

The scenes of the young writers eluding the police seem at once pathetic and comic today. From the reports in the *North China Herald,* which printed detailed descriptions of the disturbances in Shanghai, we can see how ineffective this kind of demonstration was. The slogans could make hardly any impression on the bona fide pedestrians and shoppers, who, poor prudent petty-bourgeois that they were, always tried hard to stay away from the commotion. And the handbills largely fell into the hands of the police, who, if they had not previously caught wind of what was coming, were always prompt to arrive once they were alerted. The incongruity between the pretensions and the reality was satirized by a Trotskyist paper:

Demonstration is understood to be kicking up a rumpus by dozens or hundreds of people among whom there are more long gowns or Western-style suits than there are blue denims; more party members than there are masses. There is no way to dispose of packets of propaganda material except to throw them up to the sky; thus scattered and flying up, they are to be read only by the Jade Emperor and his Celestial Hosts. To smash a couple of tramcars, so that the masses who have to travel on them are so scared that they run away like dogs—that is action. The so-called demonstration of strength is indeed demonstration of weakness.[110]

The absurdity of the situation might have struck some of the demonstrators themselves. But to them this was a strangely different experience. A demonstration on March 8, 1930, for instance, was reported in the *North China Herald.* The story begins thus:

Communist Attack on Tramcars

The now familiar form of minor demonstration which is composed of pamphlet throwing and the breaking of windows in railless tramcars was again in evidence on March 8, the occasion being International Women's Day.

Between 9:30 and 9:40 A.M. some 200 Chinese students and workers were scattered along Nanking Road between Fokien and Chekiang Roads and several of the number distributed communistic handbills bearing on International Women's Day. The arrest of three of the distributors resulted in the crowd retreating to Avenue Edward VII via Fokien Road. . . . [Then follows the story of how nine tramcars were damaged and more arrests were made.][111]

It happens that Yin Fu also wrote a sketch of the demonstration on March 8:

. . . But on the sidewalks, look, what a sight is this? A sidestreet, closest to the main avenue, and therefore the front line, reveals feet firmly planted, ranged in order, like crows huddled together on the ridge of a house against the stiff wind of a cold day—silently, steadfastly, and in good order.

[110] *Wu-ch'an-che (Proletariat,* with a subtitle in French, *Organe de l'opposition Communiste Chinoise*), Mar. 1, 1930, p. 118. (In the Hoover Library.)

[111] *North China Herald,* Mar. 11, 1930, p. 392.

Some are tall, some short. Youth, aged, students, workers. Some in suits, others only in ragged, dirty, oil-smeared shirts; some in fashionable *ch'i-p'ao,* with hair streaming down; others in shapeless denims, with yellow hair over a sickly face, or a dirty pigtail, with raw cotton still tremulously clinging to it.

Who are they? They are one body. Taken separately, each is cowardly, sickly, fatigued, feeble; each of them can be kicked into the gutters by a foot in a shining leather boot. But they are now in formation, almost hand in hand, heart linking with heart, breath mingling with breath. They are strong —they are a regiment of stalwarts—none can ever break through them. Their ranks are tough and resilient like steel . . .[112]

Yin Fu's style, as usual, has a raw vigor about it, which is more refreshing to read than the tongue-in-cheek school of British journalism. But perhaps no British reporter on that day could sense the feeling of unbreakable strength shared by the "200 students and workers." What was a joke to the Trotskyist opposition—and a nuisance to the pedestrians and riders of tramcars who haplessly found themselves trapped in a mob scene in that sector of downtown Shanghai which used to be as busy as Times Square in Manhattan—had for our young writer all the seriousness and excitement of a battle. He felt an exaltation, too, which filled out a politically infeasible "formula" with emotional meaning and completely justified it. He had the proof for it in his experience with the masses whose "spirit of struggle is running high" and who are sure to bring about the victory.

Ting Ling, in *Shanghai, Spring 1930,* presents a similar scene. Wang-wei, the young man working in a "literary organization," is ordered to give a public speech in a demonstration. The speech is never given, since the mob is dispersed when he has just started to speak. But walking slowly in the busy thoroughfare waiting for the signal (which is the shooting of firecrackers in this instance), he is assailed by powerful emotions:

He was a little excited and he could not help it. He saw, as it were, the surging waves which are rising with a force to overthrow the mountains and upset the seas. He saw, too, an erupting volcano, throwing out roaring flames to burn down this city. This is so likely to happen; no, it will soon take place: so many people are being prepared for it! And he—he will move the storm and throw the torch! Some among the crowds were known to him and their hearts had also begun to be burning. Excitement could be seen through their calm. Their faces were flushing: a certain presentiment made them all happy.[113]

We wonder whether Ting Ling, with her understanding of "leftist infantilism," did not mean to attach a note of irony to this piece of writing. Her psychology here is sound: for a young man with a simple mind and a warm

---

[112] *Yin Fu: Selected Works,* pp. 127–28.
[113] *Short Story Magazine,* Dec., 1930, p. 1733.

heart may feel happy in the face of sure defeat. But the anticlimax is cruel: all the anticipated storm and volcanic eruption wind up in a crowded Black Maria.

The bars of prison, of course, can never hold the true revolutionary spirit. But who was going to tell the happy prisoners that they had all been pursuing a wrong policy of subjectivism, adventurism, and fanaticism; that the men who issued the orders that put them to such risk were soon to be condemned as whittling away the strength of the revolutionary force; or that they were lucky to have obeyed the orders, since any demurring on their part would have incurred the wrath of the party leaders, who could be as merciless as the enemy? The Comintern, which made Li Li-san, also broke him. He resigned from the Political Bureau in November, 1930, after a letter from Moscow had convinced everyone concerned that he had to go. Earlier, there had been agitation against him, in Russia as well as in China, but the Third Plenum of the CC of the CCP, presided over by Ch'ü Ch'iu-po in late September, 1930, tried to keep him in power. Poor Ch'ü Ch'iu-po, who was dispatched from Moscow to correct the Li Li-san line after the Changsha fiasco, did nothing to satisfy either his Russian masters or the Chinese dissidents who were growing vociferous, now assured of the support of the Comintern. So Ch'ü and others who had tried to protect Li came to be known as "conciliationists," [114] a derogatory name that reduced their influence in the struggle for power that was to ensue. The main contenders were now the Ch'en Shao-yü clique and those who were called "right deviationists." The Ch'en clique won the day at the Fourth Plenum in January, 1931, but the "right deviationists," defeated at the conference table,[115] vindicated their position by establishing their own party organiza-

---

[114] "Conciliationists meant originally those who tried to work out a compromise between the Trotskyists under Ch'en Tu-hsiu and the Stalinists under Li Li-san." Otsuka Reizo, "Shina kyosanto no gensei" ("The Present Situation of the CCP"), *Kaizo,* July, 1931. The Chinese translation occurred in *Kuo-wen chou-pao* (Tientsin), July 27, 1931. After the Third Plenum of 1930, conciliationists came to denote those who tried to compromise with the Li Li-san line. See the Maoist document cited in note 92. But both Ch'ü Ch'iu-po and Ch'en Shao-yü were accused of being conciliationists by the Lo Chang-lung–Ho Meng-hsiung clique. See below, note 127.

[115] The conference lasted only fifteen hours, which did not seem sufficient for the opponents to air their opinions. (See note 93.) According to a pro-Kuomintang source, the opponents were intimidated by armed guards loyal to the Ch'en clique. "The Inside Story of the CCP Today and Its Tendency to General Collapse," *Kuang-ming chih lu (Path of Light),* Vol. II, No. 2 (Nanking, Nov. 1, 1931). (In the University of Washington Library.) Another pro-Kuomintang source indicates that Mif used Ho Meng-hsiung's influence over the rank-and-file cadres to agitate against Li Li-san after the Third Plenum. The treachery at the Fourth Plenum, which denied

tions at the central, provincial, and district levels. They refused to recognize the legality of the party apparatus under Ch'en. The party was split.

THE RIGHT DEVIATIONISTS

For some of the details of this complicated history, the reader is referred to Isaacs, Schwartz, and North. But a word about the current Maoist version of this ugly phase of the history of the Chinese Communist Party should be said. This account, probably penned by Mao himself, and sanctioned by the party under him, is found in the "Resolution on Some Questions in the History of Our Party," which has been quoted. To give the Maoist document a thorough examination should require as much research as to establish the historical accuracy of, say, Li Ang's *Red Stage*. The beautiful simplicity of the former is no less suspect than the sensationalism of the latter.

For the purpose of the present study, however, we shall content ourselves with pointing out Mao's peculiar stand on two "important questions":

1. Mao says nothing about the manipulation of the Comintern, together with its big-brotherly concern, its stupidity, arrogance, vacillation, caprice and spleen, and the effects of all of these on the Chinese Communist Party.

2. Mao makes a distinction between two kinds of "right deviationists" under attack in January, 1931. While Lo Chang-lung and other "splitters" were bad, the "twenty-odd comrades," including Li Ch'iu-shih and Ho Meng-hsiung, were actually more sinned against than sinning.

Mao's reticence on the first question is understandably diplomatic. With the Comintern thus absolved from blame, he cannot help being too severe in his strictures on Li Li-san and Ch'en Shao-yü. As evidence now strongly suggests, at least a part of the responsibility should be borne by the Comintern. But as long as Mao Tse-tung refuses to be bothered, neither Comrade Li nor Comrade Ch'en will be given a chance to defend himself on these charges.

The second question has lost none of its mystery even after Mao, whether in justice or out of sheer magnanimity, has lifted the label of "right deviationism" off the "twenty-odd martyrs." Indeed, he will have to answer many more questions before their innocence, i.e., innocence of any anti-party activities, can be established. The available information—from sources "hostile" or otherwise—all indicate that Lo Chang-lung and Ho Meng-hsiung were co-conspirators in January, 1931. It seems that the movement

---

Ho the rewards he anticipated for himself and his friends, drove him to desperation. "A Review of the Fourth Plenum of the CCP," in *Materials on Current Chinese History*, III, 210–12 (see note 10).

to split the party started after the Fourth Plenum, if not before, and that Ho Meng-hsiung supported and jointly led it.[116] Are these allegations all false? Mao Tse-tung did not attempt to disprove them. While the persistent problems remain unanswered, the document raises some fresh questions about the mishap the "twenty-odd" suffered at the hands of the Ch'en Shao-yü leadership. Did they commit anything which could be interpreted as a breach of party discipline? If not, then what was the occasion for the "blows"? Why should they have ever been identified with the true "right deviationists" group? And what were the "blows," we repeat, that could possibly fall on these guiltless ones during the fateful nine-day period?

So Mao's version does not contain much that throws light on what actually happened in January, 1931. With the limited resources at our disposal, we shall try to solve the puzzle. Our reconstruction of the events is necessarily imperfect, but the data that we have come across may now need a summation.

On matters of theory and policy, Ho Meng-hsiung does not seem to have differed noticeably from the Comintern, so far as its final stand on the Li Li-san line was concerned. He anticipated by two months the letter from the Comintern received in Shanghai on November 16, 1930, which sealed the fate of the Li Li-san line. On September 8, Ho, as a lone dissenter, criticized the said line in a letter of protest to the Central Political Bureau after he had been dismissed from the post of secretary of the Shanghai Central District Committee.[117] A great similarity in substance is discernible between the two documents. Here are "the mistakes, dangers, and evils" of the Li Li-san line, as they are listed in the Comintern letter:

1. Its failure to estimate the uneven development of the revolution in China.

2. Its neglect of the fact that the labor movement was lagging behind the peasant movement.

---

[116] Otsuka Reizo (cited above, note 114) does not mention that the Emergency Committee existed before the Fourth Plenum. But he recognizes Ho as being a co-leader of the Lo Chang-lung clique. Pro-Kuomintang sources, however, maintain that Lo Chang-lung and Ho Meng-hsiung did not organize an Emergency Committee after the Fourth Plenum; they simply made public what had already been in existence. "The Anti-Fourth Plenum Activities of the Ho Clique," in *Kuang-ming chih lu (Path of Light)*, Nov. 1, 1931; also "On the Emergency Committee of the CCP," *Society Mercury*, Jan. 10, 1933; reprinted in *Materials on Current Chinese History*, II, 266. Possibly the information in pro-Kuomintang journals was obtained from Communist renegades.

[117] Ho Meng-hsiung, *I-chien shu (Statements to the Central Political Bureau)*. First letter, dated September 8, 1930. (Hoover Library.) A summary of *A Statement of the Views of Ho Meng-hsiung* is found in Hsiao, *Power Relations,* pp. 50–53.

3. Its neglect of the tremendous role played by the imperialists; an armed uprising under the given circumstances would have meant direct clash with them.

4. An overzealousness to push through socialist programs in the Soviet areas, whereas the urgent task should be to consolidate and strengthen those areas.

5. Its failure to understand the meaning of "the workers' and peasants' Red Army"—the Red Army, as it was, was not led by the proletariat.

6. An overemphasis on armed uprising at the expense of "everyday struggle." [118]

Points 1, 2, 4, 5, and 6 here agree, respectively, with points 1, 4, 3, 8, and 5 in Ho's letter. He did not mention the imperialists, but under his point two, he recognized the necessity for "winning the conditions of a victory," while asserting that Li's "neglect of the meaning of armed uprising" was tantamount to "liquidation of the victory for armed uprising." [119]

He was worsted in his clashes with Li Li-san through the larger part of the year 1930. He wrote the letter mainly to warn the party of the disasters it was heading for, and partly to deny the charge that he was a "spy in the employ of the liquidationists" (i.e., of the Trotskyists), an aspersion that could have ruined the career of even a more worthy Communist. After the Comintern letter discovered the "spirit of Trotskyism" in Li himself, Ho might have stood a chance of being reinstated. But it is not certain how favorable to him was the "Resolution on the Question of Comrade Ho Meng-hsiung" passed by the Political Bureau on December 16, 1930, since we have not been able to locate the document.[120] The rule of Li Li-san

---

[118] See note 102.

[119] See note 117.

[120] The Political Bureau of the CCP, which circulated Ho's *Statements,* mentioned in a note that these documents should be appended to the "Resolution on the Question of Comrade Ho Meng-hsiung." The *Statements* are available at Hoover, but not the *Resolution*. Hsiao's *Power Relations within the Chinese Communist Movement, 1930–1934,* p. 95, contains a summary of *Central (Politburo) Resolution Concerning the Question of Comrade Ho Meng-hsiung:* "In the December 16 Politburo meeting, in which the four leading Russian Returned Students were rehabilitated, earlier party decisions inflicting penalties on Ho Meng-hsiung were also reversed. His statement of September 8 was re-examined and given a new explanation in the light of the Comintern line. It was found that the views of Ho Meng-hsiung were correct and that his objection to the Li-san line was in agreement with Moscow's policy. It was therefore resolved that the decisions of the Kiangsu Provincial Action Committee to remove Ho from party work and dismiss him as an alternate committeeman were rescinded. It was further decided that this Politburo resolution and Ho's statement alike were to be released. But actually these were not released until the Fourth Plenum of January, 1931."

had no doubt come to an end; but the Ch'en Shao-yü clique had emerged from obscurity, determined to show no mercy to rivals actual or potential. If Ho Meng-hsiung's name had been cleared in December, there should have been little justification for the "blows" to fall on him in the following month.

If the political party they belonged to had permitted such a technique in decision-making on policy matters, Ho and Li indeed might have enjoyed an open debate. They differed so interestingly from each other in their views on "the revolution in China." [121] But the difference between Ho and Ch'en Shao-yü did not seem so debatable. On Ho's part we have seen how he agreed basically with the Comintern, and therefore with Ch'en and his associates, who made it their avowed task to replace the Li Li-san line and the conciliationist line with the Comintern line. What had been under Li Li-san a dispute over policy, though always with an edge of personal animosity, was drained of its intellectual content when Ch'en came to power. Behind the spectacular exchange of "hyphenated invectives" (the phrase is Isaacs'), the grab for power became noisier, more disgraceful, and more relentless. The key to an understanding of the intra-party struggle in those days is found in a phrase in the Maoist document: "both that plenary session [the fourth] and the Central Committee after it promoted 'Left' doctrinaire-sectarian comrades to leading posts." In other words, comrades who were not " 'Left' doctrinaire-sectarian" were left out. The spoils were not equally divided between those who had brought down Comrade Li Li-san. The reason for Lo Chang-lung to establish "the Central Emergency Committee, 'Second' provincial committees, 'Second' district committees, and 'Second Party fractions' in Trade Unions," [122] was probably that this was the only way he could promote his friends to leading posts. Of course, Lo Chang-lung could not possibly build up the posts single-handed; it was only fair that the comrades who made up the "committees and fractions" should share his blame. We know today that at the time of his arrest, Ho Meng-hsiung was the *incumbent* secretary of the Kiangsu Provincial Commit-

---

[121] Li Li-san happened to be a diligent writer in the year 1929–30 about his own political views. See Chün-tu Hsüeh's remark about the holdings of the *Hung-ch'i* in the Hoover Library: *"Hung Ch'i:* published twice a week, this was an official organ of the CCP. It contains . . . writings of Li Li-san (Nos. 83, 86, 87, 88, 90–92, 94, 96, 98, 100, 111, 120, & 123), some of which constitute what is later known as the Li Li-san line. His writings under the pseudonym Po Shan can be found in Nos. 48, 60, 61, and 82." *The Chinese Communist Movement, 1921–1937, An Annotated Bibliography* (Stanford, 1960). It may be noted that Yin Fu, writing under his original name, Hsü Pai, was also a regular contributor to the *Hung-ch'i.*

[122] Mao, *Selected Works,* IV, 340.

tee.[123] This is one of the most surprising disclosures that has come up in our research. In September, 1930, he was still without an official position and only spending his restless days in his "pavilion room," after having been relieved from the secretaryship of the Central Shanghai District Committee, which he had held for only three months,[124] and which, we may surmise from the Yün Tai-ying episode, had probably been meant in the beginning as a demotion for a comrade of his importance. And now who promoted him to the secretaryship of the Kiangsu Provincial Committee? It could not be the Ch'en clique. According to one source, the secretaryship fell to none other than Ch'en Shao-yü himself after the Fourth Plenum.[125] Anyway, there is little likelihood that such a "leading post" would have been given away by the " 'Left' doctrinaire-sectarian" comrades to a known "right deviationist." We strongly suspect that Ho Meng-hsiung was secretary of the "Second" Kiangsu Provincial Committee, or that he was a secessionist, like Lo Chang-lung.

It should be noted that no mention is made of the "dual party organizations" in the "Resolution of the Fourth Plenum," for those came into being only after the resolution had been passed, which put the rightists to rout. Before the Fourth Plenum, the rightists still had some chance; after it, they became desperate. Some inkling of their bitter struggle is found in the resolution.

It must be remembered that although it is exceedingly important to struggle against the putschism of the Li-san line, the immediate danger of the Party at present is still the rightist tendency. . . . For these rightists are very active in distorting the CI [Comintern] line under the false banner of anti-Li-sanism, carrying on a struggle against the Li-san line on rightist grounds, denying the danger of a rightist tendency, blurring the necessity for an anti-rightist struggle, and attempting to induce some of the lower level organs to use incorrect methods of struggle in opposing Li Li-sanism. For example, they deny the necessity of shifting to practical work in the Party, and demand extreme democracy; they raise the arbitrary slogan of dismissing the whole Politburo and all the leading comrades who have committed some mistake, attempt to change the fight for principle into a fight between groups and individuals, and refuse to engage in self-criticism, etc.[126]

The "grounds" they stood on are not very clear, since, regrettably, much

---

[123] "The Blood of the Forerunners," an article by Cheng Ko, introduces the "twenty-odd martyrs" as including Ho Meng-hsiung, "who was at the time of his arrest secretary of Kiangsu Provincial Committee, CCP." *Jen-min jih-pao*, Feb. 7, 1961, p. 8.
[124] See note 117.
[125] "The Anti-Fourth Plenum Activities of the Ho Clique." See above, note 116.
[126] Conrad Brandt, Benjamin Schwartz, and John Fairbank, *A Documentary History of Chinese Communism* (Cambridge: Harvard University Press, 1952), p. 214.

of the literature issued by the rightists is not available. A pamphlet, for instance, "Fight for an Emergency Conference; Oppose the Fourth Plenum," [127] must contain their arguments in a fuller form, probably including some justification for the "dual party organizations," but until that and other materials are accessible to the researchers, it is hard to verify the nine-point platform allegedly upheld by the "Ho clique," as is found in pro-Kuomintang publications.[128] However, the quotation above at least confirms our suspicion about an "attempt to change the fight for principle into a fight between groups and individuals." The fierceness of the struggle indicates that the challenge was accepted: the Ch'en clique was ready to take on any groups or individuals who questioned its authority. Meanwhile, the rightists refused to "engage in self-criticism," i.e., refused to submit. They demanded "extreme democracy," because democracy often protects the underdog. The document does not say that the rightists were opposed to the Comintern line; they were simply "very active in distorting it." The most they did in the way of defiance was the request for the "recall and punishment" of Mif, and his replacement by a person more favorable to their views and more accommodating to their private ambitions.[129]

[127] "Letter from the Central Committee of the CCP to all members of CCP and CY" (Ch'en Ch'eng Collection, microfilm reel 14) mentions the distribution of a pamphlet under such a title, "Fight for an Emergency Conference; Oppose the Fourth Plenum."

[128] "The Anti-Fourth Plenum Activities of the Ho Clique" (note 116, above) attributes the following platform to the Emergency Committee: (1) The revolution in China has been destroyed. The crisis at present is as grave as at the time preceding the August 7 Conference of 1927. (2) The central slogan should not be to establish a Soviet regime. Slogan for economic struggles rather than political struggles should be adopted. (3) The Fourth Plenum is to be opposed because it has been conducted under the conciliationist line. It is even more despicable than the Third Plenum. (4) Mif should be recalled and punished. (5) Petition to the Comintern for the suspension of the rights and functions of the existing Central Committee which is filled with Li Li-sanists. (6) Petition to the CCP delegation to the Comintern for the convocation of an Emergency Conference. (7) The said Emergency Conference should be participated in by (a) Members of the Central Committee from the Soviet Areas; (b) Members of the CC elected by the Sixth National Congress of 1928 (thus Ch'en Shao-yü would be disqualified); (c) Active anti-Li-sanists from every level of the party hierarchy. (8) Iron discipline should be enforced. Punishment for all Li-sanists and members of the Ch'en clique, viz., Hsiang Chung-fa, Chou En-lai, Li Li-san, Ch'ü Ch'iu-po, Ch'en Shao-yü, Li Wei-han, Ho Ch'ang, etc. (9) All provincial and district committees should be reorganized. A complete liquidation of Li-sanists. Another source (*Materials on Current Chinese History*, I, 247, cited in note 10) gives a similar platform.

[129] Some of the nine points quoted above can be studied in comparison with the CC Letter (note 127) which charges, among other things, that the Party Fraction

The Resolution of the Fourth Plenum contains a useful hint about the plight of the four young writers in the sordid game of politics. It concerns the rightists' attempt to "induce some of the lower-level organs to use incorrect methods of struggle in opposing Li Li-sanism." Li Wei-sen (Li Ch'iu-shih) was, of course, a prominent target of the purge, according to the Maoist document. But Hu Yeh-p'in, Jou Shih, Feng K'eng, and Yin Fu, because they were very junior in the party, probably did not receive so much attention. How they opposed Li Li-sanism is unknown, though it was certain that they all turned against Li Li-san at a time when Li was condemned even by himself. They had sung praise for the revolutionary spirit which was manifested, under Li Li-san, in the mock-heroic demonstrations. Had they ever protested against the unnecessary risk and other arbitrary measures imposed by Li when he was still recognized as the executor of the Comintern line? If they had, their opinions were expressed perhaps only at conferences, and not in writings meant for public agitation. Anyway, they were happier under Li Li-san, since they could at least persuade themselves that they were fighting against the "enemy class," futile though the fight was. After Li's downfall, revolution took a turn for which they were little prepared. They had to be told who, among their comrades, were the rightists and who were the conciliationists. When the rightists were so unscrupulous as to attempt to teach "incorrect methods" to some of the "lower-level organs," they found it harder to keep themselves from direct involvement in the power struggle.

According to a pro-Kuomintang source, the "Ho clique" seized several organs in order to prevent them from falling into the hands of the appointees of the new Political Bureau:

> Sympathetic with that clique were the Party Fraction [of Federation of Labor Unions?], Revolutionary Mutual Aid Society, Central Preparatory Committee for All-China Soviet Congress, Delegation to All-China Soviet Congress, Delegation from Soviet Areas, Railroad Union, Maritime Union, League of Leftist Writers, etc. All these organs, at one time or another, passed resolutions opposing the Fourth Plenum, denouncing the Comintern Representative [Mif] for his preference against the Emergency Committee, proposing the convocation of an Emergency Conference, etc.[130]

---

of the Federation of Labor Unions adopted a resolution which opposed the Fourth Plenum and the Comintern representative. A fuller list of the charges will be quoted in the text. (See note 135.)

[130] "The Anti-Fourth Plenum Activities of the Ho Clique," as cited in note 116. According to "The Inside Story of the CCP Today," the District Committees of Eastern Shanghai, Chapei (Northern Shanghai) and Central Shanghai refused to be turned over to the Ch'en clique. (See note 115 for bibliographical data.) A "chin-chi

There is little doubt about the attitude of the labor unions, since the "Ho clique" is marked out as "a labor-oriented group" by North,[131] and the Party Fraction of the Federation of Labor Unions did pass a resolution opposing the Fourth Plenum and denouncing the Comintern representative.[132] One of the charges against Lo Chang-lung, who was expelled on February 2, 1931, was that "he controlled the Party Fraction of Federation of Labor Unions as a center for anti-party activities." [133]

The appearance of the League of Leftist Writers in the list is interesting, but there is no further evidence to support its inclusion, since we cannot exclude the possibility that some of its members sided with Ch'en or were simply indifferent. A more reasonable conjecture is that the League was split. Yang Ts'un-jen, a one-time leftist writer, recalled in 1932:

> In 1931, during the fight for power between Ch'en Shao-yü and Ho Meng-hsiung–Lo Chang-lung, the comrades in the Cultural Branch (*wen-hua chih-pu*) were evidently divided, since Hu Yeh-p'in, Feng K'eng, Jou Shih, and Yin Fu were close with Ho Meng-hsiung. Feng K'eng was particularly busy, running about and agitating against the Central. Though I was greatly displeased with all this, I did not join the quarrel, since I was unaffected as a worker in the Left-Wing Dramatists' League which was a mass organization, and not a branch of the party.[134]

That Hu Yeh-p'in, Feng K'eng, Jou Shih, and Yin Fu took the side of Ho

---

t'ung-kao" ("Emergency Notice") issued by the CY Central, undated, says, "In the struggle with the Li-san line, certain evil tendencies have been discovered in Shang-hai. . . . For instance, the Shanghai Central District Committee of the CCP has declared itself independent organizationally, and the Chapei District Committee of the CY has declared its own dissolution." Ch'en Ch'eng Collection, microfilm reel 14. What "incorrect methods" the rightists could use to influence a lower-level organ is illustrated by the case of Li Shao-yün. The Resolution of the CY Central on the Expulsion of Comrade Li Shao-yün (Feb. 10, 1932) charges: "Comrade Li Shao-yün, because of his mistake of opposing the Fourth Plenum, was dismissed from work by the Kiangsu Provincial Committee. . . . Later he admitted his mistake. . . . So new work was assigned him by the KPC, out of consideration for the re-education of comrades. . . . But before he left for the other province (to assume his new job), he employed the *methods formerly used by the Rightist Splinter organizations* (italics mine—T.A.H.): he gathered together a number of childish comrades under his deceitful influence; he openly opposed the new appointee by the KPC to strengthen the leadership of the Western Shanghai District Committee; he refused to turn over his work . . ." Ch'en Ch'eng Collection, reel 2.

[131] North, *op. cit.,* pp. 141, 150.

[132] See note 129 above.

[133] Otsuka Reizo, *loc. cit.*

[134] Yang Ts'un-jen, "On Leaving the Trench of Life in a Political Party," *Tu-shu tsa-chih*, Vol. III, No. 1 (Shanghai: Shen-chou kuo-kuang-she, Jan., 1933). The article bears the date November 15, 1932.

Meng-hsiung may be inferred even from the Maoist document. What is revealed here is the fact that the fight took place not so much in the League of Leftist Writers as in the party's Cultural Branch, which, presumably, controlled not only the Writers' League but other cultural organizations such as the Dramatists' League.

Interesting as the fight in the Cultural Branch was, we know little about it. Attention, however, should be called to another name on the list: the Central Preparatory Committee for the All-China Soviet Congress. That organ, as it turned out, affected the fate of the five martyrs more than anything else. And that it was deeply tainted with "right deviationism" is borne out by a "Letter from the Central Committee of the CCP to all members of CCP and CY," dated January 25, 1931. After a preamble in which it is declared:

> The Fourth Plenum has dealt merciless blows to the Rightists represented by Comrade Lo Chang-lung, Comrade Liao Mu-ch'ün, and others,

the document gives some samples of "rightist thinking":

> In our ranks have been found persons echoing the liquidationists, persons who blaspheme the Red Army and oppose the Comintern's resolution on China of last July—Kuo Miao-ken;
> who allege that the Li-san line has destroyed revolution in China and that the current situation is as grave as before the August 7th Conference [of 1927] or around the Sixth National Congress—Liao Mu-ch'ün, P'eng Tse-hsiang, and Lo Chang-lung;
> who allege that the Soviet movement has not yet become a mass movement—the Staff Meeting [*kung-tso hui-i*] of the Preparatory Committee for the Soviet Congress; and
> who—those are the most blasphemous—allege that the Sixth National Congress was conducted under the conciliationist line and that the lines pursued by the Central ever since have been a mistake—Lo Chang-lung, Wang Chung-i.
> Such allegations have often been made by men like Ch'en Tu-hsiu and P'eng Shu-chih (or the liquidationists).[135]

All these dissident opinions should be carefully studied, especially those about the Red Army and the Soviet areas, for they bear on Mao's position in the party. As they now appear in their digested, if not distorted, form, their meaning is not at all clear. Nor can it be ascertained how similar they really were to the views of the Trotskyists.[136]

---

[135] The CC Letter. See note 127 above. According to Tso-liang Hsiao, Liao Mu-ch'ün was the alias of Ho Meng-hsiung. (*Power Relations within the Chinese Communist Movement,* pp. 129, 331.)

[136] "A Letter to All Comrades of the Party from the Left Opposition of the CCP" (February 15, 1931) contains the passage clearly indicative of the irreconcilable at-

The absence of the names of Ho Meng-hsiung and Li Ch'iu-shih in the document is also conspicuous. Perhaps their opinions were not worth serious consideration. Anyway, by the time the letter was first published, they had ceased to be a threat to the party leadership. They were in prison.

But their opinion was there. Further research will reveal that the anonymous Staff Meeting of the Preparatory Committee for the Soviet Congress in the list above spoke collectively not only for Ho Meng-hsiung but also for the five martyrs. We only regret that we are unable to substantiate the thesis that "the Soviet movement has not yet become a mass movement," except for a hint found in Ho's earlier letter to the Central Action Committee (under Li Li-san) in which he stressed the necessity for introducing more industrial workers into both the party and the Red Army.[137] But since that was a principle of the Comintern line, too, we do not see why it should be regarded as rightist, not to say blasphemous. Much more must have been said by the Staff Meeting, of which we are ignorant.

CONSPIRACY WITHIN A CONSPIRACY

One of the most important events in 1930 for the Communists was the Conference of Delegates from the Soviet Areas held in or near Shanghai in the month of May. The Conference had attracted much attention ever since February of that year.[138] *The North China Herald,* for instance, reported one handbill found in the streets during the March 8 demonstration:

> Yet another handbill, in the middle of its rigamarole, contains the information that the CCP and the National General Labor Union have decided to convene a "Soviet Conference" on May 30th of this year, choosing the date as suitable because it is the anniversary of the incident in 1925.[139]

The conference actually took place on May 20, after public notice had been served to the authorities of Shanghai—a typical case of the bravado of the Communist Party under the Li Li-san line. The fact that it was carried off without a snag bespeaks a high order of vigilant discipline which enabled the delegates from the various provinces to delude the police in their travels to attend the meeting in Shanghai. Not all of them were from

---

titude of the Trotskyists: "We are opposed to the Stalinist leadership in its entirety. We are opposed to the bureaucratic conpiracy of Mif, Ch'en Shao-yü, Shen Tse-min, etc. We are likewise opposed to the bureaucratic struggle of Lo Chang-lung, P'eng Tse-hsiang, Kuo Miao-ken, etc." Hoover Library, No. 198 in the Hsüeh Bibliography.

[137] Ho's *Statements,* the September 8 letter, cited in note 117 above.

[138] An order for the convocation of the Conference was published in the *Hung-ch'i,* No. 79, Feb. 26, 1930.

[139] *North China Herald,* Mar. 11, 1930, p. 392.

the provinces, though: some were local residents. Jou Shih, for instance, attended the meeting as a representative of the League of Leftist Writers. He afterwards wrote a report on it, *A Great Impression,* which is now unavailable.[140] Feng K'eng was probably a delegate, too.[141] It was at this conference that Ho Meng-hsiung had one of his clashes with Li Li-san.[142] But the resolutions of the conference represented Li's, rather than Ho's, school of thought. The platform for a Central Soviet regime, adopted by the conference, was criticized by the Comintern in the November letter as "Trotskyist in spirit," i.e., evincing an undue enthusiasm for the realization of socialism without consideration for the consolidation of the Soviet areas. How that influenced the later "rightist" opinion of the Staff Meeting of the Preparatory Committee for the All-China Soviet Congress should be a most interesting question.

After the conference in May, active measures were taken to prepare for the first All-China Soviet Congress (which opened in Juichin, Kiangsi, on November 7, 1931, and led to the establishment of the Central Soviet government with Mao as chairman). In June, 1930, immediately after the conference, Li Wei-sen was made secretary of the "Shanghai office" of the All-China Soviet Congress.[143] Whatever the name "Shanghai office" means, he must have been important enough to sit on the Staff Meeting. Meanwhile, Hu Yeh-p'in, Jou Shih, Feng K'eng, and Yin Fu all joined the staff of the Preparatory Committee to do propaganda work for the new "revolutionary" regime in China. Special honor went to Hu Yeh-p'in in November, when he was elected a delegate to the Soviet Congress. But his elation was not unmingled with anxiety: all through the last months of his life, as Ting Ling recalled, he was worried about his wife and baby, from whom he would have been separated, had he lived long enough to make the trip to Kiangsi.[144]

Then came the meeting on January 17, 1931, in the Eastern Hotel on Avenue Edward VII. It does not seem likely that it was a meeting of the "Emergency Committee" (as in Schwartz) or a meeting of the "newly constituted Central Committee" (as in North). Our four young writers had not

---

[140] *LH,* IV, 220. A new edition of *Jou Shih ch'uän-chi,* which I have not seen, includes *A Great Impression.* It is listed in *The Daian Monthly* (Tokyo), Nov., 1961, p. 36.

[141] She is said to have attended a conference where she met delegates from various provinces. *Feng K'eng,* pp. 69–70.

[142] Mentioned in Ho's letter No. 3, dated October 9, 1930. Ho's *Statements.*

[143] *The Outpost,* p. 6.

[144] *HYP,* pp. 23–24.

yet earned enough seniority to be qualified for a meeting on such a high level; and any such meeting should have included some more of the known secessionists, namely, Lo Chang-lung, Wang K'o-ch'üan, Hsü Hsi-ken, and others, who, however, were not among those apprehended that night. Isaacs was closer to the truth when he said:

> A group of these older Party members and trade unionists, and some younger men, led by the veteran Ho Mung-shung, met at a Shanghai hotel on the night of January 17th to consider the new situation with which they were confronted.

He did not say what meeting that was. But it is now becoming clearer that it was a meeting of the Preparatory Committee for the All-China Soviet Congress. In *The Outpost,* the single-issue magazine dedicated to the martyrs, is found the passage:

> It is only months away from the All-China Soviet Congress; the revolutionary mass organizations are warmly giving their support and have enthusiastically elected their own delegates to the glorious assembly. This will be for the first time a review of troops by our government for revolutionary masses; this will be an occasion for our government to listen to the demands and complaints of the people belonging to those organizations. No wonder it has met with such warm response. Our Left-Wing cultural organizations have also elected our delegates who are ready to submit our demands on cultural affairs and on our life. But on the night when our delegates and the delegates of ten-odd organizations met to discuss the work in preparation for the Congress, they were all arrested.[145]

Though there is no further evidence to corroborate what is suggested above —that all five were delegates-elect—yet they were at least all engaged in making preparations for the Soviet Congress. The *New Masses* article contains this piece of information about Feng K'eng: "Joined Left Writers in 1930 and was in the Propaganda Committee at the All-China Soviet Congress." This statement, omitting the Preparatory Committee, is a little confusing, since the said Congress was convened nine months after her death. A clearer explanation is found in *Feng K'eng, the Martyr:*

> On the night of January 17th, crowded in a room in the Eastern Hotel . . . were over thirty men and women who were at a meeting . . . one of the meetings of the Preparatory Committee for the All-China Soviet Congress. Feng K'eng and four others were members of the "Left League" in charge of propaganda for the Congress.[146]

---

[145] Mei Sun, "A Lesson in Blood," *The Outpost,* p. 5.

[146] *Feng K'eng,* p. 83. Also, Hu Yeh-p'in sent a note from the prison, saying that he was arrested "at an organ of the Preparatory Committee for the Soviet Congress." *HYP,* p. 25.

The number of people assembled and arrested that night came to a total of 36 (including seven women),[147] and about two-thirds of them were later put to death. Among those whose lives were luckily spared, there may be some who could give an account of what took place at the meeting. If only they could be located and persuaded to talk! The main item on the agenda of that night, of course, may have been the preparations for the Soviet Congress. But the Communists were living under such tension after the Fourth Plenum that the discussion could have easily flown off in an altogether opposite direction. The presence of Li Ch'iu-shih and Ho Meng-hsiung looked particularly sinister. If they had any grievances against the "merciless blows" they had suffered wrongly at the Fourth Plenum and after, this should have been the occasion to air them. Should the Fourth Plenum be opposed and its resolutions overridden by an Emergency Conference as many of their comrades were clamoring for? They might have raised that subject too. Were they not, as rightists, looking for some lower-level organs to be induced "to use incorrect methods of struggle in opposing Li Li-sanism?" Here then was the Preparatory Committee for the All-China Soviet Congress, a lower-level organ very attractive as an object for this kind of seduction. If they had any interest in promoting the "dual party organizations," they should at least not lose hold of the thirty-odd men and women who, if won over, might add greatly to their strength.

These are not mere conjectures; on January 17 they had perhaps already been won over. It is very likely that the meeting of the night was committed to the "rightist opposition," since it is known that the Staff Meeting of the Preparatory Committee for the All-China Soviet Congress was condemned by the Ch'en leadership as "echoing the liquidationists" and uttering "blasphemy" against the Soviet movement. The first principle of propaganda for the Soviet movement, that it should emphasize "the opposition of two regimes (Communist and KMT)," [148] was perhaps laid aside at a time when factional fight compelled immediate attention. As Isaacs, Schwartz, and North have suggested, that meeting might have only aggravated the antagonism between the Communist cliques if the police of the International Settlement had not appeared in time to intervene.

That the police came on the tip-off of some Communists has remained a rumor. Since the scandal damages the reputation of the Communist Party as a whole, it is high time for the Peking regime today to deny it. But

[147] See Jou Shih's note from the prison. *LH*, IV, 373. English translation found in *China Reconstructs* (Peking), Sept., 1961, p. 7.

[148] *Hung-ch'i*, No. 112, June 21, 1930.

to the best of our knowledge, no such denial has ever been issued. On the contrary, recent Communist publications suggest that betrayal was possible. But by whom? Ch'en Shao-yü had the motive, since he was the one to benefit from the removal of his opponents. However, there is no direct evidence to support the allegation that he was the betrayer.

Wei Chin-chih recalled in 1960 that the meeting was held in high secrecy, which only deepens the mystery of how the police came to discover it.

The party meeting that Jou Shih and others attended was a secret meeting of high importance. Some of them did not tell their wives (about it); others did not tell their very intimate comrades in the party. How am I sure? For when it was found that they were not back from the meeting, wives began to look for husbands, and comrades for comrades. There was a man who was almost arrested by the detectives when he was looking for Jou Shih and Feng K'eng. What happened was like this: Jou Shih and Feng K'eng had a secret office, where Jou Shih used to spend his nights when he did not come back to the Chin-yün Li. They had a sign: if the window was open, it meant that they were in. That day when the man went to call on them, he saw that the window was open and so he shouted. But the head that appeared in the window was not Jou Shih; so the man took to his heels immediately.[149]

A different version of Wei's reminiscences appeared in 1957, which contained the name of the man who almost got into trouble because of his concern for his missing comrades. The man was Feng Hsüeh-feng who, in 1931, as a cadre in charge of a news agency under the Central Propaganda Department of the CCP, was the one to be informed of all the important meetings.[150] That he knew nothing about this one also suggests that the meeting was not sanctioned by the Party Central. The same source supports a betrayal theory with the introduction of a mysterious electrician. It also implies a denial of the possibility that a porter or some employee of the hotel informed the police who, obviously, had already known what was going to happen even before the meeting started.

When it was known that Jou Shih had been arrested, Hsüeh-feng wished to find out about Feng K'eng. The window of their house was usually shut, but that day when Hsüeh-feng approached the alley, the window was wide open, and a stranger's head appeared. Knowing that the police were lying in wait, he turned back. Further inquiries revealed that Hu Yeh-p'in had also disappeared. Only long afterwards did the information come that Jou Shih and others had held a meeting in the Far Eastern Hotel on Tibet Road (now

---

[149] Wei, "Miscellaneous Reminiscences," *Wen-hsüeh p'ing-lun,* Apr., 1960.

[150] Feng, *My Recollections of Lu Hsün,* p. 57. Feng has been denounced as a rightist since the summer of 1957; that was probably why his name was not mentioned in 1960.

converted into the Cultural Palace).[151] But it had been discovered by the enemy. Before the meeting started, somebody had walked in to investigate under the false pretense of repairing the electric light. So all who later came to the meeting were arrested.[152]

There is a court scene in *Feng K'eng, the Martyr.* Its author, who is probably Miss Feng's "lover," Hsü Ngo, using another name, Hsü Mei-hsün, assures his reader that "whatever is in this book is fact; about details such as the street number of a house or a phrase in a conversation, and especially about the identity of persons—I have been trying to preserve 100 per cent authenticity." [153] Perhaps some reservation should be made, since we do not know how anybody could overhear the interrogation quoted below, unless Mr. Hsü learned this from the survivors who came back to their comrades with this piece of dialogue:

"So you won't talk, but some comrades of yours have spilled." The re-actionary judge, his head poised, uttered his despicable lie from beneath the two halves of his mustaches.

"No, our comrades will never talk," she firmly denied.

"Then, if it was not for the information from your comrades, how do you come to find yourself here?"

"No, those who got me here are not my comrades, but my enemy—yes, my enemy, just like you!" She ended the sentence with a "Pish!" which shot at the judge like a bullet, and he lowered his head and dodged.[154]

The question raised by the judge, "If it was not for the information from your comrades, how do you come to find yourself here?" is as puzzling as ever. But what the judge said was perhaps not all lies. Among those prisoners who later escaped death, there may have been some who talked. Since the meeting they attended that night was protected by high secrecy, informers, if there were informers, could be found only among those comrades who had received the notice. Who they were and how they acted in collusion with the Ch'en clique on one hand and the KMT authorities on the other are questions not yet answered.

Our five young writers, perhaps because they refused to talk,[155] were

---

[151] This is the only source which gives for their meeting place the Far Eastern Hotel on Tibet Road. All other sources have the Eastern Hotel on Avenue Edward VII.

[152] Wei, "Time Spent in the Company of Jou Shih," *Wen-i yüeh-pao,* Mar. 5, 1957.

[153] *Feng K'eng,* p. 92.

[154] *Ibid.,* p. 90.

[155] According to Ting Ling, Ch'en Li-fu, Minister of Propaganda of the KMT, agreed to help Hu Yeh-p'in only if he would promise to live in Nanking, presumably under supervision, after his release. *HYP,* p. 28.

sent to the execution ground. They missed the great events that were to come—the Long March, the Anti-Japanese War, the Civil War after 1945 —events of such magnitude and violence as would have paled their favorite metaphors of fire, earthquake, storm, and volcanic eruption. They missed, too, much of the intra-party struggle which has actually never stopped since the time they joined the party. The repeated "rectification" under Mao may seem to belong to a distant future, as viewed from the year 1931. But they had already received some "merciless blows" in the nine days they lived under Ch'en Shao-yü. Li Li-san, the deposed tyrant, had the misfortune of subjecting himself for seven years to Ch'en's arbitrary rule, seven long years of the life of a "tremulous daughter-in-law," as he later recalled.[156] What a degradation for a fiery revolutionary indeed. Said Li in 1956:

> But, I should say, in the period of the Wang Ming (i.e., Ch'en Shao-yü) line, that evil sectarianism and patriarchal system, those methods of "cruel struggle" and "merciless blows" against the mistaken comrades were not only incapable of helping them to recognize and correct their mistakes, but also imposed such a constant pressure on their spirit that they could hardly breathe.[157]

It seems that few Chinese Communists are as frank as Comrade Li in their public utterances. It has been left to a Korean Communist to tell about his experience in China with the Wang Ming line, which should have been useful to our five writers. This Korean, who used the pseudonym of Kim San, went to prison under the Li Li-san line and upon his release found himself called a Li Li-sanist "for no reason," and then a rightist and then a Trotskyist.[158] His summary of the situation, without the aid of rhetorical embellishment, reads at least as terrible as anything found in a novel like *Tzu-yeh* where Mao Tun has done such fine work in exposing the feudalist-capitalist society:

---

[156] "I worked under Comrade Wang Ming's direct leadership for seven years, years when I led a life like that of a little daughter-in-law; fearful all the day, careful about every small detail, lest I should provoke his anger. But still, I was frequently rebuked." *Documents of Eighth Congress,* p. 411. Some of those years they probably spent together in Soviet Russia. Li Li-san was somehow reinstated in 1962. An AP dispatch from Tokyo, dated May 1, 1962, reported: "Former Chinese Communist leader Li Li-san, who has been in comparative obscurity since his disgrace in the mid-1930's, emerged Monday in the public eye in Inner Mongolia. The New China News Agency identified him as secretary of the North China Bureau of the Chinese Communist Party's Central Committee." *The Chinese World* (San Francisco), May 3, 1962.

[157] *Ibid.*

[158] Kim San and Nym Wales, *Song of Ariran, the Life Story of a Korean Rebel* (New York: John Day, 1941), pp. 185 ff.

One by one the leaders of the party betrayed [it] to the Kuomintang as they were arrested. Demoralization set in everywhere. Each man distrusted every other, and soon the work was virtually at a standstill. I had foreseen this condition, and it seemed tragically unnecessary that we did not change the line until it was too late, but the heavy mechanism of bureaucracy did not function nearly as fast as the Kuomintang.[159]

. . .

But the local Chinese leadership paid no attention to this—*ma-ma-hu-hu.* They seemed to think it was fate that turned men into traitors and that nothing could be done about it. They simply multiplied suspicion and fear and did nothing. Soon the leadership was so broken that there was no authority for anyone to do anything—and it was too late.[160]

. . .

The very men who held to the bureaucratic notion that the line could not be changed were the first to betray—for they had no deep interest in preserving and strengthening the party and revolution. They merely did their duty as they saw it—taking orders from above and refusing to take responsibility for making recommendations that might have caused them criticism from any quarter. Those who were critical were more loyal to the party than those who did not worry about the line but merely followed orders. Yet all alike were arrested and executed—the executioner does not distinguish between a head full of ideas and an empty one.[161]

BIBLIOGRAPHICAL NOTE

"Shanghai Literary Publications Association has recently put out *Tso-lien wu-lieh-shih yen-chiu-tzu-liao pien-mu* (*A Catalogue of Research Materials on the Five Martyrs of the Left League*), compiled by Ting Ching-t'ang and Ch'ü Kuang-hsi. This book, in about 200,000 Chinese characters, lists chronologically the works by the five, their translations as well as original writings, articles as well as books, and also the works on the five published from 1929 to February, 1961."

Kuang-ming jih-pao, August 20, 1961, p. 3

I have been unable to benefit from this important reference work in my research.   T.A.H.

[159] *Ibid.,* p. 185.
[160] *Ibid.,* p. 186.
[161] *Ibid.,* p. 187.

TWENTY YEARS AFTER
THE YENAN FORUM

I

IN 1962, commemorative activities were held in Communist China to celebrate the twentieth anniversary of the publication of *Mao's Talks at the Yenan Forum on Literature and Art*.[1] In the same year, a group of scholars and writers working in America and Britain gathered near Oxford to ponder over Chinese Communist literature. Though the coincidence was not intentional, it did force on one's mind a disturbing sense of history. For no review of Chinese Communist literature, from our point of view or theirs, can escape the fact of control, and the control began with Mao's *Talks*. The success of the control, of course, is something to be celebrated in Communist China, but the defects in the Chinese Communist writing, noted at the conference in England, indicate the high cost of that success. For these defects are made to order. It is beyond the power of any single writer in Communist China to correct them. He is bound to contribute to the collective errors if he wishes to avoid a political offense.

What is the political offense most commonly committed by writers in Communist China? The victims of the 1955 and 1957 purges, who were allegedly all punished for their various anti-party activities, actually made one great mistake, according to Politburo alternate member Lu Ting-i,

[1] According to Liu Hsüeh-wei, the official publication date of Mao's *Talks* was October, 1943. *Lun wen-hsüeh-ti kung-nung-ping fang-hsiang (On the Worker-Peasant-Soldier Direction in Literature)* (Shanghai, 1949), p. 90, note 5. This is probably true, since so far as I can verify, Mao's *Talks* was not available in print in 1942. But in the Chinese Communist press May, 1942, is usually given as the official publication date. "Last week literary and art workers everywhere in the country started a round of commemorative activities, to celebrate the twentieth anniversary of the *publication* [italics mine] of Chairman Mao's *Talks.* . . ." *Peking Review,* June 1, 1962, p. 1.

head of the party's Propaganda Department (who recently became a member of the party's Secretariat):[2]

We regard revolutionary literature and art as an indispensable part of the whole revolutionary task. But they, from Wang Shih-wei to Hu Feng, and then to Feng Hsüeh-feng, Ting Ling, Chiang Feng, *et al.*, all maintained the supremacy of literature and art; [they maintained] that politics should be subservient to literature and art; that "artists should lead statesmen" or that literature and art should be made an independent kingdom.[3]

The difference between "we" and "they" therefore hinged on the question of the "supremacy" or "independence" of literature and art. It is never clear to me how artists, as artists, could have the ambition to "lead" the statesmen, though from the works of the former, the latter might derive displeasure as well as pleasure, incitement to anger as well as inspiration. A plea for the independence of literature and art is understandable because political power can do so much to direct, to molest, and to persecute. But even such a plea had to be smothered for the sake of "revolution."

A leading article in *The Times Literary Supplement,* commenting on the Ditchley Manor conference, summarized well what one might think should have been the consensus of the conference:

It would be difficult to dispute the conclusion of Mr. Howard Boorman's paper giving the political setting, that "the intermeshing of doctrine and discipline . . . is as dominant in the sphere of literature as elsewhere," or to doubt that the writers who rallied hopefully and confidently to the Communist cause make "a tale of ingenuous affection deceived." [4]

What I should like to point out here is that the binding nature of Communist doctrine on writers was never certain and the wayward fancy and independent mind of a Communist writer was seldom viewed with alarm as a breach of discipline by the Chinese Communist Party until the Yenan Forum of 1942. It was in that year too that the writers who had traveled "hopefully and confidently" to Yenan began to see what great demands the party, in the person of its chairman Mao, made on them.

Liu Hsüeh-wei, a leftist critic who was purged in 1955 as a member of the Hu Feng clique, published in 1949 a commentary on Mao's *Talks.* The book, entitled *On the Worker-Peasant-Soldier Direction in Literature,* tried to allay the fears in the minds of sceptics like Hu Feng about the harm that Mao's *Talks* might do to the realistic tradition of the May Fourth Movement. Liu's disregard of the fact of party discipline made

[2] *Jen-min jih-pao,* Sept. 29, 1962.
[3] *Ibid.,* Sept. 27, 1957.
[4] *The Times Literary Supplement,* Aug. 24, 1962, p. 641.

his book an inadequate study of the real power of Mao's doctrine. Naïvely, he welcomed the reassertion of the "worker-peasant-soldier direction," which, he believed, would lead out of the theoretical confusion experienced in the Creation Society period and the years of the Chinese League of Leftist Writers. His belief in the necessity for such a doctrine seems odd in the light of his later personal tragedy, but his review of the "theoretical confusion" in the leftist literary movement in China indicates that a liberal tendency was observable even among the leftist writers before the watershed year 1942. Liu wrote:

> Without a refutation of the basic argument [that it is one's world view that determines whether one is a proletarian or not, that the establishment of world view depends on the attainment of materialist dialectics, and that to experience life is merely to acquaint oneself with the subject matter of one's writings], the leftist literary movement developed a tendency for polarization. At first, what was deemed necessary was to write according to the "materialist-dialectical method," that is, according to the formula: the description of the birth of the new amidst the old, the tomorrow in today, the conquest of the old by the new, etc. As a result of this kind of formularist theory, formularist writings (in the foreign "eight-legged" style) were mass-produced. And because of this misconception, there was also a growth of the paranoia peculiar to petty-bourgeois intellectuals. A writer might consider himself unquestionably a "proletarian writer," if he were qualified to do so by that standard. But to write about real life with this "method" meant that nothing would look life-like; to write about workers and peasants by the use of this method meant that no worker or peasant would look like one.
>
> So the need was felt to liquidate the method. It so happened that at that time the theory of the "materialist-dialectical method of creation" was liquidated in Soviet Russia. The new slogan to take its place was "socialist realism." In order to hit the weaknesses of the immediate past, there was an emphasis on the "presentation of the true reality," "the necessity to write about what one is well acquainted with," the difference or even contradiction between "world view" and the "method of creation," the difference between a Communist in politics and an actual writer for communism, etc. These were, of course, not incorrect, but we treated them with a dogmatic attitude. Under the cover of such theories and slogans, we took the opportunity gradually, subtly, and naturally to conceive a breed of liberalism. On the strength of eulogizing allusions to Tolstoy and Balzac, we began to develop a virtually uncritical worship of "classical works" and "classical writers." There began, even in the innermost hearts of the leftist writers, a reversion, an unconscious but no less true reversion to the path toward which the tendencies of the petty-bourgeois class are naturally directed. That is, we took ourselves as the first principle, while indulging in a free display of the true nature of the petty-bourgeois class. That was the process of moving from "formularism" to "liberalism," but by then we had already come to the last years of the left-wing decade. . . .[5]

---

[5] Liu, *op. cit.,* p. 17.

When the theory of "world view," which isolated theory from reality as well as from the writer, revealed its weaknesses, a remedial program to replace it was sought for in the formula "to experience life." For a long period, we took this to be the only dependable solution of contradictions; we raised it from every side to a very high eminence. Then there was introduced into China *A Letter to Beginners in Writing*[6] from the Soviet Union Literary Advisory Committee, in which the first principles were "to lay your hands on life" and "to write about what you are familiar with." We did some earnest analysis of the merits of the theory, but aside from that, we did not study the differences in conditions between Soviet Russia and China, nor did we assimilate it with a critical attitude and point out its limitations when it was applied to us. As if it had spoken out what we had in our minds, we thought that this time all problems had been solved and all doubts dispelled. As a matter of fact, from 1933 to the Yenan Forum on Literature and Art, we took this as our guiding principle.[7]

How socialist realism could lead to "liberalism" may sound paradoxical. But the realism of nineteenth-century Europe, in as diversified styles as there could be from Tolstoy to Balzac, provided a yardstick and a methodology not totally compatible with the requirements of propaganda. The hybrid known as socialist realism, if not supported by political power, could easily shift its emphasis from socialism to realism, especially when the writers who were supposed to practice it had already developed a disinterested love for the nineteenth-century masters who served as their models. Whatever the Russians said about socialist realism, the Chinese interpretation of it is surely interesting. Perhaps the Chinese leftist writers of the 1930's did feel an embarrassing sense of freedom when advice from Soviet Russia, subsequent to the dissolution of the Russian Association of Proletarian Writers, began to sound self-contradictory and therefore less dogmatic. Another possibility was that they simply followed their own bent of mind, irrespective of the Russian theory. A crop of young writers, who were published in the pages of *Wen-hsüeh* (*Literature,* 1933–37), adopted as a rule the realistic method. They were capable of independent observation and generally avoided paranoiac gesturing. Fu Tung-hua, editor of *Wen-hsüeh,* drew attention to this trend by citing a long list of its contributors which included Ai Wu, Ho Ku-t'ien (Chou Wen), Tsang K'e-chia, Wu Tsu-hsiang, Liu Pai-yü, Hsiao Chün, Tuan-mu Hung-liang, and Ch'iao

---

[6] The exact publication date is not available. But on a 1941 proscription list published by the KMT, there is the title *Kei ch'u-hsüeh hsieh-tso-che-ti i-feng-hsin* (*A Letter to Beginners in Writing*). The translator is Chang Chung-shih. See Chang Ching-lu, *Bibliographical and Historical Materials concerning Contemporary Chinese Publications,* III (Shanghai, 1956), p. 221.

[7] Liu, *op. cit.,* p. 60.

Yin (Hsiao Hung).[8] Some of these are still well-known writers in Communist China; a study of their early writings will probably bear out the observations of Liu and Fu.[9]

Later developments also show how the de-emphasis of the socialist element in socialist realism could act as a liberating force for Communist writers. Ch'in Chao-yang's critical essay "Realism—The Broad Path" (in contradistinction to the restrictive socialist realism) voiced a strong protest during the "hundred flowers" movement.[10] He quoted K. M. Simonov who, like some others, had had the audacity to redefine socialist realism in a parallel period of warm weather in Russia following Khrushchev's attack on Stalin. *People's Literature,* of which Ch'in was then an associate editor, announced the forthcoming publication, in Chinese, of Simonov's article "Concerning Socialist Realism," [11] which, however, never appeared, probably owing to a change of editorial policy as the "hundred flowers" movement changed into the Anti-Rightist movement. But Simonov's views are still available in Chinese. Another article of his, "Random Talks on Literature," was translated and published as a negative example, since it contained the "representative incorrect point of view." [12] Some of Simonov's statements (e.g., "We cannot say our literature in dealing with our postwar national life is all false; but a considerable part of our literature is half-true and half-false. And half-truth and half-falsehood is an enemy to art.")[13] must have found echoes, at least in 1957, in the hearts of Chinese writers.

Outside the left-wing groups, realism was also a method widely followed. The great changes in Chinese society dating from the late nineteenth century brought home a keen awareness of Chinese life. Not to mention the special effort made by the Chinese Writers' Union writers, the much underrated *Saturday* (*Li-pai-liu*) school of novelists, writing to entertain and little influenced by foreign models, could also turn out penetrating

[8] Fu's article is found in Fan Chung-yün (ed.), *China: The Last Ten Years* (Shanghai, 1937), p. 680.

[9] My brother gives high praise to Wu Tsu-hsiang and moderate praise to Tuan-mu Hung-liang. He is reserved about Ai Wu but censorious of Hsiao Chün. See C. T. Hsia, *A History of Modern Chinese Fiction* (Yale University Press, 1961), under the respective authors.

[10] Ch'in's article is in *Jen-min wen-hsüeh* (*People's Literature*), No. 9, 1956.

[11] See the editorial note in *ibid.,* No. 7, 1957. Simonov's "Concerning Socialist Realism" originally appeared in *Novy mir,* No. 3, 1957.

[12] In *Pao-wei she-hui-chu-i hsien-shih-chu-i* (*In Defense of Socialist Realism*), ed. Yi-wen-she (Translation Society), I (Peking, 1958). Simonov's article originally appeared in *Novy mir,* No. 12, 1956.

[13] *Ibid.,* p. 429.

analyses of the manners and mores of the newly risen petty-bourgeois class and the decaying landlord class.[14]

Independent of the realistic method, but complementing it in many instances as the *yin* principle does the *yang,* was the theme of love, whether romantic or humanitarian, which was also adopted by a great variety of writers. A touch of tenderness, a susceptibility to emotions, and an indulgence in passion and melancholy are the traditional attributes of the Chinese writer (*ts'ai-tzu,* or the man of talent); after the May Fourth Movement, the sentimental tradition was reinforced by the precepts and examples from Europe. Any unobservant or unthinking writer with limited means of expression was likely to win praise for his competency in recording his own moods or repeating some common sentiments. Novels written within a realistic framework, too, are also noted for their tender moments. This major trend does not come up in Liu Hsüeh-wei's book on the "worker-peasant-soldier direction." With an effort of will, the leftist writers could indeed frown upon the showing of affection as a sign of petty-bourgeois weakness. But they, too, sometimes lapsed into sentimentality in their supposedly "progressive" works, probably because they had a need for it in spite of their revolutionary stance.

A minor trend before 1942 was the popularity of Lu Hsün's satirical style. I call it a minor trend, because the possibilities for developing it are limited. As exemplified by Lu Hsün's *tsa-wen,* satire requires a skill in irony, epigram, economy of expression, and subtle allusion, which is usually not within the grasp of younger writers. But Lu Hsün left a brood of imitators (after his death there even appeared a magazine called *Lu Hsün feng,* or *In Imitation of Lu Hsün*).[15] The genre he made popular became a convenient vehicle to air a grievance or to register a protest at a time when occasions for grievance and protest were never lacking. One lesson that Lu Hsün taught the younger writers was how to hold emotions in check. It is clear from his writings that he seldom lost his temper or presence of mind. A skilled verbal fighter, Lu Hsün was not so particular about the code of chivalry as about the chance of victory. As a rule he

---

[14] The *Saturday* school carried on the sentimental tradition of the *Dream of the Red Chamber* and the satirical realistic tradition of *Ju-lin-wai-shih* (*The Scholars*). Its chief exponent, Chang Hen-shui, particularly deserves attention.

[15] According to Ts'ao Chü-jen, *Wen-t'an wu-shih-nien: Hsü-p'ien* (*Literary Life during the Past Fifty Years: Vol. II*) (Hong Kong, 1955), p. 154, and Lan Hai, *Chung-kuo k'ang-chan wen-i shih* (*History of Chinese Literature during the War of Resistance*) (Shanghai, 1947), p. 51, *Lu Hsün feng* (a fortnightly) was published in Shanghai before the Japanese attack on Pearl Harbor.

avoided direct clash. He would sooner have recourse to sniping than come into the open "with no armor on his naked body." But he wrote very well. Within the short compass of the *tsa-wen,* the reader usually feels a pleasurable tension. He knows that from behind the apparently civilized manner, a dart will shoot forth, but he does not see at once how or when or where. Then, after a few minutes of reading, the trick is done and someone is hit. It is the neatness of the stroke and the unexpected angle from which the attack is launched that afford the peculiar intellectual pleasure. But wit, which gives the *tsa-wen* its sting, is after all not a powerful tool. It has little respect for fact or for logic. As it is too often caught in its own cleverness to convey much of a positive idea, the *tsa-wen* was a tolerable offense in the eyes of the Kuomintang censorship. So Lu Hsün's unique genius, unhampered by those who were supposedly his persecutors, raised the *tsa-wen* to a position which almost equalled the eminence of fiction and poetry.

At the Yenan Forum, Mao endeavored to stem and deflect these three trends—realism (in fiction, and beginning with the thirties, in poetry as well), sentimentalism, and satire—which hitherto marked the "directions" of modern Chinese literature. As a matter of fact, "petty-bourgeois" realism, sentimentalism, and satire were all denounced as wrong. Henceforth, literature and art were to serve solely the party under Mao, in the name of the workers, peasants, and soldiers. Realism would be used for the praise of "progress"; love would bear the stamp of "class nature"; and satire would be directed only against the prescribed enemy. The change was great. As Chou Yang said in 1951,

Comrade Mao Tse-tung's *Talks at the Yenan Forum on Literature and Art* pushed modern literature forward into a new epoch. If it is said that the May Fourth Movement was the first revolution in the history of modern Chinese literature, then the publication of the *Talks* and the consequent changes in literary undertakings can be said to be the second, and even more sweeping and profound, literary revolution.[16]

In 1957, Yang Shuo, a defender of the party, took on two "rightists," Wu Tsu-kuang and Liu Shao-t'ang:

Wu Tsu-kuang was indeed remarkable for his kindness to save people's face. He merely rejected the literary history of the past eight years [since 1949]. I think he would utter a sigh [about his conservatism] if he compared himself with Liu Shao-t'ang who had the impudence to reject all the party's literary undertakings since the Yenan Forum on Literature and Art of 1942.[17]

[16] Chou Yang, *Chien-chüeh kuan-ch'e Mao Tse-tung wen-i lu-hsien* (*Resolutely Implement the Mao Tse-tung Line in Literature*) (Peking, 1952), p. 72.
[17] Yang Shuo, "Rise! Defend Our Party!" *Jen-min wen-hsüeh,* No. 8, 1957, p. 9.

To defenders and detractors alike, the Yenan Forum of 1942 was a major event in the determination of the nature of future Chinese Communist literature. For the first time in history, the Chinese Communist Party could boast of a "policy for literature and art." [18] All writers under the control of that policy were henceforth obliged to conform.

II

I have cited these three trends, not only because they were observable facts, but because Mao Tse-tung, as a speaker who concluded the discussion at the Forum, if not as a reader of modern Chinese literature, also noted the forces that he had to control before he could establish his authority. The striking fact about the Yenan Forum was, of course, the dominance of one man's voice. But another fact, often overlooked amidst the publicity that Mao's *Talks* receive today, was that the Forum was initiated as a meeting for the "exchange of views." [19] Of the over two hundred people invited to the conference,[20] there were, according to Mao, scores who actively participated in the discussions.[21] Though a full record of the discussion is not available, the controversy was described by Mao as "great" and the debate as "heated." [22] Some of the more interesting opinions, summarily refuted by Mao, can be found today in Mao's *Selected Works*. They represented an assortment of the views of the "petty-bourgeois" writers in the May Fourth tradition: advocates of human nature and refined sentiments, romantics with their private dreams, satirists not too careful in the choice of their target, and cool, matter-of-fact realists who wanted to expose too much for the comfort of the powers that were. They had their say at the Forum, but after that they were not allowed to repeat their old "mistakes." Their thoughts and feelings had to be transformed and remolded.

Mao's voice, which rose above and silenced the debate, had perhaps never carried so much authority as in 1942, the year of the first *Cheng-feng* (Rectification) Movement, a crucial year in his personal career, as well as in the history of his party. Boyd Compton, in his introduction to

[18] On May 19, 1942, a Yang Wei-che wrote in the *Liberation Daily* (Yenan) that the CCP did not yet have a policy for literature and art. Mao's important concluding lecture was to be given only four days later.

[19] Mao, *Talks, Selected Works* (in English) (New York, 1956), IV, 63.

[20] Ho Ch'en, "How Literature and Art in the Liberated Areas Marched toward the People," *Ch'ün-chung chou-k'an* (*The Masses Weekly*) (Hong Kong), No. 15, 1947.

[21] Mao, *Selected Works*, IV, 69.

[22] *Ibid.*, pp. 69, 92.

a collection of documents pertaining to that movement, made the following observations about the increase in Mao's power during the *Cheng-feng* Movement:

> *Cheng Feng* represented a final stage in Mao's consolidation of leadership.[23]
> Since the 1942–44 *Cheng Feng* Movement, a Mao cult has grown in China with a strong family resemblance to both the emperor cult of Imperial China and the Stalin cult in Russia.[24]

The Yenan Forum on Literature and Art was convoked as an integral part of the *Cheng-feng* Movement, and Mao's *Talks,* which came out of the Forum, fitted well into the personality cult. A dictator already in many other fields, he was now strengthening his control over literature and art. He did not state his opinion as just another speaker at the Forum; nor did he withdraw to leave the individual artists to decide for themselves after they had listened to his contribution to the discussion. He was out to reform them.

In February of that year, Mao had talked about the reform of "literary style." The so-called eight-legged style, which he attacked, the perfunctory, pedantic, repetitious, inexpressive, and high-falutin' kind of prose favored by certain Communist bureaucrats, has perhaps been the most durable style. In spite of the campaigns against it, it is still very much alive today. By including prose style as a target of his Reform Movement, Mao perhaps had in mind the "returned-students clique," composed of Moscow-trained Communists whose wide knowledge of Marxism-Leninism could be used to support their position. After their power and influence had been reduced, Mao did not really mind if his loyal followers (e.g., Chou Yang) perpetuated the "eight-legged style" in their official and theoretical writings. Indeed, the interpretations of "Mao Tse-tung's thought" are crammed with so much borrowed thought in an utterly debased language that they belong nowhere if not to the "eight-legged" school.

Mao did not take up the topic of creative literature, *belles-lettres,* drama, and fine arts until the Forum which was held in May. Here he began to attack the three trends that I have discussed. These trends, of course, produced both good literature and bad literature, and representatives of the latter always outnumbered the former. But Mao's concern was not the merit of literature as literature. His "revolution" was to take "literary and art undertakings" (*wen-i kung-tso*) out of the hands of individuals and small

---

[23] Boyd Compton, *Mao's China: Party Reform Documents, 1942–44* (Seattle: University of Washington Press, 1952), p. xxxviii.

[24] *Ibid.,* p. xlv.

groups and give them to the party. He perceived that so long as literature and art were left in the hands of individuals and small groups, however much their sympathies were professedly for the Communist cause, they had the power to cast doubts, to expose "contradictions," to raise questions about justice, to encourage independent thinking, to assert individual rights to happiness or, in a word, to undermine the power of the party. In 1942, the danger became even more visible than before. There were clear signs of disaffection.

The writers and artists who had chosen Yenan when they were seeking a refuge from the Japanese invasion were making a happy decision. In fact, it was more than a refuge that they sought. They wanted to play their parts in the war against Japan, and the Communist leadership based in Yenan looked more likely to bring about victory. Many of them had accepted Communist leadership without question. For the hardships in the barren hills and on the loess plains in the northwest, they were psychologically, if not physically, prepared when they bade farewell to Shanghai or Peking, then Peiping. They would gladly lend a helping hand to the workers, peasants, and soldiers; indeed, they would have no objection if wartime duties required them to live with them, befriend them, and learn from them. Obviously, an illusion of personal heroism helped them to make up their minds to share their fate with the Communist Party. But there was also a common ground of faith between them and Mao. When Mao advanced his arguments at the Yenan Forum, he adroitly exploited their beliefs. "Do we need Communist leadership in order to win the war? Do we want to serve the workers, peasants, and soldiers?" These were, in effect, the questions Mao put to the members of the Forum. His arguments sounded so powerful that I cannot imagine how those who were under the spell could stand up and answer "No!"

But the writers had to ask unpleasant questions when they came to Yenan. For instance, few of them had ever thought that some day they would have little to write about or that they would be even forced to cease to write. But such was their experience. Chou Yang raised a question in 1941:

> In Yenan, some friends interested in creative writing have felt that they cannot write anything any more. But the life we have here is a new, meaningful life, and creation here is free. Then why the cessation of creative activity, why is so little written? [25]

The question would have been puzzling indeed if life had been so meaning-

---

[25] *Liberation Daily,* July 19, 1941, p. 2.

ful or creation so free as Chou Yang claimed them to be. The puzzle was also noticed by Ou-yang Shan:

> To my question, "Have you written much recently?" a young acquaintance of mine who loves literature answers: "Recently my head has been so filled with revolutionary theory that not a single short poem could I produce."
>
> His immediate and unprepared answer reminded me of an article by Comrade Lei Chia in the *Wen-i yüeh-pao* (*Literary Monthly*), No. 4. He reported that the Literature Branch of the Yenan Cultural Association had put the following question at its circuit forums:
>
> Why does literary production cease after a writer has made a study of Marxism-Leninism? [26]

Since the study of Marxism-Leninism had to be free from blame, Ou-yang Shan could only explain the otherwise unaccountable phenomenon by saying that the trouble with those barren writers was that they had accepted Marxism-Leninism in a dogmatic way. If they could only relate Marxism-Leninism to "life," then one would see.

The barrenness was not immediately relieved by Mao's *Talks*. One notable example was the poet Ho Ch'i-fang, who wrote in 1940 after his conversion to communism:

> I also want to prove:
> I am a busy man,
> With several meetings a day,
> An enthusiastic administrator,
> But I am also a poet. [27]

But he could only disprove this proud statement when he explained his silence in 1944:

> Ever since the spring of 1942, I have ceased to write poetry. There are so many things more important than poetry for me to do. The most important of them is to study theory and to examine and reform myself through a number of concrete problems and concrete tasks. [28]

Ting Ling also said that she wrote nothing after "Eighteen," a short story about eighteen soldiers, a commemorative piece on the fifth anniversary of the Sino-Japanese War (July, 1942). Said she:

> Then we did not have the opportunity (*chi-hui*) to write; all of us were swallowed up in the strong tides of reform and study. This lasted until the

[26] *Ibid.*, May 19, 1941, p. 2.

[27] Ho Ch'i-fang, *Yeh-ko ho pai-t'ien-ti ko* (*Nocturnes and Songs of Daylight*) (Peking, 1952), p. 98.

[28] *Ibid.*, p. 238. However, this collection includes one poem for 1945, one for 1946, and another for 1949.

New Year of 1944 when the Party School mobilized us to write *yang-ko* plays . . .[29]

In the summer of 1944, a group of reporters from Chungking visited Yenan. Chao Ch'ao-kou, representing the independent *Hsin min pao,* commented on the literary scene:

> In fact, there are quite a number of famous writers residing in Yenan but their production does not seem to be plentiful. According to their own explanation, they are now engaged in "study." Therefore we cannot at this moment estimate the success of this literary policy. We should be fair and wait and see. We should not judge until we have seen the results of their "study." [30]

So the barrenness became all the more notable after the Yenan Forum. But why the two-year period of imposed silence from 1942 to 1944? Why did Mao subject the writers to the "strong tides of reform and study," instead of driving them to increase their productivity so as to resolve the doubts expressed by Chou Yang and Ou-yang Shan in 1941? A partial answer could be found in the general requirements of the *Cheng-feng* Movement: the party needed better Communists more than it needed better or more productive writers. To Mao, an "incorrect" production was perhaps worse than no production. He was not so much concerned with the writers' lagging productivity as with their dubious mental health. Until they were cured of the traits of individualism in their attitudes, behavior, and works, he found it necessary to keep them from publishing for the sake of public safety.

One of the "diseases" detected by Mao was the neglect of popularization. His remedy was a return to "national forms" and "national styles" which he had already championed in 1938.[31] Why individual efforts to "popularize" other forms and styles should not be permitted was never explained, except that to do so would have meant a betrayal of the interests of the workers, peasants, and soldiers. Instead of the divergent individual efforts, there would be a collective effort toward the creation of something that the people must love. Those who were to suffer from this policy were the novelists and the poets who knew their European models too well, the dramatists whose conception of their profession was limited to Western-style spoken drama, and the artists who practiced oil painting. Their audience was perhaps never large enough in the eyes of Mao, but whatever

---

[29] Ting Ling, *Shen-pei feng-kuang* (*Scenes of Northern Shensi*) (Peking, 1950), p. 92.
[30] Chao, *Yenan i-yüeh* (*One Month in Yenan*) (Shanghai, 1946), p. 114.
[31] Mao, *Selected Works,* IV, 62.

audience they might once have had was now taken away from them. For the audience had no choice, any more than the author had. They could only accept what was offered them.

According to Lu Ting-i, the immediate literary and artistic fruits of the Yenan Forum were, in the order of their appearance:

1. Folk dance and folk drama (*Brother and Sister Tilling Virgin Soil, The White-haired Girl*).
2. Woodcuts in the "national" style.
3. Novels and stories in the traditional style of storytelling (*Verses of Li Yu-ts'ai, The Heroes of the Lü-liang Mountain*).
4. Poetry in imitation of the folk-song rhythm and idiom (*Wang Kuei and Li Hsiang-hsiang*).[32]

This movement in Yenan, it seems to me, was a depersonalization movement. The search for an identification with the "people" forced the artist to neglect his own inner needs, whether moral or aesthetic. Folk art, which might have had a broadening effect, led inspiration in Yenan into a narrow alley. But it is the virtual suppression, in the years following the Yenan Forum, of other forms and styles that would seem to be the most unfortunate consequence of the power of the Communist Party.

However, the alleged neglect of popularization was a small matter in comparison with some definite signs of disaffection. From the available sources, it can be surmised that 1942 bore some similarities to 1957 as a year of crisis, a year of tolerance followed by persecution. Whereas in 1957 the Communist regime in China was alarmed by the rumblings from Europe, 1942 was also a year of great difficulty which perhaps required the stern measures of *Cheng-feng* to overcome. The seriousness of the situation, to my knowledge, has never been fully discussed, and I regret my inability to substantiate the facts quoted from *A Concise History of the Chinese Communist Party,* published in Shanghai in 1957. But these stark facts from official sources tell a great deal:

The Eighth Route Army dropped from a strength of 400,000 in 1940 to somewhat more than 300,000 in 1942. The population of the Liberated and Guerrilla Areas dropped from 100,000,000 to less than 50,000,000. Finance and economy in the Liberated Areas became also extremely difficult.[33]

The author of the *Concise History* then went on to quote a speech given by Mao in November, 1942:

[32] Lu's preface to *Wang Kuei and Li Hsiang-hsiang;* reprinted in the *Ch'ün-chung Weekly,* No. 7, 1947.

[33] Miao Ch'u-huang, *Chung-kuo kung-ch'an-tang chien-yao li-shih* (Shanghai, 1957), p. 132.

For a while we were reduced almost to the state of having no clothes to wear, no oil to cook with, no paper, no vegetables, no footwear for the soldiers and, in winter, no bedding for the civilian personnel.[34]

The difficult living conditions, together with the controls, dampened the spirit of those who had dreamed about the "new, meaningful life" of their promised land. Complaints were heard from intellectuals, traditionally the articulate group, and writers were among them. Their unhappiness, expressed in whatever medium, "popularized" or otherwise, was readily communicated. Another irony was that they automatically abolished the "eight-legged" style when they came to speak out their genuine feelings. Mao Tse-tung saw the necessity of checking their influence before demoralization, of the sort that paralyzed Chungking in the years that followed, became widespread and uncontrollable. The possible troublemakers were still a minority, but Mao did not like to see them increase in number. Faith in the future was somewhat shaken, but thanks to the organizational strength of the party, discipline was maintained. The *Cheng-feng* Movement meant a redoubled effort at indoctrination—compulsory reading of documents and compulsory discussion, which had the effect of occupying the dissident's mind with the urgent business of revolution. And the method of "criticism and self-criticism," never so widely used before by the Chinese Communist Party, was an efficient device to sound out the hidden heresy in the depth of the soul of even an apparently docile comrade.

By "criticism," Mao meant free expression of discontent, but on the condition that it should be met by strong and organized rebuttal. Here the similarity between 1942 and 1957 requires some modification. In 1957 there was a period, lasting some months, for "blooming," followed by a period of withering counterattack. In 1942 criticism was immediately countered by rebuttal. But even so, many unpleasant facts must have been exposed. Ai Ssu-ch'i, who had succeeded Ting Ling as editor of the Literary Page of the *Liberation Daily,* said on April 22, 1942:

Yenan is now engaged in the "rectification of three styles" [the style of study, the style of party work, and prose style]. One special feature of the movement has been the enthusiasm to expose facts, which is entirely necessary. [Then followed a differentiation between two kinds of facts: "substance" and "superficial phenomena."] [35]

On June 5, the same paper carried an editorial on the topic "A Summary of

---

[34] Mao, *Selected Works,* IV, 106. If the reader checks the Chinese version, he will puzzle over the meaning of the phrase "for a while" found in the official English version.

[35] *Liberation Daily,* Apr. 22, 1942, p. 4.

the Study Movement during the Past Month." It noted that one of the lessons learned in the movement was:

Maximum freedom should be granted for the expression of incorrect opinions; but there should be a readiness to organize rebuttal at any given moment.[36]

The effect of "criticism" was therefore much reduced in confrontation with an alert and organized opposition. At the same time, the dissident was required by "self-criticism" to expose his own weaknesses, that is, his "petty-bourgeois vices" according to Mao's definition, so as further to weaken the force of his "criticism."

When the Forum on Literature and Art was convoked on May 2, the *Cheng-feng* Movement had already thrown all government offices and schools in Yenan into a state of tension for at least a month. (Mao started the movement in February. On April 3 the Propaganda Bureau of the Central Committee issued an order to intensify it.)[37] How the "study groups" carried on their discussion gave some foretaste of what would happen at the Forum. The debate at the Forum was from the very beginning an unequal struggle. Before the *tso-t'an-hui* ("sit-and-talk meeting" is how the Forum is described in Chinese), Mao had prepared a number of people for what he asked of the meeting.[38] Then he delivered the keynote speech (the Introductory Lecture) to limit the discussion to five political and ideological topics (the artist's standpoint, attitude, audience, acquaintance with life, and studies in Marxism-Leninism) on which the dissidents would have had very little to say if they had wanted to avoid sounding like out-and-out reactionaries. The dissidents might have had some sort of organization and preparation, too. But the odds against them must have been overwhelming.

We should not have learned so much about the dissidents of 1942, if the case of the so-called Ting-Ch'en clique of 1957 had not reopened so many old wounds. Jealousy among writers is an age-old habit and perhaps a forgivable sin, according to the Wei Emperor Wen-ti of the third century A.D.[39] The quarrel between the two factions in Yenan, one headed by Chou Yang and the other by Ting Ling and Ch'en Ch'i-hsia, was not entirely concerned with principles. Jealousy and personal differences also played a part. The writers of the Ting-Ch'en clique did not begin as anti-Communists at all,

---

[36] *Ibid.,* June 5, 1942, p. 1.

[37] Compton, *op. cit.,* p. xxxiv and pp. 1–8.

[38] The fact is revealed in an editorial, "Commemoration, Retrospect and Prospect," of *Wen-i pao,* No. 7, 1957, p. 2.

[39] Wei Wen-ti (Ts'ao P'ei), *Tien-lun lun-wen.*

but their fight for the independence of art compelled them to take a stand incompatible with that of the Communist Party.

Therefore, to treat the disaffection in 1942 as merely a manifestation of a "sectarian" fight among writers is to ignore the issues at stake. The voices that spoke for the supra-political value of literature are still preserved within quotation marks in Mao's *Talks*. The need for "humanity," "love," and "presenting the true reality" has recurred, over and over again, all through these twenty years, to writers who were never connected with the Ting-Ch'en clique. Such a need was felt in 1942 after a shoeless and quiltless winter in the northwest had made the Communist system look all the more cold.

A great part of the literature produced in Yenan before the Forum is lost. Magazines like *Wen-i yüeh-pao* (mentioned above), *Ku-yü* (*Grain Rains*), *Ts'ao-yeh* (*Grass Leaves*), and *Shih-k'an* (*Poetry*) are hard to find. They had apparently all ceased publication by 1944, for Chao Ch'ao-kou noted that he found not a single literary magazine during his stay in Yenan. Handwritten journals posted on the wall, like the *Ch'ing-ch'i tui* (*Light Brigade*), were of course even more perishable. From the files of the *Liberation Daily* and the collections of the works of that period, I can say that much that passed for literature was simply thinly disguised anti-Japanese propaganda. (The same phenomenon was observable in Chungking.) If one is interested in individual expression rather than mass sentiment, though the latter was not manipulated so much before 1942 as after, one can recommend Ho Ch'i-fang and Ting Ling as two representatives of the May Fourth tradition. In Ho we find the suicidal progress of a sensitive soul, a Shelley in the Leninist era heaving his last sighs before he gives himself up to the historical movement. He wrote in 1940:

> And in May
> There is much too much good sunshine in daytime,
> There is much too much good moonlight at night. . . .
> I cannot get up from the bed, and walking into the woods,
> Say that each tree has a beautiful soul
> And weep with them.[40]

A mysterious urge was there, though he could not get up from the bed and cry, for whatever reason, in the woods. The tone had changed by 1942:

> And then joyously to experience
> My agonizing rebirth.[41]

[40] Ho Ch'i-fang, *op. cit.*, pp. 20–21.
[41] *Ibid.*, p. 182.

In her fiction Ting Ling exhibited sympathy and tenderness against a background of harsh reality. Her best piece of this period may be the short story "In the Hospital" (1941), which, however, has never been included in any of her collected works.[42] Perhaps she was forbidden to acknowledge it, because life in a Yenan hospital as Ting Ling understood it—the inhumanity in the system rather than the inadequacy of its material equipment—would be better kept out of the public eye from the party's point of view. But "New Belief" (1939) is a powerful, though morbid, story.[43] A village grandmother is raped by the Japanese. She becomes abnormally talkative. Wherever she goes, she prattles about her experience as well as the sadistic scenes she has witnessed. Such exhibitionism is terrible enough, but then the Communist cadres hear of it and turn the pathetic old figure into a first-rate propagandist.

That a woman, with injured body and soul, should be exploited to advance a political cause may have had personal significance for Ting Ling. Another story, "When I Was in Hsia Village" (1940) is a variation on the same theme, but with greater tenderness.[44] A lonely woman cadre (the "I" in the story) is assigned to Hsia village. There she becomes acquainted with a lonely girl who is shunned by her fellow villagers as worse than a prostitute. She has contracted venereal disease as a result of her relations with the Japanese. But she is still charged with a secret mission to go constantly behind the enemy lines, because she has Japanese friends and her youth and physical attractions can still enable her to get something out of them. A young villager loves her devotedly, but sick unto death, she has to rebuff his advances.

"Look, a Chinese woman was raped by the Japanese; so, down with Japanese imperialism!" was a theme repeated innumerable times by writers not only in Yenan but also in Chungking. Ting Ling's treatment of the theme was unique, which is a tribute to her genius. The story of the poor girl (or of the old woman) who was both a plaything for the Japanese and a tool of Communist cadres, though the latter used her only for patriotism's sake, poses a serious question about the inhumanity in human life, especially un-

---

[42] "In the Hospital" was originally published in the *Ku-yü,* No. 1, and was reprinted in *Wen-i chen-ti,* a Chungking journal. Liu Hsüeh-wei reviewed it in *Liberation Daily,* Dec. 5, 1941, p. 4. A damning criticism is found in *Wen-i pao,* No. 25, 1957, p. 11. Liu Pai-yü, also writing in 1957, said that the story was not available to him, *Jen-min jih-pao,* Aug. 28, 1957, p. 7.

[43] This story is found in two collections: *Wo tsai hsia-ts'un-ti shih-hou* (*When I Was in Hsia Village*) (Peking, 1950); *Yenan chi* (*A Yenan Anthology*) (Peking, 1954).

[44] This story is also found in the above-mentioned collections.

der the difficult conditions of war. Ting Ling's stories may have had some propaganda value at the time they were published; but their meaning remains fresh today, long after the Japanese have been defeated. The realism in her fiction supplies an interpretation of life in its totality and ambivalence, in its terror and tenderness, over and above any philosophical theory. At least, there is no room for the Communist theory of the lovable masses in her picture of an apathetic, almost cruel, crowd of villagers, drawn from a sentimentalist's innermost knowledge. Obviously, the root of evil goes deeper than the accident of Japanese aggression.

The two stories may serve as an introduction to Ting Ling's "Thoughts on March 8," [45] which, in very articulate form, saw no hope for women in the so-called Liberated Areas unless men would agree to reform themselves. Poetry and fiction from Yenan with anti-Communist undertones seldom attracted so much attention as this essay did. For "Thoughts on March 8" is a clearly written essay about the deplorable condition of women in a place where they were supposed to enjoy equality, if not happiness. But it is not a satire, a genre Ting Ling is never good at. It is only a plea from the weak to the strong.

On October 23, 1941, Ting Ling had pronounced from the editorial chair of the Literary Page of the *Liberation Daily*:

. . . It is said that this is not a suitable place for the writing of the *tsa-wen* and that what is needed here is only the reflection of democratic life and great construction.

It may be in human nature to be intoxicated with small successes or to hate to be told that one is sick or that one needs to see a doctor about it. But that is also a sign of indolence and cowardice.

Lu Hsün is dead. Customarily we say to ourselves that we should do this or that in order to live up to him. But we have not sufficiently acquired his courage in sparing no details. I think it will do us most good if we emulate his steadfastness in facing the truth, his courage to speak out for the sake of truth, and his fearlessness. This age of ours still needs the *tsa-wen,* a weapon that we should never lay down. Raise it, and the *tsa-wen* will not be dead.[46]

Here Ting Ling made a really brave gesture. She talked about "taking up the weapon"—but against whom? She went so far as to sneer at the

---

[45] *Liberation Daily*, Mar. 9, 1942, p. 4. It should be noted that on March 4, 1942, the Central Committee of the CCP gave instructions regarding the program for the celebration of the International Women's Day. The propaganda was to emphasize these points: the establishment of the international women's anti-fascist united front, the promotion of unity in China, the active part that women should play in revolution, etc. Ting Ling's essay was an open defiance against such instructions.

[46] *Ibid.,* Oct. 23, 1941, p. 4.

"reflection of democratic life and great construction," which, as is well known, had been the main theme of Chinese Communist literature all through these years. She invoked the fearless spirit of Lu Hsün. We have seen indeed a number of avatars of that spirit, but none of them have been able to maintain a career of defiance for long.

The first of the avatars was Wang Shih-wei. The day (March 13, 1942) after Lo Feng published "This Is Still the Age for Tsa-wen" as a response to Ting Ling's appeal, there appeared in the *Liberation Daily* the best-known anti-Communist literature of the year: two essays by Wang Shih-wei under the title, *The Wild Lily*. Ten days later came two more essays under the same title. About that time, Wang also published, in the *Ku-yü*, "Statesmen vs. Artists," composed of thirteen pieces of causeries also in the *tsa-wen* style.[47] Judging from the performance of *The Wild Lily* alone, I do not think Wang was a particularly brilliant satirist. In spite of his occasional obscurity, Lu Hsün is remarkable for the cool decisiveness in his home thrust, his absolute irreconcilableness, and his utter contempt for whatever came under attack. These qualities, however, are not prominent in Wang. (Among the many disciples of Lu Hsün, Hsü Mou-yung, the one he disowned, seemed to have come the closest to the master's style in the essays he published, under various pseudonyms, in the 1956–57 period.) In his attacks on the hypocrisy and corruption of Communist bureaucracy, Wang seemed still to cling to some warm hope for amelioration. He did not put himself in an extremely hostile position, as Lu Hsün might have done. The wild lily, the author explained, is the "most beautiful wild plant in Yenan"; only its bulb "tastes bitter." Hence some attractive but bitter advice he was trying to offer to the Communist Party, but the result was a long series of "struggle meetings" against the impertinent adviser until he was denounced as a Trotskyite. *The Wild Lily* had a very short life, but it anticipated the other breeds of doomed flowers by about fifteen years.

For the general literary situation at the time of the Forum, I shall cite two eyewitness accounts. These two pieces may give an exaggerated impression of the hostility and despondency prevailing in Yenan, since little is said about the staunch supporters of the regime. But what strikes us is the resemblance of 1942 to the 1956–57 period. Here we get some foretaste of the works that embarrassed the Communist regime in the later period. Works like "On the Bridge Construction Site," "Our Paper's Inside News," "Beautiful," "Realism—the Broad Path," "The Development of Realism in the

---

[47] *Ku-yü,* Vol. I, No. 4; mentioned in *Liberation Daily,* May 26, 1942, p. 4.

Socialist Age," etc., did not come from nowhere, though they were written by writers of a younger generation. They were rooted in 1942 or even earlier.

The first piece is from Ho Ch'i-fang:

One of the principal representatives of the incorrect tendency was Hsiao Chün. He based his anti-people literary activities on the arguments found in a lecture given by Lu Hsün in 1927, "The Divergence of Politics and Literature." [48] He exploited these statements of Lu Hsün's: "Literature and politics are in perpetual conflict." "Politics wants to preserve the status quo; thus it places itself in an opposite direction to literature as a symbol of discontent."

It was not Hsiao Chün alone, or people of the same color as Hsiao Chün, who were involved in the incorrect literary activities. But quite a number of writers participated. Even some writers who were party members publicly supported him. Those who did not support him theoretically still showed their affinity with this tendency in their creative works. For instance, there were works of fiction which placed the cadres of the worker-peasant-soldier classes in a very bad light but poured out heartfelt sympathy to the petty-bourgeois intellectuals. Other works of fiction denounced the principle of revolutionary organization that individuals should obey the collective; they demanded that the collective should obey individuals. The authors of such works were all members of the Communist Party. Of course, there were some Communist writers who contradicted this tendency: they opposed it with the slogan, "Praise the Bright Side!" But they were unable to combat it publicly on theoretical grounds so as to stop it completely. The "praise" found in their works still showed the more or less superficial petty-bourgeois sentiments. [49]

Here are the reminiscences of Miss Tseng K'e who joined the Yenan Branch of the Chinese Writers Anti-Aggression Association after her arrival in Yenan:

The cell which I joined for my study program was composed mostly of unreformed intellectuals who had not been in Yenan long. The great part of the more serious mistakes pointed out by Chairman Mao in his *Talks* was reflected in the Yenan branch of this Association.

The most conspicuous were people like Hsiao Chün and Ting Ling. [On another occasion, she also mentioned Ch'en Ch'i-hsia and Lo Feng.] [50] They used every means within their power to "express themselves, spread their own opinions, and demand that people remold the party and the world in their image." [51]

[48] Lu Hsün's lecture was given at Chinan University in Shanghai on December 21, 1927. It was included in his *Chi-wai-chi* (*Uncollected Works Collected*) with his approval. *Lu Hsün ch'üan-chi* (*Complete Works*), VII (Peking, 1958), 103.

[49] Ho, "Improve Our Work with Mao's Literary Theory," *Wen-i pao*, No. 1, 1952, p. 125.

[50] Miss Tseng mentioned these names at a forum sponsored by the provincial journal *Szechwan wen-i*, in celebration of the twentieth anniversary of Mao's *Talks*. *Szechwan wen-i* (Chengtu), No. 3, 1962, pp. 87 ff.

[51] Mao, *Selected Works*, IV, 91.

Even in everyday conversation, they talked about taking up the so-called weapon of *tsa-wen*. Clamorously they said that the youth and the writers should join hands in exposing the "darkness" in the revolutionary ranks and satirizing the "weakness" of the people. They wanted politics to obey the demands of art. They exaggerated the aesthetic quality as if it were something mysterious.

I remember one *tsa-wen*, "The Cock Crows," which was at once a satire on the writers who praised revolution and a diatribe of hatred against the Border Region. It was a fable about a chanticleer who longed for daylight for which he would fain sing a paean. Then he saw a glimmering and he began to sing, for he wanted to announce the daybreak. But after his crowing, he discovered that all was pitch darkness about him. The time was midnight. He had been deceived by an illusion of dawn. He began to regret his impetuosity which had led him to get all excited before he sang that song.

In the wall-newspaper, *The Light Brigade*, there was a poem-in-prose, "Cupid Comes to Yenan." An extremely malicious calumny, it ridiculed the old cadres who were supposedly wanting both in culture and in an understanding of love.

There was a poet-cum-composer who deplored the inhumanity of the Communists who, according to him, understood his emotions less than a stone or a blade of grass did. The reason was simply that the nursery attached to his office did not afford an endless supply of milk and eggs for his children.

More typical was a short story, "Beyond the Realm of Consciousness." [52] It was about a girl student who loved art. When she came to Yenan, she thought that she might now develop her artistic talent in accordance with her wishes. Instead, she was assigned the job of a nurse in a hospital, since that was what the Organizational Department regarded as more important to the revolutionary task at that time. But she could never settle down for work. All the time she was crying that she wanted to go to study at the Lu Hsün Academy of Arts, the highest institution in this field. Since permission was not granted her, she became extremely distressed. She thought that the party was strangling her talent. In her dazed state, her head was filled with poetry, music notes, the guitar, the crucifix, etc. Finally she became insane.[53]

It is interesting to note that Miss Tseng, the author of the reminiscences, was also once distressed over her failure to enter the Lu Hsün Academy. But then, she said, the Yenan Forum was convoked, and she was saved.

III

"In May, the weather in Yenan was neither cold nor hot. The River Yen had thawed; its muddy yellow waters rushed down the shallow bed, over sand and soil. The willow had turned green. The fragrance of the thorny-plum-blossoms (*tz'u-mei-hua*) filled the gullies and floated into the air. It was spring in Yenan." [54]

---

[52] This story by Fang Chi was published in *Wen-i yüeh-pao*, No. 14. A review is in *Liberation Daily*, June 25, 1942, p. 4.

[53] *Szechwan wen-i*, No. 4, 1962, pp. 65 ff.

[54] "Commemoration, Retrospect and Prospect," *Wen-i pao*, No. 7, 1957, p. 2.

Against such a background of vernal smells and sights, which punctuated the monotony of the yellow plateau, the Forum on Literature and Art was in session. From May 2 to May 23, three sessions were held in the auditorium, one of the few modern buildings in the ancient city where most people lived in caves. On the last day, the discussion stopped before dinner. The rays of the setting sun were still bright enough for a group photograph. Mao naturally took the middle seat in the front row. Before the focus was set, however, he stood up, went to Ting Ling, and gave his seat to her. Smilingly he said, "Let our woman cadre take the middle seat. We don't like to be rebuked again on March 8." Everybody laughed to Ting Ling's embarrassment. Mao's good humor somewhat relaxed the tension of the discussion. But who would speak, on the next International Women's Day, about the status of women in Yenan? [55]

When the dinner was over, it was already eight o'clock. More people than the auditorium could accommodate had come for the anticipated concluding lecture by Mao. So the meeting was moved to the open air. In the courtyard, under the petroleum-gas lamps, Mao pointed out the direction for literature and art.

Like Khrushchev, Mao has his folksy ways of speech. According to a 1949 version, he used the word "buttocks" on two occasions where we now find a less offensive word in the standard version.[56] But neither version perhaps contains everything he said.[57] His casualness and conversational tone, his deep intentions notwithstanding, are lost on those who ponder every word of his as if it were divinely inspired truth.

As I have pointed out, one does not have to quarrel so much with Mao's theory as with the fact of control. Obviously Mao could not claim any originality for his theory. Though the Russian terms were not mentioned, what he required of literature and art was the fulfillment of the familiar Russian concepts: *ideinost* (ideological expression), *partiinost* (party spirit), and *narodnost* (national character). His dialectics, based on the law of excluded middle (either for the revolution or against it), permitted no ground for writers like Ho Ch'i-fang, who had had his private tears to shed, or Ting Ling, who had insisted on telling the truth about

---

[55] The anecdote is cited by Ho Ch'en. See note 20.

[56] *Cheng-feng wen-hsien* (*Party Reform Documents*) (Hong Kong, 1949), pp. 276–77. For "p'i-ku," we find "li-tsu-tien" ("standpoint") in the standard version. Mao, *Hsüan-chi* (*Selected Works*), III, 859.

[57] In *Liberation Daily*, No. 15, 1942, p. 4, Chiang Pu quoted Mao as having complained at the Forum about the writers "having neither life, nor Marxism-Leninism." This phrase is not found in the published texts.

the revolution. The set of taboos he proposed placed a restriction even on those who favored his kind of revolution.

Concerned with the political function of art, he did not at all touch the problems of imagination, aesthetic experience, or the workings of a creative mind. He omitted these and other problems unrelated to revolution but which creative artists have to struggle with. This obvious deficiency of the *Talks* gave something of an opportunity for writers to assert their independence. Ch'in Chao-yang said at a forum in 1956 discussing the "hundred flowers" movement:

> The method of creation is to be evolved by the writers themselves; it is a subject on which no man should be allowed to place any rigid restrictions.[58]

The veteran writer Mao Tun, in an article celebrating the fifteenth anniversary of Mao Tse-tung's *Talks,* said in 1957:

> Marxism is not to replace the method of creation. That no method of creation is included in the *Talks* is only natural. The problems proposed and studied today in literary and art circles are primarily and essentially the problems of creation which arise from the act of creation and which are to be answered only through this act.[59]

From this foothold of independence, Ch'in Chao-yang later went on to question the "dogmatism in literature" when he published his "Realism— the Broad Path." But Mao Tun tried to protect himself by bringing in the "political" factor in the method of creation:

> The world view is not equal to the method of creation. But all the problems pertaining to the method of creation are related, in a myriad of subtle and devious ways, to the world view.[60]

Along the same line, Lu Ting-i said that Mao Tse-tung's *Talks* were the "foundation of the method of creation." [61] Here is what might be the main topic of Communist aesthetics: how a method of creation could be built upon the ideological foundation; but this is a topic Mao Tse-tung did not go into. "The myriad of subtle and devious ways" in which the world view affects the method of creation requires some fine analysis to develop into a literary theory. We do not get this from Mao; nor do we find it in the writings of his obedient mouthpieces, whose "eight-legged" style proves nothing but their political "correctness." Indeed, Mao Tse-tung tried to

---

[58] *Wen-i pao,* No. 14, 1956, p. 20.
[59] *Jen-min wen-hsüeh,* Nos. 5 and 6 (a combined issue), 1957, p. 2.
[60] *Ibid.,* p. 3.
[61] *Jen-min jih-pao,* Sept. 27, 1957, p. 2.

maintain a double standard—the political and the artistic—in his Yenan *Talks*. But he never explained how an imaginative work that served the workers, peasants, and soldiers could also pass the secondary—or artistic— standard. He recommended the reading of classics, both Western and Chinese—not very practical advice, since it was to be taken together with the warning against their ideological impurities. Whatever benefit, in the way of methodology, a writer might derive from the study of the classics, he must beware of their ideological content. We have already seen the danger of following too closely the examples of Tolstoy and Balzac.

We have seen, too, Liu Hsüeh-wei's discussion of the conflict between the world view and the method of creation and how it led to the failure of the leftist literature of the 1920's and 1930's. The intrusion of an ex- traneous world view has remained the most disturbing factor in Communist literature since 1942. The logical solution seems to be either a breed of liberalism which permits the writer to develop, within the limit of his talent, a method of creation which shows no respect to any particular political canon, or to write according to a formula, resulting in the complete triumph of the Communist world view. But Mao's double standard has only added to the confusion and agony of the writers. There are no doubt a myriad of ways in the relation between the artist's world view and his method of creation. But the political situation being what it is in Communist China, the myriad can be reduced to a single factor of fear. The writer in Communist China, constantly and fearfully aware of his obligation to the Communist Party, may still engage himself, as all of us do, in a private struggle with ideas, emotions, images, and words. But there is no guarantee that whatever comes out of an individual act of creation will always support the Communist world view. How to make room—and a large enough room—for the world view that the party hands him is a dis- tressing problem to the creative writer in Communist China today.

The double standard is hard to meet. Therefore, we cannot say that the Communist Party is always satisfied with the merits of the literary products under its sponsorship. In 1952, to celebrate the tenth anniversary of Mao's *Talks* the *People's Daily* editorially lamented the "ideological confusion" found in literary circles. The deplorable situation was said to be manifested in two aspects. The first was the "corrosion of revolutionary literature by bourgeois ideology." The meaning of this statement is clear, since we have seen the same corrosion in Yenan ten years earlier. The second aspect is more interesting, because it shows how the imposition of a political standard on literature and art began to reap its harvest. The "formularization" and "conceptualization" discussed in the following quotation bear some resemblance to the early proletarian literature of the 1920's, with the difference that the factor of fear was absent in the latter which was probably animated by "a petty-bourgeois enthusiasm for revolution." But a quotation at some length is needed to explain why the Communist Party was dissatisfied with the literature and art which might have been taken to be politically correct:

> Secondly, there is a tendency which seems to be in opposition to the above-mentioned [bourgeois] tendency but which actually represents also a loss of contact with the masses and with life. It is the tendency toward formularization and conceptualization in literary and art creation. This tendency comes from a Philistine (*yung-su-ti*) understanding of the political mission of literature and art. The works with this tendency have an empty content except for a medley of slogans and concepts. There is no life in them: the characters in them have neither flesh and blood nor any distinction. What is accomplished is merely a crude mixture of some superficial political concepts with a story according to a formula. Since such works are not profound reflections of real life, they do not perform the genuine educational function on the masses that they ought to. To produce such works, soon forgotten by the readers, does not require much effort. Comrade Mao Tse-tung says: "All revolutionary artists and writers of China, all artists and writers of high promise, must, for long periods of time, unreservedly and wholeheartedly go into the midst of the masses, the masses of workers, peasants, and soldiers; they must go into fiery struggles, go to the only, the broadest, the richest source to observe, learn, study and analyze all men, all classes, all kinds of people, all the vivid patterns of life and struggle and all raw material of art and literature, before they can proceed to creation." [62] But our writers of the formularization and conceptualization school are the hopeless cases. They have altogether omitted the process of going into the masses to observe, to learn, to study, to analyze, and then to organize, to concentrate, and to typify. They have never seriously engaged themselves either in the study of real life or in artistic creation. They treat only violently both reality and art with their eyes shut. They are the sloths among the literary and art workers; and of the sloths no genuine service to the people or to politics can be expected. Therefore, they are practically liquidating the genuine service that literature and art ought to do to politics. [63]

The prescription found in Mao's *Talks,* beginning with "going into the masses," etc., is not a sure remedy for formularization and conceptualization. Unlike the proletarian writers of the 1920's, who had probably more daydreams than experience, Chinese writers by 1952 had all studied some aspects of life. Among those who showed marks of "bourgeois corrosion,"

---

[62] Mao, *Selected Works,* IV, 77.

[63] *Jen-min jih-pao,* May 23, 1952; reprinted in *Hsin-hua yüeh-pao (New China Monthly),* No. 6, 1952, p. 178.

there were Ting Ling and others who had actually lived among the masses for quite a number of years. Their trouble was perhaps that they had too much experience to discover what the Communists call "the typical" and the "pattern of life." To present life as the writer understands it is hard enough; but to present life as the Communist Party orders it to be is not so easy as the editorialist of the *People's Daily* thought, unless the writer can harden himself to treat life violently and to keep his eyes shut. In 1953, Ch'in Chao-yang published an interesting book, *On Formularization and Conceptualization*. He was then not yet openly rebellious, but as an editorial assistant of *People's Literature* he was sorely disappointed at the manuscripts which it was his painful duty to read. His analysis of the basic weakness of Communist literature led, in 1956, to his conviction about the one criterion of literature, that is, reality instead of dogma. But his early opinion is also worth reading:

> I have heard that among the literary and art workers in some place there is a current jargon, namely, "to put on ideological varnish." It means that the framework of a story is like a piece of furniture and that in order to give it a better look and a better market value, some varnish is needed. . . . It is most clearly shown in the "positive speeches" that the characters in fiction have to make. . . . Sometimes, the characters have to be beaten by landlords and enemy agents; and their wives and daughters raped. . . . To strengthen the "ideological quality," it is also possible to raise the standard of the characters, even by so little, and to improve the reality, even by so little. . . .[64]

Liu Hsüeh-wei has described the formula for proletarian literature: the birth of the new amidst the old, the tomorrow in today, the conquest of the old by the new, etc. When Ting Ling sneered at "the reflection of democratic life and great construction" in Yenan she was also talking about a formula. Now Ch'in Chao-yang noted the possibility of "raising the standard of characters, even by so little, and improving the reality, even by so little." This possibility is actually a necessity for writers who are charged with the duty "to praise the bright side." To make room for the Communist world view in a literary work is to adopt Communist formulas and concepts. The difference between the required mastery of the world view and the defective presentation of formulas and concepts in a literary work is so small that I think I am not far from the truth if I say that in Communist literature there is only a difference in degree of formularization and conceptualization. At least there has not yet appeared from Communist China a critical work that explains satisfactorily the use and abuse of Communist formulas and concepts in literature.

[64] Ch'in, *Lun kung-shih-hua kai-nien-hua* (Peking, 1953), p. 60.

In 1942 Mao was quite confident of the future, though he also admitted the difficulty involved in thought reform:

These comrades still stand on the side of the petty-bourgeois intellectuals, or, to put it more elegantly, their innermost soul is still a kingdom of the petty-bourgeois intelligentsia. Thus they have not yet solved or unequivocally solved the problem "For whom are art and literature intended?" And this refers not only to the newcomers to Yenan; even among those who have been to the front and worked for a few years in our base areas and in the Eighth and New Fourth Armies, many have not solved the problems thoroughly. To solve this problem thoroughly, a long time is required, say, eight or ten years. But no matter how long it takes, we must solve it, and solve it unequivocally and thoroughly.[65]

Ten years after Mao made the vow, he saw the appearance of formularization and conceptualization. While admittedly the kingdom of petty-bourgeois intelligentsia remained in 1952, he had to divert his attention to the "republic of sloths." Now another ten years has elapsed, and Mao's problems are not yet solved; instead they have increased. To his right, in addition to the perennial bourgeoisie and the petty-bourgeois intelligentsia, there has loomed the specter of modern revisionism which, clothed as it is in Marxism or even Marxism-Leninism, gives nevertheless aid and comfort to the bourgeoisie. In 1962, commemorating the twentieth anniversary of Mao's *Talks, Wen-i pao* commented editorially:

Our literature and art must carry on an irreconcilable fight with imperialist literature and art, revisionist literature and art, and all kinds of reactionary ideology that serves imperialism and the old order. . . .[66]

According to Chou Yang in 1960, the typical revisionist among Chinese writers was Hu Feng, who echoed the views of Georg Lukács.[67] This may be true, but after the defeat of the Hu Feng "clique," I must profess my ignorance of the identity of revisionists in Communist China. If revisionism is found in Soviet Russia, as other Communist Chinese documents suggest, then Soviet literature needs a complete reappraisal, a task which seems beyond the capability of Communist Chinese critics. How the fight against revisionism will be carried out in the "literary and art circles" in Communist China will be worth watching.[68]

[65] Mao, *Selected Works,* IV, 73.
[66] *Wen-i pao,* Nos. 5 and 6 (a combined issue), 1962, p. 4.
[67] Chou Yang, "The Road of Socialist Literature and Art in Our Country," *Jen-min jih-pao,* Sept. 4, 1960, pp. 6, 7.
[68] A recent instance of the fight is an article written by Li Shu-chih, "How Modern Revisionists Follow the Decadent Bourgeois Class in Literature and Art," *Hung-ch'i (Red Flag),* No. 21, 1962, p. 21.

Then, to Mao's left, there are the so-called dogmatists who, in spite of their loyalty to the workers, peasants, and soldiers, are also said to be harmful to the party's literary undertakings. Said Ho Ch'i-fang:

Our struggle against dogmatism and the various tendencies toward crudity and violence that stem from a "left" point of view is a struggle to oppose and correct the distortion of the party's and Comrade Mao's direction for literature and art. Since this struggle belongs to the category of "contradictions among the people" . . . it has never approached the intensity of our fight against bourgeois ideology and revisionism. But the struggle has been renewed several times since the founding of the People's Republic. Those who represent this tendency also mouth their allegiance to the road of proletarian literature and art, but actually they want to take it to a dead end. They mouth support for Marxism and Mao Tse-tung's thought, but actually they are greatly distorting it, simplifying it and vulgarizing it. Their subjective desire is for the promotion of literature and art; but the result of their effort is a retardation. With their withering touch, they destroy the products of literature and art; they separate literature and art from the people. Therefore though they are opposed to it, they are actually performing the function of supporting bourgeois ideology and revisionism. When their dogmatism, their crudity and violence become disgusting, impracticable, or conducive to bad results, they provide the opportunity and condition for the growth and spread of bourgeois ideology and revisionism. Our recurrent fight in this respect is therefore unavoidable and completely necessary. Without these struggles, the party's and Comrade Mao's direction for literature and art can never be carried out and we can never hope to achieve everything in literature and art.[69]

This quotation from *Literary Criticism* (*Wen-hsüeh p'ing-lun*) says something important about the failure of Chinese Communist literature. It stands out among all the "eight-legged" essays on Mao's thought and reminiscences of Yenan that came out last year during the twentieth anniversary celebration. Since Ho Ch'i-fang refuses to mention names ("There has not yet appeared a typical 'left' dogmatist since 1949," said Ho), it would be rash for us to nail the accusation down to any single person, though, in my opinion, Chou Yang, Lu Ting-i, and others, including Ho himself (who has changed a great deal since his "rebirth" in 1942), may well qualify for the appellation of "left dogmatist." It should be noted, however, that the left dogmatists of 1962 are different from the exponents of formularization and conceptualization of 1952. The latter are the "sloths" who are simply bad writers or driven by fear or a market sense to produce what was supposed to be correct; but the former are activists in a leading position. When Ho mentions "our struggle," I do not know if he is speaking on behalf of the party. If he is, I must apologize again for

---

[69] Ho, "Chan-tou-ti sheng-li-ti erh-shih-nien" ("Twenty Years of Battles and Victory"), *Literary Criticism*, No. 3, 1962, p. 5.

my ignorance of "the recurrent struggles against 'left' dogmatists since 1949." True, complaints against them were plenty in the 1956–57 period (including a satire with a significant title "Rather Left than Right"),[70] but in no instance, to my knowledge, did the party ever support those who criticized the left dogmatists. The leftists may still belong to the "people," but the rightists, if not "reformed," never. The most significant passage in Ho's article is his explanation of the miraculous survival of bourgeois ideology and the emergence of revisionism, which should not mean after all only a new label for an old crime. When the "left" dogmatists lead literature and art to a dead end, says Ho, the rightists will then find reasons for self-justification. To discover such a gem of thought in what looks like a mire of "eight-legged" style is a great surprise. The conference sponsored by *The China Quarterly* turned out to be very critical of Chinese Communist literature. With a heavy heart, one agrees that the "crudity and violence" of Chinese Communist literary policy has provided out-siders with ample reason for adverse criticism. But if we agree with Ho here, a question will probably occur to many who have read his article: Is there a more powerful left dogmatist in Communist China than Mao? Are there literary documents more "conducive to bad results" than his addresses to the Yenan Forum?

But here is a point where logic must stop for the sake of Ho Ch'i-fang and our fellow writers in Communist China. To push the question further would be very embarrassing, indeed.

[70] An essay written by Li Feng, *Wen-i pao,* No. 9, 1957, p. 11.

INDEX

Association of Literature and Arts, 127, 129, 134*n*, 136, 138, 139, 140, 143

Benediction. See Lu Hsün
Bodhisattvahood, 15, 36, 44
Bolsheviks, 17, 30, 32, 33–34, 36, 45, 64, 77, 91
The Bottle. See Kuo Mo-jo
Buddha, 39, 157
Buddhism, 14, 15, 23

Chang T'ai-lai, 21 and *n*, 22*n*, 23, 33, 40*n*, 41*n*, 43
Chang T'ai-lei. *See* Chang T'ai-lai
Chao P'ing-fu. *See* Jou Shih
Ch'en pao, 18 and *n*, 20, 27, 33, 37, 39
Ch'en Shao-yü, 6, 168, 171, 207, 208, 216–18 *passim,* 220, 222 and *n*, 224, 226*n*, 230–32 *passim*
Ch'en Tu-hsiu, 6, 14, 17
Ch'en Yüan, 115, 137
Cheng Chen-to, 15, 17 and *n*, 22
Cheng-feng Movement, 241, 242, 246–48 *passim*
Chiang Kai-shek, 108, 119–23 *passim,* 139*n*, 166, 171, 206
Chiang Kuang-ch'ih. *See* Chiang Kuang-tz'u
Chiang Kuang-tz'u: as a romantic, vii, 60; as a Communist writer, vii, 81–84; significance of, xvii; life of, 55–58, 71–73, 97–100; *The Sorrows of Lisa,* 56, 64, 77–78, 91–93; political convictions of, 56–57; personality of, 57, 59, 60–61, 84–85; literary style and ability, 58, 59, 61–65, 70–71, 84–97; *The Moon Forces Its Way through the Clouds,* 65, 73, 80*n*, 89 and *n*, 96; *The*

Roaring Earth, 65 and *n*, 86–89, 90, 91*n*, 95; *The Wind over the Fields,* 65*n;* literary ability criticized by Communist Party, 65–67, 69–70; specific works analyzed, 73–81, 86–97; *Worship at the Unlocatable Grave,* 79, 95, 97; *The Youthful Tramp,* 80–81, 89; *The Last Smile,* 94–95; *Des Sans-culottes,* 96–97; relationship with Wu Szu-hung, 97–100; mentioned, vii, xxi–xxiii *passim*
Chinese League of Leftist Writers. *See* League of Leftist Writers
Chou En-lai, xxviii, 168, 200, 222*n*
Chou Tso-jen, 156–158 *passim,* 159–60
Chou Yang, xxii–xxiv *passim,* xxvii–xix *passim,* 107, 109, 110*n,* 111, 112*n,* 113, 118*n,* 124, 130–32 *passim,* 134 and *n,* 141, 142, 240, 242–45 *passim,* 248, 260, 261
Ch'ü Ch'iu-po: political positions and actions of, vi–vii, 6*n,* 8, 45–46, 48–51, 123; *Superfluous Words,* vii, xxix, 5, 8, 44–48 *passim,* 50–53 *passim;* significance of, xvii; relationship with Communist Party, xxix, 6 and *n,* 34, 40–41, 42–43, 47–48; *History of the Heart in the Red Capital,* 5, 18*n,* 24, 26, 33, 42, 43, 52; *A Journey to the Land of Hunger,* 5, 15, 18*n,* 23–24, 26, 52; life of, 5–6, 9–14, 16–17, 104; as man of letters, 5, 6–7, 16–17; personality of, 7–8, 44–45; mission to Russia, 18–22, 24–25, 27–29, 30–38, 40–41; personal feelings and beliefs of, 22–23, 52–54; *On the Russian Revolution,* 24; literary style of, 26–27; possible forgery of works, 51, 52; mentioned, xxi, xxii n,

xxvi–xix *passim,* 103, 105, 128, 129, 168, 216, 222*n*

Chun-mu. *See* Chang T'ai-lai

Communist Youth League, 71 and *n,* 85, 206

Cowley, Malcolm, 167–68, 176, 194. *See also* "Twenty-four Youngsters"

Creation Society, xxii, xxiii, 58 and *n,* 123, 236. *See also* Sun Society

Des Sans-culottes. See Chiang Kuang-tz'u

Diary of a Madman. See Lu Hsün

February. See Jou Shih

Feng Hsüeh-feng, xx, xxii–xxiv *passim,* 101, 103*n,* 104, 105, 107, 108–11, 113, 117, 120, 122–26 *passim,* 132, 140, 141, 144*n,* 165*n,* 167*n,* 177, 190–92 *passim,* 213, 230, 235

Feng K'eng, 163, 167, 168, 185, 197–201, 205, 206, 223, 224, 227, 228, 230, 231. *See also* Five Martyrs; Jou Shih

Five Martyrs: significance of, xvii; backgrounds of, 163, 167; historical background for, 163–66, 171–74; circumstances leading to arrest and death, 167–79, 207–32; individuals of, 174–85, 189–207; literary characteristics of, 185–88; general group characteristics of, 188–89; mentioned, xxi, xxvi, xxviii. *See also* Feng K'eng; Hu Yeh-p'in; Jou Shih; Li Wei-sen; Yin Fu

Ghost of the Hanged Woman. See Lu Hsün

"Good-bye, Brother." *See* Yin Fu

Go to Moscow! See Hu Yeh-p'in

A Great Impression. See Jou Shih

Harbin, 28–30, 31, 53*n,* 117

Hesitation. See Lu Hsün

History of the Heart in the Red Capital. See Ch'ü Ch'iu-po

Ho Meng-hsiung, 166–70 *passim,* 206, 207, 212, 217–21 *passim,* 224, 226–29 *passim*

Ho Mung-shung. *See* Ho Meng-hsiung

Hsia Tsi-an, v–ix *passim,* xv–xxiii *passim;* "The Birth of a Son," xvi *n;* "The Jesuit's Tale," xvi; *The Commune in*

Retreat as Evidenced in Terminology and Semantics, xxi; *Metaphor, Myth, Ritual and the People's Commune,* xxi; *A Terminological Study of the Hsia-fang Movement,* xxi

Hsia Yen, 109, 113, 124

Hsiao Hung, 117, 123, 238

Hsiao San, 46–49 *passim*

Hsü Mou-yung, xxii–xxiv *passim,* 107, 127, 130, 132 and *n,* 133 and *n,* 136–44 *passim,* 252

Hsü Pai. *See* Yin Fu

Hu Feng, xx, xxii, xxiv, xxv, xxix, 103*n,* 107–13 *passim,* 115, 117, 118*n,* 125, 130, 131*n,* 134, 135, 139, 140, 142–44 *passim,* 260

Hu Shih, 17, 49, 62, 76*n,* 107 and *n,* 108, 110, 112, 147, 158–60 *passim,* 180

Hu Yeh-p'in, 163, 167, 168, 170, 176, 181, 182–85, 186–87, 193, 194, 197, 203, 205–7 *passim,* 223, 224, 227, 230; *Go to Moscow!* 167, 180, 183; *Light Is Ahead of Us,* 180, 181, 183, 186–87

Huang Yao-mien, 67 and *n,* 68, 70, 71*n,* 77

Huang Yüan, 134–36 *passim,* 139, 140, 142–44 *passim*

The Human Comedy. See Jou Shih

Hung-ch'i jih-pao, 55, 59, 61, 69

I-ching, 47, 48

The Infernal Agent. See Lu Hsün

"In the Hospital." *See* Ting Ling

Jou Shih, 163, 167, 179, 185, 189–99, 203, 205, 206, 213, 223, 224, 227, 230; *The Human Comedy,* 190; "The Mother Who Is a Slave," 195, 199; *February,* 195–96, 200; *A Great Impression,* 227. *See also* Five Martyrs

A Journey to the Land of Hunger. See Ch'ü Ch'iu-po

KMT. *See* Kuomintang

Keng Chi-chih, 15, 17*n,* 22

Kiangsi, 49, 101, 119, 171, 172, 177, 227

Koestler, Arthur, xx, 5

Kuo Mo-jo, 57–62 *passim,* 73, 79, 108, 111, 118, 123, 131, 132*n,* 136*n,* 141, 144, 184, 185; *The Bottle,* 184

Kuomintang, 8, 47, 48, 51, 72 and *n*, 102, 103, 106, 113, 114, 120, 122, 123, 137, 138, 163, 165, 166, 168–70 *passim*, 174, 190, 191, 200, 201, 209, 212, 213, 222, 223, 229, 231, 233, 240

The Last Smile. See Chiang Kuang-tz'u
League of Leftist Writers, viii, xxii–xxiv *passim*, xxvii, 101–7 *passim*, 109–12 *passim*, 115, 116, 118*n*, 119, 121, 123, 124, 128, 129, 134*n*, 140, 143, 144, 167, 176, 177, 192, 193, 212–13, 223–25 *passim*, 227, 228, 236
Left(ist) League. *See* League of Leftist Writers
Left Wing League. *See* League of Leftist Writers
Li Ch'iu-shih. *See* Li Wei-sen
Li Li-san, vii, 6, 50, 168, 169, 171, 172, 209–12 *passim*, 216, 217, 219, 220, 222*n*, 223, 227, 232 and *n*. *See also* Li Li-san line
Li Li-san line, 45, 66*n*, 168, 174, 205, 207, 211, 212, 216, 218, 220, 221, 223, 224*n*, 226, 227*n*, 232. *See also* Li Li-san
Li Ta-chao, 14 and *n*, 17*n*, 18*n*, 22*n*, 165
Li Wei-sen, 163, 167, 168, 206–7, 217, 223, 226, 227, 229. *See also* Five Martyrs
Light Is Ahead of Us. See Hu Yeh-p'in
Lin Yutang, 160
Liu Hsüeh-wei, 235, 236–37, 238, 239, 257, 259
Lo Chang-lung, 169, 207, 217, 218*n*, 220, 221, 224, 225, 226*n*, 228
Lu Hsün: relationship with Communist Party, viii, xxviii, 102–7, 110–19; significance of, xvii; as a writer, xxiii, 104–5, 127–28, 156–58, 192–94; and gate of darkness, xxiv–xv, 146–47, 148, 152; literary style and ability of, xxv, 7, 43, 128–29, 147–53, 160, 162, 239–40; *Diary*, 105 and *n*, 110, 111, 112, 134 and *n*, 136, 137; death of, 106, 144–45, 251; personality of, 106, 126, 147, 154, 160–62; friendships of, 110–13, 191–92; *The Wild Grass*, 116, 150, 152, 158; *Hesitation*, 116, 128; political position and attitudes, 119–25, 129–30,

208; in Battle of Two Slogans, 130–44; *Correspondence*, 134; specific works analyzed, 150–51, 152, 153, 154–58; *Diary of a Madman*, 151–52, 153; *Benediction*, 153; *The White Light*, 153, 157; *Medicine*, 153, 162; *The True Life of Ah Q*, 153, 158, 162; *The Infernal Agent*, 154; *Ghost of the Hanged Woman*, 154–55; *Soap*, 158; mentioned, vi, xxi–xxvii *passim*, xxix, 49, 108, 109, 144, 177, 179, 189, 195, 196, 198, 203, 205, 252, 253
Lu Ting-i, 7, 246, 256, 261

Mao Tse-tung, viii, xviii, xix, xxv, xxvii, xxviii, 6 and *n*, 17*n*, 42, 60, 66, 68, 69, 82, 84, 102, 104, 107, 108, 119, 123–25 *passim*, 132, 141, 166, 171, 172*n*, 206, 207, 217, 218, 225, 227, 232, 234–36 *passim*, 240–49 *passim*, 253, 255–57, 258, 260, 261
Mao Tun, 102, 123, 130–32 *passim*, 141, 170, 172, 173–74, 176, 181, 191*n*, 211–12, 232, 256; *Midnight*, 181
Marxism, xix, xx, 31, 43–45 *passim*, 53, 68, 104, 111, 128, 129, 183, 256, 260, 261. *See also* Marxism-Leninism
Marxism-Leninism, 3, 39, 53, 72, 242, 244, 248, 260. *See also* Marxism
May Fourth Movement, xvii, xviii, xx, xxvi, xxvii, 14–15, 20, 34, 62, 63, 71 and *n*, 85–87 passim, 120, 153, 158, 159, 185, 235, 239, 240; period of, xvi, xxv, 147, 206; tradition of, xvii, xxv, 241, 249
Medicine. See Lu Hsün
Midnight. See Mao Tun
The Moon Forces Its Way through the Clouds. See Chiang Kuang-tz'u
Moscow, 28, 30–33 *passim*, 35, 36, 40*n*, 41*n*, 42–44 *passim*, 50, 86*n*, 168, 169, 183, 216, 219*n*, 242
"The Mother Who Is a Slave." *See* Jou Shih

National Defense Literature, 106, 124, 125*n*, 126–31 *passim*, 135, 140–42 *passim*, 144
"New Belief." *See* Ting Ling

On the Russian Revolution. See Ch'ü Ch'iu-po
Orwell, George, xx

Pa Chin, 134 and *n,* 136, 139, 140, 142, 143
Pai Mang. *See* Yin Fu
Peking, 9*n,* 12, 14, 21, 31, 40, 67, 72, 137, 163, 171, 177, 183, 184, 191, 192, 195, 229, 243

"Reply to a Brother." *See* Yin Fu
"Resolutions." *See* Yin Fu
The Roaring Earth. See Chiang Kuang-tz'u
Russian Language College, 14, 15, 29

Shanghai, 13, 49, 55, 62*n,* 65*n,* 67, 72 and *n,* 73, 74, 77, 85, 86*n,* 91, 95, 96, 101, 103–5 *passim,* 109, 110, 117, 120–23 *passim,* 125, 127 and *n,* 128, 133 and *n,* 134*n,* 137, 144, 164–73 *passim,* 176, 177, 183, 186, 189, 190–92 *passim,* 199, 201, 206, 210, 211, 214, 218, 226, 228, 243, 246
Shanghai, Spring 1930. See Ting Ling
Shao-po. *See* T'ien Han
Shen Ts'ung-wen, 179, 180, 184
Soap. See Lu Hsün
Socialist Youth Corps, 21, 22*n*
Socialist Youth League, 71–72*n*
The Sorrows of Lisa. See Chiang Kuang-tz'u
Spender, Stephen, xx, 5
Sun Society, xxii, xxiii, 58*n,* 123. *See also* Creation Society
Sun Yat-sen, 159, 169
Sung Jo-yü, 87, 92, 100
Superfluous Words. See Ch'ü Ch'iu-po

T'ang poets and poetry, 12, 54, 147
Taoism, 9, 19
"Thoughts on March 8." *See* Ting Ling
T'ien Han, 114, 115, 134*n,* 142
Ting Ling, xx, 49, 102, 110*n,* 122*n,* 170, 174–78, 179–81 *passim,* 182–83, 186, 190, 193, 235, 244, 247–49 *passim*

250–52, 253, 255, 259; *Shanghai, Spring 1930,* 175–76, 177, 179, 182, 183, 184, 187–88, 215–16; "When I Was in Hsia Village," 250; "In the Hospital," 250; "New Belief," 250; "Thoughts on March 8," 251. *See also* Five Martyrs
Ting Yi, 65, 70
The True Life of Ah Q. See Lu Hsün
"Twenty-four Youngsters," 167–68, 176. *See also* Cowley, Malcolm

Wang Ming. *See* Ch'en Shao-yü
Wang Shih-wei, 235, 252; *The Wild Lily,* 252
Wang Yeh-ch'iu, 126, 130
"When I Was in Hsia Village." *See* Ting Ling
The White Light. See Lu Hsün
White Terror, 170, 171, 174
The Wild Grass. See Lu Hsün
The Wild Lily. See Wang Shih-wei
The Wind over the Fields. See Chiang Kuang-tz'u
Worship at the Unlocatable Grave. See Chiang Kuang-tz'u
Writers' Association, 127. *See also* Association of Literature and Arts
Wu Szu-hung, 57*n,* 80*n,* 97–100

Yang Chi-yün, 113–14, 126*n,* 138
Yang Ts'un-jen, 57*n,* 58*n,* 114 and *n,* 115, 122, 224
Yenan, viii, 119, 121, 123–25 *passim,* 134*n,* 143
Yenan Forum on Arts and Literature, xxv, 235, 237, 240–43 *passim,* 245, 246, 248, 249, 252, 254, 255, 262
Yin Fu, 163, 167, 181–82, 185, 189, 197, 201–6, 208, 214–15, 223, 224, 227; "Goodbye, Brother," 202–3, 204, "Reply to a Brother," 203; "Resolutions," 205. *See also* Five Martyrs
The Youthful Tramp. See Chiang Kuang-tz'u
Yü Ta-fu, 58 and *n,* 59, 60, 67, 97, 98, 184–85, 192

FAR EASTERN AND RUSSIAN INSTITUTE
PUBLICATIONS ON ASIA

1. Compton, Boyd (trans. and ed.). *Mao's China: Party Reform Documents, 1942–44*. 1952. Reissued 1966. Washington Paperback-4, 1966. 330 pp., map.
2. Chiang, Siang-tseh. *The Nien Rebellion*. 1954. 177 pp., bibliog., index, maps.
3. Chang, Chung-li. *The Chinese Gentry: Studies on Their Role in Nineteenth-Century Chinese Society*. Introduction by Franz Michael. 1955. Reissued 1967. Washington Paperback on Russia and Asia-4. 277 pp., bibliog., index, tables.
4. *Guide to the Memorials of Seven Leading Officials of Nineteenth-Century China*. Summaries and indexes of memorials of Hu Lin-i, Tseng Kuo-fan, Tso Tsung-tang, Kuo Sung-tao, Tseng Kuo-ch'üan, Li Hung-chang, Chang Chih-tung. 1955. 457 pp., mimeographed. Out of print.
5. Raeff, Marc. *Siberia and the Reforms of 1822*. 1956. 228 pp., maps, bibliog., index. Out of print.
6. Li Chi. *The Beginnings of Chinese Civilization: Three Lectures Illustrated with Finds at Anyang*. 1957. Reissued 1968. Washington Paperback on Russia and Asia-6. 141 pp., illus., bibliog., index.
7. Carrasco, Pedro. *Land and Polity in Tibet*. 1959. 318 pp., maps, bibliog., index.
8. Hsiao, Kung-chuan. *Rural China: Imperial Control in the Nineteenth Century*. 1960. Reissued 1967. Washington Paperback on Russia and Asia-3. 797 pp., illus., bibliog., index.
9. Hsiao, Tso-liang. *Power Relations within the Chinese Communist Movement, 1930–1934*. Vol. I: *A Study of Documents*. 1961. 416 pp., bibliog., index, glossary. Vol. II: *The Chinese Documents*. 1967. 856 pp.
10. Chang, Chung-li. *The Income of the Chinese Gentry*. Introduction by Franz Michael. 1962. 387 pp., tables, bibliog., index.
11. Maki, John M. *Court and Constitution in Japan: Selected Supreme Court Decisions, 1948–60*. 1964. 491 pp., bibliog., index.
12. Poppe, Nicholas, Leon Hurvitz, and Hidehiro Okada. *Catalogue of the Manchu-Mongol Section of the Toyo Bunko*. 1964. 391 pp., index.
13. Spector, Stanley. *Li Hung-chang and the Huai Army: A Study in Nineteenth-Century Chinese Regionalism*. Introduction by Franz Michael. 1964. 399 pp., maps, tables, bibliog., glossary, index.

14. Michael, Franz, and Chung-li Chang. *The Taiping Rebellion: History and Documents.* Vol. I: *History.* 1966. 256 pp., maps, index. Vols. II and III: *Documents and Comments.* In press 1968.

15. Shih, Vincent Y. C. *The Taiping Ideology: Its Sources, Interpretations, and Influences.* 1967. 576 pp., bibliog., index.

16. Poppe, Nicholas. *The Twelve Deeds of Buddha: A Mongolian Version of the Lalitavistara; Mongolian Text, Notes, and English Translation.* 1967. 241 pp., illus. Paper.

17. Hsia, Tsi-an. *The Gate of Darkness: Studies on the Leftist Literary Movement in China.* Preface by Franz Michael. Introduction by C. T. Hsia. 1968. 298 pp., index.